THE MERTON ANNUAL

3

THE MERTON ANNUAL

Studies in Thomas Merton, Religion, Culture, Literature & Social Concerns

THE MERTON ANNUAL will publish articles about Thomas Merton and about matters of major concern in his life and work. Its purpose is to enhance Merton's reputation as a writer and monk, to continue to develop his message for our times, and to provide a regular outlet for substantial Merton-related scholarship. *THE MERTON ANNUAL* will also include as regular features reviews, review-essays, a bibliographic survey, interviews, and first appearances of unpublished, or obscurely published, Merton materials, photographs, and art. Essays about related literary connections or events which Merton has influenced will also be considered. Manuscripts and books for review may be sent to any of the editors.

EDITORS

Robert E. Daggy
Merton Center
Bellarmine College
Newburg Road
Louisville, KY 40205-0671

Patrick Hart, O.C.S.O.
Abbey of Gethsemani
Trappist, KY 40051

Dewey Weiss Kramer
DeKalb College
555 N. Indian Creek Dr.
Clarkston, GA 30021

Victor A. Kramer
Georgia State University
Department of English
University Plaza
Atlanta, GA 30303

ADVISORY BOARD

THE MERTON ANNUAL

Studies in Thomas Merton, Religion, Culture, Literature & Social Concerns

Volume 3

1990

Edited by

Robert E. Daggy

Patrick Hart, O.C.S.O.

Dewey Weiss Kramer

Victor A. Kramer

AMS Press, Inc.
New York

THE MERTON ANNUAL

LC 87-47815   ISBN-0-404-63800-7 (set)

ISSN 0894-4857   ISBN-0-404-63801-5 (v. 3)

THE MERTON ANNUAL, 3
was set in Chelmsford type
and camera-ready copy prepared
at the Thomas Merton Studies Center
Bellarmine College, Louisville, Kentucky

Manufactured in the United States of America

THE MERTON ANNUAL

Volume 3   1990

O

O

Contents

Contents

Contents

INTRODUCTION

The subtitle of *The Merton Annual* — Studies in Thomas Merton, Religion, Culture, Literature & Social Concerns — indicates the editors' initial plans to select from the continuing work of scholars, critics, and writers who are fascinated with Thomas Merton. The essays and reviews of volume three manifest his growth and development as a monk and writer and his awareness of a much wider world outside the confines of the Abbey of Gethsemani. His legacy reminds us of the continuing relationship of monasticism to the concerns of contemporary society.

The exchange of letters and development of friendship with Dom Jean Leclercq as well as interaction with his fellow monks as reported from the perspective of a former student and subsequent abbot help readers to see how he remained grounded in his vocation and also to understand how he sought to make all kinds of connections beyond the monastic life. It is no accident that articles have been included which inquire into Merton's religious, literary, and cultural concerns. Some are detailed textual studies and some are speculative pieces. Taken together they show something of the connections Merton made through his reading or living, praying or writing. Further, the questions he raised in his writings and through the manner of his life continue to inspire others as they adapt Merton's paradigms to their own lives.

Eleven reviews of thirteen books, including evaluations of six collections of Merton's own writing, some of which has not been previously available in print, conclude the volume. These reviews reflect the complexity of his accomplishment and the work he inspires.

Just as the various commemorations of the twentieth anniversary of Merton's death in 1988 and the First General Meeting of *The International Thomas Merton Society* in 1989 signal the continuing vitality in Merton's own work, we feel that these essays — several of which were first delivered at these commemorations and the ITMS Meeting — and reviews bode well for the next twenty years of Merton and Merton-related studies.

THE EDITORS

A NOTE ON
THE MERTON DRAWINGS
IN THIS VOLUME

In preceding volumes of *The Merton Annual*, it was our privilege to choose drawings and photographs by Thomas Merton which reflect particular aspects of his artistic temperament and which seem to evoke responses appropriate to the scholarly materials included in the volume. Thus, in volume one certain examples of calligraphy were selected because they seem to suggest aspects of Merton's fascination with the East as well as his own particular joy in life. Similarly, when we chose the photographs for volume two we did so with the idea that Merton's photography would stand by itself and also reverberate with larger aspects of his world — what he did, saw, and meditated upon.

The calligraphies, the photographs, and the drawings are familiar to Merton readers because they have been reproduced on occasion. The drawings are valuable in revealing still another facet of Merton's talent. They show that his love of drawing, which developed in childhood and continued through his college years, remained after he entered Gethsemani and that it could manifest itself in a stark, clear manner. The drawings have been chosen because they are beautiful and because they suggest patterns in Merton's artistic career as well. Most importantly, they reflect Merton's awareness that art and meditation, the artistic and the contemplative, converge.

We are grateful to the Trustees of the Merton Legacy Trust for allowing the drawings to be reproduced in *The Merton Annual*. They confirm, once again, that Merton was a figure who combined the abilities of the artist and a longing for God in many different ways — never to be fully revealed, and yet always to be appreciated.

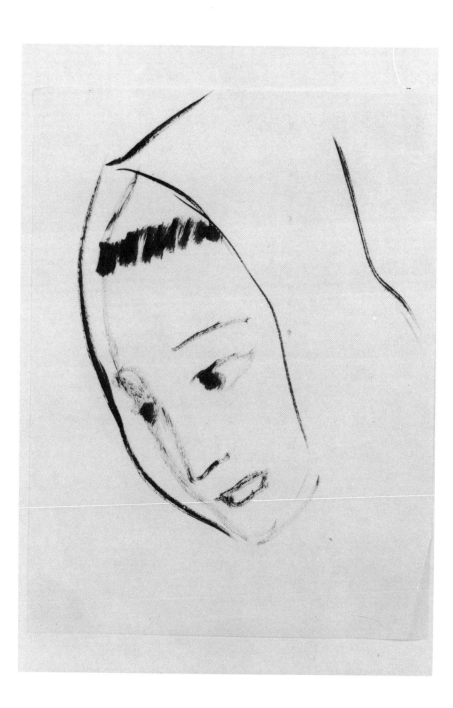

A MONASTIC CORRESPONDENCE

by **Thomas Merton & Jean Leclercq**, O.S.B.

Edited by Patrick Hart, O.C.S.O.

EDITOR'S NOTE

In a foreword to Bruno Scott James's volume of selected letters of St. Bernard of Clairvaux, Thomas Merton writes what could be an autobiographical statement: "The whole Bernard is not to be found in his letters alone: but the whole Bernard can never be known without them." Merton concludes his foreword with these equally revealing words: ". . . let us at least gather from St. Bernard that letter-writing is an art which has been forgotten, but which needs to be re-learned . . ." (Foreword to St. Bernard of Clairvaux, Chicago: Henry Regnery, 1953).

The following exchange of letters between Thomas Merton and Jean Leclercq shows us that the art of letter writing had not been completely abandoned by monks of our time. Included here are the earliest letters between Merton and Leclercq, spanning the time frame of 1950 to 1954. This is but a small sampling of the vast correspondence between these two monastic writers, one a Trappist-Cistercian monk of the Abbey of Gethsemani in Kentucky, U. S. A., and the other a Benedictine scholar of the Abbey of Clervaux in Luxembourg, who spent a quarter of a century working on the critical edition of the writings of St. Bernard.

Not surprisingly, these early letters deal in large part with the twelfth-century Abbot of Clairvaux (France), whose writings were to have such an influence on all future generations of monks, including both Merton and Leclercq. The first extant letter we have of this exchange is dated April 22, 1950, and deals with filming one of St. Bernard's Sermons from the Obrecht Collection housed at that time at Geth-semani. These manuscripts and incunabula were later transferred to the Library of the Institute of Cistercian Studies at Western Michigan University, Kalamazoo, Michigan, where they are on permanent loan.

An occasional phrase in Latin or French has been translated into English and is indicated with brackets [...]; these are supplied by the editor. But only a minimum of editing has been done in preparing this exchange of letters for publication in The

Merton Annual 3. *Merton's side of the correspondence will be published in the third volume of the Merton Letters titled* The School of Charity. *It was not possible at this time to publish both sides of the letters, but it is hoped that at some future date such a publication may be possible. Meanwhile, we have this early exchange of letters between Merton, the American Cistercian, and Leclercq, the Benedictine from Luxembourg: an engaging correspondence.* *

It is appropriate that this correspondence which deals so much with St. Bernard of Clairvaux should appear in 1990, the year in which the monastic world commemorates the ninth centenary of Bernard's birth, also known as "The Mellifluous Doctor" of the Church. We are indebted to Sister Bernard Said, O.S.B., Jean Leclercq's English-speaking secretary, for preparing the transcriptions of most of these letters, and translating where required. Actually, the majority of both sides of the correspondence was written in English. An occasional use of brackets provides a fuller editorial explanation of a term or name as seemed necessary in the context of the letters.

Although the correspondence began on the subject of St. Bernard of Clairvaux, as the years went by, these two monks explored many other related fields of mutual interest, such as renewal in the monastic orders, and the eremitical ideal of a more complete withdrawal from the world for certain monks who experienced this special vocation. Merton felt drawn to a more solitary way of life, and often wrote to Leclercq for counsel and advice as these early letters reveal. Leclercq's responses were also helpful and encouraging though prudent and cautious.

In the late 1960s Leclercq would encourage Merton as he entered the hermitage, a small cinderblock cottage on the property of the Abbey of Gethsemani. When visiting America he would frequently visit Gethsemani and was able to evaluate Merton's solitary vocation at close range.

After Dom James Fox resigned his abbatial office, and Father Flavian Burns was elected his succesor, Leclercq would continue his contacts, and was instrumental in arranging for the invitation to participate in the conference of Asian Monastic Superiors in Bangkok, Thailand, in December of 1968. Leclercq and Merton met there for the last time before the latter's accidental death. It was especially fitting that the last meeting of these monastic friends should be in the midst of Asian monks and nuns gathered to explore monasticism in the Far East, and to take advantage of the wisdom of other non-Christian monastic traditions of Asia for the sake of a revitalized monasticism in the West.

It is hoped that this sampling of a unique monastic correspondence will help us all to understand the meaning of this radical response to the Gospel, incarnated so well by these two gifted monks, and how we can in our turn live it more authentically in the years to come.

---

* For a more complete treatment of this relationship, see our essay, "A Monastic Exchange: Leclercq and Merton," in *The Legacy of Thomas Merton* (Kalamazoo, Michigan: Cistercian Publications, 1986), pp. 91-109.

A MONASTIC CORRESPONDENCE

by **Thomas Merton & Jean Leclercq**, O.S.B.

Thomas Merton to Jean Leclercq

Gethsemani
Trappist
Ky
April 22, 1950

My Dear Rev. Father:

Another film of the St. Bernard Sermons is now on the way to you. This time I looked it over to see if it was all right and it was legible on our machine. I am sorry the first attempt was not too good: you must forgive our young students who are just trying their hand at this kind of work for the first time. Pray that they may learn, because in the future many demands will be made on their talents — if any.

I might wish that your travels would bring you to this side of the Atlantic and that we might have the pleasure of receiving you at Gethsemani. We have just remodelled the vault where our rare books are kept and have extended its capacities to include a good little library on Scripture and the Fathers and the Liturgy — or at least the nucleus of one. Here I hope to form a group of competent students not merely of history or of texts but rather — in line with the tradition which you so admirably represent — men competent in all-round spiritual theology, as well as scholarship, using their time and talents to develop the seed of the word of God in their souls, not to choke it under an overgrowth of useless research as is the tradition in the universities of this country at the moment. I fervently hope that somehow we shall see in America men who are able to produce something like *Dieu Vivant*. Cistercians will never be able to do quite that, I suppose, but we can at least give a good example along those lines. Our studies and writing should by their very nature contribute to our contemplation at least remotely and contemplation in turn should be able to find expression in channels laid open for it and deepened by familiarity with the Fathers of the Church. This is an age that calls for St Augustines and Leos, Gregories and Cyrils!

That is why I feel that your works are so tremendously helpful, dear Father. Your *St Bernard Mystique* is altogether admirable because, while being simple and fluent, it communicates to the reader a real appreciation of St Bernard's spirituality. You are wrong to consider your treatment of St Bernard superficial. It is indeed addressed to the general reader but for all that it is profound and all-embracing and far more valuable that the rather technical study which I undertook for *Collectanea* and which, as you will see on reading it, was beyond my capacities as a theologian. The earlier sections especially, in my study, contain many glaring and silly errors — or at least things are often very badly expressed there.[1] If I write a book on the saint I shall try to redeem myself, without entering into the technical discussions that occupy M. [Etienne] Gilson in his rather brilliant study.[2] But there again, a book of your type is far more helpful.

Be sure that we are praying for the work you now have in hand, which is so important and which implies such a great responsibility for you. Any other material help we can give will also be a pleasure. Do not bother about any question of cost for the films. But if you do have a *tirage a part* [offprint] of one or another article by you, on your present researches into our Cistercian manuscripts, we would greatly appreciate it.

I had heard that you were helping to prepare for the press Dom Wilmart's edition of Ailred's *De Institutione Inclusarum* [Institution for Recluses] but perhaps you have put this on the shelf for the time being. Are the Cistercians of the Common Observance editing the works of Ailred? Where are they doing so and when is the work expected to be finished? By the way, about the spelling of Ailred: the most prominent English scholars seem to be spelling him as I have just done, with an "i." I wish there could be some unity on this point. My work on him is in abeyance at the moment, but when I get on with it I suppose I had better go on using this spelling. What do you think about that?

Rest assured, dear Father, that I am praying for you and that our students are doing the same. Please pray for us too. I have too much activity on my shoulders, teaching and writing. Please pray for our Lord to live and

---

1. Thomas Merton, "The Transforming Union in St. Bernard and St. John of the Cross," *Collectanea Cisterciensia* 10 (1948), pp. 107, 210; 11 (1949), pp. 41, 352; 12 (1950), p. 25.

2. Etienne Gilson, *The Mystical Theology of St. Bernard* (New York: Sheed & Ward, 1940).

work in me in such a way that all I do will nourish His life in my soul. I ask the same favor for you, in your travels and labors for His glory.

With every good wish, and in union of prayers,

Your devoted brother in Christ

fr. M. Louis, O.C.R.

Jean Leclercq to Thomas Merton

Clervaux, 5. 5. 50

Dear Reverend Father,

I was just going to write to you when I received, yesterday, your last letter. Thank you for the new film which has already arrived.

Thank you also for your prayers and encouragement. I know that some scholars and professors criticize my books because they are too "human," not sufficiently, not purely "scientific," objective: but I do not care about having a good reputation as a scholar among scholars, although I could also do pure scholarly work, and I sometimes do, just to show that I know what it is. But I also know that many monks, and they are the more monastic monks, in several Orders — Camaldolese, Cistercians, Trappists, Benedictines of the strictest observances — find my books nourishing, and find in them an answer to their own aspirations. I thank God for that, my only merit — if any — is to accept not to be a pure scholar; otherwise I never invent ideas: I just bring to light ideas and experiences which are to be found in old monastic books that nobody, even in monasteries, ever reads today.

Since you seem to want me to do so, I am sending you today some offprints, just about "monastica." As you will see, I always say and write the same thing, because only one is necessary, and it is the only thing you would find in old monastic texts. Yesterday I also received an offprint of a review of Spicq, *L'exegese medievale*; I am sending it to you as well, because in this paper there are some essential things about the monastic way of reading Scripture. I have no more copies of my first volume of *Analecta monastica*; maybe you have it. I think that what I wrote there in the general Introduction, and in the special introduction to the Cistercian commentary of Gilbert of Stanford on the Canticle of Canticles, is in the same line, and in full agreement with what you feel and what you write to me.

I think you have an important job to do at Gethsemani: first for America, and then for the whole Cistercian Order: to come back to the Cistercian idea. But there are two difficulties. The first is to keep the just measure in work, either manual or intellectual. Both forms of work, and especially the second, entail a danger of activism (mental activism), multiplicity and complexity, which are contrary to monastic "simplicity": that is a personal question which each monk has to solve for himself if he wants to work and stay a monk; some are unable to do both and have to choose to remain monks. The second difficulty is more of the historical order, if we want to study the Cistercian tradition. I am alluding to the illusion of believing that the Cistercian tradition began with Citeaux. I am becoming more and more convinced that the Cistercian tradition cannot be understood without its roots which were in pre-existing and contemporary Benedictine — and generally, monastic — tradition. That is why in my studies I never separate the different forms and expressions of the unique monastic thought and experience. For instance, if one begins to study the Mariology of the Cistercian school without taking into consideration previous and contemporary monastic thought at the time about the Virgin, then one tends to think that the Cistercians were at the origin of all true and fervent Mariology. Yet if one recalls what St. Anselm and the monks of the Anglo-Norman eleventh century wrote, then possibly one might come to the conclusion that in this field Cistercians, far from making progress may even have retrograded (I think, for example, of the Conception of Our Lady). The only way to avoid such pitfalls is to be quite free from any order-emphasis, any "order politics," and to search solely for the truth in the life of the Church of God.

Since you ask me what I think about your books, then I tell you even though I am no special authority on the matter. I suppose that the condition of our relations resides in perfect sincerity and loyalty.

I arrived back at Clervaux a few days ago, and have just had time to read the Prologue and the first two chapters of *The Waters of Siloe*. I shall read the rest and then tell you my impressions. So far, I must say that I thoroughly enjoy your pages: both what you say and the way you say it. I think that one immediately feels that you "believe" in the contemplative life, and this faith of yours is more forceful for convincing your readers than would be the most scientific treatment of the subject.

In my opinion, you point out the very essence of monastic life when you say that it is a contemplative life. The Benedictine tradition is certainly a contemplative tradition: the doctrine of Benedictine medieval writers (and almost always up to our own days — the twentieth century is an exception, alas!) is a doctrine of contemplation and contemplative life. But we must confess that Benedictine history is not entirely — and in certain periods not at all — contemplative. Nevertheless, even when Benedictines were busy about many things, they never made this business *circa plurima* an ideal, and they never spoke about it; their doctrine was always that of the *unum necessarium.*

I think you are quite right when you say that we fall short of this ideal for want of simplicity. There have always been — and there still are today —attempts to get back to this simplicity. And one such attempt has always been writing. But the danger is always there, and even today Cistercians do not always succeed in avoiding it. For instance, from the Cistercian — and even simple monastic — point of view, Orval (the new Orval) has been and remains a scandal: it is a sin against simplicity: first because it is luxurious, and then because, on pretext of observing the statutes forbidding gold and other certain materials, they have used precious and exotic materials which give the same impression as would gold, without being gold, and so on. And the festival held in honour of the consecration of Orval was also scandalous and has been felt as such even by Cistercians and Trappists. In the same way, the noise and publicity made over Gethsemani on the occasion of its centenary, and the write-up in magazines having, in the same issue, pictures of pin-up girls, was also scandalous, and has been felt as such (But perhaps that was in keeping with the "American style"). You see, dear Reverend Father, that I do not spare you. But it is in order to show how great is the temptation.

I find your pages about Rome perfectly sincere and just. I am glad that you were allowed to write so freely. Others, I know, have not had that same liberty, nor do they even now. But I hope that the love of truth will make people surrender all "order-orthodoxy" and "order-politics."

I know the Procurator General of the S. O. C. [Sacred Order of Cistercians, or Common Observance], Abbot M. Quatember, very well. He has, in my opinion, a good idea of what Cistercian life is and should be. He tries to promote this life in Hauterive, and I think he succeeds. Fortunately, till now, Hauterive has continued to be a small monastery. The danger for spiritual enterprises is always prosperity. Is the union of O. C. R. [Order of Reformed Cistercians, or Trappists] and S. O. C. an utopic dream? I would like to think not. But this re-union of brothers, who have sometimes been and sometimes remain fence-brothers, must be prepared by prayer and study in an atmosphere of search for Cistercian truth, and in an atmosphere of peace.

Yes, I did give Wilmart's transcription of Aelred's *De institutione inclusarum* to Abbot Quatember for the *Analecta S. O. C.* But I have heard nothing about this text for some years now. I will make enquiries on the next occasion. Wilmart's text is not a critical and definitive edition; but since Fr. Sage now wants to become a Trappist and give up the project of editing this text, then Wilmart's will come in useful. If you want to make a critical edition of it, let me know, and I will hold back the Wilmart text. My friend and collaborator, Dr. C. H. Talbot, has prepared the edition of Ailred's sermon for the *Analecta S. O. C.* I think it is finished and will soon be at the printer's. I have no idea about the spelling of Ailred. In French I always write Aelred, like Wilmart and everyone else. When Dr. Talbot writes to me he always writes Aelred. But if scholars write Ailred, I think you may, and should, on this point do what scholars do.

I pray for you, your monastery and the whole Cistercian order (I cannot break the unity, so strong in the Carta Caritatis; psychologically I have never accepted the schism of the beginning of the XIX century . . .) Pardon me the liberty of speech I take with you, and be sure that I am very faithfully yours in Our Lord and Our Lady,

f. J. Leclercq, O.S.B.

Excuse too my awful English, but my writing is so bad that it is easier for you to read me in English than in French.

Jean Leclercq to Thomas Merton

Bruxelles, 29. 7. 50

Reverend and Dear Father,

Retained in Brussels by the strike, I at last find time to answer your long and interesting letter of june 17.[3]

---

3. Merton's letter of June 17, 1950, has not survived in Leclercq's files or in the archives of the Merton Center at Bellarmine College.

I am glad you approve what I wrote about *lectio divina*. I do not think that we must try to settle an opposition between the spiritual and the scientific reading of the Scriptures: we must try to reconcile these two methods as was the case in the middle ages, when the same doctors explained the Bible using both methods. I tried to explain this in a paper to be published in the collection *Rencontres* (ed. du Cerf) about *L'exegese de l'Ancien Testament*:

1. In the middle ages there were two sorts of exegetics: scientific and spiritual;

2. but there were not two sorts of scripture scholars: all used the two methods;

3. and these two methods of scripture study supposed a same conception of Holy Scripture, and especially the relations between the Old and the New Testaments.

I think that the way of teaching the Bible now common in our theological colleges is merely apologetic, which was probably very useful forty years ago. Now, thanks to a reaction against this apologetic reaction, we are finding the *media via*, the *via conciliationis non oppositionis*. One of the tasks of the monastic world today is to give a practical demonstration that this reconciliation is possible: we should not reject the results of modern biblical sciences, but nor should we be satisfied with them. (I also wrote something about that at the end of my *Saint Bernard mystique*, in the excursus: S. Bernard et l'Ecriture Sainte).

Probably by now you have seen that Gilbert of Stanford is not Gilbert of Hoyland: he is one of the many unknown spiritual writers who, though not all very original, show the intensity of the spiritual life in the monastic circles of the XII century.

The right source for ordering *Analecta S. O. C.* is *Casa Generalizia S. O. C.*, Via Giacomo Medici 3, Roma 129. Write to D. Canisius. But I am sure Hauterive will answer you in the same way.

I do not know personally D. Marquis, abbot of Briquebec, of whom you speak. But I have some friends who are his friends and they esteem him greatly. I quite agree that the time is not ripe for a union (I avoid the word "fusion"; I prefer "union" which supposes distinction and differences: Distinguish in order to unite) between the S. O. C. and O. C. R. Some members of the S. O. C. are not sufficiently monks to understand the O. C. R.; but I think that this union would be good for both orders and should be prepared. Both parties should prepare an atmosphere of comprehension and sympathy, and the monastic element of the S. O. C. should come to have more influence. D. Quatember is quite favourable to this monastic element. The next general chapter of the S. O. C., in September will be of very great importance from this point of view. I think that some members of the S. O. C. have values of the spiritual and intellectual life which are quite in the Cistercian tradition . . . Fr. Neidenhoff of Lyons-Paris tells me that he received a paper from you for his special issue of *Rythmes du monde* about *l'heure des moines*. I gave him an article of which the title will suffice to tell you the theme: *Vivre a Dieu Seul* (Soli Deo vivere).

Since I am preparing the edition of St. Bernard (and to start with, the *Sermones in Cantica*), I shall have to study his sources. If you have any information about his dependence on Origen, Gregory of Nyssa and so on, you would be very kind to share it with me to help me in at least some orientations of my research. I feel the full weight of the difficulty of my work! And I am sometimes tempted to be discouraged. Everybody finds it natural to criticize, but there is no one who is willing to help.

I am not sufficently acquainted with oriental mysticism to have an opinion of yoga and St. Bernard. But since all mystical experiences are fundamentally the same, there is surely some connection; and this not only in the experience itself, but also in the expression of it. From this point of view I think that depth psychology will shed some light on these profound and universal themes of the religious representation.

I do not know your *Spirit of Simplicity*, but I would be pleased to read it if ever I get the opportunity. I read recently the *Vie de Rance* by Chateaubriand. It increased my desire to read Rance. I fear our judgements about him have been influenced by Chateaubriand and the romanticism of the monastic restorers of the last century. Whatever we may find excessive in Rance is part of his times and is to be found also in Benedictines of the same generation: the Murist and Vannist writings are very austere: too much so for our liking. I fear that what we reprove in Rance is dependent more on De Lestrange and other romantics.

The *De institutione inclusarum* prepared by Dom Wilmart will not be published: the manuscript has been lost by the printer . . . That happens in Italy.

The *Consecration monastique* de Dom Casel has not yet been published. But there is a **wonderful** book by Fr. Bouyer which has just come out: *Le sens de la vie monastique* (Coll. Tradition monastique, ed. Brepols, Turnhout, Belgium). He has also recently written a very profound book: *Vie* de St Antoine in coll. Figures monastiques, ed. de Fontenelle, Abbaye *S.Wandrille*, Seine Infre. France.

I quite understand your aspiration to a solitary life. I think there has always been an eremitical tradition in the Cistercian and Benedictine Orders. In my opinion we are not to discuss personal vocations according to principles of Community life, nor according to universal laws. We must always be very respectful for these vocations, provided they are real vocations and not illusions. Personally, though I am quite inapt for the eremitical life, I have always encouraged my confreres who aspire to such a life. Now, in France, there are some Benedictine monks who live as hermits in the mountains. Nobody knows it except God. The tradition of hermitages near monasteries or "inclusi" in monasteries seems very difficult to revive today. So we must find some new solutions to this problem. It is a permanent problem and one which is a very good sign of the monastic fervour of the times: whenever cenobia are what they ought to be, they produce inevitably some eremitical vocations. The eremitic vocations disappear in times and countries where monasticism has ceased to be monastic.

Practically, now, the solution for such vocations is nearly always to move to an eremus, a charterhouse, or the eremi of the Camaldoli, that I know for sure. Last year when I was in the eremus of Camaldoli, the master of novices was expecting an American Trappist. (I shall probably have to go again this year to the eremo at Frascati in order to study the writings of the founder). The revival of the eremitic tendency in France has led to the enquiry being made by CHOC about eremitic life. I can quite understand that your abbot would like you to find a solution within the Cistercian life. Perhaps it is a providential occasion to restore reclusion. This is still practised in Camaldoli. I saw that last year.

I would like to consult the book G. B. BURCH, *The Steps of Humility* by Bernard, second ed. Cambridge, Mass. 1940. I cannot find it in Europe. Could you find it for me and either sell or lend it to me?

With renewed greetings, very dear Father, and in osculo sancto. Please pray that my life and work will be what the Lord wishes.

f. J. Leclercq, O. S. B.

Thomas Merton to Jean Leclercq

_____

Oct. 9th 1950

My Reverend and Dear Father:

It is a long time since I received your July letter which I read and pondered on with deep satisfaction. It is a privilege for which I am deeply grateful, to be able to seek nourishment and inspiration directly from those who keep themselves so close to the sources of monastic spirituality.

Your remarks on St Bernard's ideas of Scripture are extremely important to me. I have been meditating on your appendix to Saint Bernard Mystique, and also I have been talking on this very subject to the students here. I agree with your conclusions about Saint Bernard and yet I wonder if it would not be possible to say that he did consider himself in a very definite sense an exegete. My own subjective feeling is that the full seriousness of St Bernard's attitude to Scripture is not brought out entirely unless we can in some sense treat him as an exegete and as theologian, in his exposition of the Canticle. Naturally he is not either of these things in a purely modern sense. But I think he is acting as a theologian according to the Greek Fathers' conception at least to some extent (see end of Lossky's first chapter: Theol. Myst. de l'Eglise orientale). I think that is essentially what you were saying when you brought out the fact that he was seeking less to nourish his interior life than to exercise it. As if new meanings in his own life and Scripture spontaneously grew up to confirm each other as soon as Bernard immersed himself in the Sacred Text. Still, there is the evident desire of the saint to *penetrate* the Text with a certain mystical understanding and this means to arrive at a living contact with the Word hidden in the word. This would be tantamount to saying that for Bernard, both exegesis and theology found their fullest expression in a concrete mystical experience of God in His revelation. This positive hunger for "theology" in its very highest sense would be expressed in such a text as Cant. lxxiii, 2: "Ego . . . in profundo sacri eloquii gremio spiritum mihi scrutabor et vitam" [Deep in the bosom of the sacred word I shall search my spirit and my life]. He is seeking "intellectum" and "Spiritus est qui vivificat: dat quippe intellectum. An non vita intellectus" [The Spirit gives life: indeed he gives understanding. And is not understanding life?] As you have so rightly said (p. 488) "Sa lecture de l'E. Ste prepare et occasionne son experience du divin" [His reading of Scripture prepares and occasions his experience of the divine]. But I wonder if he did not think of Scripture as a kind of *cause* of that experience, and in the same sense, "servata proportione'" [keeping due proportion], as a Sacrament is a cause of grace? Scripture puts him in direct contact with the Holy Spirit who infuses mystical grace, rather than awakening in his soul the awareness that the Holy Spirit has already infused a grace to that spoken of in Scripture. Or am I wrong? In any case, words like "scrutabor" [I shall search] and "intellectus'" [understanding] tempt me to say (while agreeing in substance with all your conclusions) that there must have been a sense in which St Bernard looked upon himself both as an exegete and as a theologian in his exposition of the *Canticle*. Although I readily admit there can be no question of his attempting as a modern author might to "make the text clear" or to "explain its meaning." That hardly concerned him, as you have shown. But do you not think, that in giving the fruit of his own contacts with the Word through Scripture he was in a sense introducing his monks to a certain mystical "attitude" towards the scriptures — not a method, but an "atmosphere" in which Scripture could become the meeting place of the Soul and the Word, through the action of the Holy Spirit?

Perhaps these are useless subtleties: but you guess that I am simply exercising my own thought in order to confront it with the reactions of an expert and this will be of the greatest service to me in the work that has been planned for me by Providence. I am also very much interested in the question of St. Bernard's attitude toward "learning," and feel that a distinction has not yet been sufficiently clearly made between his explicit reproofs of "scientia" in the sense of philosophia, and his implicit support of scientia in the sense of theologia, in his tracts on Grace, Baptism, and his attacks on Abelard, not to mention (with all due respect to your conclusions) his attitude to the *Canticle* which makes that commentary also "scientia" [knowledge] as well as "sapientia'" [wisdom]. Have you any particular lights on this distinction between science and wisdom in the Cistercians, or do you know of anything published in their regard? It seems to me to be an interesting point, especially to those of us who, like yourself and me, are monks engaged in a sort of "scientia" along with their contemplation! (It is very interesting in William of St. Thierry.)

I wish I could give you some information on St. Bernard in his relation to the Greek Fathers. I have none of my own; the topic interests me but I have barely begun to do anything about it, since I know the Greek Fathers so poorly. However, I can tell you this much: in Danielou's *Platonisme et T. M.* on pages 7 and 211 there are references to St. Bernard's dependence (?) on St. Gregory of Nyssa. The opening of St. Bernard's series of *Sermons* obviously reflects the idea of Origen and Gregory of Nyssa that the *Canticle of Canticles* was for the formation of mystics while *Proverbs* and *Ecclesiastes* applied to the beginners and progressives. I find Bernard's echo of this point an interesting piece of evidence that he considered the monastic vocation a remote call to mystical union — if not a proximate one. Then, too, Gregory's homilies on the *Canticle of Canticles* are full of a tripartite division of souls into slaves, mercenaries and spouses. Gregory's apophatism is not found in St. Bernard, but in his positive treatment of theology Bernard follows Origen. I think Fr. Danielou also told me that Bernard's attitude toward the incarnate Word is founded on Origen — I mean his thoughts on *amor carnalis Christī* [carnal love of Christ] in relation to mystical experience. I may be wrong.

A copy of *The Spirit of Simplicity* was mailed to you but my own contribution to that work is confused and weak, I believe. I refer to the second part.

I agree with what you say about Abbe de Rance and feel that my own treatment of him in *Waters of Siloe* had something in it of caricature. It is certainly true that Abbe de l'Estrange was much more austere than Rance. To my mind the most regrettable thing about both of them was their exaggeration of externals, their ponderous emphasis on "exercises" and things to be done. Nevertheless perhaps that is a sign of my own tepidity. It is true that the monastic life does demand faithful observance of many little exterior points of Rule. These can certainly not be neglected *en massé* [as a whole] without spiritual harm. But one sometimes feels that for the old Trappists they were absolutely everything.

The Desert Fathers interest me much. They seem to have summed up almost everything that is good and bad in subsequent monastic history (except for the abuses of decadent monasticism —) I mean everything that is good or bad in various monastic *ideals*.

Your news of the *De institutione reclusarum*˙ [Instruction for Recluses] — which you tell me with such detachment, is sad indeed. Do not think that manuscripts are only lost in Italy. A volume of our poems was printed by a man whose shop was in the country. Goats used to wander in to the press and eat the authors' copy. This fortunately did not happen to our poems. Perhaps the goats were wise. They sensed the possibility of poisoning.

I am extremely eager to get Fr. Bouyer's new book on monasticism, but have not yet been able to do so. I feel that our book dealer sometimes takes orders and then forgets about them — I mean for books to come out later. I liked his *Saint Antoine*. Still, I wonder if he does not overdo his interest in the fact that in the early ages of the Church people were so clearly aware that the fall had put the devil in charge of material things. Fr. Danielou's *Signe du Temple*, in its first chapter, gives a good counterpoise to that view — for heaven still shone through creation and God was very familiar with men in Genesis!

The other day we mailed Burch's *Steps of Humility* to you and it should be in your hands shortly. If you wish to send us something in return we would like to get Wilmart's *Pensees du B. Guigue*, if this is Guigo the Carthusian. I have never yet gone into him. His lapidary style fascinates me. He is better than Pascal. Yet I love Pascal.

Your page on the eremitical vocation was very welcome. Someone told me the Carthusians were at last coming to America. I know the Trappist who has gone to Camadoli. He was with me in the novitiate here. I wonder if he is happy there. His departure surprised me and I think his arrival surprised some of the Camaldolese.

Cistercian monasticism in America is of a genus all its own. Imagine that we now have one hundred and fifty novices at Gethsemani. This is fantastic. Many of them are sleeping in a tent in the preau. The nucleus of seniors is a small, bewildered group of men who remember the iron rule of Dom Edmond Obrecht and have given up trying to comprehend what has happened to Gethsemani. The house has a very vital and enthusiastic (in the good sense) and youthful air like the camp of an army preparing for an easy and victorious war. Those of us who have been sobered by a few years of the life find ourselves in turns comforted and depressed by the multitude of our young companions of two and three months' standing: comforted by their fervor and joy and simplicity, and depressed by the sheer weight of numbers. The cloister is as crowded as a Paris street.

On the whole, when the house is completely full of men who are happy because they have not yet had a chance to suffer anything (although they believe themselves willing) the effect is a little disquieting. One feels more solidly rooted in God in a community of veterans, even though many of them may be morose. However, I do not waste my time seeking consolation in the community or avoiding its opposite. There is too little time for these accidentals.

I close this long letter thanking you again for yours, which are always so full of interest and profit. I cannot place the reference to a contribution of mine to *Rhythmes du Monde*; maybe there is some mistake — or my publisher went directly to them. I would be interested in seeing your *Soli Deo Vivere!* I sent something to *Dieu Vivant.* I like them. Is the magazine *Opus Dei* worth the trouble of getting a subscription? I wish we could feel here that *Irenikon* was essential for us. Can you persuade us that it is? Or that it is important? The thought of reunion with the Greeks is one that haunts me.

Once again, dear Father, thank you for your advice and inspiration. May Jesus bless your great work for His glory and for the vitality of monasticism everywhere. Pray for me in my turn to be more and more a child of St Benedict — and if it be God's will, that I may some day find a way to be something of an eremitcal son of St Benedict! What of these Benedictines in the mountains of France? Have you more information about them? I am not inquiring in a spirit of restlessness! Their project is something I admire on its own merits.

Your devoted brother in Christ,

fr. M. Louis Merton, O.C.S.O.

Jean Leclercq to Thomas Merton

Paris, 26. 10. 50

Dear Reverend Father,

Some weeks ago I received the nice little book *Spirit of Simplicity.* We already had the French text of the report of Dom Chautard. But your volume with his notes, pictures and references and texts is precious. Thank you very, very much.

I have also received your kind letter of 9. 10. 50 and thank you for it. Of course, I agree that St. Bernard was a theologian in the traditional sense of the word: loqui Deo de Deo. This meaning has been preserved in the monastic tradition, and I explained that in my *Jean de Fecamp.* I am coming to notice more and more how much not only St. Bernard, but the whole monastic world of the twelfth century, Cistercian and Benedictine, is full of Origen. I gave a lecture on this subject three weeks ago at Chevetogne, and I have been asked to publish it in *Irenikon.* In it I pointed out this relation between the Greek fathers and medieval monasticism. I had already dealt with the question in a very general way in 1945. Now I see things better.

Maybe I shall collect everything I find on the matter and write a little article. The works of Origen which have been the most read by monks are his commentaries on Holy Scripture. And it is his exegesis, more than his doctrine, which influenced monks and Bernard.

Your distinction between *scientia* and *sapientia* is quite exact. It is a very traditional distinction, which obliged Thomas* [Aquinas] in the *In Quaestio* also to treat *theologia* as *sapientia*, although in another meaning of *Sapientia*. For him

> *sapientia* is cognitio per altissimas causas
> *scientia* is cognitio per causas immediatias.

For tradition, Poets and monks, and in the Franciscan school,

> *scientia* is cognitio per intellectum
> *sapientia* is "scientia sapida": recta sapere:

it is this savour, gustus, which we find so frequently in Bernard, William of Saint-Thierry and all other monks.

Another distinction which we often find in monastic literature is that between scientia: cognitio intellectualis

> conscientia: cognitio ad vitam

(I wrote a chapter "Science et conscience" on this in my *Pierre de Celle*.)

After further information, I now think that Rance was no Cistercian at all. So you were quite right in what you said in *Waters of Siloe*.

I am now working on the unprinted writings of Gaufridus Antissiodorensis (= Altacomba = Claravallensis): a very good witness of the second generation of Cistercians and of St. Bernard. He insists constantly on discretion. I shall publish the more significant texts.

Fr. Bouyer's new book has not come out yet. It will surely interest you. For any books you need in France, I advise you to write to:

> Librairie Sainte Marie
> 5, Rue de la Source,
> Paris XVIe

(it is our monastery in Paris). They have a service specially for that, and they send many books to Canada and elsewhere, and they do the necessary research well and rapidly. They would help you and at the same time you could help them by ordering your books there.

I hope I shall find Burch in Clervaux next week. I will send you the Pensees of Guigues, who is really Guigo the Carthusian. A nice book.

About the eremitical vocation: it is clear that the Cistercian vocation and life are, in themselves, eremitical. So a Cistercian normally, should not have to seek this anywhere else than in his enclosure. The Cistercian's solitude depends on his silence. But it may happen that for accidental and psychological reasons, for example if there are too many monks in the same monastery, or if a monk has too much to do, he longs for more silence. Then I think that the solution for him is to change his monastery and seek silence and quiet elsewhere, in another Cistercian monastery.

I do not know *Opus Dei*. But I think *Irenikon* is quite worth the trouble of getting a subscription.

My confreres in the mountains of Vercors are not making any noise. So I think all is well with them.

Do you have in your library *Histoire de l'Ordre de S. Benoit* by D. Ph. Schmitt, Maredsous 1942-1948, 5 volumes? I have a copy of it to sell. I bought it for a monastery in Germany, and afterwards they wrote and said they did not want it. It is a fundamental work though not everything is exact in it, especially concerning Cistercian origins. But the nomenclature, bibliography, and matter are complete and it is a very useful book. If you need it, I could sell it to you. Payment should be easy: I think my monastery has an account in America.

All best wishes Father. Please pray for me. Next week I am going to Germany in search of Bernard's manuscripts.

Always very sincerely yours,

f. J. Leclercq

Jean Leclercq to Thomas Merton

Clervaux, 17. 3. 53

Dear Father Louis,

It was very kind of you indeed to send your *Sign of Jonas*, thank you sincerely. I will try to answer you in my bad English, but most of us Frenchmen still write with a pen, as in the middle ages, and it takes me longer to write, even in French, with the typewriter. And I am not in the excellent condition Sertillanges requires for intellectual life: about every five minutes the bell rings and I have to go to Choir — with joy — or to wash dishes — also with joy — or something else.

As you are accustomed to receiving praise, I shall not send you one more letter of that sort. I'll just say that I surveyed your book and I liked it. I think that I shall read it when I find time. It is written with this kind of freshness, a little "primitive" that we like in Americans (I suppose you accept me speaking to you simply, like a monk to a monk). I think this book with *Seeds of Contemplation*, is exactly the kind of book you are made to write. I've got an idea. Maybe you have heard of the little collection *Tradition monastique* in which appeared the wonderful book by Bouyer, *Le sens de la vie monastique*? I am one of the directors. Maybe it would be possible to publish a translation of your *Journal* or parts of it. Would you agree (since I see that your Abbey keeps the copyright), to reserve us the possibility of publishing a French translation in this collection? It does not depend only on me. But if you give me your agreement on the principle, I will get in touch with the publisher etc.

I am ashamed to say, but I must confess that I did not read *Seven Storey Mountain*. I didn't find time. But I know that my confreres like the book, and *Seeds* as well. I suppose that you are aware of the criticism made in Europe, especially in England, on your *Ascent*, and even in France, coming from the pen of Fr. Bouyer in *Vie spirituelle*. But these are the sort of criticisms that Europeans are prepared to make. And the Church is everywhere, in the Old and the New World. In Europe we are so complicated: textual criticism has come to have such importance. We cannot even quote the *Pater noster* without putting a reference in the footnotes.

Now for some remarks and questions:

1. What is this XIV century manuscript you mention on p. 64? You sent me the microfilm of a XII century ms of a sermon of St. Bernard. Have you another one? On which folio is this picture in an "I" that you mention? I suppose that he is standing in the "I" with a book in his hand?

2. Will you publish this book you promise on p. 269? Some years ago an English Trappist, then an American Trappist asked me for permission to publish an English translation of *St. Bernard mystique*. I gave, of course, my agreement and sent both letters to the publishers, Desclee. Then I heard no more about it. I suppose, and I quite understand, that the English or American pulishers were afraid of the concurrence of Thomas Merton. The German translation will appear next week at Pustet, for the centenary.

3. On p. 159 there is a sentence on the Common Observance for which I must reproach you. I think it is an injustice: it is not exact. Let me tell

you this: I am charged with organizing a congress on the theology of St. Bernard, and I invited a Cistercian of the Common Observance, whom I know to be a Doctor of Theology and, nevertheless, a very good monk. But recently, after many months, he wrote to say that he could not accept to come because, being in charge of the monastery hens and other things as well, in addition to Choir, Chapter and so on, he had not found time to prepare a communication. On the other hand I know several Trappists who are in pretty good condition for intellectual work. It is a sin against the motto of your Order: Una caritate. There seem to be two charities: one for the Trappists and another for the Common Observance. I think that the fault lies not only (maybe not chiefly) with you, but with your censors. And since your books, even in English, are expected to be read in Europe, I would suggest that one of the censors be European. There are some points of view that a European would feel. You remember the difficulties with the French translation of the *Waters of Siloe*, and the trouble this gave P. Dimier.

I recently met in London the censor for the English books in your Order. A very sweet person, and an "echter Trappist."

Of course I understand that you are quite persuaded that the Trappist life is a very high state of perfection, and you are doing good apologetic work for it; but you must not forget that it is not the only form of contemplative life, at least in Europe.

Excuse me for all this. I give you an occasion for "gouter les humiliations." But you know that I do so because I esteem you and your life, and because I am very sincerely yours in the charity of Christ,

f. J. Leclercq

Thomas Merton to Jean Leclercq

May 18, 1953

My Dear Father in Christ:

Forgive me for my delay in answering your good letter. *Jonas* is already being translated for Albin Michel, so I regretfully decline your kind offer. It would have been an honor to appear in Tradition Monastique, in which series I already know your volume and that of Pere Bouyer. By the way, has the promised Casel volume appeared in this series yet? I am anxious to see it. Now for your questions:

1 — The XIV Century manuscript of St. Bernard is marked as n. 4 in the list of manuscripts and incunabula contributed by Dom Edmond Obrecht to the studies in *St. Bernard et son Temps*, Dijon, 1929, vol. ii, p. 133. I sent you a photograph of the page with the "I" which, in fact, is of no interest.

2 — I am not doing any work on a book on St. Bernard and there has been no announcement of any such book; hence I don't think it is in competition with your *St. Bernard Mystique*. If it gets finished — or started — before 1955 I will be surprised. The plan still exists, but I have no time to work on it.

3 — The remark about the monks of the Common Observance understanding the truth of a statement of Sertillanges on the intellectual life which Trappists are incapable of understanding does not seem to me to be an injustice. The statement of Sertillanges is true, and there is no injustice in saying that someone agrees with the truth. Nor was it intended to be disparaging. However, if it appears so to you, perhaps they will themselves be even more sensitive about it, so I will delete it from the French edition, along with a lot of other things which will be of no interest in France. One of the censors of *Jonas* was a European. Then, too, I think the book shows clearly that I do not consider the Trappist life the highest form of contemplative life, because I believe such a theory to be plainly false. The Trappist life is a solidly austere form of the monastic life, which has its limitations, which offers opportunities for a man to become a contemplative, provided the opportunities are not ruined by excessive activity within the monastery. We have something of the spirit of St. Bernard but we have no monopoly on it. From the little I know of Hauterive I am certain they are just as good a monastery and just as proper for the contemplative life as Gethsemani — with perhaps certain advantages over Gethsemani. I do not despise the Common Observance at all, nor do I despise the Benedictines (as Dom Aelred Graham seems to think).

The more I reflect on it the more I realize that all the monastic ways to God are most worthy of praise, and that, in the end, there is no point in asking who has the most perfect interpretation of the Rule of St. Benedict. In the end, however, what I most personally and intimately feel about at least my own place in the framework of things is echoed by the remarkable articles of a certain "S" in *La Vie Spirituelle* of last October and again more recently. Do you happen to know who this "S" may be, and would there be some chance of finding him and writing him a letter? (See "L'Eremitisme dans la vie spirituelle" *V. S.*, Oct. 1952). I also by the way enjoyed your article in *Rhythmes du Monde* now reproduced in *Temoignages*. I hope more and more to withdraw from the field of professional writing — or at least to appear in it only as an occasional author of disjointed meditations. But I do earnestly beg your prayers that I may seek God with greater love, and that He may deign to open to us here in America the ways of solitude, within the framework of our monasticism. This, I think, is much more important than any books. I thank you again for your letter which, as you see, was stimulating. If there is anything I can do for you about our St. Bernard manuscripts, let me know. With fraternal wishes in Xto Domino,

fr. M. Louis Merton

Jean Leclercq to Thomas Merton

Clervaux 29 may 1953

My dear Father,

Thank you for your letter of the 18th.

The book by Casel *Die Monchsweihe* will not be coming out in the near future because we are expecting a new edition which is being prepared and then we shall revise the translation according to the new edition which will have some modifications. A little book by Cardinal Schuster has just come out in the collection: *La vie monastique dans la pensee de S. Benoit*; the little book written by my abbot, *Ambroise Autpert moine et theologien*, is forthcoming. The next volume will be the French translation of *Sancta Sophia* by Dom˜ [Augustine] Baker. Then a little book by P. A. Dimier on *Les observances monastique*.

Thanks for sending me the photo of the picture of St. Bernard, in spite of the little interest it has.

I am sending you my little book *La doctrine del Beato Paolo Gustiniani* which is about the eremitical life of the Camoldolese. I recently went again to the hermitage of Frascati while I was in Rome, from where I have just got back. There is a real contemplative life there. It is not prosperity and numbers, but peace and prayer.

I appreciated your preface to *S. Bernard* of the CHOC.

I am glad that you are suppressing the allusion to Common Observance in the French translation of *Jonas*, and even I would like it to disappear in the other translations and re-editions. I am not the only one who finds it regrettable, in spite of your good intention.

The author of the two beautiful articles on the eremitical life who signs "S" is abbe J. Sainsaulieu. Of course you can write to him, 3 Rue de Clamart, Le-Plessis-Robinson (Seine) France. The first article of *Vie spirituelle*, October, is by my abbot.

Yes I pray for you because now, on account of your books, you have a responsibility which you must keep up. The news that you will no longer be a "professional writer" will please several people. You have done much good by your books, but you can also do so by the silence which you speak about. It is said that you can talk on the radio. But you have your vocation, of which no one is judge. Follow it.

A Dieu, my dear Father. I am always your fraternally in Dno,

f. J. Leclercq

If there are some letters of St. Bernard in the ms 4 of the Obrecht list, I would be pleased to know which ones; the list says: Sermones, homilae et *varia*. Anything other than letters does not interest me in a manuscript of such a late epoch.

Thomas Merton to Jean Leclercq

August 21, 1953

Dear Father in Christ:

You must think me a very churlish and ungrateful person to leave your letter so long unanswered. We have had a busy summer, with much harvesting and other farm work. In addition to that our cow barn burned down and we have also bought a new farm, so that everyone has been exceptionally busy and I am two months behind with practically all correspondence.

Our monastery would like very much to order four copies of Cardinal Shuster's _Vie Monastique_, and we will also be looking forward to Pere Dimier's book on monastic observances. I am presently dipping into a manuscript of his about his war experiences but I do not have time to read it continuously although I find it very interesting.

Above all I want to thank you for your _Dottrina del B. P. Giustiniani_. I find it most useful and am glad to have it, particularly because it would otherwise be quite impossible for me to make the acquaintance of his personality and ideas. You have given us a valuable source. I hope books will appear on all the great Camoldolese figures. Dom Giabbani sent me some pictures of Camoldoli and it is both beautiful and inspiring to me. I can well believe what you say about their having the true contemplative life at Frascati. I know nothing of that particular eremo. I would be interested in having some pictures of it as I may perhaps do an article on the Camoldo- lese — by way of exception, since I do not write for magazines any more. This would be in the hope of helping them make a foundation in this country. They are needed.

I find that in some monastic orders there is a kind of selfish and dog-in-the-manger attitude towards other orders and other forms of the contemplative life. One illusion that is very strong in this country still is the idea that the eremitical life is essentially "dangerous" and "impossible" etc. Some monks who claim to have a high contemplative ideal will actually run down the solitary life, and show a preference for the rather intense activity which is inevitable in a big, busy monastery of cenobites. It is all very well to have a big, busy monastery, but why claim that this is the highest possible ideal of contemplation! The French have a good word for that: fumisterie [practical joke].

If you want a microfilm of these letters we can easily send you one. I like Abbe Sainsaulieu's article on the Desert in the recent _V. S._ I will not bother him by writing to him. I have no time to write the letters that I am obliged to answer.

I was amused to think that I am supposed to be speaking on the radio. It is a great ordeal simply to speak to the monks in chapter. What would I do if I had to speak on the radio? I have not been out of the monastery for over a year, and then it was only for one day's journey. The only talk I have given outside the monastery was through the grille of the Louisville Carmel. I do not imagine that perfection consists merely in staying inside the enclosure, but the fact remains that I hate to go out and am very glad that I never have to do so. The last thing I would ever desire would be to speak on the radio.

Thank you for your prayers. I need them. And I hope they will obtain for me more and more solitude and obscurity and the humility proper to a true monk. I remember you also at Mass and beg Our Lard to give you every grace.

Devotedly yours in Christ,

fr. M. Louis, O.C.S.O.

P.S. I do not know anything about Ambrose Autpert; otherwise I would probably be asking you also to send your Father Abbot's work on him. I shall be very interested to hear about the St. Bernard celebrations at Lyon. I only heard a few words about the affair in May. We did practically nothing here.

Jean Leclercq to Thomas Merton

In via pacis 23. 9. 53.

Dear Father Louis,

I received your very good letter of August 21 just before leaving Clervaux for Dijon, where I had to play on the "theatrum mundi," being the secretary of the theological congress on St. Bernard. This congress has been wonderfully interesting, much more than anyone ever expected. The lectures were all of a very high standard, from the double point of view of theology and spirituality (our chief trial is to reconcile them), and above all the atmosphere was always full of charity. Everybody was pleased and peaceful: discussion never became controversial; everything finished on Saturday afternoon with a very contemplative trip to Fontenay where we all admired the style inspired by twelfth-century Cistercian life and "monastic theology." We had Fr. Danielou, De Lubac, Mouroux, Dechanet, O. Rousseau, Congar, Pacifique Delgaauw of Tilburg, Claude Botard of Orval, and others, all agreeing on the same themes of what they all called "monastic theology," all coming to the conclusion that its characteristic is fidelity to patristic sources. They all said, too, that there is no opposition at all between "monastic" and "scholastic" theology, but the former could be useful to the latter. Professor A. Forest, a layman, but very contemplative gave a very deep and beautiful lecture on St. Bernard and contemporary thought, in the style of his book which I suppose you know, *La vocation de l'Esprit* (Paris, Aubier, 1953), each page of which could be illustrated with texts of St. Bernard. I will not tell you more about this congress: in a few months time you will read, I hope, the text of all these lectures. Many of the Reverend Fathers at the General Chapter came from Citeaux for two of the sessions. On Sunday morning, at Fontaines, in the rain, I had a very short talk with your Reverend Father whom I am very, very glad to have met. And now I am on my way back to Clervaux where I shall be tonight.

I tell you confidentially that your Reverend Father asked me if I could go and preach a retreat at Gethsemani. Of course, I just made objections — and I think they were sincere — and especially I pointed out that I really do not think that I speak English fluently enough. Let's wait and see if God gives further signs of His will. But of course, if Providence arranges for me to be in the States for some time, I would be pleased not only of the opportunity of seeing Cistercian manuscripts over there, and of searching for others, but also of seeing you and your community.

Before leaving Clervaux, I had four copies of Schuster's *Vie monastique* sent to you. My abbot added his little book on Anbroise Autpert as a little present.

I have no more postcards of the Eremo of Frascati. But I wrote to my friend D. Maurizio, who is master of novices there, and I asked him to send you some. I hope you will get them. It would be a great charity if you could do something to make the Camoldolese of Monte Corona better known in America. It is not a question of propaganda; the point is rather that people who have an eremitical vocation may have the chance of living it and of knowing about this religious order.

And now, my dear Father, I leave you in peace. Let us pray for one another.

f. J. Leclercq

Jean Leclercq to Thomas Merton

Clervaux, 13. 10. 53.

Dear Father Louis,

I am writing to ask you a service. But of course you are quite free to refuse and I shall well understand.

This is what it is about: The publication of the French text of my little book about the doctrine of Blessed P. Giustiniani has been decided. The title will be something like this: Seul avec Dieu. La vie eremitique selon le B. P. Giustiniani. The book will appear in the collection *Tradition monastique*. But the publisher is a little afraid because he thinks that the book will interest only the Camoldolese. What has decided him to publish the book is that it is written by a Benedictine whom he knows has nothing of the Camoldolese vocation.

You were good enough to write that you appreciated the book. Could you write a few pages to preface it? I think that if both a Cistercian and a Benedictine agree in presenting a book of this sort, any hesitation on the part of the publisher and public will disappear. It should be made clear that though such a doctrine, such a life and in particular this form of contemplatiuve life, is an ideal not to be aimed at by all, it is a good thing that it should not be forgotten by anyone: it must remain a sign, a witness in the Church of God and in the monastic order as a whole. So I thought you could further our common ideal.

If you and your Reverend Father agree to my proposition, you could write these few (or many) pages in English and I would translate them into French.

Please convey my best regards to your Reverend Father.

Everything is going peacefully here and, as far as I hear, in all our monasteries. Our Father Abbot has just come back from the blessing of the abbot of Fontgombault a new foundation made by Solesmes. In the last century it was occupied by Trappists. The church, pure XII century style, is wonderfully clear, beautiful and peaceful. It is quite the style for our life. Here also we have one such monastery, modern but very pure.

You know, dear Father, that I am always yours in Dmno.

f. J. Leclercq

By way of a sort of compensation I am sending you a few pages I have written on St. Bernard in the Review *Camoldoli*. I think that all religious orders, chiefly monastic orders have a great deal to learn from one another.

Thomas Merton to Jean Leclercq

Nov. 5, 1953

Dear Father in Christ,

It was a satisfaction to me when Father Abbot gave me permission to write the preface for your volume on Paul Giustiniani [*Alone with God*, Farrar, Straus]. The preface is completed and is on the way to you by surface mail. I was happy to write it, and happy to go over your book again. I feel that it is especially important that the true place of the solitary in the Church should be brought out at this time when there are so many who despise contemplation and when even in the monastic orders there is a tendency to go off the right road precisely because the values for which the solitary exists are not appreciated. If my preface does not suit you, please feel free to alter or cut as you see fit, but let me know. Perhaps I could go over the proofs of this preface.

Regarding the material side of the question: may I depend on you to get this preface censored by the two censors of our Order for the French language? I do not know who they are, but Chimay could tell you. All other material questions in regard to what I write are dealt with by an agent and he will be in touch with Plon in due course.

I have been reading with great satisfaction Cardinal Shuster's little volume. It has a very fine tone, and its simplicity and solidity make it attractive as well as useful. I like it very much and feel that it is doing me good. It makes me wonder if I might not ask Cardinal Shuster to write a preface to the translation of a forthcoming book of mine on the Psalms. Does he know English? Could you let me know, and I will send him a copy if he does. A copy will also come to you. You might like it for your series, but I do not know if the agent will give Albin Michel first option on it. Probably. But they may not take it.

It would indeed be a great pleasure to receive you at Gethsemani and have you preach our retreat. I sincerely hope that Divine Providence will bring you to America and that we will have this satisfaction. I was glad to hear of the theological conferences at Dijon and look forward to seeing them in print.

Returning to Gethsemani — could the Camoldolese at Frascati perhaps send me a picture or a relic of him? Even some pictures of their *eremo*. I am still hoping to write a little something on the Camoldolese, to make them known in America. Any information or books they send will be useful to me and to their own cause.

I certainly agree wholeheartedly that the monastic orders have much to learn from one another, and we in America have much to learn from you in Europe. We are very isolated and provincial, I am afraid, and our undue sense of our own importance may perhaps delude us that we are the only monks in the world. It may not be possible for me to satisfy the desires of my own heart, but at least I can continue to have zeal for God's truth and for the monastic ideal. Pray for me, and may we remain united in Christ and St. Benedict.

fr. M. Louis

Jean Leclercq to Thomas Merton

23. 11. 53

Dear Fr. Louis,

I have received your letter, and then the Preface. I have read it and shall translate it. I think it is just what was necessary, and that will be useful for the book. May we be unanimous in the esteem for the contemplative life, even of solitary life, even if we are unable to live according to this ideal. For, as regards the easier life of activity, it will never be necessary to speak of it to monks. The natural tendency, with very good reasons, is always going to the active life. But it is necessary to recall that solitude and contemplation are also legitimate in the Church of God.

I shall send you a copy of the French translation of the Preface. And I think you will receive galley proofs.

The Prior of Scourmont [Cistercian monastery in Belgium] answers me that the censors are now anonymous. So I shall send the translated introduction to the Rev. Fr. General in Rome.

My friend, D. Maurizio, Novice Master of the Eremo at Frascati, writes me that he has been delighted to see your Rev. Fr. at the Eremo, and that he gave him some pictures of the Eremo. As regards relics of Blessed Giustiniani, I wonder if they have something, but the autographs. And there is no great literature on the subject. But I shall write to D. Maurizio about that.

Yes, on the whole, the book of Card. Shuster is really a fine book. Some details seem to be nonsense, but the general impression, surely, is authentically Benedictine.

I suppose Card. Shuster would accept to write for you a preface. He is very attached to everything which is monastic. I am going to Milan for a lecture at the Catholic University on St. Bernard, Theologian. He will speak the last day. I shall pay him a visit and ask him about your preface. And I will answer you. I suppose he does read English.

Don't think at all that you, Americans, are monks of secondary quality. On the contrary, I think that you are, and for some time, in better condition than we are as regards "sancta simplicitas'" [holy simplicity]. Here, in this old, too old Europe, we all are sophisticated, intellectual, complicated; we are dying of erudition. We have no spontaneity any more, nothing of the "spiritus liberatis" [liberty of spirit] which is necessary to any creation or renovation. There is in your monasticism something of ingenuous that we are tempted to despise; but you are right. We know all the constitutions, statutes, texts and so on, but we are quite unable to invent any thing adapted to new times. That is why I hope so much from you in America, especially as regards intercommunion; if some revival is to come, it will come from you. You have more liberty of mind, and more courage. We may have more austerity, more science, more aesthetic. But the sources of life are with you. I have not been alone; in Dijon last August, when we saw all the Trappists one got the impression that the Americans reminded us of the first Citeaux. In the first Citeaux there was also this kind of freshness, of liberty, of initiative, of courage in the life, of which you have something. You are probably not very conscious of it, but I expect that your abbots must feel it, when they come over here. And even this "unawareness of your importance" of which you speak, is a sign of vitality: you still believe in monastic life, you have the impression of having discovered it, it is a new reality for you. For us, it is an old, venerable institution which we try to preserve, like archeologists do for museum pieces. Of course, we also believe in monastic life, but in more of an intellectual way. Also, the first Cistercians believed that they were the only monks. The old, too old, Benedictines, protested. But it was true that the life had passed to the Cistercians. I, for instance, noticed from experience that you are more free from prejudices, more ready to accept history as it has been, than here in Europe. We always *fear* dangers for the uniformity, or for the reputation of the Order, or for our sentimental piety. You don't fear. You look forward to the future. Fear is proper to old people. And when we are too old, we die . . .

We are not yet dying. But I am sure that we have at least as much to learn from you as you have from us. That's why everything that helps us to know your ways and methods is useful to us.

Excuse this long digression. I am very sincerely

Yours in Christ,

J. Leclercq

[P.S.] I am gathering the texts for the volume *S. Bernard theologien*, which will result from the Dijon Congress. I think that in spite of its European erudition, it will give a good idea of St. Bernard's theology. But we still need more freshness and creative strength. We feel it, and are unable to have it. Let's do humbly what we can . . .

Thomas Merton to Jean Leclercq

December 7, 1953

Dear Dom Leclercq,

Many thanks for your very kind letter of Nov. 23. I am glad the preface satisfied you, and am still gratified at having been able to write it. Thank you also for offering to ask Cardinal Shuster about his preface.

I received a letter and some books from Dom Maurizio at Frascati. Father Abbot had left them in Rome to be posted from there and they came late. *There were no pictures.* I am very glad to be in relations with Frascati.

What you say about our American monks having a true monastic spirit is gratifying. I cannot deny that the Holy Spirit is truly at work here. And there is much spontaneity. But I do not think we have any of the solidity of European monasticism, and in our fervor there is much that is merely human enthusiasm. Also much provincialism.

I believe it is good for me to work for the *monastic* ideal as a whole, and not be a "propagandist" for any one order. Indeed, I think the more we work for unity among ourselves the better it will be.

God bless you — pray for me.

fr. M. Louis

[P.S.] Are you doing anything special at Clairvaux for the Marian Year?

Thomas Merton to Jean Leclercq

April 27, 1954

Dear Dom Jean:

I have just written to the Agent. I suspect that Plon is unjustly penalizing you because the Agent sought some kind of material settlement for the preface. I had not stopped to think that this might happen. The only reason why I use an Agent is quite obvious — it saves me an immense amount of correspondence, contract work and business worries. If I did otherwise, I would never have any time for anything except business. I simply leave all cares to the middle-man. This of course has its hard-boiled aspects, since the Agent is bent on making a living out of his percentage. I do not think it is altogether fair of Plon to retaliate by threatening the future of your series, although in a way I see where that is logical — with the logic of the jungle.

However, if it will help your series at all to publish a book by me, I have a small volume on St Bernard about to appear. It is very slight, not a formal life, simply a brief introduction to the saint and to the recent Encyclical. It has three parts — a sketch of his life and character, an outline of his works and teaching, and a commentary on the Encyclical — followed by the text of the Papal Document itself. I had not even thought of allowing this book to be published in France. When you see it, you will probably agree that it adds nothing to the number of excellent studies of St. Bernard, including your own. I do not think it will help your series except accidentally. If the appearance of the author's name is of any use to you, I will consent to let this book appear in France — without worrying about what may happen to my reputation. I will send you the book as soon as I can procure a copy. It is not yet off the press.

I can agree with what you say about the Benedictine life. The more I come into indirect contact with the Benedictine houses of Europe, like yours and La Pierre-qui-Vire, the more I appreciate the depth and solidity of the monastic spirit, and profit by contact with it. It is indeed a paradox that you do now in fact have much more real silence and peace than many a Trappist monastery. I never felt any sympathy with Rance's ideas about erudition, and I am sure that the work done by Benedictines today in this field is perfectly monastic and truly fruitful in the line of monastic spirituality.

The last thing in the world a monk should seek or care about is material success. That which I see in my own labors is as much a surprise to me as it is to anybody else. Nor can I find in myself the power to get very interested in that success. I do not claim this to be a virtue, because I never really understood money anyway. I do not know how much our books have acquired. The figures are not communicated to me and if they were I would probably not understand them anyway.

In any case I have instructed the Agent to take some kind of cognizance of the problem you mention in your letter. It is of course inevitable that such things should be said about me, and I do not see what there is to be done about it. Thank you for defending the truth. Meanwhile, I have also told the Agent that if you want the St. Bernard book, *The Last of the Fathers*, I would like you to have it on a "poor" basis. That will at least give me the satisfaction of cooperating in a work which I admire, for I have derived great pleasure and profit from reading the volumes that have reached me so far. It is quite certain that if the monastic life is to fulfil its important role in our world today there must be books that reflect the peace and sanity and depth of the true monastic tradition. Not all monastic books fulfil that function, for in every part of the Church cockle can be intermixed with the good wheat.

Please do not feel yourself obliged to write a review of *Bread in the Wilderness*. My only way of getting a copy to you was to have the publisher send you a review copy. If however you do write a review I shall feel very pleased and honored.

Please commend me to the prayers of your dear Lord Abbot and ask his blessing for me. Let us continue in union of prayers and in solitude, in limine aeternitatis [on the threshold of eternity].

Your devoted brother in Christ,

fr. M. Louis

THOMAS MERTON
AND
ST. BERNARD OF CLAIRVAUX

by **Jean Leclercq**, O. S. B.

On the occasion of the ninth centenary of the birth of St. Bernard of Clairvaux, I have been asked to suggest some parallels between him and Thomas Merton. It is not in order, I suppose, to compare St. Bernard to Merton — something that Merton himself would have abhorred — but rather to compare Merton to St. Bernard. These two men, one of the twelfth century, and the other of the twentieth, had this in common: they were both monks of the Cistercian Order. They were also writers and through their writings had great influence in their own times and afterwards. Both had a message, even a teaching, for their readers who were also their disciples.

I

It would be hazardous to compare them in the field of doctrine, if only because they lived in such very different times and cultures. We do not know — though it is not entirely nonsensical to imagine — what Bernard would have said about Merton. But we do know what Merton thought of Bernard.

From the very first letters I received from Thomas Merton, in the late 1940s, he shared the impressions he got from his readings of the works of St. Bernard and from writings about him. He asked some very good questions, which were quite pertinent. His reactions were personal ones. It was Bernard who offered me the first opportunity of contacting Merton (Fr.

Louis): I needed a microfilm of a medieval manuscript kept in the library of the Abbey of Gethsemani [this was from the Obrecht Collection, which is currently on permanent loan to the Institutes of Cistercian Studies Library at Western Michigan University, Kalamazoo, Michigan]. Our correspondence immediately became an exchange of views on Scripture, theology and St. Bernard.

Shortly afterwards, in view of the eighth centenary of the death of St. Bernard, in 1953, a very learned and bulky volume entitled *Bernard de Clairvaux*, was in preparation and the editor thought that it would reach a wider reading public if it had a preface by Thomas Merton, who was already famous as a writer. He accepted and did a good job. He was well aware of the fact that he was no historian, but he had discovered, mainly after the success of *The Seven Storey Mountain*, not only, as he admitted, that he was "an author," but also what it meant for him to be one and what it meant for his readers. The fact that he had been requested to preface an historical work was something with which the editor was immediately reproached. An illustrious European university professor — who perhaps would have liked to write the preface himself — pointed out that this American star-writer was not a scholar — as he himself was — and that he was nothing of an historian or a medievalist. However, the volume was published, and even reprinted. It is still the most valuable synthesis we have of the life and activities of St. Bernard. And Merton's preface is still being read.

In the meanwhile, Merton continued to talk about St. Bernard to the novices and juniors of Gethsemani. He also wrote a few items, articles and even books, which I have not read, on St. Bernard. His talks were tape-recorded and then transcribed. After his death they were collected and made up a little book on St. Bernard. When asked to write the introduction, I was ill at ease: would I too have to point out that he was not an expert? To my suprise, I discovered that he had gone to the heart of the matter. His powers of penentration were so great that he was immediately able to grasp the essential and to express it in a way which met the spiritual and practical needs of the present-day reader.˙ [See *Thomas Merton on St. Bernard* (Kalamazoo: Cistercian Publications, 1980)].

II

If now we turn to the biographies of Bernard and Merton, there are certain similarities which catch the eye at once. Both had lost their mothers when they were young boys.. But unlike Merton, Bernard never expressed any feeling about his mother, be it sorrow at her death or any other sentiment. All that has been written on the subject is legendary.

Both Bernard and Merton underwent a process of conversion to the monastic life when they were already young adults. And both spent several years reflecting and thinking things over before deciding to become monks. The decision was a good one and they both found fulfillment in the Cistercian life even though other possibilities were open to them. Both profited from the rich culture they had received in the years preceding their entry into the monastic life: they read widely and developed the talent of expressing their thoughts in beautiful and elegant writing. Both had a tendency towards what some people today would term mysticism, that is to say, a kind of spiritual experience and the ability to put it into words, either orally or in writing. They felt a certain need and attraction for an encounter with God, without however losing either their practical common sense or their intellectual capacities.

Eventually, in the last period of their lives — the last dozen years or so — from about 1139 for Bernard and 1956 for Merton — they became involved, more or less directly, in political activity which aimed at pacifying their contemporaries and persuading them to reduce and limit the violence inherent in their cultures. Has the Vietnam War not been compared to a crusade in favor of human rights and religious freedom? I remember being in Saigon shortly after Francis Cardinal Spellman had been there to justify with such arguments the intervention of the United States and its bombing raids. That had greatly disturbed some people, Christians and others. Furthermore, every evening a Christian minister was blessing the bombers at a base on Guam Island with no mention of the victims. When I shared my impressions on this matter with Merton in a letter, he agreed with them.

As for St. Bernard and the crusade to free the Holy Land, it is true to say that he had never thought of it until he was asked to wield his pen in this cause which, as recent studies have shown, was supported by the majority of Christians at that time. "Crusading as an Act of Love" is the title of a recent historical article quoting many texts to that effect. And another learned publication, *Criticism of the Crusades*, establishes that if any criticism was indeed made it was not about the fact of taking the Cross, but about the taxes that were sometimes imposed on the faithful to finance the expeditions. In a treatise Bernard had written earlier, *In Praise of the Templar Knights*, while justifying the fact of fighting to ensure the safety of Christian pilgrims, he endeavored to restrict as much as possible any armed

violence and reduce it to the minimum. He exhorted the Knights to resort
to violence only for justifiable reasons and with pure intentions. He warned
them never to fight for glory or through ambition and greed. I remember
having once quoted the words, at an American university, in which Bernard
says that victory can be unfortunate: *infelix victoria*. Armed violence was
part of the societies to which Bernard and Merton belonged: the latter
dreamed of suppressing all forms of violence, and Bernard did all he could
to restrict it. Both worked for peace and were in favor of those realities
which are true signs of the presence of God in and among humans: faith,
love, confidence in salvation, and assistance given to all in a truly human
and Christian culture.

Such activism on the part of these two monks made them seem to be
the "chimera" of their age while yet remaining deeply committed monks.
And indeed there is a much quoted text in which St. Bernard says of
himself: "May my monstrous life, my bitter conscience, move you to pity. I
am a sort of modern chimaera, neither cleric nor layman. I have kept the
habit of a monk, but I have long ago abandoned the life" (Ep. 250.4). This is
an authentic text, but it betrays a certain desire for literary effect — and that
too is a typically authentic Bernardine trait — by means of the use of
exaggeration. But there are other more finely nuanced texts which are
applicable to both Bernard and Merton. For example:

> That soul will be considered perfect in which are to be found these three
> things: grieving over oneself, rejoicing in God, serving one's neighbors;
> pleasing to God, prudent towards self, useful to others. But who is able to
> do all that? Please God that after some years there might be seen in each
> one of us, I do not say all these qualities, but at least one of them.
>
>   (On the Song, 57.21)

The perfect individual, the fulfilled person who has achieved his own
synthesis is the one in whom humiliating lucidity about self, illuminating
certitude about God, and work for the good of one's fellow human beings
are to be found in balanced harmony, working either alternately or simultaneously. We must not let ourselves be deceived by rhetoric. Men of this
metal have acquired self-unity, they are one with themselves, no longer at
odds with self as a general rule, though there may be some ups and downs.

III

Bernard and Merton had something to do with politics, but their
chief concern was in the field of spirituality and monastic renewal or

reform. The evolution which actually took place, in their own Order and elsewhere, shows that they were efficacious. At the bottom of this urge to intervene in these different fields of activity was the consciousness they had of their gift for writing and they considered that their "mission" was to use this talent in the service of as many people as possible, even of all human-kind. They were stimulated by the fact that people listened to what they had to say about Church matters and social issues. As one of the Desert Fathers said in antiquity: "From our cells we judge bishops." This was an avowal of the ambiguity of their position as monks and hermits. They had no role to play on the public scene. Yet they did not hesitate to do so and that without the slightest feeling of guilt. Bernard occasionally struck out at himself in irony because of the ambiguity of his position in the Church, and Merton did so too. But this did not stop them from continuing to write. To be sure, they were also aware of their own limits. Bernard had always been reluctant to take a stand in the controversies going on among professional masters in theology, in spite of the pressure that some of them exerted on him, people like William of Saint-Thierry or Guerhoh of Reichensberg. He never raised his voice against Abelard until late in both their lives. Likewise Merton was cautious not to appear as a dogmatist, a speculative or systematic theolo-gian: he wrote on the practical ways of seeking God.

Both these monks were writers and they resembled one another in several ways. They both liked to use paradox, with striking formulas, some-times not without a certain exaggeration, and even at times with biting, unjust irony. Both were poets. Bernard composed only a few hymns, but many of his pages in prose are poetic — poetry in prose, so to speak — with verses, rhymes, plays on words in sound and sense. Merton left more formal poems, but he too was generally attentive to his style, polishing the musical-ity of the words and sentences. In fact, neither he nor Bernard ever had to make an effort in that field: they had no need to struggle in order to produce literary beauty. They had a gift for it. Their literary qualities are evident even in their private letters destined for a particular person with apparently no public purpose. They were excellent letter writers and have left an enormous number of letters, many of which are valuable for their literary interest, but also as historical documents revealing something of themselves and their times. [See the first two volumes of Merton letters: *The Hidden Ground of Love*, edited by William H. Shannon, and *The Road to Joy*, edited by Robert E. Daggy. A third volume is pending publication, *The School of Charity*, edited by Brother Patrick Hart. All three volumes published by Farrar, Straus & Giroux.]

IV

Having looked at their biographies and their works, let us now turn to their characters. In both St. Bernard and Merton the awareness of having a mission in the Church and in society, as well as the talent to fulfill this mission, in spite of the cloistered life which they had chosen, engendered a sort of complexity, a questioning as to their personal identity. Bernard does not seem to have been particularly subject to depression, though he excelled in describing some of the feelings of sinfulness, limitations, "finitude" as philosophers of today say. Such feelings are common to all human beings and perhaps are more deeply experienced by Christians in the light of God. In making these descriptions, Bernard did not shy away from speaking in the first person, saying "I," as if he were describing what was going on in himself. It is not always easy to discern, in all that he says, what part is rhetoric and what part is sincerity. The result was not only a lesson in humility given by the saint writer to the reader, but also a sense of confidence in God and in self: everyone could understand that the shadow side in him or her was normal and to be found in all humans, even in Bernard. So there was no reason to despair: the grace and the forgiveness of God are stronger than our sinfulness.

Merton, especially in his later writings, was more inclined to such declarations about his life being a failure, about his psyche being full of unresolved problems. But there, too, there is an element of the rhetorical. Since the writing of *The Seven Storey Mountain*, and probably before, it was typical of Merton's style that each of his readers could identify with him. More than once, both in the 1950s and more recently, in various parts of the world, I have heard people (generally monks) say: "When reading him, I discovered that his story was my story, and I followed him all the way through the process of conversion to morality, to faith, to Christianity, to Catholicism and to the monastic life." By dint of digging into his later writings, especially the more private ones — letters and journals — it has become the fashionable and easy thing to discover, or to invent anxieties, doubts, protests, even rebellions. Now I can vouchsafe that the Merton I got to know through our conversations together was a unified, even a joyful person.

I was recently asked: "Do you have the impression of having been his spiritual father?" This question provoked my immediate and strong negative reaction! I do not know whether Merton ever had what is fashionably called "a spiritual father," and I personally am loathe to have any such relation with anyone, and I was certainly not a spiritual father for Merton. When we walked the paths of Gethsemani together, he confided himself with great sincerity, either clearly or by way of allusion. But our walks always led to joy and often we ended up joking in one way or another. The Merton I knew was much less paradoxical, much less problematic than the literary Merton may lead his readers to think, especially when Merton writes about Merton. On such occasions, as with St. Bernard, he knew that he was expressing himself in the name of many others. A nineteenth-century French poet has declared: "O insense qui crois que je ne suis pas toi" — "O you silly one, who thinks that I am not yourself!" Both Bernard and Merton confront us with the difficulty already alluded to, that of combining sincerity and artifice. I have tried to formulate the dilemma of literary interpretation in the case of St. Bernard in a book of psycho-historical essays (*A Second Look at St. Bernard*, Chapter II, Cistercian Publications, 1989). A similar and somewhat delicate endeavor should now perhaps be undertaken in regard to Merton. What makes a "poet?" That is to say, what makes a man a "creator?" Precisely his ability to voice the universal while speaking of the particular, the specifically specific.

Both Bernard and Merton were sometimes humorous and sometimes very serious, but never dramatic if drama means a tragedy to which there is no solution, no other issue than despair. There is no such thing as an easy "happy ending." But there is hope. Both Bernard and Merton wrote with great beauty using God's gift to the utmost and thus expressing all the wealth of their personal experience. They were true reformers, measuring and taking all the risks that it meant, accepting all the upheavals that such a vocation entailed. At the end of his life, in his last writings Bernard made a sort of examination of conscience, a revision of his life, a review of what he called "the state of the Church." Just as St. Augustine had managed to do, Bernard left in his final work, *On Consideration* a retraction, a "treating again" of all the causes he had served during his lifetime, and he was clearly aware of his partial failures on certain issues. Merton did not have time to write a book of retractions. He merely hinted at some points he would have liked to have gone over again. These hints are now helping scholars to linger over the figure of the posthumous Merton.

V

Both Bernard and Merton have a posterity. Bernard's has lived on over eight centuries and it is becoming increasingly difficult to discern the real Bernard from among the many conjured up by myth, legend, history, his own literary output, and those many other Bernards imagined by innumerable historians of all times and tendencies, from monastic apologists to Marxist enemies, even in these days of Glasnost, not to mention Lutheran and Calvinist admirers and recent experts in theology.

How long will Merton's posterity last? We do not know. Who can say? But already, twenty-two years after his death, several post-Mertonian Mertons have contributed to a deeper knowledge of the wealth and complexity of the real Merton. We are now discovering that there was not one Merton, but several successive or simultaneous ones, even while he was still living. Somebody asked me recently: "When he died, was he not going through a crisis?" I answered: "I think he had always been in one long continuous crisis." Hence the many aspects of his work and his character. Who was the real Merton? Towards the end he himself distinguished between the "image" of himself he had given in *The Seven Storey Mountain* and the man he really was. God alone knows the secret of Merton's grace, of Merton's own self. But one thing is certain for us: among all his writings, those which are still converting people — whether he would have liked that or not — are his early monastic books, his writings on the Psalms, on prayer and contemplation, all that he wrote to help countless people become united with God.

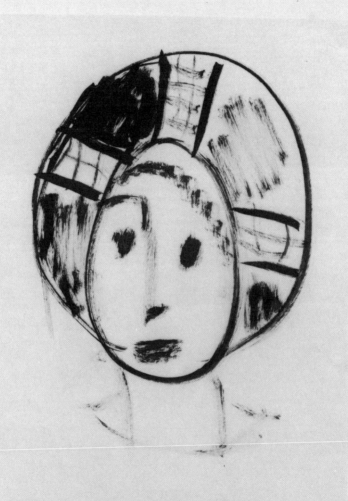

THE TENSION BETWEEN
SOLITUDE AND SHARING
IN THE MONASTIC LIFE
OF THOMAS MERTON

by **James Conner**, O. C. S. O.

In the preface he wrote for the 1962 *Thomas Merton Reader*, Merton notes the fact that his whole life was almost totally paradoxical.

> It is in the paradox itself, the paradox which was and still is a source of insecurity, that I have come to find the greatest security. I have become convinced that the very contradictions in my life are in some ways signs of God's mercy to me.... Paradoxically, I have found peace because I have always been dissatisfied. My moments of depression and despair turn out to be renewals, new beginnings. All life tends to grow like this, in mystery inscaped with paradox and contradiction, yet centered, in its very heart, on the divine mercy.[1]

And in a talk in Alaska, only a few months before his death, Merton cited Martin Buber who

> talks about the man who has a "complex self-contradictory tempera-ment" of which I could tell you much because that is a perfect description of me. It is rough to live with that kind of temperament, but a number of people have it and one should not feel too condemned to be complex and self contradictory forever." [Buber] says that in the core of our soul the Divine force in its depth is capable of acting on the soul, changing it, binding the conflicting sources together, amalgamating the diverging elements. It is capable of unifying it. He makes it quite clear that there is in the depths of our souls a power of God which can do this if we let it.[2]

1. Thomas Merton, "First and Last Thoughts: An Author's Preface," in *A Thomas Merton Reader*; ed. Thomas P. McDonnell (Garden City, New York: Doubleday Image Books, 1974): pp. 16-17.

2. *Thomas Merton in Alaska: Prelude to* The Asian Journal: *The Alaskan Conferences, Journals, and Letters*; introd. by Robert E. Daggy (New York: New Directions, 1989): p. 150.

Nowhere is this paradox and "complex self-contradictory temperament" more apparent than in the tension between solitude and sharing in Merton's life. I will limit my observations to those years when I knew him, namely, from 1949 when I entered the monastery until his death in 1968.

By August 1949, Merton had been ordained a priest only a few months. He did not have any special position in the monastery and was involved mostly in his writing and literary work. Hence it was some weeks before I was able even to identify who this author of *The Seven Storey Mountain* was. When I found out, I was quite surprised. He was the jovial monk who sometimes delighted the somber novices and others by his sign comments during the abbot's chapter talks. The monks sat in long rows facing one another, with the abbot seated at the end of the room. Hence those facing him sometimes found it more entertaining to look directly across for any witty reactions, whether by sign language or by facial expression, rather than to watch the abbot from the side. Such reactions of Merton were not directed at anyone in particular, unless perhaps his immediate neighbors. They were simply an expression of his ebullient nature as well as his spontaneous wit. Certainly his reactions were not directed to the novices since even sign communication between professed and novices was forbidden at that time.

A few months later, Merton was designated by the abbot to give some conferences to the novices on monastic spirituality. Prior to that, the main spirituality of the monastery was centered on that of La Trappe: penance, asceticism, humility, obedience and manual labor, along with a smattering of the Little Flower. Hence when Merton began giving talks on the Desert Fathers, early monastic tradition, prayer and contemplation, this was viewed by some (including the novice master!) as being "foreign" to Trappist life. There was also some tension between the enthusiastic response which Merton evoked in most of the novices and the more sober response to the novice master. Consequently these conferences ceased after some months.

During all this time Merton himself was going through a period which he characterized in *The Sign of Jonas* as being "alone in my insufficiency — dependent, helpless, contingent, and never quite sure that I am leaning on Him upon whom I depend."[3] Yet exteriorly Merton showed no signs of depression or withdrawal. Exteriorly he seemed to be his usual

---

3.   Thomas Merton, *The Sign of Jonas* (Garden City, New York: Doubleday Image Books, 1956): p. 234. Hereafter referred to in the text as *SJ*.

affable self. About this same time, he wrote in his journal: "in the depth of this abysmal testing and disintegration of my spirit, I suddenly discovered completely new moral resources, a spring of new life, a peace and a happiness that I had never known before and which subsisted in the face of nameless, interior terror" (SJ, p. 226). One can only speculate as to whether there may have been some relation between this resurgence and his new work in giving conferences and sharing with others. His work in preparing and giving conferences was always stimulating to the hearers, and also to himself. It gave him the opportunity for study, reflection and some exchange on matters which were of great importance to him.

In May of 1951, Merton was named Master of Students and in October I came under him in that capacity. His whole manner of dealing with the students was one of love, respect and encouragement. The first time that I went to him for direction, he gave the blessing, as was usual, and then simply said: "Sit down." This was a real revolution in itself, for prior to this it was customary for the monk to remain kneeling during direction. He was attentive and kind and an excellent listener. He was one who seemd to be able to perceive almost intuitively what you were trying to express and to accept anything without reproof or chagrin. He was always encouraging and also stimulating to new ways of looking at things or thinking about things. He was an excellent spiritual director.

Alice von Hildebrand, in her video called *The Tragedy of Thomas Merton*, rebuked him for his use of psychology and psychiatry when he had no training in psychoanalysis. From my own contact with him, both during this period and later when he was Master of Novices, I can attest to the fact that he never tried to use psychiatry himself nor to do any analysis as such. He had read some psychology, both Freud and Jung, but he used this knowledge more as a background than as a tool for spiritual direction. He had an interest in dreams, but never used even this in any habitual way. After he was novice master he did try to compose something on signs of neuroses in monastic life. This was the occasion for his run-in with Dr. Gregory Zilboorg at Collegeville in 1956. Even though he did not use his own notes after that fiasco, he did later compose some notes together with Fr. John Eudes Bamberger on "The Mature Conscience."

Besides spiritual direction, Merton also gave weekly conferences to the students as a group. Like the novitiate conferences, Merton developed various themes of the monastic life, showing the background and basis for such elements. Besides this, he also spoke on many varied subjects as they were timely. He also, from time to time, exposed the students to recordings of classical music, poetry and literature, so that their formation would be truly rounded in human as well as spiritual ways. He encouraged exchange with himself during the conferences, and showed obvious enthusiasm when the students became involved in the discussion. At the same time, though, he could resolutely put someone in his place if he tried to outshine him in such discussions. This was done, not in a defensive or haughty way, but in a way that showed that he had no patience with artificiality or false airs. He wanted the students to be true and well-rounded, but also humble and authentic.

In all of this, Merton shared his love for solitude. He did this both in theory, in his conferences, and also in practice. He obtained permission for the first time for the students to go out to the small woods just outside the enclosure wall. Earlier he had obtained permission to go there himself, and a small old toolshed had even been put out in the woods for his use. This became "St. Anne's Hermitage" (though it was not called a hermitage at first). Each day after dinner, any of the students who wished could go with him out to the woods, where all would scatter to various points for about an hour and a half of solitude. Later he managed to erect an old bell in the pasture so all would know when it was time to return to the monastery. Only about a half dozen students went out regularly, but he daily processed out to enjoy his time at St. Anne's. I once asked him whether it was not an impingement on his own solitude to have us go along with him. But he immediately said that he thoroughly enjoyed having us go out there and that it did not impede his own solitude at all. He rejoiced to see others respond with enthusiasm to an experience of solitude, even though so brief.

At times, on major feast days, he would obtain a truck and take any students who desired out to the large woods on the other side of the road. Sometimes this would be done under the pretext of tree planting, but even then tree planting took a minimal amount of the full afternoon that was available. Such trips were made, though, for the express purpose of having time for solitude, and conversation was still not allowed among the monks themselves. For a while the prior of the monastery (who had also been novice master when Merton gave conferences to the novices) tried something similar, but with the purpose of communication. The Rules stipulated that monks could speak to one another when they were in the presence of the abbot or the prior. So the prior organized some trips to the woods, using an extension of that rule to allow the monks to speak with one another with him out in the woods. Whether this was actually done in

conscious or unconscious competition with Fr. Louis and his trips to solitude, one cannt say for sure. But there was definitely at least something of
that present, and most were aware of it. The majority continued to choose
the solitude time, and the prior gave up after a while.

Merton felt this tension with others and was very sensitive to it. On
one occasion when I was cantor for the choir, I approached Fr. Louis and
asked him why he did not sing out more in choir. He had a very nice,
melodious voice which could be a valuable addition. He answered that
whenever he sang out more, his neighbor would shut up altogether and
visibly show his displeasure. Merton was not one to force an issue. He did
not care for conflict and usually withdrew into himself, though not in a
pouty, childish way. He was sensitive to the criticisms of others about his
dealings with the students, about his writings (he detested having to sit
through the reading of his own works in the refectory at times), about his
zeal for solitude, about his criticisms of technology in the monastery. At
such times, he frequently took refuge in solitude in an effort to go beyond
such misunderstandings. It was certainly a part of his sense of dereliction
and desolation which plagued him at times. Yet here again, he was not one
to show this in public. With others he could still be humorous and
mischievous.

One area where Merton loved to share with others was in manual
labor, particularly on the farm. He enjoyed working at cutting and shucking
the corn, at planting and cutting the tobacco, and particularly in working in
the woods. Due to physical maladies, he was not able to do this very much.
But when possible he would take part in these, both as a way of sharing with
the brethren in the work and also as an expression of a traditionally important element of monastic life. He was not the most organized person in
directing the work, and I sometimes found it rather frustrating when I was
undermaster of novices and he would suddenly decide to take part in the
work and take charge of the work detail. But he applied himself with zeal.
Only one area of work did he refuse to take part in: namely, the Farms
Building, where the cheese and fruitcake were packaged and prepared for
mailing. He felt that dependence on such a technological venture for
sustenance of a monastic community was an infidelity to monastic life. He
poked jibes at the Farms Building, such as "Cheeses for Jesus" or saying that
the letters of the Order (O.C.S.O.) meant: "Our Cheese Surpasses
Others." In this he realized that he was being impractical, idealistic and
going against the current. He even objected to tractors and other farm
machinery used in the fields. But he stuck to his position.

There is yet another area of the tension between solitude and sharing in Merton which I have never seen discussed, but which I personally feel is important. That is the area of his relations with Dom James Fox, his abbot. Many have spoken of the complexity of the relationship between these two men — and surely it was! Michael Mott, in his biography, characterizes Merton's attitude toward authority. "This was ambiguous at the deepest level. He was rebellious by nature, a born critic and changer, and yet he sought to appease . . . . He was a rebel who won and kept a reputation for obedience."[4] On the other side, he speaks of Dom James' position.

> Dom James was not a natural tyrant. Merton was not a natural victim. But two roles *are* implicit in the monastic situation. Both were emphasized by the conception Dom James held of them. The abbot is in a special sense the father, and the monks are his children. The conflicts Merton had with Dom James were not open. They could not be, because it was in the very nature of James Fox to avoid open conflict, to turn away wrath with a smile, to dissolve all surface rancor and strife in sweetness. It was the sweetness — the word is carefully chosen — that drove Thomas Merton to distraction at times . . . . Dom James, however sweetly spoken and smiling, could be ruthless. (*Mott*, pp. 279-280)

Merton's problems with the abbot, however, were not simply an "authority problem." Certainly he had some of that, in ways not too dissimilar from many of the monks. However I feel that Merton at times felt Dom James' authority as an intrusion on his own inner solitude, as a demand that he share in areas and ways that Merton was not prepared to share. In his "Notes for a Philosophy of Solitude," Merton wrote:

> One of the first essentials of the interior solitude of which I speak is that it is the actualization of a faith in which a man takes responsibility for his own inner life. He faces its full mystery in the presence of the invisible God. And he takes upon himself the lonely, barely comprehensible, incommunicable task of working his way through the darkness of his own mystery until he discovers that his mystery and the mystery of God merge into one reality, which is the only reality . . . . The words of God have the power to illuminate the darkness. But they do so by losing the shape of words and becoming — not thoughts, not things, but the unspeakable beating of a Heart within the heart of one's own life.[5]

Merton desired to be able to face this inner solitude and to be able to make decisions on the basis of what this "Heart within the heart" revealed to him. Merton tried to do this and to make his decisions on this basis, particularly

4. Michael Mott, *The Seven Mountains of Thomas Merton* (Boston: Houghton Mifflin, 1984), p. 279. Hereafter referred to in the text as *Mott*.

5. Thomas Merton, *Disputed Questions* (New York: Farrar, Straus & Cudahy, 1960): p. 180. Hereafter referred to in the text as *DQ*.

the major decisions regarding his own vocation, his writing, his eremitical life and possible travels. He knew that it was risky to do this on his own, but he felt called to such risk.

> The essence of the solitary vocation is precisely the anguish of an almost infinite risk. Only the false solitary sees no danger in solitude . . . . Too many people are ready to draw him back at any price from what they conceive to be the edge of an abyss: but they do not realize that he who is called to solitude is called to walk across the air of the abyss without danger, because, after all, the abyss is only himself. He should not be forced to feel guilty about it, for in this solitude and emptiness of his heart, there is another, inexplicable solitude. Man's loneliness is, in fact, the loneliness of God. That is why it is such a great thing for a man to discover his solitude and learn to live in it. For there he finds that he and God are one: that God is alone as he himself is alone. That God wills to be alone in him. (*DQ*, pp. 185, 190)

Merton, as anyone trained in the Rule of Benedict, certainly knew the value and role of obedience to the abbot and the customs of the monastery. Yet he was also acutely conscious of the dangers of mere social pressure. He fully realized that many people are determined by the social pressures, expectations and image of the group. But the solitary is called to avoid the illusory satisfaction of such social images.

> The man who is dominated by what I call the "social image" is one who allows himself to see and to approve in himself only that which his society prescribes as beneficial and praiseworthy in its members. And yet he congratulates himself on "thinking for himself." In reality, this is only a game that he plays in his own mind — the game of substituting the words, slogans and concepts he has received from society, for genuine experiences of his own. (*DQ*, p. 186)

All of this led Merton to a realization of the limitation of any group, even the monastic community, even the Church.

> The illusions and fictions encouraged by the appetite for self-affirmation in certain restricted groups, have much to be said for them and much to be said against them. They do in practice free a man from his individual limitations and help him, in some measure, to transcend himself. And if every society were ideal, then every society would help its members only to a fruitful and productive self-transcendence. But in fact societies tend to lift a man above himself only far enough to make him a useful and submissive instrument in whom the aspirations, lusts and needs of the group can function unhindered by too delicate a personal conscience. Social life tends to form and educate a man, but generally at the price of a simultaneous deformation and perversion. This is because civil society is never ideal, always a mixture of good and evil, and always tending to present the evil in itself as a form of good. (*DQ*, p. 182).

It led him to a conviction that

> The solitary one is one who is called to make one of the most terrible decisions possible to man: the decision to disagree completely with those

> who imagine that the call to diversion and self-deception is the voice of
> truth and who can summon the full authority of their prejudice to prove it.
> (*DQ*, p. 183)

He felt this in relation to the concrete circumstances of his own life
and his relations with the abbot.

> So that is the vow of obedience. You submit yourself also to somebody
> else's prejudice and to his myths and the worship of *his* fetishes. Well, I
> have made the vow and will keep it, and will see why I keep it, and will try
> at the same time not to let myself be involved in the real harm, that can
> come from a wrong kind of submission. There are several wrong kinds,
> and the right kind is not always easy to find. In other words, I do not agree
> with those who say that *any* submission will do.[6]

He saw fully by faith that obedience frees one, but at the same time he was
acutely aware of the fact that "there is so much that is not 'redeemed' in the
thinking of those who represent the Church" (*VOC*, p. 199). He took solace
in the experience of others who experienced the same thing.

> What about the life of [Cardinal] Newman, which still goes on in the
> refectory? It is so inexhaustibly important and full of meaning for me. Look
> what the hierarchy did for him! The whole thing is there existentially, not
> explicit, but it is there for the grasping. The reality is in his kind of
> obedience and his kind of refusal. Complete obedience to the Church
> and complete, albeit humble, refusal of the pride and chicanery of
> churchmen. (*VOC*, p. 199)

This led him to the realization of a need to be more than simply a rebel, of
the need to submit himself with peace to the prejudices and human limitations of others who may be in authority.

> I protest by obeying, and protest most effectively by obeying in an obe-
> dience in which I am not subject to arbitrary fancies on the part of
> authorities, but in which I and the abbot are aware, or think we are aware,
> of a higher obligation and a demand of God: that my situation has reached
> this point is a great grace. (*VOC*, p. 191)

The ideal that he sought went beyond the question of either agreement or
disagreement with authorities. His desire was to be able to come to an
obedience in the Spirit and to the Spirit.

> The great joy of the solitary life . . . resides in the awakening and attuning
> of the inmost heart to the voice of God — to the inexplicable quiet definite
> inner certitude of one's call to obey Him, to hear Him, to worship Him
> here, now, today in silence and alone. In the realization that this is the
> whole reason for one's existence. This listening and this obedience make
> one's existence fruitful and gives fruitfulness to all one's other acts. It is the

---

6. Thomas Merton, *A Vow of Conversation: Journals, 1964-195*; edited by Naomi Burton Stone (New York: Farrar, Straus & Giroux, 1988): p. 148. Hereafter referred to in the text as *VOC*.

purification and ransom of one's own heart that has been long dead in sin. This is not simply a question of existing alone, but of doing with joy and understanding "the work of the cell," which is done in silence, not according to one's own choice or to the pressure of necessity, but in obedience to God, that is to say, in obedience to the simple conditions imposed by what *is* here and now. The voice of God is not clearly heard at every moment; and part of the "work of the cell" is *attention*, so that one may not miss any sound of that voice . . . . When we understand how little we listen, how stubborn and gross our hearts are, we realize how important this inner work is. And we see how badly prepared we are to do it.

(*VOC*, pp. 188-189)

In this way, his tension between solitude and sharing was at the heart of his own monastic vocation, for he realized that "it demands an integration of one's own life in the stream of natural and human and cultural life of the moment" (*VOC*, p. 189). The saving factor in all of this, throughout his whole life, was his flexibility and his resilience. He could be demanding, but he could be human. Whenever people ask me what is the main trait of Merton that impressed me, I always answer: his humanity. As a monk in his dealings with both confreres and with superiors, as a superior himself, as a director or confessor, and as a friend, it was his humanity which shone through most regularly.

One example of this was when I was Undermaster of Novices working with him as Novice Master. At that time we had a program of "summer postulants." Young men could come and spend the summer as part of the novitiate in order to discover whether they had a monastic vocation. There was one young man who was seldom able to rise for Vigils and yet frequently seemed groggy and withdrawn. Merton became suspicious and sent me to check out the young man's cell. Sure enough, under his pillow I found a fifth of gin, which was about two-thirds consumed. I gave it to Merton who confronted the person and then told him he did not think he belonged in the program. A couple of weeks later, Merton told me to come to his office one evening after supper on a feast day. When I came in he had some crackers and the remainder of the bottle of gin, which we proceeded to dispose of.

At the same time, Fr. Louis could be demanding, particularly in the realm of obedience. The one major run-in I had with him was in this regard. He had planned to renovate the novitiate chapel and the novices and I did the work. On the eve of Assumption, we had finished everything except hanging the ballister and drapes behind the altar. He said to wait and finish it after the feast. However, I thought it would be a surprise to him to go ahead and finish it for the feast, and so a couple of novices and myself proceeded to finish it after Compline. Working with all the windows closed even though it was mid-August in order to deaden the noise, we proceeded to do the deed. Suddenly about 9:00 Merton loomed in the doorway with a heavy scowl. With his light sleeping, he had heard the noise and come to investigate. He was furious and first stated that he refused even to say the Mass there the next morning. Only with much persuasion did he agree to do so, but he made it clear that such disobedience was not tolerated.

Ironically, one of the major times of tension between solitude and sharing was during his time in the hermitage from 1965 to 1968. Just a few days before going full time to the hermitage, Merton looked at himself honestly and saw how challenging this new period would be. He wrote in his journals:

> The solitary life, now that I confront it, it is awesome, wonderful, and I see I have no strength of my own for it. Rather, I have a deep sense of my own poverty and, above all, an awareness of wrongs I have allowed in myself together with this good desire. This is all good. I am glad to be shocked by grace, to wake up in time and see the great seriousness of what I am about to do. Perhaps I have been playing at this; and the solitary life is not something you can play at. Contrary to all that is said about it, I do not see how the really solitary life can tolerate illusion or self-deception. It seems to me that solitude rips off all the masks and all the disguises. It tolerates no lies. Everything but straight and direct affirmation or silence is mocked and judged by the silence of the forest. The solitary life is to stand in truth.
> (*VOC*, p. 204)

The first months were a delight for him and he thrived in the realization of his long desire for total solitude. However his back problem deteriorated and he had to have surgery. Thus in March 1966, he entered St. Joseph's Hospital in Louisville again. It was here that he met the nurse, Margie, who would play such a prominent part in his life for the next four months.

In July of 1965, he suddenly recalled a young girl whom he had known in England. She was the sister of a school friend and he met her during a stay with the student at his family's home. He wrote in his journal:

> Actually, I think she is a symbol of the true (quiet) woman with whom I never came to terms in the world, and because of this, there remains an incompleteness in me that cannot be remedied. (*VOC*, p. 194)

This sense of incompleteness bothered Merton in many ways. It left a certain gnawing doubt as to whether he was really capable of true love, whether he felt that he was truly loved by others, and consequently whether his solitude was really authentic or a partial flight from the underlying despair of himself. He was honest enough with himself that he did not try to claim that divine love would totally compensate for human love. It was this realization which left him so very open to sharing and to loving: his brothers in the monastery, his friends outside, even those he knew only by correspondence. But even with all this, he was conscious of a certain "incompleteness" in himself.

Margie definitely filled this incompleteness and it was because of this that he responded as he did. He was conscious of his love for her and her love for him. He did not question his essential vocation to solitude, and yet he desired that they might be active and present in each other's lives in a profound spiritual friendship which Merton summed up in the word "devotion."

John Howard Griffin has given the main details of this period in his book *Follow the Ecstasy*.[7] He shows both how passionate the relationship became as well as the many ways that Merton went counter to that honesty with himself that had so marked his life. The tension between this sharing in an experience of human love between man and woman and his desire for solitude became almost unbearable at times. Griffin shows that

> he entered into a long series of speculations and justifications which he later viewed with dismay as not much more that rationalizations permitting him to pursue his longing with some degree of good conscience. It was deeply necessary, critical even, at this point in his life to prove to himself that he was capable of a purely unselfish love. Otherwise he would go on being haunted by the fear that he might be like certain Christians described by Leon Bloy who were incapable of loving anyone or anything and therefore persuaded themselves that they loved God. (*Griffin*, p. 84).

Merton himself wrote:

> Who knows anything at all about solitude if he has not been in love, and *in love in solitude*? Love and solitude must test each other in the man who means to live alone: they must become one and the same thing in him, or he will only be half a person. (*Griffin*, p. 84).

Merton realized that the situation was "absurdly impossible" and yet he continued on — torn between his dedication to his life of solitude and his love for her. In the end, things were resolved by being taken out of his hands. One of the brothers at the switchboard listened in on a phone call to her and reported it to the abbot. Griffin says:

> Though troubled almost to the point of panic, Merton was swept with a sense of relief that the matter was now in the open. From this viewpoint of openness, his own perspective changed. He told himself he had to face the fact that he had been wrong. (*Griffin*, p. 101)

In this way, Merton viewed the abbot's discovery as a help. Though firm on the matter, the abbot was compassionate. Yet even then, Merton felt that

---

7. John Howard Griffin, *Follow the Ecstasy: Thomas Merton, The Hermitage Years 1965-1968* (Fort Worth, Texas: JHG Editions / Latitudes Press, 1983). Hereafter referred to in the text as *Griffin*.

he should be able to work this out by himself. The abbot required that he talk with the local monk-psychiatrist. At the time Merton remarked to me how he resented both the abbot and the psychiatrist for this. He knew he had taken a great "risk" and that he had not conducted the affair rightly. Yet he preferred to work it out in his solitude himself. Later he did admit in his journals that he found the psychiatrist helpful. However, he did try to re-enter into his solitude in real honesty before the Lord.

Finally he was able to evaluate the experience in a new light. He expressed this in an essay that he re-wrote at this time. It was entitled "Love and Need — Is Love a Package or a Message." He wrote:

> In reality love is a positive force, a transcendent spiritual power. It is, in fact, the deepest creative power in human nature. Rooted in the biological riches of our inheritance, love flowers spiritually as freedom and as a creature response to life in a perfect encounter with another person.[8]

Griffin sums up the result of all this in the following way:

> Ultimately the experience confirmed for him what had before been intuitive conclusions. He could now know that his profoundest statements about love between two human beings held equally true about love between man and God, and that he himself had the capacity to love fully. He now knew that he possessed an authentic potential for love and that his religious commitment was not the subtle disguise of an emotional cripple. This provided an inner liberation. (*Griffin*, p. 121)

On September 8, Merton made a solemn permanent commitment as a hermit in the presence of the abbot. From then on he worked at deepening this life that he had been given by the Lord and which he freely accepted.

The immediate pressure was over, but throughout the remaining two years in the hermitage he still faced another kind of tension. This was brought on due to the number of visits he received from his own friends, business associates, friends of the monastery as well as others who came uninvited and unannounced. He loved having visits from his friends; and yet he felt the tension of the call of solitude. In time he began to spend more afternoons in the woods rather than at the hermitage in order to avoid unwanted intrusions. During this time he still gave weekly conferences for the monks and was a brother to his brothers. The tension finally led to his desire for greater solitude than he felt he could find there in the hermitage. At the same time that he obtained permission to travel to the East to visit monks there, he also planned to look for a possible location for a hermitage.

---

8. Thomas Merton, *Love and Living*; edited by Naomi Burton Stone and Brother Patrick Hart (New York: Farrar, Straus & Giroux, 1979): p. 34.

Some might wonder why he did not simply stay put and limit his own contacts more and thus be able to experience the solitude he sought. Perhaps that would have worked for many, but not for Merton. Just as he wanted to *experience* not only solitude but also love, so he wanted to experience for himself how the monks of the East train themselves for the kind of experience he sought. He said himself that his purpose in going to the East was to learn more, not just quantitatively but qualitatively. In the end, the tension was resolved for him only by the bolt of electricity which brought him into that full solitude and that full love.

Thomas Merton — or Fr. Louis — was a rare individual. Certainly I can say that knowing him and living with him has been one of the great graces of my own life. The fact that he still speaks so eloquently to so many over twenty years after his death shows that he truly had lived that type of solitude of which he wrote — a solitude which led him not only into his own heart but into the heart of every person. As Merton says:

> Without solitude of some sort there is and can be no maturity. Unless one becomes empty and alone, he cannot give himself in love because he does not possess the deep self which is the only gift worthy of love. My deep self is not something which I acquire, or to which I can attain after a long struggle. It is not mine, and cannot become mine. It is no "thing" — no object. It is "I." But the deep "I" of the Spirit, of solitude and of love, . . . who is always alone, is always universal: for in this inmost "I" my own solitude meets the solitude of every other person and the solitude of God. Hence it is beyond division, beyond limitation, beyond selfish affirmation. It is only this inmost and solitary "I" that truly loves with the love and the Spirit of Christ. This "I" is Christ Himself, living in us: and we, in Him, living in the Father. (VOC, p. 207)

OF MOSES' MOTHER
AND PHAROAH'S DAUGHTER:

A Model of Contemporary Contemplation

by **Joan Chittister**, O.S.B.

The Talmud instructs: "If you expect to see the final results of your work, you have simply not asked a big enough question."

Well, if the major problem of a meaningless world is narrowness of vision then, our age certainly need not fear. In the lifetime of many people, Thomas Merton laid before the world a question the scope of which may well decide its future. All of his adult life, Thomas Merton struggled — and provoked us to struggle — with the question of contemplation. His biographers record that at various stages of his life — depending on his own circumstances — Merton either made fun of contemplation or lusted after it, or argued its meaning or poked at its veneer, or wrestled with its demands.

Merton read about contemplation and wrote about contemplation and talked about contemplation everywhere he could. He researched the ancients on it and moved to the woods to find more of it and then left the woods both to teach it and learn it. And, in the end, went to the East to plumb it only to discover there that he had already identified it and left it at home.

He said of contemplation: "It is the mark of the true mystic that, after their initiation into the mysteries of the unitive life, they are impelled, in some way, to serve humanity." And in the course of it all, in one of the most chaotic moments of history, Thomas Merton, contemplative, influenced more people than any other religious figure of his time.

---

* This address, delivered on 12 November 1987. was the tenth annual *Thomas Merton Lecture* of the Merton Center at Columbia University.

He questioned often whether or not his own contemplative order was really contemplative. He struggled to find a balance between contemplation and social activism and most of all, by the honesty of his grappling and the tenterhooks of his very singular, very double, very separated, very involved life, he called the rest of us to contemplation as well.

The question is: What is it to be called to contemplation? And why? And where is such a thing to be found? Well, Merton's call is not a new one. The call to contemplation is, in fact, the basis of every great wisdom of the world. Among the sayings of Hasidim it is written: "What matter that the eye be sound if the heart is blind." And the Sufi tell of the disciples who asked the master for a word of wisdom that would guide them through life's journey. And the master smiled knowingly and said, "Of course. Awareness." But the disciples were only more perplexed. "That's far too brief," they said, "couldn't you expand on that a bit?" And so the master, fixing his gaze on them, said, "Well, then: Awareness, awareness, awareness." "But what do these words mean?" the disciple said. And the master said, with no small amount of agitation: "Awareness, awareness, awareness means *AWARENESS*."

Contemplation, it seems, is the ability to see through, and to see into, and to see despite and to see without blinders. In America today, perhaps as never before, there is a great need for seeing hearts, for contemplative awareness of the kind of world we are creating today for tomorrow. In the United States, there is an awesome kind of blindness in vogue. In this culture the blind count happiness in things. The American philosophy of happiness, it seems, teaches that life must always be easy and life must always be comfortable and life must always be personally fulfilling and life, at least American life, must always be secure, and life must always look the way we think it should look.

In this world, consequently, it is success, not learning, that has become the goal of education. In America, it is the salary scale rather than the work itself that has become the measure of the job. And money rather than character has become the standard of success. And things rather than values have become the mark of personal achievement. And what we can't take with us rather than what we have left behind so that others can live has become our definition of the quality of life. And what we got for ourselves instead of what we helped to provide for everybody else has become the boast of our ability. And, as a result, pathological individualism and materialism cloud the vision and choke compassion.

And, out of that way of seeing, consequently, we have created the end of the world and we're storing it in the cornfields of Kansas and we call it "defense." Out of that way of seeing, we have the mentally ill sleeping on the heating grates of our cities and we call it "personal freedom." Out of that way of seeing, we have thousands dying from AIDS and we ignore them in the name of morality. Out of that way of seeing, we have women by the score living in poverty because our welfare programs are designed to punish people who need help rather than to help people whom life has already punished enough and we call it "motivation" or "woman's role." Out of that way of seeing, we have an entire generation of youngsters underfed, undereducated and underdeveloped because we care more about giving money to the contras than we do about providing services for our own children. We spend more on bombs than we do on babies; we allocate more for human destruction than we do for human development. And, oh, yes, our pride is that we are not a welfare state; but we can, apparently, be a warfare state and not even have the grace to blush. Indeed, there is blindness aplenty in us.

And what should we do about it? I suggest that we must begin to struggle, as Merton did, with the difference between complacency and contemplation. We must begin to struggle, as Merton did, with the difference between true and false contemplation. Because indeed there is a contemplatiopn that is for its own sake. This kind of contemplation seeks comfort in prayer and consolation for the spirit and interventions by God to save us from things not created by God but by ourselves. That kind of contemplation is, at its best, some kind of transcendental complacency that is at least lulling, but probably infantile and certainly unconscionable. That kind of contemplation makes a blessing out of blindness and anoints the unaware who, in the name of Christianity, practice civil religion instead, and who, in the name of citizenship, sell their souls to the separation of conscience from civil life. That kind of contemplation cares more for ritual than for righteousness and maintains law rather than justice.

But there is another kind of contemplation that came to the prophets but was expected of watchers on the city walls as well. Ezekiel writes:

> If someone hears the sound of the horn, but pays no attention, the sword will overtake them and destroy them and they will have been responsible for their own death. If, however, the sentry had seen the sword coming but had not blown the horn and so the people are not alerted and the sword overtakes them and destroys them, the latter shall indeed die. But I will hold the sentry repsonsible for that death. And I have appointed you as sentry . . . . (*Ezekiel*, 33: 1-7)

I have appointed you to contemplate the situation, I have appointed you to search for the truth behind the truth, the whole truth. I have appointed you to see the whole truth, to grasp all of what is there. I have appointed you to be aware. That kind of contemplation is not for its own sake. On the contrary, as the Sufi say, "The candle is not there to illuminate itself."

But where shall we go for a model of that kind of contemplative consciousness; we who often feel more weak than we ever do strong; we who usually feel more alone than part of a rising human consciousness; we who commonly rank ourselves more with the powerless than with the powerful.

I suggest that what the world needs anew is to reflect on the model of contemplation that illuminates the life of two simple women who lived in a world environment not very unlike our own. I suggest as a model of contemporary contemplation the biblical figures of Moses' mother and Pharoah's daughter. Moses' mother and Pharoah's daughter were two unlikely contemplatives if ever the world were in search. The scripture reads:

> Now a certain man of the house of Levi married a Levite woman who conceived and bore a son. Seeing that he was a goodly child, she hid him for three months. When she could hide him no longer, she took a papyrus basket, daubed it with bitumen and pitch and putting the child in it, placed it among the reeds on the river bank. His sister stationed herself at a distance to find out what would happen to him. Pharoah's daughter came down to the river to bathe, while her maids walked along the river bank. Noticing the basket among the reeds, she sent her handmaid to fetch it. On opening it, she looked, and lo, there was a baby boy, crying! She was moved with pity for him and said, "It is one of the Hebrews' children." Then his sister asked Pharoah's daughter, "Shall I go and call one of the Hebrew women to nurse the child for you?" "Yes, do so," she answered. So the maiden went and called the child's own mother. Pharoah's daughter said to her, "Take this child and nurse it for me, and I will repay you." The woman therefore took the child and nursed it. When the child grew, she brought him to Pharoah's daughter, who adopted him as her son and called him Moses. (*Exodus* 2: 1-10)

The implications are clear. Moses' mother was a member of the outcast people. Pharoah's daughter was pure establishment. But both of them had plenty to lose from seeing. Moses' mother, who had nothing, risked the loss of even more — not simply her child's life, but her own life, and the life of her family, and the life of her entire people. They were low class now; to confront the law could only make them even lower. And Pharoah's daughter? Well, Pharoah's daughter risked the loss of everything, too! Pharoah's daughter risked the loss of status and approval by "the right people" and acceptance by her family and the judgment of orthodoxy. And her future: what would the Pharoah do when he discovered her defiance? What would the people think about her consorting with the enemy? What would the neighbors say about her raising a minority child? How would the government respond to her harboring a refugee?

Here in a situation where the law is very clear that these kinds of people, these foreigners, these defenseless ones are to be controlled because it is good for the government, and it is good for the economy, it is good for all the security and power and affluence we value — that's why! And because it was even good for the Jews themselves, surely, whose role in life — God-given we must obviously presume — was to be a slave. Here in a situation like this two women defy the political nothingness that being female implied — then, as now, now as then.

Because they saw life differently than did the people around them, two women — one inside an oppressive system and one outside that oppressive system — simply joined hands across national boundaries to subvert a sinful system. Two women are aware of the sinfulness of the system and simply refuse to accept it; two women contemplate a greater good and simply must respond to it; two simple, contemplative women save the Jewish people — not simply Moses.

So why did they do it? And what does their doing it have to do with us? The answer, I believe, lies in the nature of contemplation and the nature of the times. The answer lies, I think, in what Merton means when he says: "Contemplation is sudden gift of awareness, an awakening to the real within all that is real." When Moses' mother and Pharoah's daughter saw the circumstances, suddenly they saw a law above the law, a life above life, an end without end, a sight beyond what was seen. Together two contemplative women cut through the male system of nationalism and patriarchy and extermination. The Jewess entrusted her baby to the enemy. The Egyptian saw value in the Jew. The kingdom of God became the native country of both. And power came to the powerless to confront the powerful whatever the cost.

It was a moment that spoke of the presence of God in life. It was a very contemplative moment. "Contemplation," wrote Merton, "is the response to a call, a call from the God who has no voice, and who speaks in everything that is, and who, most of all, speaks in the depths of our own being words meant to answer to God, to echo God, and even in some way, to contain God and signify God." Contemplation, in other words, is the ability to see as God sees. Contemplation is the awareness of the divine in the natural. Contemplation is the call to co-creation. And contemplation, therefore, — if the model of Moses' mother and Pharoah's daughter — has any meaning at all, must obviously have four dimensions. For contemplation to be real, it must have consciousness, conviction, courage, and constancy.

To see the cosmic sin of the obliteration of the Jewish race in the death of its first-born males was an instance of contemplative consciousness. But contemplation means that consciousness compels. To take the child from the bullrushes and commit oneself not only to save the child but to save the tradition rather than to need to convert or control it — "Yes, go; get one of his own to nurse him," — Pharoah's daughter decides — is an act of contemplative conviction. Contemplation means that consciousness commits. To judge the system and then to fly in the face of the system, as Moses' mother did when she challenged the conscience of one of its own, and as Pharoah's daughter did when she used her position in behalf of the innocent, is an act of contemplative courage. Contemplation requires that consciousness cry out in witness. To commit themselves to the long-term cost of seeing the vision through — despite the pain and the losses and the dull, dull demands of dailiness — is an act of contemplative constancy. True contemplation, you see, demands that conscience contend to the end.

Contemplation is the ability to see a whole world instead of a partial one. Contemplation is the awareness of the holy in everything. Contemplation is conscience co-creating. The problem is that the people are in peril again and contemplation, it seems, is today at a premium.

Three issues of our time call in a special way for contemplative consciousness:

Nuclearism — the notion that massive evil can be permitted in the name of resistance to evil;

Globalism — the notion that those who starve in Africa while our barns are full of wheat have claim on our conscience; and

Feminism — the notion that women are just as graced and as gracing as men.

The simple truth is that in a world that is linked by a single camera, under the threat of destruction from a single trigger, drawing from a single resource pool, and ruled only by the male model, no one can with integrity ignore the call to contemplate the effects of all this on creation and our own commitment to it.

We ignore at our peril the biblical frieze of Moses' mother and Pharoah's daughter who saw their situation, contemplated its implications in the light of eternal truth, confronted the powerful in their sin, cooperated across differences, refused to demonize one another, mentored the next generation in their midst, preserved the enemy and saved the nation.

As sure as the baby in the bullrushes, the signs of the fragility of our own world and the chaos in our own system are everywhere. Women are the poorest of the poor, in this country as well as everywhere in the world, because their work is undervalued, their talents are overlooked, their life development is circumscribed and, right to the end, even when they have done exactly what the system wanted them to do — stay home, raise a family, be a good wife and mother — the system conspires to cheat them out of social security monies by giving the widow less than the widower of money that was supposed to have been jointly theirs. Who can contemplate such a contradiction, who can see with the compassionate eye of God, and do nothing?

Or, imagine in your mind's eye three tin pails: now in the first tin pail, drop 2 BB's. Those BB's represent the total amount of firepower — including the two atomic bombs — that was used in all of World War II. Now, go to the second tin pail and, one at a time, slowly, drop into that bucket 32 BB's. Those 32 BB's represent the amount of firepower it would take to unleash nuclear winter on this planet and destroy all life on earth. Finally, in your mind's eye, stand in front of your third tin pail. Into that pail, slowly, one at a time, drop 2, 32, 100, 1,000, 1,500, 2,000, 2,500, 3,000, 3,500, 4,000, 4,500, 5,000, 5,500, 5,600, 5,700, 5,800, 5,900, 6,000 BB's. Those 6,000 BB's represent the total amount of nuclear firepower now existing in American and Soviet arsenals.

And while the poor the world over struggle to eat, and the illiterate struggle to get educated, and families struggle to raise children, and the homeless struggle for their dignity if not their dreams, the superpowers build and buy five more nuclear bombs each, every single day.

With the factory system what it is, why? With agriculture what it is, why? With the national debt what it is, why?

"Hatred," the philosopher wrote, "is simply a slower form of suicide."

Isn't it time to contemplate what it is that makes our enemies enemies?

And who decided it?

And over what?

One day they told us that the Japanese were fundamentally dishonest and that Germans were essentially cruel. The next day, the Germans and the Japanese became our most important allies and our most ardent supporters. What happened to the "fundamentals?" Whatever became of the list of "essential elements?" Isn't the "enemy" really only whoever someone else tells us that they are?

Young men die in old men's wars, they say. And that's true. But only after enough brainwashing and enough fear and enough demonizing of the enemy has been done to send German boys against Russian boys unthinkingly; or American boys against Vietnamese boys uncaringly; or Palestinian boys against Israeli boys willingly — with great ideals in mind and the drumbeats of glory in their ears.

The problem is that in a world where every decent thing that humankind has ever done is now in peril — both our future and our past — both Shakespeare and the space shuttle — we may no longer have the luxury of allowing our government to choose our enemies for us. Hate is indeed simply a slower form of suicide and in our society we are already beginning to feel its atrophying effects.

SDI is already the largest item in the Pentagon budget while funds for education, and food stamps, and subsidized housing, and day care — all women's issues and children's issues — get smaller every day.

Who can truly contemplate such a situation, who can see what creation was meant to be but is not, who can see with the compassionate eye of God and say nothing?

A polluted planet, the growing numbers of poor in the Garden of Paradise, the lust for a kind of "progress" that diminishes the prospects of the next generation all cry for contemplative consciousness.

According to World Watch Institute's "State of the World, 1987," in the tropics, ten trees are being cut for every one tree planted. As a result, forests are shrinking at a fairly predictable rate. Large-scale depletion of the ozone shield and the development of chlorofluorocarbons, population concentration and the overtaxing of local water sources, fuel supplies and disposal capacities all bring into relief the fact that the very notion of "progress" is ripe for redefinition.

Who can contemplate poverty in affluence; power for profit; women, as a class, in oblivion throughout the world; or prejudices enthroned as morality? Who can contemplate all this with the compassionate eye of God and do nothing, say nothing, change nothing, stand for nothing?

But contemplation is not without cost. To see what should be instead of what is; to see what could be instead of what will be if things go on as they are; to see what is possible instead of what is probable; to be conscious and compassionate and courageous and constant about it, costs.

"The duty of the contemplative life," Merton wrote, "is to provide an area in which possibilities are allowed to surface and new choices beyond routine choice become manifest." "Contemplative time," he went on, "is compassionate time; contemplative time is time open to others."

But to do the civil disobedience, the "citizen diplomacy," the act of conscience of Moses' mother and Pharoah's daughter, to cry out like the sentry in the night, takes its toll. But once we begin to see, what other choice is there? Once we become seeing souls, how can we not? An Arab proverb reminds us: "I will set my face to the wind and scatter my handful of seeds. It is no big thing to scatter seeds, but I must have the courage to keep facing the wind."

Yet in the midst of all the effort that consciousness, conviction, courage and constancy take to become compassion, the monastic literature of the ancients shows us clearly what it takes to rise to heights of contemplative awareness.

The story is told that a young person came to the monastery disillusioned with life but wanting to find a short cut to enlightenment for fear that a hard, slow process of study and meditation would only lead to failure. And so the Elder said: "Ah, yes, there is a shorter way to enlightenment. I will put you to playing chess with one of our old sisters. Whichever one of you loses, I will cut off your head. If the old sister loses she will wake up in Paradise. If you lose, since you have done nothing so far with your life, you will simply deserve it."

When the game began the youth played for her life. The chessboard became her entire world; she was totally concentrated on it. And though the early stages of the game were a near equal struggle, the youth finally took the advantage and the old sister's position began to crumble. And then the young person saw the worn face of her opponent and its intelligence and its sincerity and a wave of compassion came over her. And deliberately she began to make one blunder after another in her opponent's behalf until finally her own position was completely defenseless. And then the master leaned forward and upset the board. "There is no winner and no loser," the Elder said. "There is no head to fall here."

"Life requires of us only two things," the master said to the youth, "concentration on what is important and compassion for the other, and you have just learned both. Pursue that spirit and your enlightenment is sure."

That's the kind of contemplation that put Moses in the river and that's the kind of contemplation that took him out. And that's the kind of contemplation for which Merton called. And that's the only kind of contemplation with its consciousness, and conviction, and courage and constancy that will preserve this planet and its peoples in our own time.

That's the awareness, that's the insight, that's the call to alarm, that's the kind of contemplation that must grow in our lives. And it is, I believe, that kind of contemplative consciousness to which Moses' mother and Pharoah's daughter in this time call us all.

Why?

Because there truth is alive; there all creation is one; and there God's face shines — as it should — in us.

MERTON'S CONTRIBUTIONS AS TEACHER, WRITER AND COMMUNITY MEMBER:

An Interview with
Flavian Burns, O.C.S.O.

Conducted by Victor A. Kramer

Edited by Dewey Weiss Kramer

Flavian Burns, O.C.S.O., former Abbot of Our Lady of Gethsemani, Trappist, Kentucky, entered that monastery in 1951. After his ordination, he was a student of Canon Law at the Gregorian University in Rome. He served as Abbot from 1968 to 1973, and has also acted as temporary superior at other Cistercian monasteries. He lives at present in a small hermitage at Gethsemani.

Kramer: What was your association with Thomas Merton?

Burns: It was twofold, in a sense, because I entered Gethsemani at nineteen years old, and in my first years as a monk, Fr. Louis was my teacher. He was Master of Scholastics.

Kramer: That was in 1951?

Burns: 1951, 52, 53, 54, those years. And then when he went to the Novitiate, I was somewhat out of contact with him, except for the normal

---

* This interview has been edited from a tape first made for the *Thomas Merton Oral History*. The interview was conducted at the Cistercian monastery, The Abbey of the Holy Cross, in Berryville, Virginia.

community life. But in the 1960s I became the Father Prior of the monastery and then our relationship was in a different situation. Then I was his superior, and Father Confessor for a while, and eventually his Abbot. For a year and a half we were fellow hermits, from 1966 to 1968, when I was in the hermitage. He mentioned that in some publications. So that's pretty much the association; I think we grew closer when I got out of the stage of being just one of the many students he had. He had about forty at the time. And then of course, people who had him in the Novitiate were a different group. Like Jim Finley had him in the Novitiate. So, I would say my best years with him were the last two or three years when we were more peers working together for the good of the monastery and acting together. I always treated him pretty much as my teacher even when our roles were reversed technically, let's say.

Kramer: Right. And during that period towards the end, you saw him very frequently, would you say?

Burns: The last year, yes, especially after being Abbot, I was seeing him quite a bit. He was on the Council and he was one of the main people I was going to lean on when I accepted the job of being Abbot. Of course the Lord didn't see fit to let that work out.

Kramer: Could you describe the monastery during the earliest years that you were there, in the early 1950s?

Burns: Well, I think he's described that very well in *The Seven Storey Mountain* and *The Sign of Jonas*. It's pretty much the way life was. That's what I entered into; and there are books which describe the life — probably you could find them in one of the monastic libraries — our old Book of Usages. And if you read that Book of Usages you would see the type of thing that we had to live with, and rules that we lived by. It was very meticulously spelled out, and we followed that routine and regime. I think it would help a lot of people, you know, who are doing studies on Merton if they would read that old Book of Usages, give them a feel for the place.

Kramer: How would you say some of the other monks thought of Merton during the period when he was becoming well known as a writer?

Burns: Well, I don't think he got any special treatment, maybe a little razzing even from some. We lived a very silent life in the early years. I heard from one priest who was very close to Fr. Louis that he didn't even realize that he was a famous author until he got a job in the Guest House and had to deal with the guests. Because at the monastery, he was Fr. Louis, and there were some who didn't realize that Thomas Merton was Fr. Louis. Even if they knew of Thomas Merton. And we didn't have his books around. It took me quite a while to find out. I entered under the influence of *The Seven Storey Mountain*. So I'd say it took me a couple of months to find out who Thomas Merton was.

Kramer: Actually to identify him physically?

Burns: Because there was a big crowd there. I wasn't thinking about him anyway, and his name, as I say, in the monastery was Louis, and a lot of the times Latin names were used in the monastery for official appointments, the name was done in Latin. So Ludovicus, you know, was a little lost on me as being Thomas Merton. But, as I say, he didn't stand out, I think he was well loved in the community. But he was a type who was a boyish type in a community of pretty staid people. If he stood out at all, it would be as a certain charmer who was a little bit different from the ordinary run of people you commend to young people. I don't think he was disliked for that. But he certainly got no special attention as being a famous author —even from people like myself, you know, though I was impressed by this when I first entered. After you enter the community life, you just took him for granted as a ordinary monk. (**Kramer:** But he was . . .) He played that role. In fact it would be humorous seeing people try to figure out who is the famous author. They'd never pick him. He would be the least likely candidate to be the famous author.

Kramer: But there were very few monks who would actually be writing on a regular basis. There were a few others.

Burns: But you didn't know that from the monastery point of view. He did all the ordinary things. A lot of people had secretarial jobs in the monastery. And, so what he did during the work time, he did all the other ordinary chores the monks were doing, the outdoor work.

Kramer: Well, he wrote somewhere that during those years he had maybe six or eight hours per week actually to write.

Burns: Yes, he was amazingly fast. People can't believe what he would turn out; I can, after watching him, both read and write. Even on the typewriter, he simply was fast.

Kramer: Could you say something about his physical appearance? If you had to say some little bit about the way he looked, what kind of thing stands out in your mind?

Burns: Well, I would say that most of the time he looked very cheerful. I remember when I tried to identify the body, when it returned, and it took me a while to look at this corpse. And I said to the others, "Are you sure that that's Fr. Louis?" And they said, "Oh, yes. Look at the forehead" And when I got back , I looked at the picture I had of him by John Howard [Griffin], and I realized that what was missing was the eyes. For me, that dominated his whole face . . . the eyes, the twinkle in his eyes. So he was a very lively person, and to me very humorous, funny. But he could be equally serious. I think Matthew Kelty has described him — I like his description in the little essay he did. (**Kramer:**   In *Flute Solo*?) No, in the one that Patrick Hart put out; he has the first chapter in that.[1] He describes him physically.

Kramer: Yes, he does, Could you say something else about his sense of humor. You said that he had a twinkle in his eye.

Burns: You know he was an artist with words both in writing and in speaking. This was true even in ordinary conversation. He was very lively in his speech. Sometimes I wasn't always happy with his sense of humor because I felt a little bit that he used it to keep you at a certain distance. A lot of people do that — especially I think the English and the Irish — people that keep you at a certain distance by humor. But for the most part, it was pleasant and enjoyable. And he couldn't sit still, you know. The monastery is rather a serious place and you have a lot of reading in public and a lot of speaking in public and there's a lot of things going on and most of the monks keep their eyes down; don't let on what's going on. He wasn't like that. He'd let on. He'd comment on everything, if it was only by eye movements, a surprised look, something like that.

---

1.   Matthew Kelty, "The Man." In *Thomas Merton, Monk: A Monastic Tribute*; ed. by Brother Patrick Hart (New York: Sheed & Ward, 1974), pp. 19-35.

Kramer: Do you think he got a little bit bored sometimes?

Burns: Yes. It was harder for him, I'm sure, to get through some of those things without a sort of commentary on it or contribution to it.

Kramer: But he was always aware, too, I'm certain, of himself and what he was doing.

Burns: I think it was mostly when things would tend to be too artificial and he would do something like that so as not to be artificial. Because in church, now, he would be more quiet than anyone. He could sit without restlessness or moving around.

Kramer: You said earlier that he was a fast worker. What do you mean, that when he actually would write something, he could write it very rapidly?

Burns: Even his script was [abrupt]. He didn't hesitate. Like if he typed things up, he might go over it and correct some things. Most of us, if we write a letter, we'd think about it and we'd weigh which phrase to use. I don't think he did that. He did these things like that (snaps fingers). And if he didn't like it, maybe he would throw it away, but usually he'd let things stand. And he wrote his journal notes in a ledger . . . precisely, I think, so that he couldn't be pulling pages out and throwing them away. And if he was going to correct something that he said or take it back or anything like that, well, he'd do it on the next page . . . so that the shifting opinions or thoughts would be all there. He seemed to have the honesty of doing this journal business I remember when I was a young monk asking him about the advisability of my keeping a journal. And he said, "Oh, I wouldn't do that." I said, "Well, why not?" He said, "You'd waste too much time." And I said, "Well, you keep a journal." He said, "Yeah, but I write real fast." And I think it was exactly true. I didn't appreciate it at the moment, but, on reflection, I accept it as being very accurate.

Kramer: So he knew he could accomplish it in a short period of time, so he felt comfortable with it. Do you think that it was in any way hard for him to be a writer and a monk?

Burns: Oh, yes. I don't think it was really relative to being a monk, you know, the actual physical act of writing. I think that suited him fine. But being a published writer is certainly very complicated in the monastery. And it was one of the reasons I never accepted any kind of invitation to get into that. (**Kramer**:   Did he ever talk about this?) Oh, yes. It's well documented in the journals; even in *The Sign of Jonas* it is a big struggle. Then, of course, his ambitions, the ambitions to be a published author. I read something just recently. I guess it wasn't published earlier, or was it *The Secular Journal*, something I hadn't read before he entered the monastery, sending one of his novels around different places, and he got rejected everywhere he sent it. He ends with . . . (**Kramer**:   Yes, yes. It's from *The Secular Journal*. That's where it's from.) That's where I was reading it just recently. But he would say, "All these bad books get published, why can't my bad book get published?" I think that's a good example of both his ambition and his humor even at his own expense. But you can tell that in *The Seven Storey Mountain* where he's talking about seeing his own stuff in print for the first time. I guess most writers go through that. But he had certainly outgrown that. But later in life, I think the problem became the reading public and then the sense of responsibility of what his words were doing — (even seeing all of us come to the monastery) — maybe many that he could tell didn't belong in a monastery, and being there, by reason of his influence. That must certainly have come across to him that he was responsible for this. Then, of course, the whole peace movement, with people like Dan Berrigan and Phil Berrigan. That was one of the things they could use on him. Well, you have this audience, people who listen to you. You have an obligation to speak because, you know, everybody doesn't have that audience, but you have it. So it puts burdens on him which don't belong on a monk. But they were his personal vocational burdens. I think they were in that sense. But it happens to different people. I find being an Abbot is a hindrance to the way I like to live the monastic life, and I have now twice been called to be an Abbot. Somebody has to be Abbot. And other people have talents or abilities or lack of them, and they make it — being a monk —different from someone who is very famous and tries to be a monk.

Kramer: One thing that disturbed Merton was that he was always ahead of his readers, and so he could never get away from the books he had written earlier.

Burns: I remember when he finally got the book *Faith and Violence* published. It took him a long time to get it out from the time he had it written and, in the meantime, the whole climate had changed in the nonviolent community. They had moved to more violent stands, and he was telling me — I think I was Prior at the time — he said, "Oh, these people at Notre Dame. I'm getting my book out so late. All my friends are going to be mad at me when they see this 'cause it's going to look like it's coming out in the face of their changes in attitude." And then, as you say, his opinions changed. But he learned to live with that. I think somewhere it's documented about that. He wrote to somebody, and he more or less told them that you have to be willing to do what you're doing, be happy with what you're saying, and let it go. But he was a constantly changing person in that sense . . . and would have been if he had lived longer. (**Kramer:**   So there was conflict, but it was something he was learning to accept.) I think it was inevitable. And I personally don't feel that he did change that much. There were little things and a style, or way of saying things. Sometimes a person can be very [insensitive]. When I go back over things that I say, I realize in the face of all this women's lib, that women would say how sexist my language is. But I'm talking to a male audience most of the time, talking about a man who does this, and a man who does that, instead of "person" which would be more suitable for a wider audience.

Kramer: I wonder if you could comment about Fr. Louis' work habits, if there's anything that stands out in your mind. We talked about how he worked rapidly and he learned to revise quickly, and he didn't worry too much.

Burns: I think you have a better witness to that in Matthew Kelty because he worked with him as a secretary and he describes how he did his writing, [even] redoing it in different color inks. Someone wrote recently that Fr. Louis would leave these first draft things and let the secretaries fill it all in. I don't think that's true. It just doesn't correspond to him at all. (**Kramer:**   I don't think that's true.) And he didn't have that much secretarial help.

Kramer: We know the interests Merton had on the basis of what he wrote. I wonder if there were other things in which he was interested — in terms of how he actually lived as a hermit or within in the monastery — that he didn't write about? Do you think he wrote about most everything in which he was interested?

Burns: I suspect his interests are well documented. I can't think of anything unless you have something specific in mind.

Kramer: I was thinking especially about the final years when he was living by himself. He really seemed to derive a lot of pleasure just from being out with the birds and the trees.

Burns: I think he always enjoyed that. We used to have these arguments occasionally about living the contemplative life in the city, in high rise apartments or something like that. I thought it could be done and he said he couldn't do it without the trees and the woods. One time he spent about a week or so out on the Pacific coast and I remember his response to that was it's interesting because he said that it was better. It was even better than the woods here because all you had was sand and sea and sky, not the distraction of the birds and the trees, things like that.

Kramer: But how long could you go on living on a beach? He also realized that people in the city need to have a contemplative way of life.

Burns: Yes, I think he was speaking more for himself, that he would prefer [a certain way of life]. I suppose a lot of people are like that. But, as Matthew Kelty pointed out, he was very disciplined in his use of time. He wasn't a time waster. There were a lot of these things that he had preached to himself and made a big sacrifice to practice.

Kramer: I've heard some stories about how he would get impatient when people would come in and interrupt him at various times.

Burns: I think that manner was partially for others. Those people were his novices and he felt they should be living disciplined lives too. I remember one time we had a council meeting discussion when he was Fr. Master of Novices. I was Prior and there was a complaint on the part of one of the other members of the Council that he, Merton, wasn't around when the novices needed him. He answered that by saying that he saw each of the novices — and there were quite a number at that time — once a week or whatever the time period was. He didn't think it was right for him to be sitting there so they could run in to him whenever they had any little problem. He said, "We're training these people to be able to live the solitary life to some extent . . . life alone with God. We'd better find out in the first couple of years that they are here whether they can do that or not." So even if he seemed impatient, I think he was actually a very patient man. He was certainly patient with me. But I think he was not willing to accept falsehood or people wanting to talk when there was no reason for it and things like that. He used to tease us occasionally about things that we would do, for example, in passing one another. We were supposed to be living in silence. There was a prescribed little bow that you made so you didn't act like you weren't there. But usually the American outgoing manner, or self-consciousness, which was more or less what he was telling us it was would engage us, and we would have to make some joke or passing remark. I remember one time he was telling us that we didn't really believe in silence if we felt it was necessary to do that. One should be able to pass somebody in silence. Most of his relationships with the younger monks, at least, were as a teacher, a monastic father. It was really part of his job to point these things out to us. But I think he was a very patient person actually, considering all that he had going on in himself. I read things now in his writings and I check the date and I realize what my conversations were with him on those very topics, and I'm embarrassed how out of it I was, and yet how patient he was.

Kramer: Do you feel that his contact with persons outside the monastery made it more difficult or less difficult for him to live his life?

Burns: Oh, I'm sure it made it difficult. But he didn't have too much of that until later in his career. He didn't see too many outsiders. But he was the type that, if somebody came, he would give that person everything he had, all of his time, all of his energy. Well naturally, when he returned to his quietude, he'd feel that. So, it was important for him, I think, to have a lot of physical solitude because otherwise he would just run himself out. I'm not built like that and I can handle a little more of it. (**Kramer:** He really would just give everything to whatever it was he was doing at the moment.) And so the only way you could really keep him to himself was to protect him to some extent from himself. A lot of the people who complained about the old Abbot [Dom James Fox] and all that are not being very realistic to the providence that God had in mind. And even Fr. Louis realized that if he hadn't had that he could have used himself up very easily on superficial things. And this is why, even when I was Abbot, my aim was to get him a more private place because I knew that if he had more physical solitude, he would use it well. But if he was going to be where people could get at him, he was going to respond to that.

Kramer: Fr. Thomas Fidelis said once that he thought one of Merton's most important contributions was in showing other monks about a life of solitude which had in some way been forgotten. The life in many monasteries had become so active. It's a real paradox then that Merton did that by being terribly active himself in writing all these books.

Burns: He spent his time well. If you go over his schedules in the hermitage, for example, another writer might get up in the middle of the night and write books and things like that, but he spent his time well; [frequently] in prayer. He spent his time walking in the woods. I remember going to speak with him following the first time I myself walked in the woods with him and the group of Scholastics. He asked how I liked it. I said, "Well, it was all right but by the time we got out there and I got settled I didn't get much reading in." And he sort of looked at me with mock horror and said, "Reading? You brought a book?" The time was so scarce in those days, and we had so much that we were supposed to read and study that the thought of just going out and wasting a whole afternoon walking through the woods was something that we found a little hard to do. (**Kramer**: But he found it quite acceptable?) Yes, he did, and he urged us to do it. And there were certain times of the day when he would say you should never touch a book, before such and such a time, or this, or that. (**Kramer**: That would have been a relatively unusual attitude.) Yes. I think most people felt that they had to use their time "well." They didn't have the idea of "holy leisure" that he had. And that's been pretty nicely documented by Brother David Steindl-Rast in his little essay about God with us, and that's reminiscent of a lot of things that Merton said to us as Scholastics.

Kramer: If you had to pick one thing that you felt was really quite important to be remembered about Fr. Louis, is there any one remembrance that comes to mind, whether by your association with him or just about him in general?

Burns: I may read these things differently from other people, but I think so far he's been pretty well documented. My overwhelming impression is of a good man, a very good person, a very friendly person, very natural and spontaneous and likable. I haven't met that many people like that in my life experience. He was very unpompous. I've met people, even in this monastery, who know Thomas Merton only from the books and hearsay, and they would say that they didn't like him or I had heard that they didn't like him. Since I've been at Holy Cross Abbey near Berryville, Virginia, and talking about him and getting to know these people, I can see that they often have a completely false image of Thomas Merton. (**Kramer:** They have superficial ideas about Merton, I mean, even some monks who maybe haven't read his writings?) I suppose a lot of it has to do with the person in question. As Our Lord says, "He who has ears to hear, let him hear." Anyone listening is making the thing into his own image and likeness, and inevitably I suppose, they create these things. I remember the first time I read *The Seven Storey Mountain*, I was tremendously impressed by it and I had an interesting experience. I was working in an office building in a summer job with a lot of other young college people. We had a little group whose members were exchanging all the best sellers. That's how I came across *The Seven Storey Mountain*. I used to get the books from this black girl, and when she got them, I knew when I could expect to get them. I got it very quickly, so I knew she hadn't spent much time with it. When she gave it to me, I asked her, "How did you like it?" And she said, "It's all right, if you like that kind of thing." But it was obvious that she didn't like that kind of thing. So I read it. I was completely taken by it. And as you do with something that you're completely taken by, you give it to other people that you care about. So I gave it to my mother to read, and she didn't like him at all. She was turned off by him. So I figured, well, she's another generation, and she's kind of square and probably this is too different. So I gave it to my sister who's only a year or two different from me in age and she didn't like it either. And I said, "Well, what's wrong with it?" I could argue with her a little better than I could with my mother. And she said, "He's so egotistical ...I...I...I... and everything revolves around him." So I said, "Well, it's an autobiography. You have to write about yourself." But there seemed to be very few people at that time who liked the book or were moved by it. And later I heard these same things said, even today. People criticized the book as being too this, or too that, and naturally that's the way he would seem to them. And of course, what came across to me was probably a caricature, too, in the sense that I had imagined a much less lively person, despite all the obvious things in the book. So I expected to see a much quieter monk than I encountered when I got to the monastery. (**Kramer:** Do you think other people were surprised the same way?) I don't know. I never compared notes with too many people. But when I got over this initial misconception, I was happy with what I found .

Kramer: When Fr. Louis was Master of Scholastics, what exactly did he do day-by-day?

Burns: Aside from living the ordinary monastic life, which left you about two hours in the morning and two hours in the afternoon for special work, I'm sure he did some writing. That was when he had the vault where he could do his writing. But he had about forty Scholastics, and he saw each of us once a week or so. So that was an awful lot. (**Kramer**:   He would see you for almost half an hour or something?) At least, at least that. (**Kramer**:   So that's twenty hours right there.) Yes, right there. Now that wasn't just in two-hour periods, but it took a lot of his time. And then, of course, he was preparing conferences. I'm sure he had to do a lot of reading for that to get his notes ready. His orientation notes were from those years. And then there were other meetings. He had to meet with the Abbot and the Council. There were a lot of hours in choir in those days. And occasionally he would have to do outdoor work with the monks, all-out workdays. So, again, as I say, if you take those Old Usages and his schedule . . . When you know the particular job a person had in the monastery, you know how the person had to spend his time.

Kramer: It's quite clear from what you've been saying that you feel your personal association with Fr. Louis was very valuable over the years.

Burns: Oh, yes. It was my salvation. I owe him more than I owe any other human being, I think, for what I really treasure in my life. I don't see how I could have gotten the insights into various things without his help. So, I haven't a bad thing to say about him.

Kramer: He must have always been able to take enough time. Fr. Thomas [Fidelis] told me a nice story about how he had written a letter to Fr. Louis about the Jesus Prayer. I don't know exactly when this was, probably early 1960s, or there about. Fr. Louis wrote him a long letter back, saying, yes, fine, but you know you're not a Russian mystic. You're an American. Fr. Thomas mentioned that letter a couple of times in the last year or so, and I think the letter was very important at that time in his life. I think there must be other examples of that, where he went ahead and talked with people or wrote to them. Can you think of any other anecdotes about Merton and how he worked, or things that he did, which might be of value for persons who might be writing about him in the future? Are there any stories you can remember that say something about his manner, or his way of working? I was thinking, for instance, about these Sunday afternoon conferences which are taped and the enthusiasm which is reflected in all of those tapes and the fact that it's kind of unusual that a monk would be willing to commit himself to that kind of project over a long period of time. I mean, wouldn't you say that's unusual?

Burns: The taping was accidental to some extent. (**Kramer:** What do you mean "accidental?") I mean it wasn't part of the program that he should be taped. In fact, when I was a young Scholastic, one of the monks brought that up. We were talking about how to raise money for something or other, and one of the young monks asked jokingly, "Well, we could tape all these talks, you know, that you've given us, and we could sell them and make a lot of money." And we all just laughed, it sounded so outrageous, so ridiculous. He shook his head at the monk and said, "I don't think you've been moved by the Holy Spirit." But the origin of the taping was interesting because one of his novices, after he made profession, was put in charge of the lay brothers. The brothers had a work period in the morning when they had to go down to the kitchen and peel potatoes and things like that. They usually had readings, and the attendance wasn't very good. So he decided to ask Fr. Louis if he could tape the talks that he gave to the novices and play them for the lay brothers. It worked very nicely. The brothers had never been exposed to Fr. Louis. He had the Scholastics. That was the origin of the tapes. I don't know how they did it . . . (**Kramer:** You mean there was no machine in the room?) The microphone that he would use for speaking was the same microphone that was being taped. He wasn't conscious as I would be now of being taped. Since we had brothers and priests, we had different types of people in the monastery. The cooks cooked the meals, the others ate them, things like that. I remember him telling me that he felt that we, priests in the monastery, had an obligation to do a lot of reading and share this with the brothers who didn't have as much time for reading and study and maybe not the inclination. So, he felt it was part of his duty. When I became Abbot, he asked me if I wanted him to continue and I told him yes. By that time he was just giving Sunday talks, though. I think he saw that as his role in the community, to give those talks. I think he liked it best when the group that came were voluntary, so that he didn't have to worry about being imposed on people. (**Kramer:** Was it mostly voluntary?) Except for the novices. Of course, they had to go. But Sunday afternoons were free time. He always had a good audience. And he had enthusiasm. What's curious, if you listen to the tapes and reflect on it is that the enthusiasm is mostly him, himself. The audience was probably all just sitting there, and that's hard to sustain, that kind of enthusiasm in the face of an audience which isn't applauding you or showing a whole lot of interest. There are some pictures. I was looking through some books here along with some brochures. I think there are some photographs in another book which show the audience he had. You can see these monks sitting at the table, looking up at someone. I think there's a group of young people sitting around the table, all looking at a speaker. You don't see the speaker in the picture.

Kramer: Do you think that Merton was an innovator, or do you think that he was able to synthesize things? Do you think that he was actually making contributions in terms of interpreting monasticism?

Burns: I think he translated the tradition into a language that this generation, or my generation at least, could understand. I thought of him as a popularizer of what had always been taught. But I also remember one time I had a visit while I was Abbot at Gethsemani from John Tracy Ellis, a historian of the Church, and I was making conversation with him. This was after Fr. Louis had died. I said that I was surprised that there were so many people doing theses on Merton. His answer was, and he's published this somewhere, "It doesn't surprise me at all because he is one of the five original thinkers of our century — at least in Catholic thinking." I didn't think to ask him who the other four were. That was news to me, but I respect John Tracy Ellis' opinion, as an outsider, as an historian of what's been going on. Later in an interview with somebody else that turned up in one of the papers, Ellis said the same thing, more or less, not about Merton, but saying just in general that there were only about five really original thinkers in our century, and he said, for example, Teilhard de Chardin and Thomas Merton. So Teilhard was one of the five. I don't know who the other three are. But that places Merton in a kind of original company. I don't know if everbody would accept that judgment. I even have problems, you know, seeing it. But I do believe that he was original in his context. There was nobody else at Gethsemani preaching what he was preaching. There was nobody in our Order who was preaching what he was preaching.

Kramer: Do you think his work at Gethsemani actually caused specific changes in the way the monastery was?

Burns: I think he changed a whole generation's attitude toward how to live the monastic life. He changed mine completely.

Kramer: You mean changes in terms of more individual responsibility, each person living within a community, but not just following rules?

Burns: Well, to some extent it was a question of getting to the heart of the matter. It's not a good analogy perhaps — you have the Jews getting the law from Moses and their tradition is waiting for the Messiah and then you have Jesus Christ coming on the scene, and to all appearances he's upsetting the whole thing. But that's not what Jesus says. Jesus says, "I haven't come to do away with these things. I come to fulfill them. But you people have missed the point." I think that was more or less what Fr. Louis was saying: "I'm not here to upset the monastic life but what is the meaning of these things?" I think that was new. I couldn't have survived if I hadn't found some meaning, or if I had survived physically, I wouldn't have been anything I'd like to be at this point. So, to me, he was a very providential man. His spiritual writings at least will survive, I think, as part of the heritage of the Church.

Kramer: They are surviving. I noticed recently in *Sojourners,* published in Washington, D. C., that they still offer several of Merton's books through their book club. When we had the conference in Atlanta in 1980 there was a lot of talk about passages in his book *Contemplation in a World of Action,* references to adaptation of the monastic life to the modern world, and even references to a kind of adaptation of the monastic life for people who aren't monks. I was wondering, and this would be a speculative question, what connections there are between that group, the Families of St. Benedict, who are presently living adjacent to Gethsemani and Merton's writing? I would think there must be some connection.

Burns: I think there's some influence, but not entirely. Their inspiration came really from a different source. They were in contact with their generation of people wanting to do something besides what society is offering. Their first contact with community living was with Protestant communal groups. I forget their names, but they're there in Pennsylvania. They lived similarly. Others wanted something like that within the Catholic forum. So I don't think they were really following Merton. They didn't read something in Merton and then go off and try to do it.

Kramer: Right, there are some similarities between the Families of St. Benedict and others. I already asked this question in a different way, but I'll ask it again with different language. Do you think Merton has had an effect upon the way monks actually live day-by-day as compared to the Gethsemani he entered in 1941?

Burns: Yes, I think he did. I think, in fact, that he was one of the main influences. You must realize that the great influx came earlier. They always talk about pre-Vatican and post-Vatican, but we started the changes long before the Vatican Council, in the 1950s, and they were demanded by this whole new generation of people who were coming in. I'm not saying that everybody came in because of Merton's influence, but I had never heard of the Trappist monks until *The Seven Storey Mountain* was written, and I'm sure a lot of people could say the same thing. So, just by that physical thing of so many people coming into the Order and new houses being made, even if they didn't like Merton or it didn't have anything to do with him, they were still there and this new blood and these new people forced the old monks to change a lot of things. We had to adapt and I lived through all of that. I entered in 1951 and we had over 200 monks at Gethsemani. All of a sudden these fifty people in a community which had had very few Americans, as you can tell from the history, had 150 Americans coming in. I had imagined myself entering a small place with a lot of old people walking around, and I got in there and the place was crawling with youth, everybody with new ideas. So, in that sense, I do believe that he was influential, although people don't want to give him all the credit, and maybe he doesn't deserve it . . . other people had ideas, too . . . but certainly at Gethsemani, very subtly, he was the man who was behind changing attitudes. Of course he changed things. He had influence on the generation coming in, myself included, and we became the future superiors. I went to General Chapter and was influential in making changes. I wouldn't have been there if it weren't for him, and I wouldn't have had those attitudes if it hadn't been for him.

Kramer: Sometimes people say that Merton was easily swayed and that sometimes he would write one thing and then later he would write something else or he would contradict himself in journals, even in journals that are published and so on. The implication is that he was too impulsive or too spontaneous. Do you have any feeling about that kind of criticism?

Burns: For the most part I find it superficial because he was spontaneous and impulsive and in certain areas, I think, naive. He tended not to be too good a judge of people. I mean in the sense of being critical with people.

He would give them a better judgment perhaps than they deserved. But I think what they missed mostly, and I've said this before, is that he addressed himself to the people to whom he was speaking here and now, and, you know, if you're talking to a group of people who are too conservative, you will say one thing. If you're talking to a group of people who you feel are being too liberal, you'll say another thing. Now people can take those two things and say, well, he's contradicting himself. But he isn't. If you sit down and listen to what he's saying, he's still saying the same thing but to two different people. You have to say "yes" to one and "no" to the other. And if you observe him as I did, I think his best writing — and his life — was as a spiritual master. A spiritual master is speaking to people for *their* welfare. He is going to have to address them where they're at, or where they're coming from. They should do some of the things they do for Scripture and other literary sources. They study literary genres and all that, but they don't do that with Merton. They want to take statements out of context.

Kramer: Do you think he thought of himself as a spiritual master?

Burns: Yes. I think he did. Not maybe in the sense of perfection. I think he would see it more as a job. That was his job. And I remember once that a group of nuns was trying to get him to come and give some talks, and I wasn't too much in favor of it because, as he said himself very often, "There's all this talk about prayer and spirituality and everybody's talking about it. Why don't we just go and do it?" I said, "You're just going to be another one. They'll have another speaker, and then there will be just more talk. You'd do better to tell them you can't come because you've got to practice." But in the course of that conversation, I remember him saying, "Well, these people, they don't know anything about these things. I'm not saying I know a lot about it, but I know something about it." He wasn't the type who took himself too seriously, but he was honest. He was realistic to know what he knew and what he didn't.

Kramer: Do you think he felt the same way about his poetry, that is, that he knew a good bit about writing poetry?

Burns: I think he believed in his poetry a lot more than most people believe in it, maybe. I don't know what the objective judgment will be eventually, but I think he really thought of his poetry as good. This may be the better part of his writing. I can't pass judgment on poetry at all. But I've listened to different people at different times — they don't think he was a good poet.

Kramer: They have not read the poetry carefully, either. People interested in Merton within Merton circles, or Catholic circles, or people in American poetry circles who also don't know anything about Merton or Catholicism — in all three instances, I think, they haven't really read the poetry.

Burns: I was listening to one of the published tapes recently — it's about community life — and he was talking about examples of community life. Then he mentioned his experience of solidarity with poets, how poets have this kind of sense of one another. It was like a little club, a community. And I know that that was very strong in him. It wasn't something I could share with him because I wasn't a poet, and I couldn't understand his poetry for the most part. But I know it meant a lot to him. As I say, I don't know what the final judgment on him as a poet will be, but I feel his reputation is secure as a spiritual writer. People are still reading John of the Cross and other authors like that, whereas famous authors of their own times come and go, yet there are certain basic spiritual truths that have been articulated.

Kramer: Would you say this is why you think most people are interested in Merton?

Burns: I wouldn't know about that. That's *my* interest in him. And I think people in the peace movement are more interested in some of the other things, the social things that stand for relevance to their time, and others could be more interested in the poetry or in art or something like that. We had an interesting event, if you are interested in anecdotes. It was at Fr. Louis' funeral. We had a good many of his friends there. Br. Patrick [Hart], I think, has told the story to someone. It is one of the things that impressed me, and I've been told it impressed some others there. It was how incompatible we were; we who were Merton's friends and didn't think we could very easily be on an intimate basis with one another. We had such different interests and tastes, yet he had the ability to relate to all kinds of different people. So, I don't know. I don't know what you can do with this oral history project, or if it's going to work. But it's worth a try. I personally feel, and I've told people this who haven't had the opportunity to know Merton, that I who have had the opportunity to know him personally, and on as intimate a basis as he's been known, that he's better known through his writings. I think he reveals himself more in his writings than he did face to face. Because I think on a face to face personal level he kept a distance. He had to relate to them differently. But he was very protective, very modest; whereas in his writings, I sensed, that this man is talking from his heart. And it's all laid out there. I think that's what people pick up. Maybe that's what made him so protective. He knew himself that he was "doing it." Naturally you read something, and you're touched, and then you want to sit down and talk to the man. You feel you're going to get right on that level with him. Well, you can't. He wasn't up to doing that with complete strangers, whereas he could do it in his books. I think that's a good point to remember.

FOUNDATIONS FOR RENEWAL:

An Analysis of the Shared Reflections

of Thomas Merton and Ernesto Cardenal

by **D. R. Letson**

I was ordained a priest to come and establish the community here* [at Solentiname]. It was Thomas Merton who gave me the idea. He had been a monk for twenty years and had written a great deal about that life but had become unhappy with monastic life . . . . He knew it was a medieval, anachronistic lifestyle. Ridiculous. So he wanted to found a different kind of contemplative community outside the U. S. Merton was an enemy of the U. S., of Yankee Civilization and everything it represented. He hated the bourgeois mentality most monks had.[1]

Words of Ernesto Cardenal: poet, minister of culture in Sandinista Nicaragua, and a man whom Thomas Merton, Cardenal's one-time novice master, praised as "one of the rare vocations we have had here [at Gethsemani] who certainly and manifestly combined the gifts of a contemplative with those of an artist."[2]

Indeed, Thomas Merton and Ernesto Cardenal shared much in common. Both were religious converts of sorts who responded to a call to a religious vocation as mature men of the world. Both had their writings censored (one by an ecclesial, the other by a governmental authority). Both were significantly influenced by a Cuban experience (Merton by the warmth of 1940 pre-revolution Havana, Cardenal by the community-

---

1.   Margaret Randall, *Christians in the Nicaraguan Revolution* (Vancouver: New Star, 1983), p. 41.

2.   Thomas Merton, "Ernesto Cardenal," in *The Literary Essays of Thomas Merton;* ed. Brother Patrick Hart (New York: New Directions, 1981), p. 323.

*   This paper was delivered on 27 May 1989 in the session, "Merton and Human Dignity," at the First General Meeting of *The International Thomas Merton Society* in Louisville, Kentucky.

mindedness of 1970 post-revolution Cuba).[3] Both were inspired by a theology of love. Both had developed a deep admiration for the spiritual and communal traditions of the Latin American Native Indian. Both genuinely admired Gandhi and his philosophy of nonviolence. Both were poets — Columbia University-trained poets who ultimately shared an Augustinian-Bonaventurian affection for nature and a liberationist thirst for social justice. So strong was the Merton-Cardenal association that Dom James Fox is said to have frowned upon it as being an "ami intime." The abbot was clearly intent on putting an end to an epistolary friendship which was becoming too hot to handle.[4]

As Ernesto Cardenal's spiritual director during the Nicaraguan's two-year apprenticeship with the Gethsemani Trappists (1957-1959), Thomas Merton displayed a keen interest in Cardenal's knowledge of Nicaraguan poets, of the Somoza dynasty, of Nicaraguan geography, and of matters Latin American in general. Indeed, Cardenal's spiritual director was destined to change the course of his novice's life irreversibly, his life as contemplative and his life as artist. Through Merton's guidance, for example, Cardenal quickly grasped the inherent fusion of contemplation and poetry, of the active and contemplative life which Merton himself had long struggled to reconcile. According to Cardenal, Merton "saw no conflict in the contemplative life and a life of action."[5] Indeed, Cardenal notes of his mentor that "Merton transformed me completely during the two years I was a novice under him . . . ." Merton had convinced Cardenal that he (Cardenal) needed to renounce nothing, that there was no contradiction in being simultaneously a poet, a contemplative, and a political activist (*Wilkes*, pp. 36-37). Like the Desert Fathers and like St. Bernard whom Merton had so admired, Thomas Merton and Ernesto Cardenal dreamed of new foundations, new forms of religious expression — foundations embodied in part at least at Solentiname.

Solentiname would become a contemplative foundation with the potential to transform the lives of those it touched, a community which

---

3. Merton discusses his Cuban experience in *The Seven Storey Mountain* and *The Secular Journal*, but perhaps more to the present point Ernesto Cardenal compares their reactions in his *In Cuba*; trans. by Donald D. Walsh (New York: New Directions, 1974), pp. 8-9.

4. Michael Mott, *The Seven Mountains of Thomas Merton* (Boston: Houghton Mifflin, 1984), p. 340.

5. See Paul Wilkes, *Merton, By Those Who Knew Him Best* (New York: Harper & Row, 1984), p. 36. Hereafter referred to in the text as *Wilkes*. It is a theme Merton developed often. See, for example, "Poetry and Contemplation: A Reappraisal," in *The Literary Essays of Thomas Merton*: "In actual fact, true contemplation is inseparable from life and from the dynamism of life" (p. 339). See also his "Marxism and Monastic Perspectives" in *The Asian Journal of Thomas Merton* (New York: New Directions, 1973).

would provide the contemplative pause for the nurturing of research and the inspiration of writing, research and writing which would, in turn, promote new social foundations blossoming from the teachings of Vatican II and rooted in the gospel of love.[6] The spirit of St. Benedict would be reshaped once more, this time to serve the needs of a nuclear world stalked by the shadows of Gog and Magog. Solentiname is the physical manifestation of Merton's 1963 observation on Cardenal, the contemplative and the poet, that

> the poet remains conscious of his relation to the world he has left and thinks a great deal about it, with the result that one recognizes how the purifying isolation of the monastery encourages a profound renewal and change of perspective in which "the world" is not forgotten but seen in a clearer and less delusive light. (*LE*, pp. 323-324)

As Cardenal observes from the tentative security of his 1977 exile in Costa Rica, the menace of Solentiname then reduced to rubble by Somoza's National Guard, "Contemplation means union with God . . . . Contemplation also brought us to the revolution."[7]

When Ernesto Cardenal's uncertain health forced him from Gethsemani in 1959, Merton encouraged him in his quest for priesthood — "the church was still very clerical, so it would be important to be a priest in the kind of community we had in mind" — and Merton also encouraged him in the pursuit of their common vision (*Randall*, p. 43). As for Cardenal's departure from Gethsemani, Cardenal asserts that Merton saw it as a good thing: "If you leave before making your vows then you won't have a problem [of dispensation] I do being a monk from the Trappist order." As for Merton, he would follow as soon as permission permitted: "We are planning to leave anyway, now you can leave early" (*Randall*, p. 42). And so Cardenal recalled for Michael Higgins and me how Merton petitioned Rome for permission to establish his Latin American foundation, but John XXIII, while approving of the idea itself, insisted that the Trappists were not the order to realize the vision, a different order with a different charism was

---

6. In his "Poetry and Contemplation: A Reappraisal," *The Literary Essays of Thomas Merton*, Merton has much to say about poetry which echoes Cardenal's convictions perfectly. Contemplation, Merton explains, "brings us into the closest contact with the one subject that is truly worthy of a Christian poet: the great Mystery of God, revealing His mercy to us in Christ" (p. 343). Merton also says of the Christian poet that "All good Christian poets are then contemplatives in the sense that they see God everywhere in His creation and in His mysteries, and behold the created world as filled with the signs of God" (p. 345). Like Merton, Cardenal frequently uses his poetry to analyze the function of the poet. Like Merton, he concludes that the roles of the contemplative and of the poet will merge necessarily. The ideas noted above are evident in the themes of the liberation theologian which become more and more a part of Cardenal's poetry. They are especially explicit in his *Psalms*, and they are reflected on in his *Love*.

7. Ernesto Cardenal, *The Gospel in Solentiname*; vol. 1; trans. by Donald D. Walsh (Maryknoll, New York: Orbis, 1976), p. 267. Hereafter referred to in the text as *GIS*.

required.[8] Merton agreed, and petitioned to leave the Trappists, a dispensation he was so confident of receiving that a Merton-Cardenal rendezvous was determined for Mexico. One day before the Mexican meeting, Merton informed Cardenal that Dom James had lobbied Rome successfully — Merton was bound by obedience both to silence and to his cloister (*Conversation*, pp. 35-36). Merton, however, remained forever restless, eager to develop new forms of contemplative life. He continued to yearn for Solentiname. New plans were made, and Cardenal had prepared a cottage for his would-be companion in Solentiname where he was to stay for several weeks following his return from Asia and on route to Chile where he was to investigate the potential for establishing a Latin American Trappist foundation. It was another meeting destined to remain unfulfilled.

Inspired by Thomas Merton's vision, however, Ernesto Cardenal pursued the dream. He was ordained a priest in Managua on the Feast of the Assumption of Our Lady in 1965. On February 13, 1966, he founded his religious community, Our Lady of Solentiname.[9] And from Cardenal's leaving Gethsemani until Merton's departure for Asia, the two corresponded regularly. At first they discussed matters related to poetry and to the publication of poetry, but the topics soon included Latin American issues, social corruption, the politics of Gethsemani, and the development of Solentiname.

The evolution of Merton's thinking with respect to Solentiname makes for interesting reading. At the outset, Merton clearly shares the spark of excitement he has fanned in Cardenal, and surely intends to leave Gethsemani to join his former pupil; but by 1968 he has begun to waver, to waver seriously, so that the enthusiasm Cardenal clearly exhibited in his 1984 conversation with Michael Higgins and me concerning Merton's joining him in Nicaragua seems no longer to have been a mutually-shared one by the time Merton left for his Asian pilgrimage. Merton's 17 August 1959 letter to Cardenal is only the first of a series of what were to become a virtual "Dear Ernesto" genre.[10] In this instance he could not join Cardenal in Mexico where he was studying at Cuernavaca — problems at Gethsemani:

---

8.   Michael W. Higgins and Douglas R. Letson, "A Conversation with Ernesto Cardenal," *Gamut* 6 (1984), pp. 30-43. Hereafter referred to in the text as *Conversation*.

9.   February 13 is the date recalled by members of the Solentiname community (*Randall*, p. 48). Robert Pring-Mill records February 16 in his thorough introduction to Cardenal's *Marilyn Monroe and Other Poems* (London: Search Press, 1975), p. 18.

10.   All references to the Merton-Cardenal correspondence are to material researched at the Thomas Merton Studies Center, Bellarmine College, Louisville, Kentucky. The letters file includes the Robert Pring-Mill records of the Merton-Cardenal correspondence prepared by Pring-Mill in Managua and deposited at the Merton Center.

"We have no right to escape into happiness that most of the world cannot share. This is a very grim and terrible country, and in it we must suffer sorrow and responsibility with the rest of the world."

Still, on 8 October 1959, Merton is planning to enter Mexico on "a regular visa . . . as a permanent resident." Undaunted by occasional set-backs, Merton and Cardenal have proceeded with their plans to establish a new foundation and have chosen as their site Corn Island, the subsequent CIA jumping-off point for the abortive Bay of Pigs fiasco. Corn Island was an isolated territory in the Atlantic, northeast of Bluefields, Nicaragua. Then, on 24 October 1959, Merton wrote to Cardenal to break the news. According to Merton, Dom James had apparently intervened and had scuttled their plans by warning the bishop of Bluefields "to steer clear of anyone who wanted to leave Gethsemani. The bishop really sounded frightened." The advice: turn our eyes to Ometepe, a large island in the westerly region of Lake Nicaragua, and not far distant from the Solentiname archipelago. To reinforce the present thesis, Merton points out that Pablo Antonio Cuadra agrees with him that the new foundation must "be rooted in the Indian and Latin cultural complex in a very definite way."

24 November 1959: awaiting an indult, but no news of it. Father Abbot has gone to Rome and "is evidently opposing everything with all his power." In the meantime, "Gethsemani is *terrible* . . . ." 17 December 1959: the response from Rome is negative; I "can only accept and obey." Merton suspects that psychiatrist Gregory Zilboorg is at the root of the problem since he has advised the abbot "of my desire of solitude that I just wanted to get out from under obedience and that if I were allowed a little liberty I would probably run away with a woman." Nonetheless, Merton has not lost his consistently-expressed enthusiasm for Cardenal or their project, consoling Ernesto that "I know we will always be united in prayer, and I assure you of all my affection and of the joy I have in our association."

Over the next two years, Merton mentions Corn Island and Ometepe on several occasions, but centers more on poetry, peace, his headaches, and Latin America. The issue of their jointly-sponsored undertaking is renewed in earnest, however, when Cardenal is ordained a priest on 15 August 1965 and immediately sets about to realize their plan for a newly-formed religious foundation in Nicaragua. Fate and finances present the archipelago of Solentiname in Lake Nicaragua and (providentially, in Cardenal's mind) a partially completed church on one of the thirty-eight islands. It is an opportunity which Cardenal explains to Merton in a letter from Managua dated 28 December 1965.

Merton replies to Cardenal's news on 8 January 1966, suggesting that Cardenal proceed with the foundation, that he "should do everything that is required, leaving all the rest to Divine Providence." As for his joining Cardenal in Nicaragua, Merton suggests flexibility about the timing of the petition to Rome, adding that "at present my feeling is that it should be put off until 1967." Anyway, it would be best if Cardenal, himself, got "off to a good start before I came, and meanwhile we could freely correspond about the problems and difficulties that presented themselves." For his part, Merton could foresee a major problem: "I am a North American. I know that I am not a typical North American . . . . But I do not want to be in any sense a kind of occult cultural ambassador for this society, and I cannot help being so in some involuntary sense." One year hence, in 1967, Merton explained, he would petition Rome for a six-month permission, "after which I could get the regular permission from Rome according to the usual routine."

So, as promised, by 14 October 1966, Merton is writing to give advice to Cardenal, encouraging him to accept the bishop's invitation that he become pastor to the people of Solentiname, to establish a small community with no bureaucracy, and to attract "a beautiful community of the poor around the monastery." For his part, as a sign of foundational renewal and of identification with his people, Cardenal abandoned the trappings of the traditional monastic setting, resurrecting for the communal habit the *cotona*, the traditional shirt of Nicaragua's peasants (*Randall*, p. 67). And the foundation flourished, raising Christian consciousness, becoming a center of Nicaraguan native art, the haunt of poets and professional artists, and, ultimately, a center for Sandinista revolutionaries, radicalized, as Cardenal explains, by the Gospel (*GIS*, p. 268).

3 July 1966: Gethsemani is taking control of a monastery in Chile. Now that the Trappists are in Latin America, Merton suggests, perhaps he and Cardenal will finally meet in Solentiname. But, Merton adds to temper the optimism, "Dom James believes my place is here." Warning signs of second thoughts. Then, on 15 March 1968, Merton writes to Cardenal celebrating Father Flavian Burns' elevation to the position of abbot of Gethsemani, and noting that, as a result, he may be able to join Ernesto in a few weeks. Still, Merton interjects another sign of waning interest: "It seems wrong to escape the immense rottenness, the evil, the judgment, that are inevitable here." Then Merton adds by way of further caution: "If I were to leave here, I would want to disappear completely and go where I was not known at all, and cease to have any kind of public existence

whatever." At the same time, he continues to encourage Cardenal, rejoicing that the foundation includes a married couple: it's "just tremendous. I think the whole future of monasticism depends on some broadening of perspective like this."

Finally, on 15 March 1968, Merton sees the real possibility of travel, and even of joining Cardenal in Solentiname. His enthusiasm has diminished considerably, however, and Merton begins to backtrack in the face of a long-held anticipation about to be realized. He explains to Cardenal:

> I would be ashamed to be in a Latin American country and to be known as a North American. But in any case, apart from all these ideas one way or the other, it is necessary to see whether or not God really wants me there. In so many ways this seems to be the place for me, here. But I want to come to Solentiname and see what it is like, see if it seems to be where God wants me, though I rather doubt it. For one thing, I believe I would be a kind of tourist attraction, and would have to be seeing people all the time. It is bad enough here.

Peculiar ideas, these, about the comings and goings on an all-but-deserted island in the lower reaches of Lake Nicaragua, and this during the height of Somozan repression. Merton grasps for a *deus ex machina*. He is consistent, nonetheless, in his repeated expressions of admiration for the Latin American Native, in his revulsion towards North American society, and in his care to temper Cardenal's expectations concerning his own arrival while simultaneously exulting over developments in Solentiname.

Then, on 21 July 1968, Merton informs Cardenal that he is leaving for Japan, thence to Thailand, with various visits in the Far East. If, however, his travel plans do not unfold as expected, "I may get to Nicaragua for a few weeks with you." On the other hand, Merton adds — taking with the left hand what he gives with the right — Dom Flavian is thinking of starting a hermitage in California, "or somewhere hidden." Dom Flavian's proposition sounds attractive to Merton, forgetting altogether that three months earlier he had cautioned Cardenal that Gethsemani now "seems to be the place for me." Characteristically, however, Merton leaves a ray of hope: the pursuing of the California concept will rest on Father Flavian's suggested location "remaining really hidden." So, Merton concludes, "I hope to see you either in June 1969 or the following year." "Or the following year": Merton has now maneuvered a two year delay! Clearly, Merton has shoes hot to travel, but decidedly cool to travel to Nicaragua. A tragic final chapter, this, to what seemed destined to be so fortunate a tale.

Nevertheless, the association of Thomas Merton and Ernesto Cardenal was surely a providential one since they complemented one another's needs and interests so remarkably. In addition, the foundation which they planned did not reside merely in physical structures. Solentiname, for example, provided Cardenal with the time and the resources to study the religion and society of the Native Peoples of North America, as well as to teach his people the message of Christ's love. Projects close to Merton's heart since in these people he saw the potential for revitalized social foundations and a living example of Christ's love for his people.

Thomas Merton's and Ernesto Cardenal's shared enthusiasm for the Native life-style echoes throughout their correspondence between 1962 and 1965. On 12 July 1962, for example, Merton assures Cardenal that:

> It is first of all important to listen to the silence of the Indian and to admit to hearing all that has been said for five hundred years. The salvation of our lives depends on it. The thing you wrote about the San Blas Indians was marvelous. There is no doubt that you have a providential task in this work of understanding and of love, a profound work of spiritual reconciliation and atonement.

The essential redemptive and healing work which Merton feels is to be done with the Natives of Latin America begins with hearing because, he contends, the "confusion, hatred, violence, misinformation, blindness of whole populations comes from having no one to listen to them. Hence they speak with knives, as the Negroes are now doing . . . ."

Later that same year, Merton writes once more in praise of Cardenal's poetry of the Latin American Indian, noting in his letter of 17 November 1962: "I have not forgotten about the Indians and all that they mean to us both . . . : [T]he Indians . . . the poorest and humblest people . . . may remain to pray God to pardon and revive the human race." The Indians whom Cardenal is researching during his seminary studies in Colombia Merton contrasts with the "great criminals with enormous power [who are] . . . in a death struggle with each other" and who populate the rest of the world. On 25 February 1963, Merton once more celebrates the Latin American Indian, noting that it is the challenge of the greatest missionaries to "enter into the thought of primitive peoples and to love that thought and spirit as Christians, thus bringing the spirituality of these people into the light of Christ where, indeed, it was from the start without anyone realizing the fact." 10 March 1964, Merton writes to congratulate Cardenal on an interview with Yabilinguina, and to write in lavish praise of the Latin American poetic tradition:

> [T]his movement of poets and artists toward a new spiritual consciousness is certainly the most hopeful thing that I have seen in the world lately . . . . We simply cannot look to the established forms and structures at the moment for any kind of constructive and living activity. It is all dead, ossified, corrupt, stinking . . . . But Miguel [Grinberg] and the poets have

shown genuine integrity and love which are the same longing for life and truth is manifesting itself everywhere at the same time and idependently.[11]

North America, Merton concludes, must learn to hear "the voices of the Andes and the Amazon." It is a letter flowing with praise for the Native and grating with condemnation for the non-Native. Then, on 24 April 1965, Merton warns that Cardenal should expect clerical criticism for his work with the Indians. It is a caution, Merton assures him, spoken from painful experience. The warning is, in fact, a tactful follow-up to Merton's 2 March 1965 correspondence with Pablo Antonio Cuadra in which he outlined his concern that Ernesto's ordination was in jeopardy — Ernesto is to "stop publishing anything about the Indians at once." Rome has been informed. On 10 May Merton consoles Cardenal once more. He too has been censored. It is friendly advice intermixed with the bitter disclosure that he feels confined to the uttering of officially sanctioned catechetical statements or to the mouthing of vacuous expressions of social pleasantries. Nonetheless, Ernesto is ordained on 15 August 1965 and proceeds both with the religious foundation as planned, and with the study of Latin America's Native People as a foundation for a renewed social order.

Of course, Merton discussed his interest in Latin America, its people and its poets, with correspondents other than Cardenal. Stefan Baciu, for example, clearly documents this interest when he quotes, among other things, Merton's statement that "Latin American poets really seem to me to be alive, to have something honest to say, to be sincerely concerned with life and with humanity. There is some genuine hope left in them...."[12] The sentiments reflect those contained in his February 1964 "Message to Poets" in Mexico City as well as in Merton's 10 March 1964 letter to Cardenal. Ernesto Cardenal's name appears naturally in the short list of authors provided to Stefan Baciu by Thomas Merton to verify the accuracy of his observations about poets of life and humanity (*Baciu*, p. 21), as it does in Merton's undated "Prologo."[13] Similarly, Robert E. Daggy's introduction to *Day of a Stranger*, a brief book written by Merton in response to a request from Latin America, also sketches Merton's affection for Latin America and

---

11.   One month earlier Merton had written his "Message to Poets" who were meeting in Mexico City and had presented them with a similar meessage. In that letter he exhorted his poetic colleagues: "Let us obey life, and the Spirit of Life that calls us to be poets, and we shall harvest many new fruits for which the world hungers — fruits of hope that have never been seen before" (*LE*, p. 373).

12.   Stefan Baciu, "Latin America and Spain in the Poetic World of Thomas Merton," *The Merton Annual 2*; ed. Daggy, Hart, Kramer & Kramer (New York: AMS Press, 1989), p. 17. Hereafter referred to in the text as *Baciu*.

13.   Thomas Merton, *The Collected Poems of Thomas Merton* (New York: New Directions, 1977), p. 744. Hereafter referred to in the text as *CP*.

his disaffection for the culture of the United States.[14] But it is Thomas Merton himself, especially in his "Letter to Pablo Antonio Cuadra concerning Giants," who best expresses his philosophy of life, death, and Latin America. In Merton's eyes the Latin American races reject the apocalyptic forces of Gog and Magog. Instead they take "a totally different outlook on life, a spiritual outlook which is not abstract but concrete, not pragmatic but hieratic, intuitive and affective rather than rational and aggressive" (*CP*, p. 380). In our inability to see in these simple people a superior rather than an inferior race, we and those who came before us have failed to "*encounter Christ* already potentially present in the Indians" (*CP*, p. 381).

It was Cardenal's concurrence with Merton's thesis which spurred him to research the sources of Latin America's Native civilization while at Cuernavaca, Mexico, and La Ceja, Colombia, which caused him to amass a library of half a million books in Solentiname from which he could contemplate the history of the Incas and the Aztecs. And it was Cardenal's personal meditation coupled with his scholar's admiration for the Native way of life which produced numerous poems about the Native People of Latin America, most of which are collected in his *Homage to the American Indian*. In it, Cardenal sings of individuals and tribes who live essentially egalitarian lives without money, without conflict (conflict being the direct result of acquisition), without walls. He sings of people living communally, reflecting a oneness with nature and with each other. He sings of "Lost Cities," of civilizations destroyed by white man's greed for power and possession.

> and because there was no money
> there was neither prostitution nor plunder
> the doors of the houses stayed open
> there was no Administrative graft nor embezzlement
>
> . . . .
>
> No Indian was ever sold
> and there was *chicha* for everybody [15]

Because Cardenal is a Latin American poet, a poet of hope and life, his poems may well describe the destructive forces of Gog and Magog, but they will also almost invariably embody lessons of hope, of resurrection, and will often conclude with a resurrection motif:

---

14.   Thomas Merton, *Day of a Stranger*; ed. Robert E. Daggy (Salt Lake City: Gibbs M. Smith, 1981), pp. 12ff.

15.   Ernesto Cardenal, *Homage to the American Indian*; trans. by Monique & Carlos Altschul (Baltimore: Johns Hopkins University Press, 1973), p. 36. Hereafter referred to in the text as *HAI*.

> but in the glass case of the Museum
> the Mummy still squeezes her pouch of grain
> in her dry hand.   (*HAI*, p. 43)

And so in the last words of "The Ghost Dance," Cardenal embraces his theme and his mentor:

> and the old chief smiled sadly (and understood me)
> (fall 1965, my trip to the usa to see
> Merton and the indians).   (*HAI*, p. 111)

In a similar way, whether knowingly or unknowingly, Natalia Sequeira, a member of the Solentiname community, echoes the resurrection motif which permeates Cardenal's poems, poems like "Death of Thomas Merton," and she anticipates the resurrection celebrations of those who fell in the Sandinista uprisings eternalized in many of Cardenal's *Flights of Victory* poems, and others.[16] Speaking to Margaret Randall, Sequeira comments: "One time, someone mentioned Che Guevara. And I said: 'Che died, but he didn't die. He remains alive because there are others who follow him'."[17] There is here a spirit of hope, of resurrection, a hope which inspires Cardenal to rejoice in his "Death of Thomas Merton": "At last you've reached Solentiname (it wasn't *practical*)" (*Marilyn Monroe*, p. 133). And, indeed, Thomas Merton had reached even to Solentiname.

But if the contemplative and poetic lives of Merton and Cardenal had been in some ways sketched in the stars, one might legitimately wonder whether their paths would have parted when it came to questions of Marxism and to questions of revolution. Such issues deserve more time and space than such an article can provide, as indeed do those introduced above, but we can here at least be suggestive, though hardly definitive.

Although his earlier inclinations were to call himself a socialist, with the maturing of liberation theology Cardenal began openly to declare himself a Marxist. It was no easy transition for Cardenal who had been a social activist in the 1950s, but whose "conversion" to Roman Catholicism had put him at arm's length from social revolution — Marxist theory implies revolution. In fact, Cardenal's reply to Carlos Fonseca's invitation that Cardenal join the FSLN consisted in the gift of a biography of Gandhi

---

16. Ernesto Cardenal, *Flights of Victory*; trans. by Marc Zimmerman (Maryknoll: Orbis, 1985).

17. *Randall*, p. 69. For a similar resurrection motif in *Flights of Victory*, see, for example, "Flight over the Homeland without Stopover," "Landing with Epitaph," "Vision of a Face," "To Donald and Elvis," "Elvis," "A Very Screwed Up Trip," "In the Tomb of the Guerilla Fighter," "Vision from the Blue Window." It is worth noting that in his *In Cuba* Cardenal recalls that Haydee Santamaria, Director of the House of the Americas, had assured him that "If Fidel was alive, her brother, her fiance, and all the others had not died, they would live in Fidel, who was going to make the revolution" (p. 28).

(*Randall*, pp. 80-81). But his 1970 experiences in Cuba had had a profound impact on Cardenal and had convinced him of the possibility of a fusing of Christianity with Marxism. He returned from Cuba singing its praises in tones remarkably similar to his celebration of the Latin American Native. Contrasting Havana with capitalist cities he had seen, Cardenal marvels: "Here I see the immense joy of a metropolis without poor people, without misery. And the joy of everyone being equal" (*In Cuba*, p. 6). It is a city where people are given according to their needs and in which people provide according to their ability. On the relationship between capital and acquisition, he records the reflections of a Cuban companion: "There's a curious change in mentality produced in a people when you take away commercial advertising. They no longer desire to make unnecessary purchases. They no longer want to get ahead of others by buying more things or owning the best things" (*In Cuba*, p. 10). In Cuba, he says, there is plenty of money, but little to buy. As a result, there is no greed, no materialistically-based discontent, no struggle for power, no swelling of Gog and Magog. As for food rationing, the whole undertaking reminds him of his monastic asceticism. He remarks to Margaret Randall: "This system that delights you because you're a communist delights me because I find it evangelic. I also am fond of scarcity: I am a monk. I hope you will never have too much abundance. These rations are like what they eat in Solentiname" (*Randall*, p. 14). And so, Cardenal concludes: "In Cuba the new name for charity is Revolution" (*Randall*, p. 15).

Merton, of course, had provided early reflections on Marxism in his "Letter to Pablo Antonio Cuadra concerning Giants," but he develops his idea in detail in his Bangkok presentation "Marxism and Monastic Perspectives," recorded in *The Asian Journal of Thomas Merton*. In this talk he argues that, like the Marxist, the monk is by definition someone who "takes a critical attitude toward the world and its structures" (*AJ*, p. 329). Both look to the world as open to change, but "[t]he difference between the monk and the Marxist is fundamental insofar as the Marxist view of change is oriented to the change of substructures, economic substructures, and the monk is seeking to change man's consciousness." The distinction, of course, is at the heart of liberation theology, a theology embraced by Cardenal and responsible for his activity in Nicaragua. The monk, Merton adds, is one who "knows the secret of liberation and can somehow or other communicate this to others" (*AJ*, p. 333). Liberation involves a transformation of people, a recognition of the need to live the life of love: "The whole purpose of the monastic life is to teach men to live by love" (*AJ*, p. 333). At the same time, the monk is to seek liberation from the world while simultaneously liberating the world — such a liberation involves the transformation of habit and the recognition of the Christ Who dwells in all beings. Many of these ideas Merton repeats in the preface to Cardenal's book entitled *Love*, ideals he suggests are vivified in the Solentiname community, a community "located precisely at a place where it is most needed — in Central America, where there are no contemplative religious orders."[18] The opening words of *Love*, "All things love one another," teach the presence of the Word in creation, as do the young Solentiname boy's assurances to his mother: "Mother, some young people will have to die, like Christ, to end the injustice that we have in Nicaragua" (*Randall*, p. 86). Cardenal's poetic reflections dedicated to Bishop Pedro Casaldaliga make a similar point:

> One arrested in the bakery.
> Another one waiting for a bus to go to work.
> A long-haired boy falls in a Sao Paulo street.
> There is reseurrection of the flesh.

In that same poem, Cardenal suggests that:

> For Communists there is no God, only justice,
> For Christians, there is no God without justice.[19]

It is a dangerous message, this fusion of contemplation and action, of love and revolution, a message which created rumors about CIA involvement in Merton's death, and which earned Cardenal an honorable mention in the CIA document *Psychological Operations in Guerilla Warfare*[20]

It is true that the Sandinista-supported attack on San Carlos, Nicaragua, was launched from Solentiname with the support of Ernesto Cardenal, a disciple of love and admirer of Gandhi. Nonetheless, Cardenal insists that "Merton would have supported the Sandinista revolution" and adds that Merton had "told us that Gandhi had said that his method of nonviolence would not have worked in Hitler's Germany" (*Wilkes*, p. 391). It is true that Merton did praise the Danes for their nonviolent resistance to Hitler, that he did write in praise of Gandhi, and that he did reject Augustinian and medieval notions of just war, especially as they applied to a nuclear age. But it is also true that Merton did not rule out the possibility of a just war. In his

---

18.   Ernesto Cardenal, *Love*; trans. by Dinah Livingstone (New York: Crossroad, 1981), p. 18.

19.   Ernesto Cardenal, "Epistle to Monsignor Casaldaliga," *Zero Hour and Other Documentary Poems*; trans by. Paul W. Borgeson, Jr., Jonathan Cohen, Robert Pring-Mill, & Donald D. Walsh (New York: New Directions, 1980), pp. 88, 89.

20.   Taycan. Translated by CRS Language Services. As presented to the United Nations Security Council by Nicaraguan Ambassador to the United Nations, Javier Chamorro Mora, 22 October 1984.

essay "Faith and Violence," in fact, Merton argued that "[t]he theology of love must seek to deal realistically with the evil and injustice in the world, and not merely to compromise with them .... A theology of love may also conceivably turn out to be a theology of revolution."[21] Merton's preference was clearly for a nonviolent victory as the ideal solution to conflict since only in such a victory will one have altered the minds and hearts of one's enemies, thereby sowing the seeds for lasting peace. It is not without justification, therefore, that Cardenal insists that Merton would have supported the initiatives of the Sandinistas. It is worth observing, too, that in his open letter to the people of Nicaragua, Gaspar Garcia Laviana, missionary priest of the Sacred Heart who died in battle against Somoza's National guard, insisted that: *"This is a just war, one which the holy gospels see as good and which my conscience as a Christian says is good, because it represents the struggle against a state of affairs that is hateful to the Lord our God"* (Randall, p. 27).

One can only speculate about how Merton may have reacted to the Solentiname community's affiliations with the FSLN, since Merton did in fact not reach Latin America, Nicaragua, or Solentiname. Still, Merton's influence on Cardenal is so apparent in much of what Cardenal has done, in the philosophical positions he has taken, in the poetry he has written that Cardenal is surely correct when he observes in his "Death of Thomas Merton": "At last you've reached Solentiname."

---

21.   Thomas Merton, *The Nonviolent Alternative*; ed. by Gordon C. Zahn (New York: Farrar, Straus & Giroux, 1980), pp. 189-190.

THOMAS MERTON AND
THE RENEWAL OF RELIGIOUS LIFE

by **Thomas F. McKenna**, C.M.

In a considerably discussed 1987 article, Albert DiIanni wrote about the renewal of religious life from the disturbing perspective of the precipitous decline in its vocations.[1] In his view, a basic flaw had skewed much of the post-Conciliar drive for reform, and it was the fallout from this distortion which had so lowered the attractiveness of modern religious life. Some conventional wisdoms being offered for the decline, he thought, were not so much reasons as excuses. Attributing the loss to consumerist attitudes of the younger generation and to their general inability to commit themselves to anything begged the question about the Orders themselves. Equally questionable was the tendency to explain away the numerical success of some highly conservative groups by a blanket dismissal of their applicants as inadequate and sheltered personalities in search of quick role status and a risk-free life style. The core reason for the falloff, he argued, was that in their desire to be one with the modern world, many communities had lost what it was that originally made them valuable to that world. The heart of their particular brand of presence to their culture had been cut out in an overaccommodation. DiIanni argued for the reappropriation of whatever it was that galvanized the group in the first place and set it in relief against its world. Only a move at this level would anchor the "right kind of renewal."

Reaction to his article was spirited, to say the least. Some complained he had unduly discounted the results of the reform so painstakingly set into

---

1. Albert DiIanni, "Vocations and the Laicization of Religious Life," *America* 156 (14 March 1987), p. 207ff.

* This paper was delivered on 15 October 1988 at *Thomas Merton: A Symposium*, St. John's University, Jamaica, New York.

motion after the Council and had too conveniently forgotten the distortions of the era before. For these people, Dilanni was sounding the restoration trumpet and was arguing for a journey back to the "ancien regime." Others responded in an opposite direction, applauding what they took to be a well deserved repudiation of all the "experimentation." They heard a clarion call to return to the tried and true and if anything, thought Dilanni had been too lenient. Pricking sensitivities in both camps, his logic resisted quick categorization.

One especially relevant aspect of Dilanni's article is the context it gives to the present status of renewal in Religious Orders. The nerve he struck reveals how dated the glory-sounding language of its post-Conciliar youth now sounds and how the effort presently moves in a stormy, perhaps young adult stage. Paralleling the mood in economics and politics, much of the heroic tone has dropped away and reform is now pursued with a decidedly pragmatic edge. Does religious life have a future at all, and if so, what forms will bear it into the next century? A final piece is the air of contestation brought on by the so called backlash factor, lending even more ambiguity to the effort and pressing still more insistently for feasible directions.

Onto this scene we introduce Thomas Merton. Our contention is that from his pre-pragmatic 1960s view of renewal, he laid out a number of constants which paradoxically enough serve all the more usefully as beacons to see through the present murkiness. And interestingly enough, he too was found to be slippery as to position. At one time he took issue with the so called progressives, labeling them dabblers in "superficial pastimes" and engagers in "spurious and adolescent forms of spontaneity.[2] In other instances — and more commonly — he ruffled the right, accusing them of medicrity and of being purveyors of a "safe institutionalized life in which there are many ways of evading reality . . . and of living a sort of indifferent, loveless life" (*CWA*, p. 238).

Curiously enough, a direct entrance into Merton's convictions about renewal is through the recruitment question. He held a number of clear views about what was happening at the outer edge of his community, at that intersection between Trappist existence at Gethsemani and the lives of the entering candidates with whom he himself was working. There was real turbulence brewing there, and within it Merton caught the lines of a

---

2. Thomas Merton, *Contemplation in a World of Action* (Garden City, New York: Doubleday Image Books, 1973), p. 238. Hereafter referred to in the text as *CWA*.

wider picture concerning renewal about which he had been writing for years.

He counselled paying close attention to the best of the entrants, to the ones who were coming for the right reasons and who showed themselves on a genuinely spiritual search. They were exerting a pressure on life in the enclosure and as Merton saw it, it was the pressure of a prophet. Annoying and disturbing, their demands were generating a countermove to sweep their criticisms under the rug. But ultimately they were a saving grace for the monks, the Lord Himself coming in the guise of a stranger.

Merton analyzed the elements churning at this pressure point. Initially, there was the instinct to slough off such complaints by attributing them to the "influence of the world" out of which the young men were coming. The postulant was simply wrongheaded and until he was cleansed of his secular strain, he had nothing of substance to say to the Order. Merton insisted that, in many respects, exactly the opposite was the case (*CWA*, pp. 101-109).

He heard the objections of the novice as a voice of renewal. A number of entrants came because they felt they had that deep call to be "new men" and had realized that their previous way of living could not rise to that demand. The attractiveness of Trappist life was the journey it appeared to be toward an expanded Christianity. But when the newcomers arrived, they were subjected to a regimen which revealed itself to be yet another version of the same locked-in lifestyle they had left behind — only now it was called "religious." A number of them, Merton sadly testified, were driven to the paradoxical decision that to respond to the deeper demands of the cloister, they would have to leave the cloister (*CWA*, p. 122ff). What blessings were lost, he rued, when these unselfconscious prophets, having a firmer fix on the Trappist vision than did many Trappists, departed to pursue their goal elsewhere. Merton observed that there were many potential Trappists abroad in the world, anonymous monks as it were, who would flock to the monasteries if those institutions would lose some of their tentativeness in embarking upon that much sought inner quest (*CWA*, p. 13ff).

Within this analysis of the recruitment situation can be found Merton's more general vision of renewal. To allow monastic life its true attractiveness, the monks must regain their founding experience. But the access to that comes only through vital linkage with the current culture. That is to say, Trappists of today must make the spiritual experience of people like Anthony of Egypt, Pachomius and Benedict both available and engaging. But these qualities come to the fore only on the condition that such spiritual experience is in a type of symbiosis with the twentieth century world of meaning. For the fact is that the original vision arose precisely from its interchange with the third century culture. In a nutshell, that core spiritual encounter must be both a root one, getting back to the inner lives of the early monks, and a real one, in dialogue with the pressing issues of the present day.

Charting a renewal course by this formula brings its own kinds of benefits and costs. We cite them here summarily and will develop their implications in the remainder of the article. In the first place, the retrieved experience provides the base from which to critique both present and proposed structures. Secondly, its reassimilation by some people will provoke resistance from others attached to the arrangements and attitudes currently in possession. Thirdly, a particular kind of disciplined creativity will be required both to get at and then channel the primitive inspiration. And finally, even though new and competing structures will be generated from the energy set loose by renewal, the struggle between them and the older ones will avoid destructive polarization because both can be seen to spring from the same spiritual ground.

MERTON'S RENEWAL FORMULA

We note at the outset that while monasticism is not the only embodiment of religious life, it is certainly a basic form of it and has at its center something essential to all the others. Merton's guidelines, even though about the rebirth of monastic existence, can therefore shed light on reform issues for most all varieties of vowed life.

A. REGAINING THE CORE EXPERIENCE

In recent years, Gerald Arbuckle has written extensively from the stance of cultural anthropology about the need for the refounding person in religious orders.[3] A far-seeing individual who by word and action can build bridges between the old and the new, this "second founder" has laid hold of the power of the originating myth but, perhaps more importantly,

---

3. See, for example, Gerald Arbuckle, *Strategies for Growth in Religious Life* (New York: Alba House, 1987); *Out of Chaos* (New York: Paulist Press, 1988); and various articles.

has been able to recast it into some culturally resonant expression. Twenty years earlier, as a monastic theologian, Merton had made much the same point. For him, the refounders are those who regain that "wilderness perspective" of the early monks at such a deep level that they are able to appreciate any particular historic form the monastic impulse has taken, but also relativize it and thus be free to discover more relevant embodiments (*CWA*, p. 28).

Merton is lyrical in his description of these truly charismatic individuals. The new founders are those who in detachment and purity of heart become attuned to the depths of human experience (*CWA*, p. 118). They are those who focus on the interior quality of life rather than on its quantity, those who explore the inner ground of human love and understanding and, on their journey there, reach new centers of motivation for knowing and loving (*CWA*, pp. 27, 175). They are the ones who go on a pilgrimage to the source of human truth, who struggle with the death within them all while trying to find something deeper than death (*CWA*, pp. 212, 306). They are the courageous pioneers, borrowing from Claude Levi-Strauss, who "dip into the ocean of unexploited forces which surround a well ordered society and draw from it personal provisions of grace and vision" (*CWA*, p. 196).

One corollary here is the useful norm a distinctive founding experience provides for deciding which form of religious life might be best for a given individual. Much of Merton's spiritual journey was a growing awareness that his own search for meaning had followed much the same path laid out by the early monks. Nothing so strongly confirmed his choice to be a Trappist as the realization that his life's project (i.e., the struggle for his genuine self wrested from the heap of the illusory ones) was meshing with theirs. Discernment involves a putting on of the primitive spiritual experience.

Still another effect is the way in which the originating insight indicates the whereabouts of anonymous pockets of monasticism in the twentieth century. Merton would search them out among the future oriented people, those natural allies of the monks, who, because they chose not to line up with the established powers, are "free to roam" and to critique present arrangements from the vantage point of what of God is beginning to appear from the hidden ground of their own human experience (*CWA*, p. 235).

B. THE PRIMITIVE EXPERIENCE TAPPED BY THE PRESENT CULTURE

A second thrust of reform is the correlative of the first. Living contact with the prevailing culture, according to Merton, is the indispensable door of access to the riches of the past. The only stance from which monastic experience can be reappropriated is critical and intimate engagement with the contemporary world.

Over the years, Merton's thinking shifted in regard to the place from which access to the founding experience is given. Early on, his prime insistence was that "worldly matters" deflected the monk from his true purpose and that many of the answers the culture gave to questions of meaning were shallow and dangerously deceptive. One had to establish a distance from that ethos in order to see it as it truly is. One had to peer into the *saeculum* through the "doors of perception" opened by deeper encounter with God.[4]

But as the years passed, Merton also began to assert that the place for encountering that primitive experience was not just, and not even primarily, within the walls of the enclosure. "The monastery is not a ghetto and will not profit by being kept as one," he argued (*CWA*, p. 218). The monastic vocation will grow to the extent that it stays in vital touch with "what and who in the world is open to change" (*CWA*, p. 327).

As mentioned earlier, Merton sensed an affinity between the monastic insight and certain future oriented groups in the culture. He gives special attention to three of them. First are the people who find themselves in the various faith crises set off by modernity. Struggling with the absence of God and the very ability to believe at all, these are the journeyers who like the first monks are walking in hope through empty places of the world (*CWA*, p. 201). Much is to be gained, he claimed, by standing with these pilgrims who first let go and then endure the bleakness which follows before recovering on a new level the nearness of the God whom they have come to know through their painful unknowing (*CWA*, p. 178).

Second is the group with whom Merton himself felt much kinship. These were the so called unpropertied intellectuals who are on the one hand beneficiaries of culture but who, because they are not totally vested in it, are nevertheless able to take the long view and maintain a relatively

---

4. "If you want to pull a drowning man out of the water, you have to have some support yourself. Nothing is to be gained by simply jumping in the water and drowning with him." "Marxism and Monastic Perspectives," *CWA*, p. 341.

disinterested stance at society's edge. From this vantage they not only can critique the power establishment but even take up the cause of the marginated (*CWA*, p. 235ff).

The third group is the most general of all. Those individuals who, in some sustained way, give themselves over to the self-transcending aspirations of humanity are, for Merton, the hidden comrades of the monk (*CWA*, p. 200). Solidarity with this widest of human pursuits again recalls his insistence that the intersections between the visible monastery and the deeper lying monastic quest are those junctures in the social fabric which show themselves especially supple to the first stirrings of God's Absolute future.

The danger in any renewal attempt is that it follow only one of its two roads; i.e., either simply reaches back into history for the founder's insight or simply marches forth into society to encounter spiritual breakthroughs. The authentic program, more difficult because bivalent, is to keep one's feet on both paths at the same time. For Merton, the very survival of monasticism depends upon its simultaneously attending to its ancient vision and to the wisdoms of its current eschatological sympathizers. Interestingly, the very conflicts arising from this tension lend a distinctive and sobering twist to the notion of charism. That energizing signature of a particular community is without a doubt a gift of the Spirit. But in this case, givenness means anything but complacency (*CWA*, p. 237). "One must struggle to preserve and keep the gift," Merton warns, walking a fine line between the disciplines of solitude and prayer so needed for internalizing the gift and the continual efforts to dialogue with those outside the cloister who embody it in the culture (*CWA*, p. 239).

C. STRUGGLING FOR THE CHARISM: COSTS AND REWARDS

To the extent that a religious community sets its course by both bearings, it will inevitably bear fruits which, though initially bitter, will one day be enlivening. The foundational one, of course, is that the Order will have more in hand its touchstone for discernment. That anchoring vision, caught from within and without the cloister, becomes the internal norm for critiquing both its present arrangements and future proposals.

It is from such a base that Merton began to assess current Trappist practices. He reserved his most biting criticisms for the exaggerated worth he judged placed on certain historic forms then in practice.[5] Focus is to be in the monastic religious experience, he insisted, and not on the monastery itself, as if the individual had come to serve the institution and not that pursuit of God which gave rise to the institution in the first place. Merton observed, for instance, that the efforts at renewal since the Reformation had normed themselves, not by the wisdoms of the desert monks, but rather by traditions of later times, notably the Carolingian reforms of Benedict of Aniane (*CWA*, p. 196). He also noted a distinctively American managerial atmosphere which he thought had gained a strong foothold in the cloister. Suffused by it, the monastery was imaging itself as a kind of machine, a "spiritual dynamo" well oiled and smoothly ticking (*CWA*, p. 38). The critique had not gone deeply enough.

Merton directed his most stinging criticisms of historic forms at what he termed "the accepted spirituality." This meant the whole world of assumptions at Gethsemani, attitudes not exactly official but nonetheless given common credence, or behaviors supposedly foundational but in actuality justifications of the present community (*CWA*, p. 102ff). The comfort which such a world view held out only served to reinforce its hold on the group and, like every ideology, disguised its own intent. In truth, however, this spirituality was losing, not only its nurturance, but most drastically its power to mediate genuine love to the monastic vocation. While it sustained some of the monks, it did not give life to many others. The newer entrants especially intuited this and observed impoverishments in the humanness of veteran monks because of it. In any case, the reigning wisdom had little reference to the deeper realities of life. It conspired to eliminate the risk factor so fundamental to monastic existence. Both the conventional spirituality and the institution built to reinforce it only insulated the monks, creating a hothouse within the cloister (*CWA*, pp. 199). According to Merton, the system committed the unpardonable sin of "substituting the penultimate for the ultimate," or, more colloquially, of making the announcement that "I am going to go to the North Pole and then proceeding to take a walk around the block" (*CWA*, p. 204). Still further, it narrowed the monk's appreciation for authentic asceticism, distorting useful disciplinary practices into perfectionistic excess or, in his words, into "mere methodologies of will and concentration" (*CWA*, p. 120). Not surprisingly, his antidote for monastic decay was return to the

---

5. See Jean Leclercq, "Introduction," *CWA*, p. 12.

originating experience. The whole point of desert life was the exact opposite of security and comfort. Its formative thrust was to train the monk precisely for walking with God in the wilderness, for "wrestling with Satan in vulnerable freedom." It was designed to make the individual as unguarded as possible before the "unpredictable and unexplained illumination that flashes out of the ground of one's being" (CWA, p. 201). For Merton, the loss of such unsettlement causes the life to grow mediocre and loveless, and in time, to shrink into "organized narcissism" (CWA, p. 233).

Merton was not naive about resistance to reform. He saw clearly that ingrained practices would not be dislodged by clear arguments and historical insights alone and predicted a struggle that would severely tax the cohesiveness of the institute. In his assessment, monastic orders were among the most stable forces in the church, but their blessing of stability did not come unmixed (CWA, p. 23). A certain compulsion to organize members' spiritual energies so tightly that their "outbreaks of the Holy Spirit" were literally legislated away was the prime instance (CWA, p. 226). Such repression could often enough surface in a certain unconscious identification with one particular class in society. In proportion as the monastery became institutionalized, Merton observed, there was always some unreflected alignment with one or another social stratum. A number of cloisters, for instance, had identified with certain reactionary groups, absorbing their attitudes and ideologies (CWA, p. 233). Such alliances were hardly socially neutral and, in fact, stood in the way of any real chance of solidarity not only with the future oriented types noted earlier, but sadly enough with the world's poor.

Typically, Merton did not restrict his criticisms to the right. To him the activism of the left threw up as formidable a barrier to renewal. When monks tended to justify their existence by the amount of outside service they engaged in, they too lost access to the core experience. Such activity, looking apostolic but rooted too shallowly to merit the name, only served to spread "the contagion of one's own obsessing aggressiveness, ego-centered ambitions, prejudices and ideas" (CWA, p. 179). Merton's analysis of obstructions is hard headed and recognizable. Resistances to renewal are alive and well, take many virtuous guises, and if not approached intelligently will tear apart the fabric of any community. Only when the reform anchors itself in the founding experience will the divisions over rebirth be overcome.

D. A DISCIPLINED CREATIVITY

Merton would have the Order be faithful, not to a past set of practices, but to the inner life out of which those activities grew. In his words, the monk's journey is to be "a living ascent to that current of uninterrupted vitality" (*CWA*, p. 42). But far from a tranquil inner climb, this ascent is hard work and requires its own kind of discipline. Reform is anything but "drifting along . . . , a lackadaisical floating with events which excludes those dimensions of life which in fact cannot be found unless the monk to some extent works hard to uncover them" (*CWA*, p. 126). Neither is it abstract prognosticating nor, in Merton's image, a distributing of maps which sketch out the exact way. The project rather is the more ambiguous one of honing up one's sense of direction so that ". . . when we really get going, we can travel without maps" (*CWA*, p. 127). To drink from the true fount of renewal is to imbibe heady waters. The creativity unleashed will run wild unless channeled by that rigorous discipline of nurturing the inner life and doggedly pursuing one's authentic self.[6]

E. NEW FORMS

When moving to the more practical matter of structural renewal, Merton is not half so expansive. He is much more the theorist than the organizational designer, and in fact never participated in any of the world wide reforms of the Trappists. In addition, the few suggestionss he did make are dated, something certainly to be expected at this remove of more than twenty years. But granting even these qualifications, he still shows a prescience which only testifies to the depth of his insight.

Merton saw the need for transitional forms and spaces. He argued for a certain breathing spell during which the deeper motivations and purposes of the experiments would be allowed to surface (*CWA*, p. 127). Throughout such times, generosity of spirit was needed by those who preferred the older forms; e.g., a willingness to make space for the others who could not be silent and meditative in the same exact way (*Conner*, p. 178).

Merton wrote frequently about the role of authority in renewal. In general, he advocated a more grass roots participation in reform efforts

---

6. Tarcisius [a.k.a. James] Conner, "Monk of Renewal," in *Thomas Merton / Monk: A Monastic Tribute;* ed. by Brother Patrick Hart (New York: Sheed & Ward, 1974), p. 184.

and, in addition, proposed that religious power be reinterpreted as openness to the demands of love as found in the needs of the neighbor (*CWA*, pp. 101, 128). His more specific suggestions to extend the monastic invitation to married couples and to conceive it as temporary were radical in their day, even though these outer groupings would be centered around a permanent nucleus of celibate monks (*CWA*, p. 208). The religious vow also interested Merton. The promises which the monks made were not to the religious institution, he pointed out, but rather to the eschatological fidelity of God. Any focus falling short of this covenantal relationship could not justify the renunciations involved nor bring about that total inner transformation at which monastic life aimed (*CWA*, p. 337). The worth of any structure was to be judged according to how it did or did not promote "faith in God alone."

CONCLUSION

We return to our beginning issue, why it is that religious communities are not appealing to the religious aspirations of young people today. Thomas Merton would deny the fault is to be found in what is most precious about the Orders; i.e., the alluring experience which gave rise to their existence in the first place. Neither is it to be found in the alleged shrunken religious capacities of modern men and women (*CWA*, p. 29). On the contrary, faith should be renewed in precisely their ability to *be* monks.

His criticism is that, while the capacity for living religious life is present in today's world, an enabling manner of living it is not. The imagination of the culture will again be captured by monastic life when the vitality which got it underway in the first place is made both clearer and more accessible. Efforts at renewal must therefore be: (1) radical, getting down to the roots of the experience and scraping away whatever covers them over; (2) existential, being in touch with issues of meaning for the twentieth century person; (3) courageous, struggling in darkness through predictable resistances; (4) creative, arising from the wellspring but in a disciplined way; and finally, (5) paschal, hopeful that the dying involved will issue in more abundant life.

And to be sure, Merton remained hopeful, and even in awe, as to the outcome. This communal and Spirit-directed recovery of meaning will bring a renewal entailing much more than wise legislation and innovative processes. In the last analysis it will be "a kind of miracle of water in the desert'' (*CWA*, p. 200). For Thomas Merton, this ongoing miracle, so hard won in its making, is the real, saving and perennial attraction of religious life.

THOMAS MERTON
AND HANNAH ARENDT:

Contemplation after Eichmann

by **Karl A. Plank**

As for the liar, fear him less
Than one who thinks himself sincere,
Who, having deceived himself,
Can deceive you with a good conscience.
Thomas Merton

When everybody is swept away unthinkingly by what everybody else does
and believes in, those who think are drawn out of hiding because their
refusal to join is conspicuous and thereby becomes a kind of action.
Hannah Arendt

He who believes can experience no miracle. During the day one does not
see any stars.

Franz Kafka

VOICES HEARD IN SILENCE

Human life bears the freight of dialogue. Whether we live alone or in the near company of each other, our lives are shaped by a speaking and hearing that involve us in realities greater than ourselves. Uttered dialogue, in its living immediacy, bridges the separateness of selves with words of relation and calls us to respond to a voice not of our own making. Solitude, as well, may welcome a voice heard in memory or held by the imagination and thereby host the presence of an other in its silent domain.

---

*   This paper was delivered on 27 May 1989 in the session, "Merton and Human Dignity," at the First General Meeting of *The International Thomas Merton Society* in Louisville, Kentucky.

As he reflected on the promise of his Mount Olivet hermitage, Thomas Merton acknowledges the company of voices heard in silence. He writes:

> There is a mental ecology, too, a living balance of spirits in this corner of the woods. There is room here for many other songs besides those of birds .... Here is heard the clanging prose of Tertullian, with the dry catarrh of Sartre. Here the voluble dissonances of Auden, with the golden sounds of John of Salisbury. Here is the deep vegetation of that more ancient forest in which the angry birds, Isaias and Jeremias, sing. Here should be, and are, feminine voices from Angela of Foligno to Flannery O'Connor, Theresa of Avila, Juliana of Norwich, and, more personally and warmly still, Raissa Maritain. It is good to choose the voices that will be heard in these woods, but they also choose themselves, and send themselves here to be present in this silence.[1]

Merton's paean to "the voices that will be heard in these woods" — in essence, a list of authors with whose works he was seeking intimacy — provides no meager metaphor for the solitary's dialogue. Reading may remove us from the context of living speech but, no less than conversation, holds the potential to call us into response. In reading we encounter something external to ourselves, a text whose meaning may lead us into self-examination, stirring feelings of kinship or inciting profound change. Once chosen, such texts intrude into our lives. They "choose themselves, and send themselves here to be present." We cannot easily ignore them, for once we admit them into our consciousness, they become part of the fabric of our identity. From that point on, these texts assume a voice that haunts and consoles, but rarely lets us alone.[2]

Readers become writers. In solitude they respond to the presence of other voices with texts of their own. Merton recognized the responsive character of writing and understood even his personal notebooks to have the character of "implicit dialogue." In the preface to *Conjectures of a Guilty Bystander* he writes:

> ... these notes add up to a personal version of the world in the 1960s. In elaborating such a version one unavoidably tells something of himself, for

---

1. Thomas Merton, *Day of a Stranger*; ed. by Robert E. Daggy (Salt Lake City: Gibbs M. Smith, 1981), pp. 35-37.

2. The distinction between oral media and written communication has become a commonplace in hermeneutic theory. See, e.g., Paul Ricoeur, *Interpretation Theory: Discourse and the Surplus of Meaning* (Fort Worth: Texas Christian University Press, 1976), pp. 25-44 and Walter J. Ong, S.J., *The Presence of the Word* (New York: Simon & Schuster, 1970). This distinction, however, should not lead us to diminish the significance of reading as a dialogic act, albeit one with its own dynamic. The point parallels the monastic tradition's seriousness about *lectio* as an activity that involves the reader's whole person with the power of a text (i.e., Scripture), an involvement that leads to self-knowledge, conviction, change, and profoundly, to *oratio*. See Jean Leclercq, *The Love of Learning and the Desire for God*; trans. by Catherine Misrahi (New York: Fordham University Press, 1982), pp. 71-73 and "Western Prayer and Contemplation," in *Christian Spirituality. Origins to the Twelfth Century*; ed. by B. McGinn & J. Meyendorff (New York: Crossroad, 1985), pp. 417-419.

> what a man truly is can be discovered only through his self-awareness in a living and actual world. But these pages are not a venture in self-revelation or self-discovery. Nor are they a pure soliloquy. *They are an implicit dialogue with other minds, a dialogue in which questions are raised.*[3]

Though Merton's writing characteristically constructs "a personal version of the world," that version itself admits and responds to the presence of other voices. Neither their puppet nor their profligate, Merton writes with a sense of engagement, a coincidence of hearing and speaking. The questions which would ensoul his writing emerge in no vacuum, but from his encounter with other voices in a shared world.

Although Merton does not mention her among the feminine voices in his corner of the woods, one of his earlier partners in the "implicit dialogues" of *Conjectures* is the Jewish political philosopher, Hannah Arendt.[4] Indeed, Arendt's voice, familiar from previous readings of *The Human Condition* and *The Origins of Totalitarianism*, continued to compel Merton's attention from 1963 forward in the form of her haunting portrait of Adolf Eichmann, the S. S. officer in charge of deporting millions of Jews to the death camps of the Third Reich.[5] In this paper I focus upon Merton's reading and appropriation of Arendt, particularly her Eichmann report, and explore the notion of contemplation as a response to the Eichmann predicament as they both understood it.

THOMAS MERTON AND HANNAH ARENDT

We do not know what, if anything, Merton knew of the life of Hannah Arendt. For instance, no correspondence seems to have occurred between them, a surprising fact given Merton's inclination to write authors whose works compelled his interest. If he had known of her biography one finds it easy to imagine his sense of being a marginal self resonating with her affinity for the "pariah." Arendt's biographer, Elisabeth Young-Bruehl writes:

> The friends of every sort and also the historical figures with whom Arendt felt special affinities, like Rosa Luxemburg and Rahel Varnhagen, had one

---

3.   Thomas Merton, *Conjectures of a Guilty Bystander* (Garden City, New York: Doubleday Image Books, 1968), p.5. Emphasis is my own.

4.   Note *Conjectures*, especially pp. 285-290 which concern Merton's response to Arendt's Eichmann report.

5.   Arendt's report of the 1961 Eichmann trial originally appeared in *The New Yorker* during February and March 1963. In May 1963 her material was published in book form under the title *Eichmann in Jerusalem: A Report on the Banality of Evil* (New York: Viking Press, 1963). Hereafter cited in the text as *Eichmann*.

characteristic in common: each was, in his or her own way, an outsider. In Hannah Arendt's personal lexicon, *wirkliche Menschen*, real people, were "pariahs." Her friends were not outcasts, but outsiders, sometimes by choice and sometimes by destiny. In the broadest sense they were unassimilated. "Social nonconformism," she once said bluntly, "is the *sine qua non* of intellectual achievement." And she might well have added, also of human dignity .... Hannah Arendt maintained her independence and she expected her friends to do the same.[6]

In this respect Merton resembles Arendt's friends and she those free persons with whom he felt deep kinship.

By 1963, when Merton first encountered Arendt's *New Yorker* series on Eichmann, he already knew certain of her major works. On 13 May 1960 he wrote to John Harris: "I have been reading a fabulous book, *The Human Condition* by Hannah Arendt, the one who wrote such a good one on *Totalitarianism*. This is very fine, once one gets into it. And for once someone is saying something really new, though it is also really old. I recommend it."[7] According to Michael Mott, the next day's journal entry similarly indicated that he was reading *The Human Condition* and that this "had disturbed [him] as greatly as reading Shirer's *The Rise and Fall of the Third Reich*."[8] If, in Merton's eyes, Shirer had chronicled the Nazi collusion of technology and death, Arendt's analysis of modernity described an eclipse of genuinely political (and thus, for her, human) value for which the Nazi program might furnish the most blatant instance.[9] The "fabulous" character of *The Human Condition* — that which Merton might have found to be "really new" and yet "also really old" — rests in Arendt's stubborn refusal to surrender the meaning of human activity to the constraints of its modern context and her retrieval of the Greek notion of free "action" as a distinguishing feature of human life. Merton could only have read of these things with a sense of collegiality.[10]

---

6. Elisabeth Young-Bruehl, *Hannah Arendt: For Love of the World* (New Haven: Yale University Press, 1982), p. xv.

7. Thomas Merton, *The Hidden Ground of Love: Letters on Religious Experience and Social Concerns*; ed. by William H. Shannon (New York: Farrar, Straus & Giroux, 1985), p. 395.

8. Michael Mott, *The Seven Mountains of Thomas Merton* (Boston: Houghton Mifflin, 1984), p. 396. Hereafter referred to in the text as *Mott*.

9. For Merton's interest in this aspect of Shirer, note *Conjectures*, pp. 241-242. For Arendt's analysis of modernity, see *The Human Condition* (Chicago: University of Chicago Press, 1958), pp. 248-325. We should note that, for Arendt, the term "political" implies *not* our usual connotation of "governmental," but refers more fundamentally to that which occurs whenever men and women act freely with and in the midst of one another (thus *Human Condition*, pp. 192-207).

10. The philosophical and public tone of Arendt's writing should not divert us from seeing in *The Human Condition* a commitment kindred to Merton's own. Arendt's refusal to accept the constraints of modern culture as a definitive context for human life exercises the same impulse as Merton's "world-renunciation" or detachment as, for instance, when he writes: "... what I abandoned when 'I left the world' and came to the monastery was the *understanding of myself* that I had developed in the context of civil society — my identification with what appeared to be its aims" (*Conjectures*, p. 47). Moreover, Arendt's

Regardless of interest, Merton's reading of *The Origins of Totalitarianism* and *The Human Condition* did not issue in significant written response.[11] Such is not the case, however, when he takes up Arendt's Eichmann report. His journal entry for 27 March 1963 indicates that he is reading Arendt's *New Yorker* articles and is devastated by them (*Mott*, pp. 396 and 625, n. 308). That devastation gave rise to several different writings which have their roots in Arendt's account of the Eichmann trial: a) the reflections published in *Conjectures of a Guilty Bystander*; b) the poem, "Epitaph for a Public Servant;" and c) the essay, "A Devout Meditation in Memory of Adolf Eichmann." Following a discussion of Arendt's own thesis regarding Eichmann, we will consider each of the writings in turn.

ARENDT AND THE "BANALITY OF EVIL"

Merton was not the only one called into response by Arendt's Eichmann report. The publication of *Eichmann in Jerusalem* created a vitriolic controversy whose fallout continues to be evident in studies of the holocaust.[12] In certain respects, the complex burden of the Eichmann trial made controversy inevitable. Before its attendant legacy of incomprehensible suffering and atrocity, no judgment could be adequate nor interpretation of events satisfactory. Moreover, any judgment or interpretation could only risk intrusion upon, if not betrayal of, the intensely personal memories

---

notion of "action" as an expression of a distinctive human freedom and *not* of necessity ("labor") nor utility ("work") locates that which is peculiarly human in a realm familiar to the Merton who writes: "He who receives the grace of this kind of religious illumination is given a freedom and an experience which leave him no longer fully and completely subject to the forces of nature, to his own bodily and emotional needs, to the merely external and human dictates of society, the tyranny of dictatorships. This is to say that his attitude to life is independent of the power inevitably exercised over him, exteriorly, by natural forces, by the trials and accidents of life, by the pressures of a not always rational collectivity" (*Conjectures*, pp. 88-89).

11.   His references to these works is largely citational or allusive. See, e.g., the quotations from *Totalitarianism* in *Conjectures* (pp. 104 and 108) and the reference to *The Human Condition* in *Gandhi on Non-Violence* (New York: New Directions, 1965), p. 7. Note also Merton's passing references to Arendt's article, "Truth and Politics," in *Faith and Violence* (Notre Dame: University of Notre Dame Press, 1968), pp. 249-250; and to her introduction of Bernd Naumann's *Auschwitz* in "Auschwitz: A Family Camp," *The Nonviolent Alternative* (New York: Farrar, Straus & Giroux, 1980), p. 150. On the taped lecture, "Second Century Apologists: Tertullian," Merton refers to Arendt as the one who wrote the extremely good book on Totalitarianism and acknowledges her "subtle, deep classical background." He goes on to say in a manner that will be familiar to listeners of the taped lectures, "She sounds like Tertullian, though Tertullian writes about ten times better than she does." See Tape # 14a, Thomas Merton Studies Center, Bellarmine College, Louisville, Kentucky.

12.   For an overview of the controversy, see Young-Bruehl, pp. 347-378. Note also the following: *Die Kontroverse* (Munich: Nymphenburger, 1964); Randolph L. Braham, *The Eichmann Case: A Source Book* (New York: World Federation of Hungarian Jews, 1969), pp. 144-174; and Hannah Arendt, *The Jew as Pariah: Jewish Identity and Politics in the Modern Age*; ed. by Ron H. Feldman (New York: Grove Press, 1978), pp. 225-279.

of horror that surrounded the trial.[13] When coupled with Arendt's bold style and subtle use of concepts, these seeds of controversy yielded bitter, aggressive conflict.

The controversy focused primarily on three dimensions of Arendt's report: a) her guiding thesis that Eichmann, in his utter normality, manifested the banality of evil; b) her criticism of the conduct of the *Judenraete*, the Jewish councils, during the deportation stage of the "final solution;" and c) her probing inquiry into legal and political dimensions of the trial. Though each of these aspects raised acute issues, much of the actual conflict was exacrebated by her critics' blatant distortion of what she had written. Arendt's own view of the trial challenged certain "versions of survival," interpretations of an event made by thos epersons whom the event has victimized.[14] Thus, what she had written could not provoke, because it called into question basic assumptions out of which other persons had sought the meaning of their own profound suffering.[15] But what she did not say also provoked as, in the controversy, her critics unfairly took the banality of evil for the banality of suffering and her unfortunate discussion of the *Juderaete* for comment on the Jewish people as a whole, including those victimized in the camps.

Arendt's thesis concerning the banality of evil dominated Merton's attention more than did her historical and political questions. Accordingly, we will point our discussion toward exposition of this thesis. For Arendt, reflections on the banality of evil began withe her perception of the ordinariness of Eichmann. The obscene atrocity of Auschwitz seemingly required in the human imagination a diabolical beast to account for its horror and Eichmann's prosecutor stood ready to deliver such a beast with repeated declarations of "and there sits the monster responsible for all this."[16] But no amount of rhetoric could transform "the figure in the glass booth" into a dark villain of hatred or psychpathic fury of malevolence. To everyone's

---

13. In this regard, see Elie Wiesel, "A Plea for the Dead," in *Legends of Our Time* (New York, Schocken, 1982), pp. 174-192. Michael Berenbaum has argued that Wiesel intends this essay as an attack upon Arendt's work but, even so, the point would transcend the limitations of her book to include virtually any attempt to interpret the holocaust, especially from socio-historical perspectives. See *The Vision of the Void: Theological Reflections on the Works of Elie Wisel* (Middletown, Connecticut: Wesleyan University Press, 1979), pp. 194-200.

14. On "versions of survival," see Lawrence L. Langer, *Versions of Survival: The Holocaust and the Human Spirit* (Albany, SUNY, 1982).

15. In particular, her thesis that Eichmann's evil had its source in an all too ordinary banality challenged attempts to underscore the extraordinary character of the suffering by pointing to an extraordinary agent.

16. Arendt's quotation of Gideon Hausner, *Eichmann*, p. 8. Arendt recognized that the prosecution's strategy presupposed Eichmann to be a "perverted sadist" and thus intended to "display Bluebeard in the dock" (p. 276).

surprise, including Arendt's, Eichmann displayed virtually no extraordinary capacity for hatred or anything else. Young-Bruehl notes that Arendt's "first reaction to the 'man in the glass booth' in Jerusalem was that he was *nicht einmal unheimlich*, 'not even sinister,' not inhuman or beyond comprehension. She was startled."[17] So were many others when the unmasking of Satan showed him to look and act much like the rest of us.

Eichmann's ordinariness went beyond appearance to claim a chilling psychological normality. In his environment he "fit in;" he behaved as expected and more or less like everyone else. As Arendt depicted him, the Nazi bureaucrat adapted so well to his milieu that he became virtually indistinct from it, buying a certain absence of personal turmoil through an obedient adjustment to atrocity. Free from obsession with base motives and hatred, unplagued by demons of conscience, and loyal to the norms of his social context, Eichmann was certified by at least six psychiatrists as "normal":[18]

> "More normal, at any rate, than I am after having examined him," one of them was said to have exclaimed, while another had found that his whole psychological outlook, his attitude toward his wife and children, mother and father, brothers, sisters, and friends, was "not only normal but most desirable" — and finally the minister who had paid regular visits to him in prison after the Supreme Court had finished hearing his appeal reassured everybody by declaring Eichmann to be "a man with very positive ideas." Behind the comedy of the soul experts lay the hard fact that his was obviously no case of moral let alone legal insanity. (*Eichmann*, pp. 25-26)

Eichmann's normality reflected only that he was no exception within the Nazi regime, a fact that created a dilemma which Arendt saw clearly. The corollary to Eichmann's well-adapted normality was simply that "under the

---

17.   *Hannah Arendt*, p. 329 (from a letter of 15 April 1961 written by Arendt to her husband, Heinrich Bluecher). The perception was not Arendt's alone. Avner Less, who interrogated Eichmann for the Israeli police, recalls: "My first reaction when the prisoner finally stood facing us . . . was one of disappointment. I no longer know what I had expected — probably the sort of Nazi you see in the movies: tall, blond, with piercing blue eyes and brutal features expressive of domineering arrogance. Whereas this rather thin, balding man not much taller than myself looked utterly ordinary." *Eichmann Interrogated: Transcripts from the Archives of the Israeli Police*; ed. by J. von Lang; trans. by R. Manheim (New York: Farrar, Straus & Giroux, 1983), p. v.

18.   One of the haunting dimensions of the Eichmann case is that his gross crime is motiveless, at least in the sense of lacking any particular animus toward the Jews whose extermination he was bringing about. Were orders given to annihilate some other group Eichmann would have complied just as easily (*Eichmann*, p. 25). Moreover, not only did he lack base motives toward his Jewish victims (p. 30), but he lacked real motives altogether in his general conduct. For example, "he did not enter the Party out of conviction, nor was he ever convinced by it — whenever he was asked to give his reasons, he repeated the same embarrassed cliches about the Treaty of Versailles and unemployment; rather, as he pointed out in court, 'it was like being swallowed up by the Party against all expectations and without previous decision. It happened so quickly and suddenly.' He had no time and less desire to be properly informed, he did not even know the Party program, he never read *Mein Kampf*. Kaltenbrunner had said to him: Why not join the S. S.? And he had replied, Why not?" (p. 33). Arendt notes, "as for his conscience, he remembered perfectly well that he would have had a bad conscience only if he had not done what he had been ordered to do — to ship millions of men, women, and children to their death with great zeal and the most meticulous care" (*Eichmann*, p. 25; note also, pp. 91 and 95).

conditions of the Third Reich only 'exceptions' could be expected to react 'normally' " (*Eichmann*, pp. 26-27). Could Eichmann, in and precisely because of his normality, know the criminal nature of his acts? In his sanity could he judge right from wrong?

If Arendt saw that Eichmann's evil resulted not from psychological aberration nor from gross and willful malevolence — that he was "not Iago and not Macbeth" (*Eichmann*, p. 287) — she certainly perceived that his evil was nonetheless evil, terrible and terrifying in its normality.[19] This evil of Eichmann, as she understood it, grew from banality and mirrored a "sheer thoughtlessness" (*Eichmann*, p. 287) that pervaded the total behavior of this ordinary doer of monstrous deeds. As the Eichmann example made clear to Arendt, banality, not harmless stupidity, becomes evil in its eclipse of the fundamental activities which allow a human being to judge right from wrong, to know what one is doing, and to be linked meaningfully to others in a community of discourse. Eichmann did not set out to do wrong, but sacrificing to banality his ability to think and speak, neither could he do right — an impairment which, in his "normal" situation, meant also that he could not *not* do wrong. Therein he becomes an agent of atrocity; therein, his evil.

For Arendt, banality was tantamount to the inability to speak or think (*Eichmann*, p. 49). In Eichmann's case this took the form of being devoutly oriented toward cliches, toward the stock phrases and formulas which seemed to elate, but which could only, in effect, isolate him from any reality that might provoke or disturb. What cliches he had not inherited from his environment he unwittingly forged on his own through endless repetition of his own references to incidents which potentially offered elation. Thus, in a rare moment of at least accidental clarity, Eichmann commented: "Officialese [*Amtssprache*] is my only language." Arendt continues, "But the point here is that officialese became his language because he was genuinely incapable of uttering a single sentence that was not a cliche" (*Eichmann*, p. 48). Where cliches furnish the basic rules of play for one's action, thought

---

19. The motiveless crime is not less scandalous, but all the more so for its underlying indifference robs victims of the distinctiveness and, if one may speak of it in this way, the dignity that even honest hatred confers. Thus Elie Wiesel writes, "To be indifferent — for whatever reason — is to deny not only the validity of existence, but also its beauty. Betray and you are a man; torture your neighbor, you're still a man. Evil [what Arendt would term "wickedness"] is human, weakness is human; indifference is not." *The Town Beyond the Wall* (New York: Schocken, 1982), p. 177. Martin Buber suggests a comparable distinction when he writes, "Yet whoever hates directly is closer to a relation than those who are without love and hate . . . Primal man's experiences of encounter were scarcely a matter of tame delight; but even violence against a being one really confronts is better than ghostly solicitude for faceless digits! From the former a path leads to God, from the latter only to nothingness." *I and Thou*; trans. by Walter Kaufmann (New York: Scribners, 1970), pp. 68 and 75.

will appear unnecessary and, in its critical function, undesirable. It will vanish along with the prospect for judging right from wrong and thereby knowing what one is doing.[20] Where language is given over to slogan, the genuine speech which relates persons and guards their sense of reality also ceases to exist. Its loss, marking the reign of illusion, prevents a basic accountability for human affairs and denies human beings the task of justification — the possibility of making sense to themselves and each other.[21] Such an exile of speech and thought leaves a void within which banal selves surrender their power not to do evil and thus become ever vulnerable to agency in monstrous deeds.

Banal selves such as Eichmann can function well in any situation that offers clear rules of play and allows for conduct to assume the nature of a cliche. But once thought and speech have been eclipsed these same persons can no longer judge the rules nor act in contexts where the formulas of right behavior do not apply. Thus Arendt noted:

> In the setting of Israeli court and prison procedures he [Eichmann] functioned as well as he had functioned under the Nazi regime but, when confronted with situations for which such routine procedures did not exist, he was helpless, and his cliche-ridden language produced on the stand, as it had evidently done in his official life, a kind of macabre comedy. (*Mind*, I:4)

Banal persons cannot function in an environment in which they are free to be responsible for the norms of conduct and to act with creative discernment amid human ambiguity. Inevitably seeking *some* context within which they can attain normality, they can be no better than the ethos which they would serve and, having yielded critical capacities, will embody its worst tendencies without compunction. Without speech and thought such persons lack the power to act differently. More pointedly, once they surrender self to the tyranny of normality's cliche, they forfeit the power to *act* at all.

In Eichmann's case this banality results in a stark loss of self-

---

20. Thoughtless agents are "unknowing" not in the sense of ignorance or stupidity, i.e., that they do not see the consequences of their action, but that they have given up the vantage point of critical discrimination and thus may deceive themselves that, in its normality, a monstrous deed is somehow right. They know, for instance, that the releasing of Zyklon B in sealed chambers leads to the death of those trapped within, but somehow no longer know that this act of normal political obedience is also heinous murder. Arendt notes that the Nazi affinity for so-called "language rules" [*Sprachregelung*] — "what in ordinary language would be called a lie" — goes hand in hand with the rhetoric of cliche and combines to obscure the reality of any deed (*Eichmann*, pp. 85-86, 287).

21. On the suppression of reality by cliche, see Arendt, *The Life of the Mind* (New York: Harcourt Brace Jovanovich, 1977), I:4. Note also Arendt's reminders that where speech is denied its power to reveal the personhood of its speaker (as in the case of every cliche), the collusion of words and violence are never far behind (*Human Condition*, pp. 179-180).

cognizance (the basis for the "macabre comedy" Arendt perceived). Left perforce to role-play himself Eichmann's cliches mired him in blatant contradictions which reveal not so much guile as alarming self-deception. Nowhere does the absence of self-cognizance appear more striking than in the gallows rhetoric of Eichmann. Wishing long life for Germany, Argentina, and Austria, Eichmann concluded his last words with the cliche reserved for funeral oratory: "I shall not forget them." Elated by the slogan, he had failed to perceive that this was his own funeral. Accompanying such a total blank of insight, Eichmann's final statement demonstrated to Arendt a "grotesque silliness" and seemed to summarize "the lesson of the fearsome, word-and-thought-defying *banality of evil*" (*Eichmann*, p. 252).

If the force of banality could be seen only in its reflection of the banal person, then we would view in Eichmann a "pathetic comedy," a perverse drama within which the actor never attains the gravity of self-awareness or serious intent. As Arendt saw, Eichmann dies as a victim to his own banality, ultimately trivializing even his own death. But, in effect, banality such as Eichmann's does not confine itself to the banal person. It enters the common world with serious consequence for all those who live therein and depend upon human responsibility for the sustenance and quality of life. On the one hand, banal persons cannot genuinely act in response to another human, for their conduct is circumscribed by the rules governing their self-serving normality. On the other hand, this limitation means that not only have the banal become a cliche to themselves but, in their eyes, every other has become similarly objectified, robbed of the pertinence of his or her own speech and thought and the rights that such confers. Given any authority, the deeds of the banal can only turn oppressive, for banality cannot tolerate human distinctiveness — that which makes us all exceptions — any better in others than in its own herd. The human distinctiveness which makes speech and thought vitally necessary challenges the rhetoric of cliche and the normal conduct which issues from it. Accordingly, in a season of banality the distinct presence of others must be suppressed along with that human voice lost somewhere within the banal self. In the pursuit of normality the banal may banish from their world those real persons which call them to speak and think as unique selves. The status of normality will assure them that to destroy the alien or the exceptional is no mistake. As Arendt's portrait of Eichmann ever reminds, here the pathetic comedy of banality becomes the haunting tale of evil, grave and consuming.

MERTON'S CONTEMPLATION OF EICHMANN:

CONJECTURES ON THE BANALITY OF EVIL

Merton's reflections collected in *Conjectures of a Guilty Bystander* contain several discussions of the holocaust including his consideration of Arendt's Eichmann report.[22] These pages, along with the poem "Epitaph to a Public Servant" and the essay "A Devout Meditation in Memory of Adolf Eichmann," comprise Merton's written response to Arendt's depiction of Eichmann and are the only places where he so explicitly engages in dialogue with her text. In *Conjectures*, as in the other writings, he appropriates Arendt's thesis as a base from which he articulates certain implications of the Eichmann event.

Noting the shattering power of Arendt's text, Merton finds in Eichmann's case an indictment of the world's conscience that gives the trial a scope larger than the reckoning of Eichmann's individual fate. Merton gleans the trial's global indictment from the seeming inadequacy of any judgment rendered to Eichmann. In confronting Eichmann, not only do the "stereotyped answers fall all to pieces" but so do the forensic concepts of morality and the legal machinery they would authorize (*Conjectures*, pp. 286 and 288). Accordingly, at one level, the trial indicts the Western world for the impotence of its moral and legal traditions: they cannot sufficiently respond to Eichmann's atrocities. But at another level, as Merton saw, the limitation of those traditions share in the making of Eichmann, or at least in the creation of his conspicuous sense of guiltlessness. Echoing Arendt, Merton writes:

> What judgment could *add anything* to the judgment already implied in the fact that a man who was by certain accepted standards quite honest, respectable, sane, and efficient could do the things he did without feeling that he was wrong? The judgment falls not on Eichmann alone, but on our whole society. (*Conjectures*, p. 288)

That "certain accepted standards" failed to challenge Eichmann's sanity indicts those standards and the persons allegiant to them. In this way the social dimension of Eichmann's case issues in an accusation of the world which hosted his crimes against humanity.[23]

---

22.   In addition to Merton's discussion of Arendt (pp. 285-290), note the comments on W. L. Shirer's *The Rise and Fall of the Third Reich* (pp. 241-243) and Quasimodo's poem, "Auschwitz" (pp. 57-58).

23.   The social dimension of the Eichmann case is customarily put in terms of the relation between Eichmann's activity and the immediate social ethos of Nazi Germany. Yet that social ethos, no isolated or remote entity, brings with it the larger traditions of Western culture. The crisis of that culture's religious,

Merton's concern is not to diminish Eichmann's guilt, but to include the guilty bystander in its responsibility. No one can assume a safe vantage, detached from the implications of the Eichmann trial: Eichmann has been and remains a part of our world. Here Merton recognizes that in certain of our own seemingly acceptable activities we act in ways that resemble Eichmann. Not only do we host the company of Eichmann, but we ourselves *become* Eichmann in moments of banality or blind obedience. Thus, Merton brings near the spectre of Eichmann, pointing to its presence even in the context of monastic life. He writes:

> The awful details of this case can give monks food for thought. Are novices not sometimes trained to "do everything as if the abbot were watching you?" Are monks and priests not sometimes extremely upset over acts that are in fact good, not bad, but which happen to violate some tiny detail of a conventional code of observance. Is it not after all familiar to see that, when there is a choice between real charity and human compassion on one hand, and the violation of a punctilious usage on the other . . . they will prefer to violate charity rather than the observance? Violation of the observance would make them feel far more guilty . . . .
> (*Conjectures*, pp. 287-288)

Merton's reference to monastic communities, however, provides only a case in point for his warning that *wherever* habits of complacency or conformity supplant critical commitment Eichmann gains a posthumous long life. Though the banalities of cliche and blind allegiances have not everywhere erupted into programs of genocide, they pervade religious and political life in such a way that resist any facile separation of Eichmann's situation and the banalities of seemingly moral communities. Merton's point is simply that banality is banality: its benign forms differ from Eichmann only in degree, not in kind, and therefore themselves remain vulnerable to complicity in deeds of destruction.

Merton emphasizes in *Conjectures* that one cannot confine Eichmann's verdict to him alone: at best, the world is Eichmann's guilty bystander; at worst, his witting or unwitting compatriot in a banality ripe for evil.[24] If this global indictment warns Merton's readers of the dangers of

---

political, and humanistic traditions are here manifest both in the defendant and the world of those who must judge not only him, but indirectly themselves. It is in this respect that Merton speaks of the trial as an indictment of the Western conscience. It should go without saying that the crisis of judgment which Merton detects belongs to the bystander's world and not that of the victim. Indeed, from a basis that transcends the concepts of morality and law, the victim's experience judges both Eichmann and the Western bystander.

24.   It is in this last sense that Merton interprets Eichmann's words at the gallows as a refusal to be dismissed from the world, a refusal tantamount to saying, "Your world is full of me, I am all over the place, I am legion; and you, whether you like it or not, are going to take the same long course in wickedness and study all its details. When you have finally, with great labor learned it all, you will be even more banal and more appalling than I" (*Conjectures*, p. 290). Arendt would have agreed with Merton's sense of the legionary existence of Eichmann, but would not have ascribed such awareness to Eichmann himself.

their own indifference, it also intends to make them wary of interpreting the human situation in terms of moral principles which themselves may become banal and enslaving. On the one hand, those principles are shattered by the Eichmann trial itself, by Eichmann's appeal to his own moral virtues (*Conjectures*, p. 287). On the other hand, in their abstraction from particular human contexts, such principles may encourage an ethical banality that finds one, like Eichmann, engaging in concrete evil though with moral principles fully intact. Though Merton does not want to give up morality to a nihilism "that only opens the way to a more complete surrender to a more absolute irrationality, a more total cruelty" (p. 286), the Eichmann story makes untenable for him any retreat into moral confidence based on the rationality of principles. For Merton, one cannot respond to Eichmann with moral answers for, in a certain sense, they themselves are the problem. As such, *Conjectures* calls not only for a nightwatch against banality, but for a mode of ethical deliberation that insists upon "an existential respect for the human reality of each situation" (p. 288) and interrogates the conscience with claims of the concrete world. One forgets with peril that, in the abstract, Eichmann was a morally principled man.

EPITAPH FOR EICHMANN

In 1961, the year of the Eichmann trial in Jerusalem, Merton had written his signature Auschwitz poem, "Chant to be Used in Processions around a Site with Furnaces."[25] This poem experiments with a technique common in "found art" or *assemblage*, a sculpture movement popular in the 1950s.[26] As "found art" sought to take various common objects — whatever one might "find" — and unite them in one aesthetic form, here Merton takes verbal litter from his reading of Shirer's *The Rise and Fall of the Third Reich*, constructing from quotations of Rudolf Hoess a haunting portrayal of a death camp commander.[27] This same technique shapes Merton's poem, "Epitaph for a Public Servant," which bears the motto, *"In*

---

25. *The Collected Poems of Thomas Merton* (New York: New Directions, 1977), pp. 345-349. The poem appeared in *The Catholic Worker* during the Eichmann trial and its wide reprinting included publication in Lawrence Ferlighetti's first *Journal for the Protection of All Beings* (1961). See Therese Lentfoehr, *Words and Silence: On the Poetry of Thomas Merton* (New York: New Directions, 1979), p. 44.

26. For the designation of "Chant" as a "found poem," see *Mott*, p. 364.

27. Therese Lentfoehr suggests the probability that Merton had Eichmann in mind as the protagonist of "Chant" (p. 44). The poem's method of construction, however, would lead to another conclusion. Merton clearly bases his poem on Shirer's quotation of Rudolf Hoess, the commandant of Auschwitz. Moreover, the commandant role so evident in the poem cannot be seen as Eichmann's, though the links between the atrocities of Hoess and Eichmann should be obvious enough.

Memoriam — Adolf Eichmann." In "Epitaph" Merton takes direct quotations from Arendt's *Eichmann in Jerusalem*, fragmenting them, isolating them from their discursive contexts, and repeating them endlessly in various juxtapositions.[28]

Read straightforwardly, "Epitaph" makes little sense. An exercise in anti-poetry, it does not intend to.[29] The poem's semantic content, like Eichmann's own speech, is vacuous, but its effect stuns: without the diversion of discursive comment the reader confronts starkly the banality of Eichmann's slogans, the procession of cliche and empty confession. If Merton's *Conjectures'* entry articulated the implications of Eichmann's banality, "Epitaph" leads the reader to experience it verbally, to weary at its repetition, and thus prepares to protest against its continuance. The poem, though, is not simple. Merton presents Eichmann's slogans in such a way as to insure perception of their banality and the absurdity of their meaning when taken together. Thus, more than repetition, "Epitaph" brings about a synoptic reading of Eichmann's sayings — a near fugue of banality — that exposes the shallowness and ironic contradictions of Eichmann's speech.

The following example should convey the spirit of the poem and illustrate Merton's technique in "Epitaph."[30] When, in a discussion of Himmler's 1944 offer to exchange a million Jews for ten thousand trucks, Eichmann was asked if he himself had expressed any pity for the Jews, he replied: "Not out of mercy did I launch this transaction" (*Eichmann*, p. 25). "Epitaph" opens with Arendt's direct quotation of this reply and proceeds to repeat various fragments of it in relation to other aspects of Eichmann's behavior. Thus, the second stanza of the poem finds these fragments modifying the psychiatrist's testimony that Eichmann's family relations were "not only normal but desirable," (*Eichmann*, p. 26), a counselling minister's assessment that he was "a man with very positive ideas" (*Eichmann*, p. 26), and Eichmann's own claim that his "whole education through [his] father and mother had been strictly Christian" (*Eichmann*, p. 30) and

---

28. See *Collected Poems*, pp. 703-711. "Epitaph" was first published in the May 1967 issue of *Motive*, the magazine for the Methodist Student Movement. Its actual date of composition, however, is problematic. Therese Lentfoehr's contention that "Epitaph" was written at about the same time as "Chant" (1961) cannot be correct (*Words and Silence*, p. 44). Merton bases "Epitaph" on Arendt's Eichmann report in the same way as he had used Shirer's *Rise and Fall* as the source for "Chant" [see Appendix]. Thus "Epitaph" could not have been written by Merton before March 1963 when he first encountered Arendt's work.

29. "Epitaph" is anti-poetic in its use of fragmentation and dislocation, insisting that a reader reconstruct reality from disordered bits of direct experience. The materials of the anti-poem are cut free from the customary sense-making conventions out of the poet's concern not to impose meaning on experience, but to let that experience bluntly speak for itself.

30. For further display of Merton's technique, see the appendix ("The Source for Merton's 'Epitaph for a Public Servant' ") provided at the end of this article.

that "he 'personally' never had anything whatever against Jews; on the contrary, he had plenty of 'private reasons' for not being a Jew hater (*Eichmann*, p. 26). This second stanza reads as follows:

> Relations with father mother brother
> Sister most normal
> Most desirable
> Not out of mercy
> A man
> With positive ideas
> (This transaction)
> A Christian
> Education
> (Not out of mercy)
> With private reasons
> For not hating Jews   (*Collected Poems*, pp. 703-704)

The juxtaposition of Eichmann's claim to the merciless transaction with these other assertions empties them of any meaning they might have held in some other "language game." The juxtaposition mires these utterances in the contradiction of a Christian education that yields no mercy, of a capacity for positive ideas that coexists with motiveless genocide, and of a normal, desirable family life that coincides with an indifference to millions of Jews that could send them to the gas chambers or exchange them for trucks both with equal compunction.

At the same time, the repetition of Eichmann's reply leads the reader to suspect something of the assertion's own banality; that it, too, exists as a slogan that may have no congruence with truth. The illusion is not that somehow Eichmann retained a secret mercy, but that in the elation of the cliche he ascribes to himself the more powerful role of Himmler: in truth, neither with nor without mercy does Eichmann "launch this transaction" (*Eichmann*, p. 25). Yet, as the effect of "Epitaph" makes clear, the scandal lies not in simple falsehood, but in the absurdity that reigns whenever truth and language part company. With no less than nineteen citations from Arendt's *Eichmann in Jerusalem*, Merton weaves the fabric of "Epitaph" that recreates for its reader the tangle of Eichmann's absurdity and makes unavoidable the weary perception of evil's banality.[31]

---

31. The numerous quotations of Arendt (and her quotations of Eichmann) suggest that one might further study "Epitaph" in the context of documentary art, i.e., art which constructs its representation of reality primarily from fragments of *realia* such as documents, letters, transcripts, newspaper and broadcast reports, etc. Documentary art, a prevalent mode of holocaust literature, can be seen in such works as Peter Weiss's drama, *Die Ermittlung* (Frankfurt am Main: Suhrkamp. 1965); English version, *The Investigation* by Jon Swan and Ulu Grosbard (New York: Atheneum, 1966). Weiss bases his play extensively and in detail on the court records of the 1964-65 Auschwitz trials in Frankfurt. On documentary art and holocaust literature, see Sidra Ezrahi, *By Words Alone: The Holocaust in Literature* (Chicago: University of Chicago Press, 1980),

THE DEVOUT MEDITATION

The third text in which Merton responds to Arendt's volume, "A Devout Meditation in Memory of Adolf Eichmann," amply paraphrases her depiction of Eichmann's sanity, his lack of disturbance that is itself so disturbing.[32] While sending millions of Jewish men, women, and children to their deaths, Eichmann experiences no guilt; he eats and sleeps well. Devoted to his duty, he has pride and a certain peace of mind gained in the knowledge that he is normal, that within his context he acts in the same manner that anyone else would. While Merton adds little to Arendt's description, he proceeds to make explicit and unavoidable the implication of her study: namely, that such sanity as Eichmann's, derived from arbitrary social norms, has nothing to do with being in one's right mind. "Fitting in," or not being "impeded by [one's] disordered emotions from acting in a cool, orderly manner, according to the needs and dictates of the social situation in which [one] finds [oneself]" can scarcely guarantee right-mindedness for, as Merton puts it, the banal "can be perfectly adjusted even in hell itself" (*Raids*, p. 47). Anxiety, that disturbing voice so conspicuously absent in Eichmann, if not a constitutive feature of human identity, remains the only voice in touch with reality when human identity is threatened by inhumanity. At such times it is not dis-ease, but the peaceful no-mindedness of banality that denies true sanity and with it, the prospect of love and compassion. Perceiving no threat to one's own humanity — not even in a world gone mad — one remains blind to what imperils the life of another. For this reason, Merton reminds, in certain contexts "the worst insanity is to be totally without anxiety, totally 'sane' " (*Raids*, p. 49).[33]

Though it is only a case in point, Merton clearly has in mind here the context of life after Hiroshima, life in the midst of nuclear threat. The spirit of Eichmann, for Merton, lurked dangerously within the issue of the bomb,

---

pp. 24-48; and James E. Young, *Writing and Rewriting the Holocaust: Narrative and the Consequences of Interpretation* (Bloomington: Indiana University Press, 1988), pp. 64-80.

32. In *Raids on the Unspeakable* (New York: New Directions, 1966), pp. 45-49. Hereafter referred to in the text as *Raids*. For an interpretation of this essay, see Karl A. Plank, "Meditating on Merton's Eichmann," *The Christian Century* 102 (9 October 1985): pp. 894-895.

33. Merton's point shares a clear affinity with certain contemporary works of fiction such as Ken Kesey's *One Flew Over the Cuckoo's Nest* (New York: Viking, 1962) as well as psychotherapeutic literature such as R. D. Laing's *The Politics of Experience* (New York: Ballantine, 1967). If the critique of normality was broadly current at the time of the "Devout Meditation," the antecedents for Merton would seem to date back a decade earlier to his first reading of Erich Fromm's *The Sane Society*. Thus, in a 1955 letter to Fromm, Merton writes: "I certainly agree with you that we ought to scrap the notion that mental health is merely a matter of adjustment to the existing society — to be adjusted to a society that is insane is not to be healthy" (in *Hidden Ground*, p. 313). On Merton's use of Fromm, see David D. Cooper, *Thomas Merton's Art of Denial: The Evolution of a Radical Humanist* (Athens: University of Georgia Press, 1989), pp. 244-251.

embodied within those who with "perfectly good reasons, logical, well-adjusted reasons" might actually "press the buttons that will initiate the great festival of destruction that they, *the sane ones* have prepared" (*Raids*, p. 46). Merton's hermeneutic move from Auschwitz to Hiroshima, from Eichmann to those who parlay nuclear arms, emphasizes again the insight of *Conjectures* with immediacy and urgency: the banality of evil does not stop with Eichmann, nor is it a peculiar feature of our enemies. It is *ours* in every instance in which we eschew the responsibility for thinking what we are doing or compromise the humanness of life in the name of our own shallow well-being.

CONTEMPLATION IN DARK TIMES

During the Eichmann trial the testimony of the Jewish poet and resistance fighter, Abba Kovner, yielded an unusually dramatic moment. Kovner, when asked how he had first heard of Eichmann, mentioned that he had learned of this man who "arranges everything" from a German sergeant named Anton Schmidt. As Kovner proceeded to tell the story of Schmidt's heroic assistance to members of the Jewish underground — assistance for which he was eventually arrested and executed — a reverential silence settled over the courtroom. Struck by the preciousness of this story and its power to dismantle Eichmann's appeal to the necessity of his obedience, Arendt commented:

> . . . the lesson of such stories is simple and within everybody's grasp. Politically speaking, it is that under conditions of terror most people will comply but *some people will not*, just as the lesson of the countries to which the Final Solution was proposed is that "it could happen" in most places but *it did not happen everywhere*. Humanly speaking, no more is required, and no more can reasonably be asked, for this planet to remain a place fit for human habitation. (*Eichmann*, p. 233)

Though legion, Eichmann's spirit is not absolute. While conditions of domination may imperil the human capacity to act uniquely and banality may lull the impulse for doing so, the story of Anton Schmidt reminds that in the most desperate of seasons persons remain charged with a responsibility for the human quality of life and endowed with the freedom to preserve that humanity or at least to protest its violation.[34] As Arendt later wrote:

---

34. On the function of such protest, see Karl A. Plank, "Raging Wisdom: A Banner of Defiance Unfurled," *Judaism* 36 (1987): pp. 323-330.

> Even in the darkest of times we have the right to expect some illumination,
> and that such illumination may come . . . from the uncertain, flickering,
> and often weak light that some men and women, in their lives and works,
> will kindle under almost all circumstances and shed over the time span
> that was given them on earth.[35]

If Eichmann manifested sheer thoughtlessness, dark times, Arendt
believed, could yet host a spirit of thinking — not so much that of the
professional philosopher, but of the person of conscience, like Anton
Schmidt, whose uneasiness births a critical attitude toward ideology and
piety. Thinking, as Arendt understood it, constitutes the self's own dialogue
with itself, a reflexive interrogation that brings to bear a multiple perspective upon whatever matter confronts the self (*Mind*, I: 179-193). Such
thinking, in its dyadic character, engenders a conscience — an awareness of
a critical voice within oneself — that both accuses and liberates. As accusing, the thinking conscience takes away any complacent satisfaction with
cliched answers that may console or elate but cannot stand the ordeal of
examination. As liberating, the thinking conscience frees one from the
tyranny of oppressive ideologies by exposing at once their relativity and the
prospect of acting in new and surprising ways. Anton Schmidt, as he
supplied papers and vehicles for the Jewish partisans in Poland, embodied
not only the spirit of the courageous actor, but of Arendt's thinker. His
capacity to judge good and evil and to act accordingly presuppose the prior
activity of thinking, a habit of conscience that required suspicion of Nazi
morality, no matter how dominant in his environment, and a recognition of
a basic freedom to act independently of that morality. At dangerous odds
with his environment and unwilling to forsake the self-examination of
conscience, Schmidt could not claim the ease of Eichmann's sanity; but in
his capacity for thinking he was redeemed from the banality of evil and for a
righteous martyrdom.

Arendt devoted her final writing, *The Life of the Mind*, to an account
of this activity of thinking, explicitly casting it as the singular alternative to
Eichmann's banality.[36] Where Arendt moves from the Eichmann predicament to a constructive response in her writings on thinking, we might look

---

35. Hannah Arendt, *Men in Dark Times* (New York: Harcourt Brace, 1968), p. ix.

36. Posthumously published, *The Life of the Mind* was a lengthy development of the concerns Arendt
had already showed in her seminal article, "Thinking and Moral Considerations," *Social Research* 38 (1971):
pp. 417-446. Here, as in the subsequent book, she specifically justifies taking up the category of thinking as a
response to the thoughtlessness of Eichmann. Her inquiry into thinking shows a clear moral trajectory as she
asks, "Do the inability to think and a disastrous failure of what we commonly call conscience coincide?" and
"Could the activity of thinking as such, the habit of examining and reflecting upon whatever happens to
come to pass, regardless of specific content and quite independent of results, could this activity be of such a
nature that it 'conditions' men against evil-doing?" ("Thinking," p. 418).

for a comparable move in Merton's prose and poetry. While Merton's writings that explicitly treat Eichmann have focused on the predicament and its implications, his writings on contemplation provide an apt basis for a critique of the banality of evil that gives insight into the nature of Eichmann's banality and offers an alternative to it. Indeed, Merton's notion of contemplation, like that of Arendt's thinking, stands over-against Eichmann as a source of light in the darkest of times.

Though Merton does not specifically consider him in writings other than those we have discussed above, Eichmann appears allusively in much of Merton's prose as an unnamed anti-type of the true contemplative: he is the guiltless ape, pulling levers in space and being "bothered by no metaphysical problems" (*Conjectures*, pp. 60-61).[37] He is the self of the crowd who "does not talk [but] produces conventional sounds when stimulated by the appropriate noises," the one who "secretes cliches."[38] He is one of those who "will live 'good lives' that are basically inauthentic.... In order to avoid apparent evil, [he] will ignore the summons of genuine good."[39] As Eichmann's *persona* had shaped the countenance of the "sane" ones that Merton so feared, so as anti-type does it inhabit his contemplative writings in the guise of those who have surrendered to false selfhood, the orientation utterly contrary to contemplation.

As Merton perceived him, Eichmann's behavior would show him to be a totally false self, one who is defined exclusively by his social function whose security he protects at all costs (*NS*, pp. 34-36). As such his banality differs from simple shallowness or political naivete and cannot be abstracted from the crisis of existential life which all persons face. For Merton, human life, in its myriad forms of finitude, frightens with a dread that does not go away:

> ... underlying all life is the ground of doubt and self-questioning which sooner or later must bring us face to face with the ultimate meaning of our life. This self-questioning can never be without a certain existential 'dread'

---

37. The parallel to Eichmann becomes obvious when read in tandem with "A Devout Meditation." If, in that essay, Merton pointed to the danger of Eichmann's sane heirs launching nuclear destruction convinced that "it is no mistake," here he moves from the obedient, guiltless ape to those who may enter space and with obedient guiltlessness blow up the world: "We will not feel guilt in space ... From Mars or the moon we will blow up the world, perhaps. If we blow up the world from the moon we may feel a little guilt. If we blow it up from Mars we will feel no guilt at all. No guilt at all. We will blow up the world with no guilt at all. Tra la. Push the buttons, press the levers! As soon as they get a factory on Mars for banana-colored apes there will be no guilt at all" (*Conjectures*, p. 61).

38. Thomas Merton, *New Seeds of Contemplation* (New York: New Directions, 1962, © 1961), p. 55. Hereafter referred to in the text as *NS*.

39. Thomas Merton, *Contemplative Prayer* (Garden City, New York: Doubleday Image Books, 1971), pp. 103-104. Hereafter referred to in the text as *CP*.

— a sense of insecurity, of 'lostness,' of exile, of sin. A sense that one has somehow been untrue not so much to abstract moral or social norms but to one's own inmost truth . . . a profound awareness that one is capable of ultimate bad faith with himself and with others: that one is living a lie.
(*CP*, p. 24)

False selfhood arises as an inauthentic response to that dread, an attempt to avert the crisis of "the ultimate meaning of [human] life" with projects that would intimate human power and determination. False selfhood, that mode of "ultimate bad faith," would supplant the fact of human finitude with the illusion that human beings control the terms of their existence. As such, the false self lives the lie which ignores the reality of its own death. Seen as a false selfhood, the Eichmann predicament cannot be posed as the simple banality of Nazi answers, as if some other ideology would have redeemed this bad faith. Concerned to "fit in" to whatever ethos would take away the dread of existence and give him a secure identity, Eichmann's predicament was to be a slave to banality as such; to serve that pervading, corrupting force that falsifies and deadens whatever reality it would hold. Moreover, slavery to banality, when seen from Merton's contemplative perspective, reflects a deep fear of life and the God who creates its condition. Ethical in its ramifications, the Eichmann predicament is theological at its core.

The life of contemplation counters Eichmann's false-selfhood in a double-edged way. First, as an act of renunciation, contemplation negates the defenses which armor persons against their finitude and thus, also, against the humanity of their life. Contemplation begins with and keeps in view the anxiety from which Eichmann would flee into banality. Second, if contemplation challenges defenses such as Eichmann's, it strikes further at the fearful vision of life which would seemingly warrant defensiveness. No eradicator of anxiety, contemplation seeks instead to enable one to perceive a deeper ordering of life within which one's undeniable finitude can be trusted and accepted.

Renunciation, the first aspect of contemplation that would arrest Eichmann's banality, expresses its roots in a tradition of *contemptus mundi*, an eschatological orientation that holds the world's activity to be ultimately inadequate for human salvation.[40] As Merton appropriates this tradition, its meaning lies not in a resentful hostility of the world, nor in a detachment from the life which occurs in it, but in a protest of the world's aims as being

---

40. For Merton's discussion of *contemptus mundi*, see *Conjectures*, pp. 45-53.

sufficient to sustain human life. For the contemplative, *contemptus mundi* means a renunciation not of the world but of its ultimacy: a constant struggle with the human tendency to identify with its values and a firm nonacquiescence when those values are held with absolute seriousness. As such, contemplation takes on an iconoclastic character, destroying the idolatrous links human beings forge with the world in an attempt to escape the threat of finitude. Human emptiness cannot be filled with worldly activity, for projects of the world have no more finality than the fragile person who seeks in them a consoling permanence or significance. "No pain-killer," contemplation is a "steady burning to ashes of old worn-out cliches, slogans, rationalizations . . . a terrible breaking and burning of idols, a purification of the sanctuary, so that no graven things may occupy the place that God has commanded to be left empty" (*NS*, p. 13).

Contemplation, as iconoclasm, has a self-consuming character that refuses to stop at critique of the world or any of its given objects. It aims not simply at *contemptus mundi*, but at a basic openness of the self to God's presence and thereby must challenge whatever the self would hold as idol. Not only worldly activity, but the pursuits of faith may be conscripted by the self in quest of its own security and at that point stand as idols to be renounced in contemplation.[41] The final idol to be overcome, if "the place that God has commanded to be left empty" is indeed to be empty, is simply one's own self, for there is generated the fear that leads one to seize the world, secular and religious, as a source of refuge; there, in the self, is found the bits and pieces of finite reality that no one wants to take with less than ultimate seriousness. In contemplation, *contemptus mundi* becomes a self-critique, fundamental and thorough.

Deprived of the world as a defense, the contemplative is turned back upon his or her own resource and discovers starkly the ultimate emptiness of the self. Yet this only confirms the suspicion that had prompted false selfhood in the first place and so the contemplative experiences anxiety, the dreadful sense of having no haven from his or her deepest fear. Accordingly, Merton warns, "Let no one hope to find in contemplation an escape from conflict, from anguish or from doubt. On the contrary, the deep, inexpressible certitude of the contemplative experience awakens a tragic

---

41. The point parallels the insight of J. D. Salinger's memorable character Zooey who says: ". . . as a matter of simple logic, there's no difference at all, that I can see, between the man who's greedy for material treasure — or even intellectual treasure — and the man who's greedy for spiritual treasure. As you say, treasure's treasure, God damn it, and it seems that ninety per cent of all the world-hating saints in history were just as acquisitive and unattractive, basically, as the rest of us are" [*Franny and Zooey* (Boston: Little, Brown, 1961), pp. 147-148].

anguish and opens many questions in the depths of the heart like wounds that cannot stop bleeding" (*NS*, p. 12).[42]

The contemplative's anxiety, intensified in the renunciation of defenses, distances him or her from the undisturbed sanity of Eichmann. Like Arendt's thinkers who must question all answers — including and especially their own — the contemplative faces a heightened uncertainty that knows keenly the provisionality of the human self: born to die, no self can know, articulate, or live the final truth which is God's to reveal — a mystery. Thus, where Eichmann invests the Nazi mythology with the authority of final truth and the power to secure the meaning of his existence, the contemplative's anxiety issues in a basic doubt of any worldly truth and its cheap promise of security. Where Eichmann can, without guilt, deport millions of Jews to their death, contemplatives awaken to the constant reality of their own bad faith and the burden of responsibility. Where Eichmann, asleep to what threatens himself, can acknowledge no jeopardy to others in his mad world, the contemplative's dread provides a source for compassion for those with whom they share the sleepless night. Though profoundly disturbing in experience, the truth of the contemplative's anxiety humanizes in effect. Those who can face it without illusion cannot be seduced by false gods to slay that which is human in themselves and each other.

Still, the contemplative's capacity for anxiety does not fully resolve the predicament of false selfhood. Anxiety, for Merton, was not the goal of contemplation but, rather, the condition within which the contemplative finds freedom from false attachments. So liberated, the contemplative might then discern a deeper vision of life that breaks the compulsion to conform to orders that may themselves be false or empty. By combatting not only human defenses, but the need for defensiveness, contemplation brings to bear its second challenge to Eichmann's banality.

Eichmann's predicament reflects a captivity to illusion about himself, the world of human others, and the ultimate meaning of created life. Seen starkly, life's mortality condemns and the nearness of others endangers with reminders of limitation and futility. So threatening is this perspective that it leads some to flee from life — the very condition which poses the

---

42.   Merton understands that the anxiety which combats false selfhood, an existential anxiety rather than neurotic, has a creative function necessary for growth. Thus, while devastating in its attack upon the false self, such anxiety must be affirmed as a beckoning to maturity. See Merton's review article which treats the work of Reza Arasteh: "Final Integration: Toward a Monastic Therapy," in *Contemplation in a World of Action* (London: Unwin, 1980), pp. 205-217. Note also Cooper, *Art of Denial*, pp. 179-185.

crisis of mortality — and surrender to a banality which promises distraction from the pains of finitude. In his banality, Eichmann binds himself to a vision of a secure self and a world in which others either promote that security or become enemies to be destroyed without compunction; seeking the solace of illusion, he denies death in himself and freedom in the actual others with whom he shares the world.

The contemplative cannot deny the perception of finitude: too rending is the anguish that tears the soul "like wounds that cannot stop bleeding." Yet, where Eichmann's banality represses this basic conflict of mortality, the contemplative turns toward the darkness of the human condition and enters its heart more deeply. Accordingly, though Eichmann and the contemplative share a common human condition, they perceive it from different vantage points, a difference which decisively shapes the actions which each undertakes. In flight from finitude, Eichmann escapes to a shallowness that thins life so as virtually to guarantee its collapse, rhetorical warranties notwithstanding. Where all things are viewed under the lens of superficiality no substantial meaning can emerge to frame the darkness which frightens unto banality. The actions of one so frightened can only harbor an unceasing defensiveness that may maim and kill to protect the illusion of security. The contemplative, however, seeks intimacy with the depth of life, especially its darkness. From the vantage of depth the glimpse of any meaning holds the prospect of an enduring truth within the darkness itself. Such a prospect opens the contemplative to the world of human others whose presence may bring darkness near and to the God whose light appears in the shadows of human existence.[43]

Only by risking life, its finitude no less than its promise, does one gain the vantage from which can be seen an illumination of darkness. Eichmann's banality mires itself in a desperate cycle, for in the fearful flight from life's depths he only superficially avoids the crisis of his humanity while remaining completely outside the domain where its meaning is won or lost. The contemplative, however, liberated from false attachments, knows a freedom to pursue life's depth and thereby finds access to a vision which the banal deny themselves. For Merton, the contemplative enters a desert of darkness and there stands open to a deeper perception of reality, a *paschal* order that finds the presence of God bringing life from death in all its permutations (*CP*, pp. 34 and 106). There in a human wasteland, the

---

43.   For a congenial consideration of depth, see Abraham Joshua Heschel, *God is Search of Man* (New York: Harper & Row, 1955), pp. 3-23.

contemplative knows what Eichmann cannot: that one loses life not by death but by fear; that where God brings life from death no human insecurity can finally threaten or estrange, or can ever warrant the flight from the depth of human life; that darkness is not all. Death and anxiety — finitude in all its forms — remain in the contemplative's world as part of life's own mystery; but gone is the defensiveness that would seek to flee these realities; banished is the fear that would find shaken souls hiding from God and each other in a tangle of desperate banalities.[44]

Put simply: Eichmann's evil does not grow from his humanity, but from his dreadful attempt to escape it. Contemplation, as Merton understood it, enables one to see that such an escape is futile, destructive, and ultimately unnecessary. The contemplatives who have no need to fit into structures of oppression become conspicuous actors, guardians of the human, in their non-compliance with the world's evil. Not only do they resist the legacy of Eichmann, but they embody light in dark times, sanity in seasons of madness. In this the vocation of the contemplative, as well as of the thinker, becomes one with the human calling.

---

44. For discussion of this perspective in a biblical context, see Karl A. Plank, *Paul and the Irony of Affliction* (Atlanta: Scholars Press, 1987).

APPENDIX

THE SOURCE FOR MERTON'S
"EPITAPH FOR A PUBLIC SERVANT"

As the following parallels make clear, Merton bases his Eichmann poem on quotations taken from Hannah Arendt's *Eichmann in Jerusalem* (New York: Viking, 1963).

Merton's "Epitaph for a Public Servant"	Arendt's Eichmann in Jerusalem
"Not out of mercy Did I launch this transaction"	Eichmann was asked: "Mr. Witness, in the negotiations with your superiors, did you express any pity for the Jews . . .?" And he replied: "I am here under oath and must speak the truth. Not out of mercy did I launch this transaction." (p. 25)
Relations with father mother brother Sister most normal Most desirable Not out of mercy A man With positive ideas (This transaction) A Christian Education (Not out of mercy) With private reasons For not hating Jews	[One of the psychiatrists] had found that his whole psychological outlook, his attitude toward his wife and children, mother and father, brothers, sisters, and friends, was "not only normal but most desirable" — and finally the minister who had paid regular visits to him . . . reassured everybody by declaring Eichmann to be "a man with very positive ideas." (pp. 25-26)
"Not out of mercy did I Launch this" Christian education Without rancor Without any reason For hating	". . . for my whole education through my father and mother had been strictly Christian." (p. 30) He "personally" never had anything whatever against Jews; on the contrary, he had plenty of "private reasons" for not being a Jew hater. (p. 26)
"I ENTERED LIFE ON EARTH IN THE ASPECT OF A HUMAN BEING AND BELIEVED IN THE HIGHER MEANING"	"Today . . . I begin to lead my thoughts back to that nineteenth of March of the year 1906, when at five o'clock in the morning I entered life on earth in the aspect of a human being" . . . an event ascribed to a "higher bearer of meaning." (p. 27)

Without any ill-feeling
Or any reason for
This prize-winning transaction

"I ENTERED LIFE ON EARTH"
To launch a positive idea
"But repentance is for little children"

He had never harbored any ill
feelings against his victims. (p. 30)

[Eichmann] proposed "to hang myself
in public as a warning example for
all anti-Semites on this earth." By
this he did not mean to say that he
regretted anything: "Repentance is
for little children." (p. 24)

I entered life on earth
Bearing a resemblance
To man
With this transaction
In my pocket
Relations most normal
Most desirable
Father mother brother sister
In the aspect
Of human beings
One and all without any reason
For ill will or discourtesy
To any Hebrew
Or to Israel
But without
Ideas

"Repentance is
For desirable
Little children"

Without any transaction

ii

"I NEVER HARBORED ANY ILL FEELING
AGAINST THE JEWS DURING THIS ENTIRE
 TRANSACTION
I EVEN WALKED THROUGH THE STREETS
WITH A JEWISH FRIEND

HE THOUGHT NOTHING OF IT."

"Even in my elementary school, I had
a [Jewish] classmate with whom I
spent my free time . . . The last
time we met we walked through the
streets of Linz, I already with the
party Emblem . . . in my buttonhole,
and he did not think anything of it." (p. 30)

iii

Yet I was saddened at the order
I lost all joy in my
Work

To regain my joy
Without any reason
I joined the Party
I was swallowed by the

"I lost all joy in my work, I no
longer liked to sell, to make calls." (p. 31)

"It was like being swallowed up by
the Party against all expectations
and without previous decision. It
happened so quickly and suddenly." (p. 33)

Party
Without previous
Decision and entered
Upon my apprenticeship
In Jewish
Affairs.

Saddened at the Order
And the merciless
Affairs
Of my learning
Fast
To forget
I resigned from various
Associations dedicated
To merriment lectures
And Humor refined
Humor!

When Kaltenbrunner suggested that he
enter the S. S., he was just on the
point of becoming a member of an
altogether different outfit, the
Freemasons' Lodge Schlaraffia, "an
association of businessmen,
physicians, actors, civil servants,
etc., who came together to cultivate
merriment and gaiety . . . Each
member had to give a lecture . . .
whose tenor was to be humor, refined
humor." (p. 32)

From then on
Official orders
Were my only language

"Officialese is my only language." (p. 48)

iv

I lost all joy
In my work
And entered life on earth
In the aspect of a human
Believer

They were all hostile.
The Leader's success alone
Proved that I should subordinate myself
To such a man
(Relations most normal)
Who was to have his own thoughts in
        ˙[such a matter?]
In such a transaction?
Who was I
To judge
The Master?

"At that moment, I sensed a kind of
Pontius Pilate feeling, for I felt
free of all guilt." Who was he to
judge? Who was he "to have [his] own
thoughts in this matter"? (p. 114)

I lost all joy
I believed in destiny
I learned to forget
The undesirable Jew.

v

I was born among knives and scissors

He was born on March 19, 1906 in
Solingen, a German town in the
Rhineland famous for its knives,
scissors, and surgical instruments. (p. 27)

One of the few gifts fate
Bestowed on me is a gift
For truth in so far as it
Depends on myself.

I make it depend
On myself.

Gifted.

They were all hostile.

Repentance is
For little children

Depending on knives and scissors

vi

To grant a mercy death
Institutional care

Not out of mercy
Did I dare

To launch an institution
Or the gifted Leader's
Solution
Not out of mercy
Did I dare

O the carefree relation
The well-run instutution
The well-planned
Charitable care

To grant a mercy killing summer
Vacation
To the hero nation
Not out of mercy
Did I dare

I welcomed one and all
To the charity ball
In the charitable foundation
For the chosen nation
I spent sleepless nights
In care

Who was to have his own thoughts
I granted
To very many
A mercy death
With institutional
Care.

"One of the few gifts fate bestowed
upon me is a capacity for truth
insofar as it depends upon myself."
(p. 54)

The gassing in the East — or to use
the language of the Nazis, "the
humane way" of killing "by granting
people a mercy death" began on almost
the very day when the gassing in
Germany was stopped . . . . None of
the various "language rules,"
carefully contrived to deceive and to
camoflage, had a more decisive effect
. . . than this first war decree of
Hitler, in which the word for
"murder" was replaced by the phrase
"to grant a mercy death." (p. 108)

I never asked
For any reward.

vii

At the end
A leaderless life.

No pertinent ordinances
To consult

Not out of mercy
Did I launch this transaction

No pertinent orders
Lolita? "An unwholesome book"

Repentance is for little children

"I sensed I would have to live a
leaderless life, I would receive no
directives from anybody, no orders
and commands would any longer be
issued to me, no pertinent ordinances
would be there to consult — in brief,
a life never known before lay before
me." (p. 32)

. . . the young police officer in
charge of his mental and
psychological well-being handed him
Lolita for relaxation. After two days
Eichmann returned it, visibly
indignant; "Quite an unwholesome
book," he told his guard. (p. 49)

viii

As I entered it
So I left it
LIFE
In the aspect
Of a human
Being

A man with positive
Ideas
With no ill will
Toward any Jew

A man without reason
To hate his fellow citizen
Swallowed up by death
Without previous decision
A believer

Long live Argentina
Long live Germany
We will meet again
And again
We have been chosen partners
Not out of mercy
Amid knives and scissors
In a positive transaction
Without any reason
For serious concern

"After a short while, gentlemen, we
shall all meet again. Such is the
fate of all men. Long live Germany,
long live Argentina, long live
Austria. I shall not forget them."
(p. 252)

WHO THEN SHALL CHERISH HIS OWN
    THOUGHTS?

Gentlemen Adios
We shall meet again

We shall be partners
Life is short
Art is long
And we shall meet
Without the slightest
Discourtesy

Repentance is
For little children.

THOMAS MERTON,

LOUIS MASSIGNON,

AND THE CHALLENGE OF ISLAM

by **Sidney H. Griffith**

Among the books that Merton was reading on his Asian journey was Louis Massignon's classic study in comparative mysticism, *Essai sur les origines du lexique technique de la mystique musulmane.*[1] It is a book that concentrates on the technical vocabulary of Islamic mysticism in the Arabic language. But along the way the author clarifies the terms he studies by comparing them to earlier Christian usages, and sometimes by putting them side by side with the expressions Hindus and Buddhists use to describe similar mystical phenomena. By 1968 such an approach to the study of Christian religious life was, to say the least, very congenial to Merton. And in *The Asian Journal of Thomas Merton* there are two quotations from Massignon's book that neatly point to the two themes of the present essay.[2]

Merton was struck by the Islamic critique of monasticism, expressed in part in the famous phrase attributed to Muhammad, "there is no monasticism in Islam" (*Essai*, pp. 145-153).[3] Early Muslim mystics had to justify their own behavior in the light of this dictum, and to explain its original import.

---

1. Louis Massignon, *Essai sur les origines du lexique technique de la mystique musulmane* (Paris: J. Vrin, 1964). Hereafter referred to in the text as *Essai*.

2. Thomas Merton, *The Asian Journal of Thomas Merton*; ed. by Naomi Burton Stone, James Laughlin & Brother Patrick Hart (New York: New Directions, 1973), pp. 263-264. Hereafter referred to in the text as *AJ*.

3. See also, for a different view, Paul Nwiya, *Exegese coranique et language mystique: nouvel essai sur le lexique technique des mystiques musulmans* (Beirut: Dar el-Machreq, 1970), pp. 55-56.

* This paper was delivered on 26 May 1989 in the session, "Merton and Islam," at the First General Meeting of The International Thomas Merton Society in Louisville, Kentucky.

They advanced in response the notion that what was wrong with Christian mysticism was, as Merton put it, the substitution of "human institutions for divine providence" (AJ, p. 263).

Here is just one example of the insightful challenge to Christian life and thought that one can find abundantly in Islamic texts. Given Merton's concern for the reform of monastic life, it is no wonder that his eye lingered long enough over Massignon's discussion of the issue in the works of early Muslim writers to mark the spot and to highlight a telling phrase or two. The issue reminds the reader of the even more far reaching critiques of Christianity one can find in Islamic texts. And the Muslim critic sometimes opens a way to a deeper appreciation of truths at the very heart of the Christian's own response to God. We shall explore below another instance in which Merton followed the guidance of Louis Massignon into just such a matter, the mystic center of the human being that Merton, following Massignon, called "le point vierge."

Another passage in Massignon's *Essai* that took Merton's attention in 1968 and caused him to reach for pen and notebook is one in which the author explained his approach to the study of the early Muslim mystics. He was after "experiential knowledge," he said, by an "introspective method" that seeks to examine "each conscience 'by transparency'..." The method was to search "beneath outward behavior of the person for a grace which is wholly divine" (*Essai*, p. 138; AJ, p. 263). Again, this idea struck a responsive chord in Merton. It expressed the sympathy Merton felt for Massignon himself that persisted from their first acquaintance in 1959, through Massignon's death in 1962, right up to Merton's final months in 1968.

The purpose of the present communication is twofold: to sketch the outlines of the relationship between Louis Massignon and Thomas Merton; and to give an account of the significance of Massignon's phrase, "le point vierge," which Merton found so evocative that he appropriated it for his own purposes. The emphasis here will be on Massignon, whose biography is not so well known to Americans as is Merton's. And while Merton's use of Massignon's pithy phrase "le point vierge" has received attention, its origins in the study of the martyr mystic of Islam, al-Husayn ibn Mansur al-Hallaj (d. 922), has gone unremarked for the most part.[4]

---

4. See M. Madeline Abdelnour, S.C.N., "Le Point Vierge in Thomas Merton," *Cistercian Studies* 6 (1971), pp. 153-171; Donald Grayston, *Thomas Merton: The Development of a Spiritual Theologian*; Toronto Studies in Theology, vol. 20 (New York & Toronto: Edwin Mellen Press, 1985), p. 9; Anne E. Carr, *A Search for Wisdom and Spirit: Thomas Merton's Theology of the Self* (Notre Dame, Indiana: University of Notre Dame Press, 1988), pp. 69 and 157.

I

MERTON AND MASSIGNON

Thomas Merton was known in the French Catholic intellectual circles in which Louis Massignon was a major figure for almost a decade
before they started writing to one another. In the early 1950s Merton
published several pieces in the Parisian journal, *Dieu Vivant*, on whose
editorial board Massignon served for five of the ten years of the journal's
life.[5] And even after his break with Marcel More, *Dieu Vivant's* moving
spirit, Massignon remained friends with many of the magazine's regular
contributors. One of these was Jacques Maritain, whom Merton first met in
New York in the spring of 1939, and was not to meet again until the
philosopher visited the monk at Gethsemani in 1966, although the two had
by then been in correspondence for years.[6] And it was Maritain who,
already in 1952, prompted Massignon to visit Merton when Massignon was
on a lecture tour in the United States and Canada.[7] Unfortunately, they
never met. But, as we shall see, the writings of Louis Massignon on Islam and
other subjects exerted a considerable influence on Merton's thinking in
the 1960s. And throughout 1960 they corresponded with one another on an
almost monthly basis.

It would be impossible in the small time and space available here to
provide even a quick sketch of Professor Louis Massignon (1883-1962) of the
College de France that could in any way do justice to him. Like Merton, he
was a man of many faces, to borrow Glenn Hinson's apt characterization of
the numerous roles the monk seemed to assume for the many different
people who knew him.[8] And what is more, for all their manifest differences,
there are some remarkable parallels in the biographies of Merton and
Massignon.[9] This feature of their compatibility would have appealed to

---

5. See Thomas Merton, "Le moine et le chasseur," *Dieu Vivant* 17 (1950), pp. 95-98; "Le sacrement de l'avent dans la spiritualite de saint Bernard," *Dieu Vivant* 23 (1953), pp. 23-43. See also E. Fouilloux, "Une vision eschatologique du christianisme: *Dieu Vivant* (1945-1955)," *Revue d'Histoire de l'Eglise de France* 57 (1971), pp. 47-72.

6. Michael Mott, *The Seven Mountains of Thomas Merton* (Boston: Houghton Mifflin, 1984), pp. 121-122, 461. Hereafter referred to in the text as *Mott*.

7. Letter of Massignon to Merton, 3 September 1959, Thomas Merton Studies Center, Bellarmine College, Louisville, Kentucky. Hereafter referred to as *TMSC*.

8. See E. Glenn Hinson, "Merton's Many Faces," *Religion in Life* 42 (1973), pp. 153-167.

9. A. H. Cutler called attention to the parallels in an appendix to his English translation of Giulio Basetti-Sani, *Louis Massignon (1883-1962): Prophet of Inter-Religious Reconciliation* (Chicago: Franciscan Herald Press, 1974), pp. 170-177.

Massignon, who was very interested in biography, and liked to plot on the graph of history and current events what he called the "curve of life" of persons whose stories attracted his attention for one reason or another.[10]

A — MASSIGNON'S "CURVE OF LIFE"[11]

Louis Massignon was the son of an artist, a sculptor, who was an agnostic, but his mother was a Catholic, and she reared Louis in the pious style conventional among her kind in nineteenth century France. This is an important item in Massignon's story, one that will have a strong effect at a later turning point in his life. Meanwhile, the father too was a strong influence, playing no small role in encouraging his son's academic career. Furthermore, it was the senior Massignon's network of friends among artists and writers that brought about Louis Massignon's meeting with the convert-novelist Joris Karl Huysmans (1848-1907) in 1900. Although the meeting was brief, even fleeting, the young Massignon appealed to the novelist, and the memory and influence of Huysmans remained with Massignon for the rest of his life.[12]

Massignon's first substantive academic project took him to North Africa in 1904 to investigate the terrain in Morocco described by Leo Africanus in the sixteenth century. This enterprise led him to write an appreciative letter, and to send a copy of his thesis on Leo's geographical work to the earlier explorer of the Sahara, Charles de Foucauld, who was then living as a hermit in the desert regions of the southern Sahara.[13] And the hermit became a major formative influence in Massignon's spiritual development.

---

10. Massignon discussed his idea of the "curve of life" in the context of other major premises of his work in the preface to the new edition of his major life's work that was published only after his death. See Louis Massignon, *La passion de Husayn ibn Mansur Hallaj* (Paris: Gallimard, 1975), I: 26-31.

11. Among the available biographies of Louis Massignon one might note the following: Jean Morillon, *Massignon* (Paris: Editions Classiques du XXe siecle, 1964); *Massignon* (ed. by J.-F. Six), Cahier de l'Herne (Paris: l'Herne, 1970); Vincent Monteil, *Le Linceul de feu* (Paris: Vega, 1987) — hereafter referred to in the text as *Monteil*. In English there is available the book by Basetti-Sani cited in note # 9 above. The best biographical sketch of Massignon in English is by Herbert Mason in the "Foreword" to his translation of *La passion de Hallaj*: Louis Massignon, *The Passion of al-Hallaj: Mystic and Martyr of Islam* (Princeton: Princeton University Press, 1982), I: xix-xliii — hereafter referred to in the text as *Passion*.

12. See Robert Baldrick, *The Life of J.-K. Huysmans* (Oxford: Clarendon Press, 1955), pp. 286-287. See also B. Beaumont, *The Road from Decadence: From Brothel to Cloister, Selected Letters of J. K. Huysmans* (Columbus, Ohio: Ohio State University Press, 1989).

13. For an orientation to the life and work of Charles de Foucauld, see R. Aubert, "Charles de Foucauld," in the *Dictionnaire d'Histoire et de Geographie Ecclesiastique* (Paris: Letouzey et Ane, 1971), XVIII: cols. 1394-1402. See also D. Massignon, "La Rencontre de Charles de Foucauld et de Louis Massignon d'apres leur correspondance," and J.-F. Six, "Massignon et Foucauld," in *Presence de Louis Massignon: hommages et temoignages*; ed. by D. Massignon (Paris: Maisonneve et Larose, 1987), pp. 184-191, 201-206.

Difficulties on his North African journey prompted Massignon to master the Arabic language, both the classical tongue and the modern spoken dialects. Eventual success in this purpose led him to Cairo for further studies in 1906. While there he made the acquaintance of yet another spiritual giant. This time the person was long dead, having been executed for blasphemy in the year 922 A. D. He was a Muslim mystic, whose life and teachings it would become Massignon's vocation to explore and to make known not only in the world of Western scholarship, but among Muslims as well. His name was al-Husayn ibn Mansur al-Hallaj (858-922). Eventually Massignon's study of this holy man was published in 1922 as his doctoral dissertation, under the title *La Passion de Husayn ibn Mansur Hallaj: martyr mystique de l'islam*.[14] It became a landmark book that was almost singlehandedly responsible for arousing scholarly interest in the west in Sufism and Islamic mysticism. It would be impossible to overstate the book's importance and influence. There were repercussions even in Roman Catholic theology, in that Massignon's advocacy of al-Hallaj's cause raised the question of the recognition of genuine mysticism beyond the church's formal boundaries.[15]

Long before the publication of *The Passion of al-Hallaj*, there were dramatic changes in Massignon's personal life. While on an archaeological expedition in Iraq in 1908, he became entangled in a skein of dramatic circumstances that disoriented him to the point of attempted suicide. But in these very circumstances, Massignon himself had a mystical experience, an encounter with God, with "the Stranger," as he often said, after the manner of Abraham in the story of the visit of the three angels at Mamre, recounted in Genesis XVIII. This experience issued in Massignon's conversion from agnosticism, and a certain moral libertinism, to the Catholicism of his upbringing.[16] He attributed his conversion to the intercessory prayers of his mother, Joris Karl Huysmans, Charles de Foucauld, and to the advocacy of al-Hallaj. Thereafter Massignon lived an intense religious life, supported

---

14. Louis Massignon, *La Passion d'al-Hosayn-ibn Mansour al-Hallaj, martyr mystique de l'islam* (Paris: Geunther, 1922), 2 volumes. Massignon continued to work on a new edition of this book until he died *in medias res* in 1962. After his death, the new edition was assembled by a group of scholars working together with Massignon family members and friends. Louis Massignon, *La Passion de Husayn ibn Mansur Hallaj, martyr mystique de l'islam*; 2nd ed. (Paris: Gallimard, 1975), 4 volumes. The new edition was translated into English by Herbert Mason: *Louis Massignon, The Passion of al-Hallaj: Mystic and Martyr of Islam* (Princeton: Princeton University Press, 1982), 4 volumes.

15. Massignon was pleased by the judgments expressed by J. Marechal, *Etude sur la pschologie des mystiques* (Paris: Desclee de Brouwer, 1937), II: 487-531. See also L. Massignon, "Mystique musulmane et mystique chretienne au moyen age," *Opera Minora*, II: 470-484.

16. See the discussion by Daniel Massignon, "Le Voyage en Mesopotamie et la conversion de Louis Massignon en 1908," *Islamochristiana* 14 (1988), pp. 127-199. Hereafter referred to in the text as *Mesopotamie*.

by a rather strict Roman Catholic orthodoxy, purified, as he believed, by the sharp religious challenge of Islam. He recognized in Islam a genuine heritage from the kindred and ancestral faith of Abraham. And on this foundation he built his lifelong campaign for better mutual relationships between Christians and Muslims.[17] The fruit of his efforts is to be seen in the eirenic references to Muslims in the Vatican II documents, *Lumen Gentiuum* and *Nostra Aetate*, as well as in the ecumenical efforts of the present day Secretariat for Non-Christian Religions and of the Pontifical Institute for Arabic Studies in Rome.[18]

After his conversion, Massignon continued his scholarly career. He married in 1914, after some hesitation over the possibility of a religious vocation. After the First World War, because of his Arabic skills, Massignon assumed a role in behalf of France comparable to that of T. E. Lawrence for England in the Sykes-Picot accords in Syria/Palestine in 1917-1919.[19] All the while he continued both his scholarly and religious interests. In the years 1924-1928, he played a major role in promoting interest in the ideals of Charles de Foucauld, including the publication of the latter's rule for religious life, *The Directory*.[20] In 1931, Massignon became a third-order Franciscan, and on the occasion of taking the habit, he also assumed the religious name "Abraham." He professed his private vows in 1932. Meanwhile, in 1931 in Paris Massignon had met Mohandas Gandhi, in whom he recognized a kindred, genuinely spiritual man. In the struggles of the Algerian War, Massignon adopted the non-violent confrontation methods of Gandhi to protest the human rights violations of the French government.[21]

In 1934, Louis Massignon, together with his longtime friend and associate in Cairo, Mary Kahil, founded a religious movement dedicated to prayer and fasting on the part of Arabophone Christians, in behalf of the Muslims under whose political control they lived.[22] The organization was called in Arabic, *al-Badaliyyah*, a word that in Massignon's use of it be-

---

17.   See the authoritative study of Massignon's religious thought in Guy Harpigny, *Islam et christianisme selon Louis Massignon*; Homo Religiosus, 6 (Louvain-la-Neuve: Centre d'Histoire des Religions, 1981). See also Maurice Borrmans, "Louis Massignon, temoin du dialogue islamo-chretien," *Euntes Docete* 37 (1984), pp. 383-401.

18.   See Robert Caspar, "La vision de l'islam chez L. Massignon et son influence sur l'eglise," in *Massignon*; ed. by J.-F. Six (Paris: Cahier de l'Herne, 1970), pp. 126-147.

19.   See Albert Hourani, "T. E. Lawrence and Louis Massignon," *Times Literary Supplement* 188 (8 July 1983), pp. 733-734.

20.   See D. Massignon, "La rencontre de Charles de Foucauld," p. 191.

21.   See Camille Drevet, *Massignon et Gandhi, la contagion de la verite* (Paris: Le Cerf, 1967).

22.   See *Louis Massignon, l'hospitalite sacree*; ed. by Jacques Keryell (Paris: Nouvelle Cite, 1987). This volume includes selections from the letters of Massignon to Mary Kahil, along with many documents from the foundation of the Badaliyyah. Hereafter referred to in the text as *L'hospitalite*.

speaks a form of mystical substitution of one person and his merits and prayers for the salvation of someone else. The doctrine of mystical substitution was very prominent in the works of late nineteenth century French writers, especially J. K. Huysmans, who had a considerable influence on Massignon.[23] What is more, Massignon found the doctrine in the thought of al-Hallaj. So it became the focus of his efforts to bring real fasting, prayer, and religious dedication to the joint Christian/ Muslim effort to bring about mutual trust and fidelity between Christians and Muslims.[24] In Cairo the *Badaliyyah* movement had a center for its activities run by Mary Kahil, under the name *Dar as-Salam*. There were meetings, prayers, conferences, discussions and fasts held under its auspices. The center also published the bulletin, *al-Badaliya*, as well as a more formal periodical, *Mardis de Dar as-Salam*. In later years Massignon arranged for copies of these publications to be sent to Thomas Merton.[25]

The better to align himself with other Arabophone Christians, particularly those living in the Islamic world, Massignon received in 1949 the permission of Pope Pius XII to transfer his allegiance from the Latin rite to the Greek Catholic Melkite rite. In 1950, with the tacit permission of the Vatican and the full cooperation of Patriarch Maximos IV, Massignon was ordained a priest in the Melkite rite. To offer the eucharistic liturgy was for Massignon the perfect way to integrate his personal act of mystical substitution for others with Christ's own gratuitous act of vicarious suffering in substitution for the whole of sinful humanity.

In his scholarly career, Massignon never missed an opportunity to integrate his researches with the aims and purposes of his religious apostolate. A case in point is the work he did to search out all he could discover about the early Christian devotion to the Seven Sleepers of Ephesus. According to their story, they slept concealed in a cave through centuries of the persecution of Christians by the Roman authorities, until the Empire itself became Christian and they awoke to testify to the resurrection of justice. Their cult was popular among Christians in the East from the fifth century onward. What attracted Massignon to their story was the fact that it also appears in the *Qur'an*, in a chapter (or *surah*, XVIII) that Muslims recite

---

23.   See the relevant chapter in Richard Griffiths, *The Reactionary Revolution: The Catholic Revival in French Literature* (London: Constable, 1966), pp. 149-222. It is noteworthy that Louis Massignon is one of the three people to whose memory the author dedicates his work.

24.   See Guy Harpigny, "Louis Massignon, l'hospitalite et la visitation de l'etranger," *Recherches de Science Religieuse* 75 (1987), pp. 39-64. See also his *Islam et christianisme*, pp. 161-191.

25.   Massignon requested Fr. Joachim Moubarac to send copies of the *Mardis de Dar el Salam* to Merton. Letter of Massignon to Merton, 2 August 1960, TMSC.

every Friday, the day of their communal assembly. So both Muslims and Christians are devotees of the cult of the Seven Sleepers, and crowds of them come to pay their respects at the shrine of the Sleepers in Ephesus to this very day. Massignon bent every effort to trace the devotion in Christian piety. And in his own native Brittany he found a church dedicated to them at Vieux-Marche near Plouaret, where he often led pilgrimages of Christians and Muslims together, especially in his later years when he was protesting French atrocities in the Algerian War.[26]

From 1953 until his death in 1962, Louis Massignon was engaged in active resistance to the war by every non-violent means at his disposal, in public and in private. His antiwar activities earned him both respect and obloquy, as one might expect. It is important to observe that for Massignon it was not only pacifism and non-violence that motivated him. The Algerian War was a conflict between Muslims and Christians, people who are brothers and sisters in the faith of Abraham whom love and hospitality should bring together. Most painful to Massignon was France's own broken word to the Muslims. To resist the war, to give aid to its victims was a religious act for Louis Massignon, and every demonstration or "sit-in" where he appeared was an occasion to practice the mystical substitution that was at the heart of his devotional life.[27]

Throughout his career Massignon remained very much the French academic, the professor of the College de France. His scholarly work was enormously influential. And in this role he was almost another *persona*. It is no exaggeration to say that he was among the twentieth century's most important Orientalists, especially in the area of the study of Islamic mysticism and sociology.[28] To this day many academics find it almost impossible to reconcile the two sides of the man, the indefatigable researcher, and the passionate believer, a confessor of the faith.[29] But they were the same man. Massignon was that rarity in the modern world, a truly saintly scholar.

---

26.   See L. Massignon, "Les 'Sept Dormants', apocalypse de l'islam," and "Le culte liturgique et populaire des VII dormants martyrs de'Ephese (ahl al-kahf): trait d'union orient-occident entre l'islam et la chretiente," in L. Massignon, *Opera Minora* (Beyrouth: Dar al-Maaref, 1963), III: 104-180. In the latter article Massignon collected, among many other items, prayers from the liturgies of the "Seven Sleepers." Thomas Merton called his attention to prayers composed by St. Peter Damian. See "Le culte liturgique," p. 180. Massignon asked Merton for this information in his letter of 16 May 1960, TMSC.

27.   See especially the relevant chapters in Monteil, *Le Linceul de feu.*

28.   See Jean-Jacques Waardenburg, *L'Islam dans le miroir de l'occident* (Paris: Mouton, 1963). Massignon is one of the major figures to the study of whose scholarship this book is devoted. See also J.-J. Waardenburg, "L. Massignon's Study of Religion and Islam: An Essay a propos of his *Opera Minora*," *Oriens* 21-22 (1968-1969), pp. 135-158.

29.   See Edward W. Said, "Islam, the Philological Vocation, and French Culture: Renan and Massignon," in *Islamic Studies: A Tradition and Its Problems*; ed. by M. H. Kerr (Malibu, California: Undena, 1980), pp. 53-72; Julian Baldick, "Massignon: Man of Opposites," *Religious Studies* 23 (1987), pp. 29-39.

Massignon's bibliography as a scholar is an impressive one. To read down the list of his publications, books, articles, lectures, and reviews, is to see first-hand how broad his interests were.[30] It would be out of place even to attempt to sketch the profile of his output here. Suffice it to call attention to two collections of articles and essays that, in addition to his scholarly books, present the essential Massignon to the reading public. The first and most important of them is called *Parole donnee*, a collection that Massignon himself supervised, but which appeared only after his death.[31] The pieces included in this volume reflect the whole spectrum of his interests, both religious and scholarly. From the perusal of them one truly gets a sense of the man. What is more, Massignon himself was virtually responsible for the interviews with the author that introduce the book and that are ascribed to the editor, Vincent-Mansour Monteil (*Monteil*, pp. 18-29). So we have for all practical purposes a self-portrait.

There are two other collections of Massignon's essays and articles to mention. The first is the three volume *Opera Minora* that Moubarac assembled and published long before Massignon's death.[32] These volumes contain more than two hundred Massignon pieces, many of which are hard to find otherwise since they appeared originally in little known or no longer existent journals. And finally one must mention the recent publication of a selection of Massignon's most important essays in English translation.[33] This volume should go a long way toward bringing the personal side of Louis Massignon more to the attention of Americans than has hitherto been the case. It is somehow not surprising that long before the translations, it was Thomas Merton who knew and spoke of Massignon to the American reading public.

B - MASSIGNON AND MERTON IN CORRESPONDENCE

In the mid-1960s it must have brought a wry smile to Merton's lips to

---

30. See Youakim Moubarac, *L'Oeuvre de Louis Massignon*; Pentalogie Islamo-Chretienne I (Beyrouth: Editions du Cenacle Libanais, 1972-1973). It is interesting to note that in an epilogue to this volume, Moubarac has published the original English and a French translation of Thomas Merton's poem, "The Night of Destiny," pp. 204-207.

31. Louis Massignon, *Parole donnee: precede d'entretiens avec Vincent-Mansour Monteil* (Paris: Julliard, 1962). The book has appeared in two subsequent publications: Paris: Coll. de poche 10/18, 1970; and Paris: Le Seuil, 1983. Hereafter referred to in the text as *Parole*.

32. Louis Massignon, *Opera Minora*; ed. by Y. Moubarac (Beyrouth: Dar al-Maaref, 1963; Paris: Presses Universitaires de France, 1969).

33. *Testimonies and Reflections: Essays of Louis Massignon*; ed. by Herbert Mason (Notre Dame, Indiana: University of Notre Dame Press, 1989).

read in his personal copy of *Parole donnee* what Massignon wrote in 1949 about Trappist asceticism. In that year, when *The Seven Storey Mountain* was holding up the Trappist way of life to Americans as a beacon of spiritual health for all, Massignon was maintaining that "in the face of the growing social perversity and the mystery of iniquity at the present time, the ultimate recourse of humanity is right there," in Trappist asceticism (*Parole*, p. 257). What is more, Massignon went on to say of the Trappists: "When the convents of the strict observance become weak, as we have seen in France prior to 1789 and in Russia prior to 1917, society itself falls into decay" (*Parole*, p. 259).

In context, Massignon was commending to his readers the purifying prayer and fasting that Trappist monasteries preserved in modern times from the long tradition of Christian asceticism that traced its line of descent in the West from Armand de Rance, St. Bernard and St. Benedict, all the way back to St. Augustine, St. Basil, and Pachomius. Massignon thought this was a pedigree of sanity for the modern world. He saw its effects in the lives of those who exercised the most spiritual influence on him, J. K. Huysmans, Leon Bloy, and Charles de Foucauld. So it was perhaps inevitable, given their common friends both ancient and modern, that Merton and Massignon would meet, if only by correspondence.

Jacques Maritain had urged Massignon to visit Merton in 1952.[34] But the two men did not in fact meet until the summer of 1959, and then it was only by letter. The person who brought them together was a young American writer, Herbert Mason, who was in Paris for research interests of his own in 1959. He wrote to Merton on 21 May 1959 in connection with his work on St. John of the Cross. And it was not long before Merton and Mason were exchanging letters and poems on a regular basis.[35] In a letter dated 2 August 1959 Mason told Merton about his own enchantment with Louis Massignon and presumably sent him an offprint of one of Massignon's articles on the "Seven Sleepers of Ephesus."[36] For by the end of the month Merton wrote Mason to say: "One of the most fascinating things I have had my hands on in a long time is that offprint of Louis Massignon about the Seven Sleepers" (*Memoir*, pp. 117-118). And in the meantime Merton had sent a reprint of his Pasternak article to Paris. In a letter of 31

---

34. Massignon to Merton, 3 September 1959, *TMSC*.

35. See Herbert Mason, *Memoir of a Friend: Louis Massignon* (Notre Dame, Indiana: University of Notre Dame Press, 1988), pp. 62-63. Hereafter referred to in the text as *Memoir*.

36. Mason's letters to Merton are in the archives of the *TMSC*.

August 1959 Mason mentions receiving it and promises to show it to Massignon. By 3 September 1959 Massignon himself is writing to Merton to thank him for the "Pasternak," and with this letter the Merton-Massignon correspondence began.[37]

In the archives of the Thomas Merton Studies Center there are fourteen letters from Louis Massignon to Merton, written in English, and dating from 3 September 1959 to 26 April 1961. They are brief letters for the most part, but they reveal much about the two correspondents. It is clear that they are both searching for holiness, and they are both convinced that their search for it must include some attempt to address themselves to the evils of their own societies. By this time Massignon was actively engaged in his protests against the atrocities of the Algerian War. On 2 August 1960 he explained his ideas about civil disobedience to Merton: "Peace could not be gained by rich means, but through the outlawed, and it was required of us 'to assume their condition' (spiritually I mean), in 'substitution' as our dear Lord did in Gethsemani."[38]

In this brief paragraph Massignon neatly put a practical point on one of his most cherished convictions, the notion of "mystical substitution," an idea that he had spent a good deal of time expounding in his writings over the years. It is not unlikely that Massignon's thinking on this point had an effect on Merton. Already in a letter to Mason, dated 3 September 1959, the same day of Massignon's first Merton letter, Merton wrote: "I want to say how deeply moved I am at this idea of Louis Massignon's that salvation is coming from the most afflicted and despised. This of course is the only idea that makes any sense in our time" (*Memoir*, pp. 122-123).

By spring of the following year, Merton in Gethsemani was fasting in solidarity with Massignon's political actions on behalf of the afflicted and despised North Africans in Paris. On 21 April 1960, Merton wrote to Jean Danielou:

> Louis Massignon strikes me as a grand person. He has been writing about all the causes in which he is interested and I am going to try and do a little praying and fasting in union with him on the 30th of the month when there is to be a demonstration outside Vincennes prison — even Gabriel Marcel participating. This is one way in which I can legitimately unite myself to the *temoignage* and work of my brothers outside the monastery.[39]

---

37. Merton wrote two pieces on Pasternak in 1959. See *The Literary Essays of Thomas Merton*; ed. by Brother Patrick Hart (New York: New Directions, 1981), pp. 37-83.

38. Massignon to Merton, 2 August 1960, TMSC.

39. Thomas Merton, *The Hidden Ground of Love: Letters on Religious Experience and Social Concerns*; ed. by William H. Shannon (New York: Farrar, Straus & Giroux, 1985), p. 134. Hereafter referred to in the text as *HGL*.

There are other issues in the correspondence that were of more interest to Massignon than they were to Merton. One of them is Massignon's devotion to St. Charles Lwanga and his companions, young Christian men of the royal court of Uganda who in 1886 forfeited their lives rather than renounce Christianity or yield to the sexual requirements of their nominally Muslim ruler.[40] Immoral sexual practices in Christian societies, and even in the priesthood, were of great concern to Massignon. He told Merton in a letter of 30 April 1960 that he had spoken of his concern about these matters to Pope Pius XII in 1946. Now he wanted Merton to help him find out whether or not there was a Trappist monastery in Uganda or neighboring parts of Africa, where prayers and fasting would be offered in solidarity with the sacrifices of Charles Lwanga and his companions.[41] Such an interest was typical of Massignon. It reminds one that for Massignon himself, and for his spiritual friends such as Huysmans, Bloy and de Foucauld, not to mention Merton, Trappist discipline had been their own means of conversion from lives in which incontinence had been a debilitating factor (*Mesopotamie*, p. 189).

One result of the exchange of letters between Merton and Massignon was their widening network of mutual friends. A notable instance is Massignon's encouragement of the Pakistani Ch. Abdul Aziz to write to Merton on 1 November 1960. Merton replied on 17 November 1960, and so there began a correspondence that was to continue until 1968, and one in which Merton revealed much of his inner life in contrast to his usual reticence about his personal religious practices (*HGL*, pp. 43-67). On 31 December 1960, Massignon wrote to Merton to say: "Ch. Abdul Aziz (he is the son of a converted Hindoo) wrote mé [of his] joy to come in touch with you. He is a *believer* in Abraham's God without restriction."[42]

Merton and Massignon continued to correspond until 1961. And Merton mentioned Massignon with some awe in letters he wrote to other people. But Massignon died on 31 October 1962, thus bringing to an end their correspondence. Nevertheless, there were still Massignon's numer-

---

40. On Charles Lwanga and his companion martyrs, see the documents in the *Acta Apostolicae Sedis* 56 (1964), pp. 901-912.

41. Massignon to Merton, 30 April 1960; July 1960. On 3 April Massignon sent Merton a prayer card dedicated to Charles Lwanga and companions. On 3 June 1960, Merton said Mass "for Louis Massignon and for his project for African boys, under the patronage of Blessed Charles Lwanga. I happened in a curious and almost arbitrary manner to pick June 3d, and only today did I discover by accident that June 3d is the Feast of the Uganda Martyrs." Thomas Merton, *Conjectures of a Guilty Bystander* (Garden City, New York: Doubleday Image Books, 1968), p. 144; hereafter referred to in the text as *CGB*. We know the date from Merton's letter to Mason on 1 June 1960 (*Memoir*, p. 158).

42. Massignon to Merton, 31 December 1960, *TMSC*.

ous articles and books. Merton was reading them up until and even during his journey to the East.[43] They had begun to exchange books and offprints at the very beginning of their acquaintance. At that time Herbert Mason was often the go-between. After Massignon's death, he continued to be Merton's contact with the world of Louis Massignon. But already in 1959 Mason was receiving such requests as the following one from Merton: "By the way, I want to put something about Hallaj in the book I am writing, and have nothing at hand. Can you lend or send me anything?" (*Memoir*, p. 124).

By the spring of 1960 Merton had received Massignon's *Akhbar al-Hallaj* and *Diwan de al-Hallaj*. Massignon thought the former book in particular had shaken Merton, and he wrote to Mason: "Tom is not mistaken in believing that my thought can be found through the curve of my life substituted by the Hallajian thought" (*Memoir*, p. 152).[44] It was probably somewhat earlier that Merton had received a copy of *La passion d'al-Hallaj*. By August of 1960, when Herbert Mason visited Gethsemani, Merton had already read much of it and, as Mason says: "Hallaj and M[assignon] himself struck him deeply as 'knowing the way.' I think Merton sensed M[assignon] was spiritually revolutionary for future Islamic/Christian influences."[45]

It was al-Hallaj, the Muslim mystic, who had fired Massignon's enthusiasm and who played a role in his conversion back to his own ancestral Roman Catholicism. Hallaj the Muslim showed him the way back to God. This was the point that struck Merton: the fact that a compassionate encounter with another, a seeker of the God of Abraham in another tradition, could open a way for one to reach God in one's own heart. The challenge of Islam then meant a challenge to open oneself to the "Other." This was the challenge of *La passion d'al-Hallaj* for Merton, as Herbert Mason reports it: "Merton told me himself of the far-reaching effect this book had on his life, coming at a particularly critical moment for him, in helping turn his attention toward the East."[46]

Merton also had a copy of Massignon's *La parole donnee*, the collection of essays Massignon himself chose to represent the spectrum of his thought, although it was published posthumously. The copy is now in the

---

43. Merton dedicated his next published book: "*In memoriam*: Louis Massignon 1883-1962." Thomas Merton, *Life and Holiness* (New York: Herder & Herder, 1963).

44. There is a copy of Massignon's *Akhbar al-Hallaj* in the "Marginalia Section" at the *TMSC*. Unlike the copy of *Parole donnee*, however, the only other Massignon title in the collection, there are no reader's marks by Merton in the *Akhbar*.

45. Herbert Mason to Sidney H. Griffith, 21 October 1988.

46. Herbert Mason, "Merton and Massignon," *Muslim World* 59 (1969), p. 317. Hereafter referred to in the text as *Mason*.

collection of the Thomas Merton Studies Center at Bellarmine. In certain sections of the book Merton marked passages that particularly appealed to him, especially in the essays on Foucauld, al-Hallaj, and Gandhi, although there are marks scattered throughout the book, indicating a relatively thorough reading. It is clear that reading Massignon did not restrict Merton to Islam. In a letter to James Forest on 20 May 1964, a single sentence makes the point: "I am reading some fantastic stuff on Islam by Louis Massignon, and Buddhist books which I now have to review for [a] magazine of the Order" (*HGL*, p. 280).

So it is clear that the Merton/ Massignon correspondence was a fruitful one. Each one of them gave his impression of the other man to yet other correspondents. Merton had sent some of his poems to Massignon, who spoke of them to Herbert Mason, saying: "[H]e couldn't judge the verses' merit but they showed he was a poet rather than a dry theologian" (*Memoir*, p. 143). This was a mark of respect on Massignon's part, who had a dim view of merely academic theologians. As for Merton, he wrote of his respect for Massignon in a letter to Abdul Aziz, just about two months after Massignon's death:

> The departure of Louis Massignon is a great and regrettable loss. He was a man of great comprehension and I was happy to have been numbered among his friends, for this meant entering into an almost prophetic world, in which he habitually moved. It seems to me that mutual comprehension between Christians and Moslems is something of very vital importance today, and unfortunately it is rare and uncertain, or else subjected to the vagaries of politics. I am touched at the deep respect and understanding which so many Moslems had for him, indeed they understood him perhaps better than many Christians. (*HGL*, p. 53)[47]

II

LE POINT VIERGE

Conjectures of a Guilty Bystander, published in 1966, is the book in which one finds the most explicit published trace of Merton's colloquy with Louis Massignon. This is not surprising since he compiled *Conjectures* from notes, correspondence and reading from the previous decade (*Mott*, pp. 429, 631, n. 470).[48] He had been in correspondence with Massignon

---

47. Merton himself published this letter in "Letters in a Time of Crisis," *Seeds of Destruction* (New York: Farrar, Straus & Cudahy, 1964), no. 27, "To a Moslem," pp. 300-302.

48. William H. Shannon, "Thomas Merton and the Living Tradition of Faith," in *The Merton Annual 1*; ed. by R. E. Daggy et al. (New York: AMS Press, 1988), pp. 90-93. Hereafter referred to in the text as *Shannon*.

throughout 1960, and he was reading and marking books by Massignon well into 1964, as we have seen. And in *Conjectures* the passage that most commentators cite as evidence of Merton's debt to Massignon is the following one:

> Massignon has some deeply moving pages in the *Mardis de Dar-es-Salam*: About the desert, the tears of Agar, the Muslims, the *"point vierge"* of the spirit, the center of our nothingness where, in apparent despair, one meets God — and is found completely in His mercy. (*CGB*, p. 151)

One must hasten to point out that contrary to what one sometimes reads, *Les Mardis de Dar-es-Salam* is not the title of a book by Louis Massignon, but the name of the periodical edited by him and published in Paris and Cairo under the auspices of the *Badaliyyah* movement.[49] In 1960, Massignon arranged for copies of the journal to be sent to Merton.[50] And in the volume for 1958-1959, there is an article by Massignon on the subjects Merton mentions in the quotation from *Conjectures*.[51] The phrase, *"le point vierge,"* duly appears in the article, but Massignon uses it only in passing here, and one must look elsewhere in his writings to learn what it really means.[52] Clearly, the phrase caught Merton's fancy when he had read it in this place and elsewhere in pieces by Massignon.[53] The vague reference to *Mardis de Dar-es-Salam* must then have been simply the closest reference to hand when Merton made the note that appears in *Conjectures*. For he clearly understood the deeper significance of the phrase, and it will repay one to see how Massignon himself used it before returning to Merton's appropriation of it for his own purposes.

In the sense in which Massignon employed the phrase *le point vierge*, it has its roots in the mystical psychology of Islam, especially as one finds it in the thought of the martyr-mystic, al-Husayn ibn Mansur al-Hallaj, to the study of whom Massignon dedicated so much of his scholarship. Massignon was fond of quoting a saying of al-Hallaj to the effect that "our hearts are a virgin that God's truth alone opens."[54] To understand the saying,

---

49. See the citations in n. 4 above.

50. Massignon to Merton, 2 August 1960, *TMSC*.

51. Louis Massignon, "Foucauld au desert: devant le Dieu d'Abraham, Agar et Ismael," *Les Mardis de Dar-es-Salam* (1958-1959), pp. 57-71. The article is reprinted in *Opera Minora*, III: 772-784.

52. In context, Massignon is speaking of the training both he and Foucauld had received to gather intelligence in North Africa for the sake of the government's military purpose there, a purpose that Massignon now said he thought of "comme d'un 'viol du point vierge' des Musulmans." Massignon, "Foucauld au desert," p. 59; *Opera Minora*, III: 774.

53. Merton marked and underlined the phrase when he read it in his copy of Massignon's essay on Gandhi in *Parole*, p. 132.

54. He quotes it in this form in a letter to Mary Kahil, 26 March 1948, *L'hospitalite*, letter 134, p. 249. As we shall see below, Massignon quotes this saying in several forms.

one must know how al-Hallaj thought of the mysticism of the heart. Massignon offered the following explanation:

> Hallajian psychology . . . allows man the guiding rule and basic unity of an immaterial principle: *qalb*, heart, or *ruh*, spirit . . . . How does man bring about the purification of his heart? Hallaj retains the vocabulary of previous mystics who, preoccupied with their asceticism, subdivided and parceled out the heart into successive "boxes," running the risk of confounding it and destroying it with its "veils" out of desire to reach beyond it to God. Hallaj retains and expands the Qur'anic notion that the heart is the organ prepared by God for contemplation. The function cannot be exercised without the organ. Thus, if he mentions the successive coverings of the heart, he does so without stopping at them . . . At the end, he declares mystical union to be real; far from being the total disappearance of the heart, . . . it is its sanctifying resurrection . . . . The final covering of the heart . . . is the *sirr*, the latent personality, the implicit consciousness, the deep subconscious, the secret cell walled up` [and hidden] to every creature, the "inviolate virgin." The latent personality of man remains unformed until God visits the *sirr*, and as long as neither angel nor man divines it. (*Passion*, vol. III, pp. 17-19)

This long quotation from *La passion d'al-Hallaj* has been necessary for it to become clear that for al-Hallaj and for Massignon, "the virgin" is the innermost, secret heart (*as-sirr*) — the deep subconscious of a person. It is to this heart that the saying of al-Hallaj applies: "Our hearts, in their secrecy, are a virgin alone, where no dreamer's dream penetrates . . . the heart where the presence of the Lord alone penetrates, there to be conceived."[55]

If the innermost heart is "the virgin," the other term in the phrase we are investigating, "the point," puts one in mind of "the primordial point" (*an-nuqtah al-asliyyah*) of which al-Hallaj and other Muslin mystics often speak. It is the apophatic point of the mystic's deep knowledge of God.[56] So the "virgin point," *le point vierge*, in Massignon's parlance, is by analogy the last, irreducible, secret center of the heart. The phrase used in this way begins to appear in Massignon's writing in the 1940s, where he uses it even to express a profoundly Christian sentiment. For example, at Christmas 1948, he wrote to Mary Kahil:

> The return to our origin, to the beginning of our adoption — by re-entering our Mother's womb, as our Lord told Nicodemus, to be born again — by finding again at the bottom of our heart, the virgin point (*le point vierge*) of our election to Christianity and the action of God's will in us. (*L'hospitalite*, p. 257)

---

55. For this form of al-Hallaj's saying, see Louis Massignon, "Le 'couer' (*al-qalb*) dans la priere et la meditation musulmanes," in *Le Coeur; Les etudes carmelitaines* (Paris: Desclee de Brouwer, 1950, p. 97. Massignon's article is reprinted in *Opera Minora*, II: 428-433.

56. Louis Massignon, *Kitab al-Tawasin par abou al-Moghith al Hosayn ibn Mansour al-Hallaj* (Paris: Paul Geuthner, 1913), pp. 196-197.

Perhaps the clearest expression Massignon was to give to what he meant by the phrase *le point vierge* came in an essay he published in 1957, in comparing Muslim and Christian mysticism in the Middle Ages. He wrote:

> The "science of hearts," the early nucleus of the methodological traits of mysticism in Islam, began with the identifying of anomalies in the spiritual life of the believer who prays, who must be simple and naked; the early technical terms served to designate the errors of judgment, the mental pretences, the hypocrisies, . . . The "heart" designates the incessant oscillation of the human will which beats like the pulse under the impulse of various passions, an impulse which must be stabilized by the Essential Desire, one single God. Introspection must guide us to tear through the concentric "veils" which ensheathe the heart, and hide from us the virginal point (*le point vierge*), the secret (*sirr*) wherein God manifests Himself.[57]

Having found this felicitous phrase well apt to evoke al-Hallaj's thoughts about the meeting place of God and man in the human heart, Massignon used it often in other contexts. Presuming its primary sense in al-Hallaj's mystical psychology, Massignon then borrowed the phrase, so to speak, to give sharper focus to the discussion of other issues. For example, he spoke of the faith of Abraham as the very axis of Islamic teaching, the "true virgin point (*point vierge*) that is found at its center, that makes it live and by which all the rest is sustained invisibly and mysteriously."[58] And in the passage to which Merton referred in the article in *Les Mardis de Dar-es-Salam*, the "virgin point" is the manly honor of the Muslims, expressed in the rules of sacred hospitality, that by 1960 Massignon was prepared to say he and Foucauld had raped by their "rage laique de comprendre, de conquerir, de posseder" before the First World War (*L'hospitalite*, p. 155, n. 73).

Massignon's friends also adopted the phrase. In a letter to Merton, Herbert Mason wrote: "More and more I understand the visiting of prisons; for once the soul has been dragged out to its virginal point by the sharpest sin, as a friend here said," grace may enter in.[59] The friend was most probably Massignon himself. And it was in offering praise to Massignon's memory that Fr. Georges Anawati, O.P., used the phrase in a way that recalls its true mystical meaning. He spoke of Massignon's own personal ability to

---

57. Herbert Mason, *Testimonies and Reflections*, p. 127. For the original see Louis Massignon, "Mystique musulmane et mystique chretienne au moyen age," in *Orient e Occidente nel Medioevo* (Rome: Accademie Nazionale, 1957), pp. 20-35. The piece is reprinted in *Opera Minora*, II: 470-484.

58. Louis Massignon to Robert Caspar, 12 November 1955, quoted in Caspar, "La vision de l'islam chez L. Massignon," p. 132.

59. Undated letter from Herbert Mason to Thomas Merton, *TMSC*. The letter must date from the second half of 1959 or the first half of 1960, when Mason was still in France.

discern the problems of other people, "to touch within them,' ' he said, "the virgin point where the conscience is affected and disarmed before the living God."[60]

Merton too found the phrase both apt and untranslatable. In view of its mystical sense, it is noteworthy that Merton chose it to help express what he had experienced on 18 March 1958, on the famous occasion of his sudden "realization" at the corner of 4th and Walnut in Louisville. He later wrote of this event in *Conjectures*, describing how he realized that "I loved all those people" crowding the center of the shopping district. And toward the end of the account he wrote:

> Then it was as if I suddenly saw the secret beauty of their hearts, the depths of their hearts where neither sin nor desire nor self-knowledge can reach, the core of their reality, the person that each one is in God's eyes . . . . Again, that expression, *le point vierge*, (I cannot translate it) comes in here. At the center of our being is a point of nothingness which is untouched by sin and by illusion, a point of pure truth, a point or spark which belongs entirely to God . . . . This little point . . . is the pure glory of God in us . . . . It is like a pure diamond, blazing with the invisible light of heaven. It is in every body. (*CGB*, pp. 156-158)

Reading this passage it is not surprising to learn that Merton was composing this section of *Conjectures* in 1965 by which time he was already steeped in Massignon's thought and had already adopted the phrase *le point vierge* as his own (*Mott*, pp. 310-311). He used it in another place in *Conjectures* in a way one cannot quite imagine finding it in something Massignon would have written, but it is true to al-Hallaj's thought. Merton wrote:

> The first chirps of the waking day birds mark the *"point vierge"* of the dawn under a sky as yet without real light, a moment of awe and inexpressible innocence, when the Father in perfect silence opens their eyes. They begin to speak to Him, not with fluent song, but with an awakening question that is their dawn state, their state at the *"point vierge."* Their condition asks if it is time for them to "be." He answers "yes." Then, they one by one wake up, and become birds. (*CGB*, p. 131)

The phrase lingered in Merton's thoughts and appeared later in another published piece as a theme in variation. In *The Asian Journal* one finds the following statement about the contemplative life:

> It should create a new experience of time, not as stopgap, stillness, but as *"temps vierge"* — not a blank to be filled or an untouched space to be conquered and violated, but a space which can enjoy its own potentialities and hopes — and its own presence to itself. One's own time. (*AJ*, p. 112)

---

60. Quoted by Jacques Jomier, "Le centenaire de la naissance du professeur Louis Massignon, sa celebration au Caire (11-12 octobre 1983)," *Islamochristiana* 10 (1984), p. 43.

To follow the trail of a single catchy phrase in Merton's work shows the searcher how inventive a writer he was. It is clear that he met and communicated well with such an idiosyncratic thinker as was Massignon. But Massignon was only one of many persons whose works Merton read, with whom he corresponded, and whose happier phrases he made his own. He was truly a man of many faces. But Massignon was not wrong to have thought "he was a poet rather than a dry theologian."

III

THE CHALLENGE OF ISLAM

One thing Massignon and Merton surely had in common was an interest in other people, both in the present and in the historical past. Both of them conducted a vast correspondence with like-minded persons around the world, and both of them spent an enormous amount of their time in research in works written by scholars and saints, not only from the past, but from several religious traditions, not to mention numerous language communities. What is more, this interest in persons, in biography one might say, was not just a passing fancy. For both Merton and Massignon understood that their own access to God ran through the hearts of other people. In the first place, of course, there is the heart of the incarnate Son of God to lead one into the depths of the divine. But for both Merton and Massignon, in addition to their faith in Jesus Christ, their encounters with other people who had met God were also of great moment. And nowhere was this more the case than in their encounters with people of other religions. For both of them, other religions were other people, and not just sets of other doctrines.

It was through Massignon initially that Merton came to know Muslims, Islam, and something of the Sufi mystical tradition. Massignon put Merton into touch with Abdul Aziz, the Pakistani scholar of Islamic mysticism, who was the person who elicited from Merton the clearest description we have of his own prayer practices (*HGL*, pp. 63-64). But it was not Islam that was the other religion which most enticed Merton. Taoism and Zen Buddhism probably enchanted him more. Nevertheless, there are those who believe that it was Massignon's relationship with al-Hallaj and his evocation of the Muslim's life of holiness that helped Merton to see the powerful force of the other, the religious stranger, as one who can kindle one's own fires anew (*Mason*, p. 317).

Massignon was fond of saying in so many words that it was not he who possessed al-Hallaj, but al-Hallaj who had co-opted him. The Muslim mystic captured his fancy when he was a young man still living a life of incontinence, and still an unbeliever. Al-Hallaj was present to him at his conversion, and remained the focus of his life work in the scholarly world. In his religious life he wrestled not only with questions of vocation and holiness, but with how to find a place for al-Hallaj with him in his Catholic life.[61] On his death bed he was still exhorting his friends to do whatever they could do to make al-Hallaj better known in the world.[62]

Massignon's personal relationship with al-Hallaj brought him to the very heart, one might say *le point vierge* of the Muslim world. With al-Hallaj he encountered Muhammad, who was caught up with a word of God he was compelled to recite. The *Qur'an*, coming to the Arabic-speaking world by way of Muhammad's experience of God, brings one face to face with Abraham, his concubine Hagar, his son Ishmael, who were also recipients of God's blessing and promise. Massignon had the sense of a deep personal relationship with Abraham and, as we have seen, took his name when he became a third order Franciscan. He informed Merton of this fact in his second letter to him, dated 9 September 1959.[63] Of Massignon's relationship with Abraham, one modern historian of religion has written: "In short, it seems to us that for him the religion of Abraham was the "natural religion," or the nature of religion; mysticism is its essence, and sacrifice is its end."[64]

Massignon brought all of his personal relationships somehow back to Abraham: al-Hallaj, Muhammad, the Seven Sleepers, St. Francis, Huysmans, Bloy, de Foucauld, Gandhi.[65] And it is in this context too that one sees how the religious values of "substitution" and "compassion" functioned for him.[66] "Substitution" is personal. It requires meeting another person in what Catholics would call the communion of saints. It involves carrying one another's burdens, putting oneself in another's place, accepting another's help. Within the embrace of the immortal communion of the saints, such a

---

61. See the very revealing letters in *Paul Claudel / Louis Massignon (1908-1914)*; ed. by Michel Malicet; Les grandes correspondences (Paris: Desclee de Brouwer, 1973).

62. See Louis Gardet, "Esquisse de quelques themes majeurs," in *Massignon*; ed. Six, p. 78.

63. Louis Massignon to Thomas Merton, 9 September 1959, *TMSC*.

64. Jacques Waardenburg, "regards de phenomenologie religieuse," in *Massignon*; ed. Six, p. 148.

65. See especially Louis Massignon, "Les trois prieres d'Abraham, Pere de tous les croyants," *Parole*, pp. 257-272; English translation in Mason, *Testimonies and Reflections*, pp. 3-20.

66. On these themes see especially J.-F. Six, "De la priere et de la substitution a la compassion et l'action," in *Presence de Louis Massignon*; ed. D. Massignon, pp. 155-166.

personal encounter is a mystical experience. One might say the same thing for "compassion." For Massignon, "compassion" meant getting it right, feeling the other person's predicament to the point that it provokes oneself to action. Massignon's own action in the last years of his life consisted in prayer, fasting, public demonstration and civil disobedience in behalf of the victims of the Algerian War. The supreme model for Massignon, the one to whom Abraham points, is, of course, Jesus the Christ, God Incarnate.

It is at this point that Massignon meets the challenge of Islam. In a letter to Merton, Herbert Mason once wrote that Massignon used to say that communism is a "cross examination of Christianity."[67] One can say much the same for Islam on the religious level, especially in reference to the testimony of the truth about Jesus Christ. For Muhammad and the *Qur'an*, Jesus, Mary's son, is but a man, a messenger of God. In terms of Massignon's thought, it is instructive to observe the role he sees for al-Hallaj in this regard: "Muhammad halted at the threshold of the divine fire, not daring 'to become' the Burning Bush of Moses; Hallaj took his place out of love."[68]

But Islam's challenge to Christians still stands. In this regard Massignon was struck by what happened on one occasion when a body of Christians came from the old Arabian city of Najran to meet Muhammad at Medinah. The *Qur'an* only alludes to that event, but Islamic tradition has it that on that occasion Muhammad proposed an ordeal by fire to test who was telling the truth about God and Jesus the Christ, with the Christians themselves and Muhammad and his family ready to be holocaust victims. The Christians withdrew from the challenge on that occasion (*Parole*, pp. 147-167). But for Massignon the challenge still stands. He noted that in November 1219, at Damietta, St. Francis of Assisi stood to the challenge on the Christians' behalf once again, in the presence of the Muslim Sultan. They let him go, and he returned to Italy to receive the stigmata. But in our own day, the same challenge is still before us.[69]

Massignon, together with his friend Mary Kahil, formed the *Bada-liyyah* as a way in which Arabophone Christians might themselves accept the Islamic challenge — to put oneself in the place of the other and to take the consequences. He once tried to explain his actions in one of his letters to Merton:

---

67. Herbert Mason to Thomas Merton, no date, *TMSC*.
68. Quoted in Six, "De la priere," p. 156.
69. See Louis Massignon, "Mystique musulmane et mystique chretienne," *Opera Minora*, II: 483-484.

> My case is not to be imitated; I made a duel with our Lord, and having
> been an outlaw (against nature in love), against Law (substituted to Mos-
> lems), and Hierarchy . . . (leaving my native proud Latin community for a
> despised, bribed and insignificant Greek Catholic Melkite church), I die
> lonely in my family, for whom I am a bore . . . . I am a gloomy scoundrel.[70]

This is not a statement of despair, but a summary statement of his own
situation, as Massignon saw himself. It was all part of the price of putting
himself in the other's place, following al-Hallaj, J. K. Huysmans, — Jesus
Himself. It was his way of facing the challenge of Islam.

As for doctrine, Massignon was convinced that contrary to much
Christian polemic against the Muslims, Muhammad was a prophet, a negative prophet he used to say, summoned to challenge the Christians and
other religious people to the truth of the natural religion of Abraham, and
to warn them away from their moral errors. As for the *Qur'an*, it points to
Christ for Massignon. But it is a revealed scripture only in terms of the truth
it contains. He called it "an Arabic edition of the Bible with a conditional
authority" — conditional because in the end it excludes the full revelation
of Jesus the Christ in the Gospel and in the Church.[71]

From Massignon's perspective, Islam and Islamic mysticism, encountering the God of Abraham, pose a challenge for purity of heart to Christians. In concrete terms, Sufism poses this challenge to Christian monasticism. Perhaps that is why in Merton's case he began, in 1967 and 1968,
reading steadily in Islamic literature and giving lectures to the monks at
Gethsemani on Sufism (*HGL*, p. 97). And it is why he was still reading
Massignon and wondering about the Islamic view of Christian monasticism
on his Asian journey. Merton finally thought he understood it this way:

> The Moslem interpretation of this: that Allah did not prescribe the monas-
> tic life but some disciples of Jesus invented it, with its obligations, and
> once they accepted its obligations they were bound to them in His sight.
> The moral being: how much more will He require others to keep what He
> has prescribed. (*AJ*, p. 264).

This is the point at which we began to follow the course of the Merton/
Massignon correspondence. It is a good point at which to bring it to a close.
Their dialogue was a fruitful one. It continued past the point of no return
for both of them.

---

70. Louis Massignon to Thomas Merton, 31 December 1960, *TMSC*.

71. See M. Hayek, "Louis Massignon face a l'islam," in *Massignon*; ed. Six, pp. 188-199' Martin Sabanegh,
"Le cheminement exemplaire d'un savant et d'un chretien a la recontre de l'islam," in *Presence de Louis
Massignon*; ed. D. Massignon, ppp. 113-128. On these subjects, see some of the ideas of Massignon in Giulio
Basetti-Sani, *The Koran in the Light of Christ: An Interpretation of the Sacred Book of Islam* (Chicago:
Franciscan Herald Press, 1977).

St John
Baptist

MERTON AND THE REAL POETS:

Paradise Re-Bugged

by **Michael W. Higgins**

In a letter to his friend W. H. "Ping" Ferry, dated 14 September 1967, Merton observes, vis-a-vis the copy of the David Jones *Agenda* "Ping" has sent him: "As I told you, I did not know him at all. This has me felled. It is just what I have looked for so long: better than Bunting. With Jones, Bunting and Zukofsky we have the real poets and I wonder where they have been hidden."[1] Characteristically, Merton responds to his friend's generous gift with his usual mixture of intense interest, wonder, and hyberbole. How seriously do we take him?

The beginning of Merton's interest in Louis Zukofsky appears to be dated 20 July 1966; and his interest in Basil Bunting is first recorded in the *Restricted Journals* shortly after that. Michael Mott notes: "Merton first mentions Basil Bunting: RJ, Oct. 16, 1966. The previous day he had found Bunting's work at the University of Louisville Library, 'very fine, tough, Northumbrian, Newcastle stuff of the Kingdom of Caedmon'."[2] His interest in Jones was dependent only in part on Ferry, for he had in the person of A. M. Allchin not only a keen admirer of Jones's fully Catholic genius, but the individual who would introduce him to many fine Welsh poets, including the estimable Ronald Stuart Thomas. Merton writes to Allchin on 16 June 1967: "R. S. Thomas is for me a marvelous discovery. A poet like Muir,

---

1. Thomas Merton, *Letters from Tom: A Selection of Letters from Father Thomas Merton, Monk of Gethsemani, to W. H. Ferry, 1961-1968*; ed. by W. H. Ferry (Scarsdale, New York: Fort Hill Press, 1984), p. 61. Hereafter referred to in the text as *Ferry*.

2. Michael Mott, *The Seven Mountains of Thomas Merton* (Boston: Houghton Mifflin, 1984), p. 640.

* This paper was delivered on 26 May 1989 in the session, "Merton and Poetry," at the First General Meeting of The International Thomas Merton Society in Louisville, Kentucky.

perhaps better than Muir, with such a powerful spirit and experience, so well conveyed. I must try to write something on him: is there anything about his life, or who he is?"[3]

And so we have it — new models, new voices. It would be futile, however, to argue that the evolution of Merton's poetics was profoundly affected by his discovery of Jones and Thomas, but it is important to note the points of convergence, the shared sensibility, the common vision. With Zukofsky there is a healthy interchange of ideas, and a correspondence that underlines a mutual aesthetics. Bunting, like Edwin Muir, reminds Merton of the centrality of the particular, of the concrete, of the individual in the mass age. What he writes of Muir in his essay, "The True Legendary Sound: The Poetry and Criticism of Edwin Muir," is as true of Bunting as it is of himself:

> The power of the poet's imaginative vision (in which of course the reader can participate) is that it directs our eye to beings in such a way as to "*feel the full weight and uniqueness of their lives.*" Here as a matter of fact the poet has a prerogative which the speculative and abstract metaphysician might be tempted to deny him out of envy: the power to see being *in the concrete* and not by pure abstraction; to see it in its *individual actualization* — and even to express it as its concreteness. Both the vision and the expression of the individual evade technical and discursive ontology.[4]

Their common dread of theorizing — of the powers of abstraction and generalizing — which prevents the imagination from seeing being both "in the concrete" and in its "individual actualization" is a dread, an abhorrence, rooted in Blake, Merton's *magister spiritus.*

For the purpose of this article, however, I would like to concentrate mainly on Zukofsky and his cosmology, with some attention to the significance of Jones and Thomas for the theme of unity and sapiential vision. Zukofsky's cosmology is paradisal, Franciscan, and Blakean. His poetry, as a consequence, is celebrative, vital, and wholistic. In his review-article on Zukofsky's *All: The Collected Short Poems, 1956-1964* (first published in *The Critic* under the title "Paradise Bugged" in February-March 1967, and subsequently re-titled "Louis Zukofsky — The Paradise Ear"), Merton argues that "all really valid poetry . . . is a kind of recovery of paradise," that the paradise poet effects a renewal of vision through a new poetics, a new art, a new form. "Here the world gets another chance."

---

3. Thomas Merton, *The Hidden Ground of Love: Letters on Religious Experience and Social Concerns;* ed. by William H. Shannon (New York: Farrar, Straus & Giroux, 1985), p. 28.

4. Thomas Merton, *The Literary Essays of Thomas Merton;* ed. by Brother Patrick Hart (New York: New Directions, 1981), p. 34. Hereafter referred to in the text as *LE.*

And the world needs another chance. In various of his critical essays and prose poems Merton sounded the alarm bell, the *tuba mirum*, announcing Death's ruthless hegemony. Only the poets can successfully resist the blandishments, the allure, of Death's clever minions — technology, advertising, corporate and political power. The poets must obey life

> and the Spirit of Life that calls us to be poets .... In the Republic of Plato there was already no place for poets and musicians, still less for dervishes and monks. As for the technological Platos who think they now run the world we live in, they imagine they can tempt us with banalities and abstractions. But we can elude them merely by stepping into the Heraklitean river which is never crossed twice.
>
> When the poet puts his foot in that ever-moving river, poetry itself is born out of the flashing water. In that unique instant, the truth is manifest to all who are able to receive it .... Come, dervishes: here is the water of life. Dance in it.[5]

These passages were addressed to a gathering of Latin American poets in Mexico City in 1964, and they underscore the importance Merton attached to Latin American verse, in sharp contrast with the deadly, self-preoccupied, and sterile poetry emanating from the United States. In "Prologo," a prose poem dedicated to Ludovico Silva, Merton sarcastically reminds us that "we must continue to taste the lamentable experience of those in whom death has failed, O twenty poets, O ten poets, O five poets, O Ludovico Silva and Ernesto Cardenal."[6]

The poet is the celebrant of life in the theater of death. The poet must disclose the holy at the heart of the mundane.

> In the Kingdom of Death the poet is condemned to sing that in the midst of death he, the unsuccessful, remains in the midst of life. All the others are embalmed in the vast whispering perfumed cybernetic silence of the millenium of death. (*CP*, p. 743)

And for Merton it is the Portuguese and Spanish-speaking poets of Latin America to whom one turns to hear the sounds of life, the promise of Eden; to these poets and a few others scattered throughout the Kingdom of Death, principal among whom is Louis Zukofsky.

In a letter to Zukofsky dated 11 March 1967, Merton speaks of the poet's "A" 7 as a Easter fugue, "with the kind of secularity that is in Bach," and goes on to speak of the resurrection reality that authentic art is all about: "the victory over death." "This is the real witness to the world and

---

5. Thomas Merton, "Message to Poets," in *Raids on the Unspeakable* (New York: New Directions, 1966), pp. 160-161.

6. Thomas Merton, "Prologo," in *The Collected Poems of Thomas Merton* (New York: New Directions, 1977), p. 744. Hereafter referred to in the text as *CP*.

you are the one who is saying it most clearly: which is probably one reason why as yet too few have heard it."[7]

Zukofsky's poetry is a sustained revelry in the particular, a celebration as Zukofsky would have it of "Shakespeare's clear physical eye against the erring brain," and a forceful repudiation of the tyranny of abstraction:

> *Out of deep need*
> Four trombones and the organ in the nave
> A torch surged-
> Timed the theme Bach's name,
> Dark, larch and ridge, night:
> From my body to other bodies
> Angels and bastards interchangeably
> Who had better sing and tell stories
> Before all will be abstracted.[8]

Zukofsky's cosmology of love rejects nothing as alien. As Merton notes in his review-article on Zukofsky:

> Franciscan, he knows that only when you accept the whole thing will evil be reduced to the last place in it . . . . Zukofsky's poems are about this wholeness, therefore they spring from a ground of immense silence and love which extends beyond them infinitely in all directions. (*LE*, p. 131)

The particular; the child; the angel; paradise; Blake — this is Zukofsky's cosmology and it is that of Merton's *Cables to the Ace.*

Cables to the Ace underscores Merton's cosmic eschatology. The cables are "cosmic cables without interception" sent to those who can see, for "It is written: 'To see the world in a grain of sand'" (Cable 4). Only those truly liberated from a "narrowing of vision, a foreclosure of experience" can understand the necessity for a "new form of theological understanding." Like Blake, Merton worked for the dethronement of Urizen or Nobodaddy, the permanent casting out of the devils of a secular logic, law, and generalization from the spiritual and unimaginative life, the creative revitalizing of the tension of separation (the latter being the legacy of the Fall), and the redeeming of the Contraries or "the marriage of heaven and hell." Of the Contraries Merton observes, in his "Blake and the New Theology":

> True holiness and redemption, for Blake, lie in the energy that springs from the reunion of Contraries. But the Negation [Urizen, the "Abstract objecting power that Negatives everything" (*Jerusalem*)] stands between the Contraries and prevents their "marriage." Holding heaven and hell apart, Urizen infects them both with his own sickness and nothingness. True holiness, faith, vision, Christianity, must therefore subvert his power

---

7.   Thomas Merton Studies Center, Bellarmine College, Louisville, Kentucky. Hereafter referred to in the text as *TMSC*.

8.   Louis Zukofsky, *"A" 1 - 12* (Garden City, New York: Doubleday & Company, 1967), p. 132.

to Negate and "redeem the contraries" in mercy, pity, peace. The work of
this reversal is the epiphany of God in Man. (*LE*), pp. 7)

But this reversal of the power of Urizen, of a fallen history, though it be seen
in the epiphany of the Incarnate Word, must not be seen as occurring
outside human history and consequently succumbing again to the abstract
reasoning of Urizen. The radical reversal of fallen history requires not only
the acceptance of the Fall as an ontological fact but an acceptance of the
world as the geography of redemption:

> A reading of Blake's Prophetic Books will show clearly enough how radical
> is the reversal . . . . The reversal comes from within history accepted, in its
> often shattering reality, as the focus of salvation and epiphany. It is not that
> the world of Auschwitz, Vietnam and the Bomb has to be cursed and
> repudiated . . : [rather] that very world has to be accepted as the terrain of
> the triumph of love . . . .[9]

For the world to be seen as "the terrain of the triumph of love" there must
be something other than the apocalyptic fire that razes. There must be the
fire that cleanses, transmutes, and restores: "Learn to love the fire. The
alchemical fire of transmutation . . . . The apocalyptic fire: 'Meditate on the
make-believe world as burning to ashes, and become *being above
human*'."[10] In Cable 82, a powerfully Blakean poem, Merton has St. Theresa
of the Heart victimized by the servants of Urizen who seek to constrain pure
vision within the walls of reason:

> And the prelates, mayors, and confessors wanted the doors
>   closed.
> The tongue of her heart, they said, must proffer insults to
>   the vision
> So they built four walls of cold rain around the vision.

Theresa alone, however, "pierced by a thousand needles of fire," trans-
forms herself into a dove that flies "into the fiery center of the vision" while
the "prelates, mayors, and confessors" wrap their minds "in the folds of the
black storm." Determined to resist the declaimers of passion, affection, and
imagination, Theresa, mystic and visionary, knows true vision in the burning of the world, an apocalypse of love. She sees with the eye of love, the
Spiritual Eye or Divine Vision, and all is burnt up in a glance. As Blake says in
his conclusion to "A Vision of the Last Judgement":

> Error is Created. Truth is Eternal. Error, or Creation, will be Burned up, &
> then, & not till Then, Truth or Eternity will appear. It is Burnt up the

---

9. Thomas Merton, "The Death of God and the End of History," in *Faith and Violence* (Notre Dame, Indiana: University of Notre Dame Press, 1968), p. 258.

10. Norman O. Brown, *Love's Body* (New York: Vintage Booka, 1966), pp. 178-179.

> Moment Men cease to behold it. I assert for My Self that I do not behold
> the outward Creation & that to me it is hindrance & not Action; it is as the
> Dirt upon my feet, No part of Me. "What," it will be Question'd, "When
> the Sun rises, do you not see a round disk of fire somewhat like a Guinea?"
> O no, no, I see an Innumerable company of the Heavenly host crying
> "Holy, Holy, Holy is the Lord God Almighty." I question not my Corporeal
> or Vegetative Eye any more than I would Question a Window concerning
> a Sight. I look thro' it & not with it.[11]

Although one looks *through* the corporeal eye and observes the ruin and
misery of matter one does not *see* with this eye but with the eye of
Imagination. In an instant, Error (Auschwitz, Vietnam, etc.) is burnt up for
there is only Truth, the "terrain of the triumph of love."

It is similarly not with the corporeal but with the spiritual eye that
one sees angels. For Blake, who had commerce with them often and not
only as a child, angels are holier than men and devils "because they do not
Expect Holiness from one another , but from God only." For Merton, angels
are "heavenly departures" who accompany him "through the shivering
scrap-towns" (Cable 77). For Blake they are the host of systematic religion
but for Merton, "an entire sensate parcel / Of registered earth" (77), they
are "nine fond harmonies" that "never leave me alone":

> For Merton the angels are the "farmers of the mind." He says "they walk
> with me" and although he denies "word magic . . . an impurity of lan-
> guage," the angels are
>> The midnight express
>> Bringing Plato, Prophets, Milton, Blake,
>> The nine daughters of memory.   (Cable 83)
> They are the *Sanctus* sound, the solemn music of creativity, "the abyss of
> brass, the sapphire orchestra," that accompanies the emerging image into
> consciousness:
>> Bear the hot
>> Well-fired shot
>> Roaring out
>> Of the cool-dark   (83)
> Angels for Blake and Merton are part of their vision and not only a
> sacramental metaphor. They exist because they are seen by intuition. It is
> the language of Zen that they speak and not that of the *Cogito*.[12]

And it is with the spiritual eye that one will see paradise in the very midst of
the "burning garden;" one will discover Christ coursing "through the
ruins," "speaking to the sacred trees," and know

> The Lord of History
> Weeps into the fire   (Cable 80)

---

11.   William Blake, *Complete Writings* (London: Oxford University Press, 1969), p. 617.

12.   See Michael W. Higgins, "A Study of the Influence of William Blake on Thomas Merton," *American Benedictine Review* 25: 3 (1974), p. 382.

The poet will recover paradise because he loves, because his heart is "pierced by a thousand needles of fire." In Cable 74 Merton the poet/lover rejects the allure of an unsuitable romanticism:

> O God do I have to be Wordsworth
> Striding on the Blue Fells
> With a lake for sale and Lucy
> Locked in the hole of my camera?

and declares that

> I am sustained
> By ravens only and by the fancies
> Of female benefactors

Although the poet is nurtured "by the fancies / Of female benefactors," these benefactors are in fact emanations from the one female, Sophia / Virgin / Urthona, the love of whom is paradise. To see paradise, to know wisdom, one must love and wait for the *point vierge*, "that moment of awe and inexpressible innocence." The "unspeakable secret," this "ace of freedoms," is the poet's discovery, the full perfection of which means death. In a powerfully Jungian and prophetic conclusion to Cable 74 Merton speaks of the mandala, the ancient symbol of integration and fulfillment, in connection with the "distant country" of his approaching death:

> Better to study the germinating waters of my wood
> And know this fever: or die in a distant country
> Having become a pure cone
> Or turn to my eastern abstinence
> With that old inscrutable love cry
> And describe a perfect circle

Before the poet's annihilation by Wisdom, an experience which he describes as "a perfect circle," "having become a pure cone," he assists in the recovery of paradise through his poetry — the language of his vision, the sacrament of his "discovery" — freeing Imagination from the shackles of Urizenic perception. Authentic paradisal poetry explores new possibilities through a daring revitalization of idea, word, and sound and, in his antipoetic epics, Merton attempts to give "the world another chance." In doing this, *Cables to the Ace* qualifies by Merton's own definition as truly "valid poetry." In his Louis Zukofsky piece, Merton justifies his own Blakean purpose as a poet:

> . . . (poetry that is fully alive, and asserts its reality by its power to generate imaginative life) is a kind of recovery of paradise. Not that the poet comes up with a report that he, an unusual man, has found his own way back into Eden; but the living line and the generative association, the new sound, the music, the structure, are somehow grounded in a renewal of vision and hearing so that he who reads and understands recognizes that here is

> a new start, a new creation. Here the world gets another chance. Here
> man, here the reader gets another chance. Here man, here the reader
> discovers himself getting another start in life, in hope, in imagination, and
> why? Hard to say, but probably because the language itself is getting
> another chance, through the innocence, the tenacity, the good faith, the
> honest senses of the workman poet. (*LE*, p. 128)

Merton's "own way back into Eden" is like Blake's, through the
imagination, the spiritual eye, perpetually recovering in verse the *point
vierge* — the paradisal moment. Zukofsky, the paradise poet, attends to
reality. "Here is an unspeakable secret: paradise is all around us and we do
not understand. It is wide open. The sword is taken away, but we do not
know it . . . . "Wisdom," cries the dawn deacon, but we do not attend."[13]

Zukofsky does attend, to the particular, the minute, the forgotten,
the commonplace.

> Each poem is very much the same question, but brand new. Because here
> is a poet who has the patience and the good sense to listen. And look
> around at the Brooklyn he loves. And write a perfect poem about a dog
> looking out of a brownstone window. (*LE*, p. 133)

Merton was impressed not only by the purity and craftmanship of Zukofsky's art, but by its comprehensiveness, its epic integrity. In a letter to
Zukofsky, written on 5 April 1967, Merton comments on the Blake-like
quality of "A" 10, and observes further that: "It is true, we none of us
interpret our dream: but you do it in 'A.' It is a long, careful, valid, patient,
humble, penetrating interpretation of your dream. It helps me to interpet
my own" (*TMSC*).

And Merton *was* in the process of interpreting his own, as the
subsequent correspondence between the two clearly indicates. In a letter
to Zukofsky dated 30 August 1967, Merton inquires: "Where did you get
the Melanesian stuff?" (*TMSC*). He then proceeds to speak about his own
interest in the Cargo Cults and the work of Claude Levi-Strauss. Zukofsky
responds on 2 September 1967 that indeed the Melanesian stuff is from
Malinowski and that perhaps he should read Levi-Strauss, but then concludes with the irreverent twist: "But maybe better to leave it to chance
— as it's not *larnin* one wants however one respects it" (*TMSC*). Zukofsky
wears his erudition lightly.

He also warns the younger poet apropos the South Canto or the Cain
poem which Merton had sent him: "[I]f you're experimenting, as I'm sure
you are, pay no attention to me and find your own answer" (2 January 1968,

---

13. Thomas Merton, *Conjectures of a Guilty Bystander* (Garden City, New York: Doubleday Image
Books, 1968), p. 132. Hereafter referred to in the text as *CGB*.

TMSC). Merton accepts the advice, but only in part. He knows that the task he has set himself is fraught with risk, he knows that "the Cain poem . . . does indeed need some more work. Part of a big long mixed up thing that will come together in time, I hope. I need to soak in 'A' again and deepen my understanding of how to get at such a venture" (2 February 1968, *TMSC*).

That venture of which he speaks is *The Geography of Lograire*, which is about unity, final integration, "ingathering." It is about a spiritual locus, a spiritual rootedness. It is about a geography of the imagination, a geography of the spirit, and a geography of place. In his "The Prologue: The Endless Inscription," Merton "identifies the source of his imaginative gift: his Welsh heritage and its Celtic love for the mythical and the visionary."[14]

Merton had written before the composition of *The Geography of Lograire* of his unique bonding to Wales in *Conjectures of a Guilty Bystander*: "It is the Welsh in me that counts: that is what does the strange things, and writes the books, and drives me into the woods" (*CGB*, p. 200). A. M. Allchin remarks: "Must one not, despite Merton's reported disclaimer, see some reminiscence of the Welsh name for England, *Lloegr* (in medieval French and English *Logres*) in the title of the poem?"[15] This might suggest then that the "geography of England" might be a more accurate reading of the title than "geography of Wales." It is Wales, however, that is central to the poet's memory. It is Wales that awakens the poet to his roots. It is Wales that is the lever, the intersection where the opposites conjoin in harmony:

> Plain plan is Anglia so must angel father mother
> Wales Battle grand opposites in my blood fight hills
> Plains marshes mountains and fight
> Two seas in my self Irish and German
> Celt blood washes in twin seagreen people . . . .
>
> And another child of Wales
> Is born of sea's Celts.   (Prologue, p. 5)

But what did Wales *mean* to Merton?

> Merton was accomplishing two things: a recognition of another perennial source of his inspiration, the Welsh visionary tradition that he held in common with Henry Vaughan and Dylan Thomas, and a reaffirmation of the importance of the *cantus firmus*, the steady base or principle in one's life, revealed in the creative remaking by the imagination of the culture

---

14. See Michael W. Higgins, "The Silent One and the Poetics of Unity: Thomas Merton's Last Poem," *Gamut Three* (1983), p. 35. Hereafter referred to in the text as *Higgins*.

15. A. M. Allchin, " 'The Cloud of Witnesses': A Common Theme in Henry Vaughan and Thomas Merton," *Cistercian Studies* 2 (1976), p. 128.

> that nourishes one . . . . "The geography of Lograire" is "the geography of
> Wales," if we mean by Wales that *cantus firmus* without which the imagi-
> nation and the spirit wander directionless. In the kingdom of Wales
> Merton will unite all men in himself because he will have relived the
> history of his family: "Wales all my Wales a ship of green fires / A wall wails
> wide beside some sex / Gold stone home on Brecon hill or Tenby harbor /
> Where was Grandmother with Welsh Birds / My family ancestor the
> Lieutenant in the hated navy / From the square deck cursed / Pale eyed
> Albion without stop" (Prologue, p. 7).
>   In the poet's particular history can be found the general history of
> humanity; in the poet's personal vision can be discovered the universal
> mythdream. The poet knows, however, that "in holy green Wales there is
> never staying" and he must move on to other lands. (*Higgins*, pp. 35-36)

And Merton does "move on to other lands" surveying the legacy of Cain.

From Wales to the world, from the particular to the universal — this is
the movement of *The Geography of Lograire*. It isn't only Wales that
captures the Trappist's attention. The steady and illuminating correspondence between Allchin and Merton results, as has already been indicated,
in the discovery of R. S. Thomas and in a growing fascination with kindred
spirit David Jones. There is great affection for Jones on Allchin's part and he
writes to Merton with such an infectious zeal that Merton, none too
resistant to any kind of zeal, could hardly avoid response.

Although Allchin comes to Jones rather late, 1967 to be precise, his
enthusiasm grows quickly. Not only is he resolved to acquaint Merton with
the full range of Jones's artistic and poetic genius, he takes a personal and
solicitous interest in the aging artist's well-being. In his last letter on the
matter he remarks:

> We must talk about D. Jones. I think something from you (are there any
> copies of Cassiodorus still?), could be very important to the old man, who
> is genuinely grieved and puzzled by everything that goes on, (rather in a
> Maritain way, but without Maritain's capacity for articulating it).
>   (26 March 1968, *TMSC*)

Merton is right when he recognizes the singularity of Jones's genius,
the peculiar isolation of a writer at variance with contemporary ideologies
and fashions. Having read the complex epic, *The Anathemata*, Merton, in
the very midst of working on his own "summa of offbeat anthropology,"
writes to "Ping" Ferry:

> I have gone right into *The Anathemata* and it is a fine poem: curious from
> the Catholic viewpoint right at this time!! I hope at least one or two
> Catholics read it one of these days and keep their sense of continuity with
> the past. He says everything. And has the sap and solidity of Romanesque
> sculpture, too. (*Ferry*, p. 63)

For there to be unity, there must be continuity; for there to be
personal integration, there must be cultural integration. In describing *The*

Anathemata as a work of universal anamnesis, a work of uniting the disparate, as he does in his article "A Discovery of David Jones," Allchin could just as appropriately be describing the structure, intention, and poetic modalities of *The Geography of Lograire*.

> At first there may be only a few things which come sharply into focus. Much is unclear; there is so much detail; it is difficult to place oneself in such a rich and complex universe. The texture of the writing has as many dimensions as the reality it describes. Again, the secret is to take time. No one could hope to read these poems and understand them all at once. We have to learn not only to see what they say, but how they say it . . . . For David Jones is one who is determined to gather up the fragments so that nothing be lost, as he himself writes in one place: "Gathering all things in, twining each trussed stem to the swaying trellis of the dance, the dance about the sawn lode-stake on the hill where the hidden stillness is at the core of the struggle . . . ."[16]

Jones and Merton were engaged in a common task: reparation of our disordered vision and the healing integration of memory, holiness and communion. Their epics — complex, recondite, allusive — are sacramental, symbolic, designed

> to express and to encourage man's acceptance of his own center, his own ontological roots in a mystery of being that transcends his individual ego. But when man is reduced to his empirical self and confined within its limits, he is, so to speak, excluded from himself, cut off from his own roots, condemned to spiritual death by thirst and starvation in a wilderness of externals.[17]

For it is not only Jones who is at variance with his time.

The Welsh parson-poet, R. S. Thomas, was another of Merton's latter day finds. Allchin was singly responsible. As was so often the case, Merton's appetite for the new discovery was insatiable. Merton wanted more of Thomas's books and all the information about the poet he could get his hands on. Allchin obliged as best he could with various of his own impressions about the solitary, profoundly pastoral, and frequently melancholy Anglican priest-poet.

Allchin urged Merton to write to Thomas as he had urged him to write to Jones, but to no avail. Allchin informed Merton of Thomas's contempt for the twentieth century and for England [he is, in fact, a Welsh nationalist]:

> The only time I met him and we had a long talk, he certainly made me feel that I should be leaving the promised land and descending onto some

---

16. A. M. Allchin, *The World is a Wedding* (New York: Oxford University Press, 1978), p. 160.

17. Thomas Merton, "Symbolism: Communication or Communion?", in *Love and Living*; ed. by Naomi Burton Stone & Brother Patrick Hart (New York: Farrar, Straus & Giroux, 1979), p. 65.

pretty Sodomish kind of plain on my 150 mile drive back to Oxford . . . . But he's a very nice man; gloomy, with a great craggy face, and all the sensitive perception that you can see. One of the things that struck me was the extraordinary seriousness and workmanlike way in which he regards his own parish work. (20 July 1967, *TMSC*)

What I think Merton discovered in the poetry of R. S. Thomas was a voice not unlike his own: sapiential, pastoral, anti-technology. Merton saw in the lacerating disclosures of Thomas's despair, in the fierce dialectic between faith and doubt, in the doomed struggle to preserve a culture's memory in the face of brutal modernization, a struggle strangely reminiscent of those cultures laid to waste by the sword and the cross of the *conquistadores* — "archaic wisdom" sundered.

I think it was the "sapiential vision" he found in the pastoral lyrics of the Welshman with a taste for Kierkegaard that most struck Merton. I am speculating only, of course. But there are enough striking resonances, convergenecs, commonalities between the two poets to suggest that had Merton lived longer, had he written on Thomas as he proposed, indeed, had they corresponded as Allchin urged, they would have discovered how much they are alike. But it was not to be.

What do I mean by their sapiential vision?

The wisdom that is sapiential is childlike; it is penetrative, immediate and unaffected. The child knows not only through the intellect but primarily through the imagination with the empathy and freedom it grants. *Sapientia* is the way of the poet, the child, the innocent dreamer, and Christ: it is the mode of knowing for the religious pastoralist, the Zen master, the visionary and the mystic. When the poet knows in the highest way and loves in the deepest way the poet has tasted the innocence of *Wisdom*.[18]

It is this sapiential vision and his Zukofskian cosmology that provide the stuff of Merton's new poetics, but only insofar as they are integrated into that mature synthesis that constitutes Merton's "Prophetic Books," his antipoetic epics, his Blakean mythdream, the map of paradise regained.

---

18. See Michael W. Higgins, "The Laboratory of the Spirit: Pastoral Vision in the Age of Technology," *Cistercian Studies* 16: 2 (1981), p. 122.

THOMAS MERTON:

THE MONK AS A CRITIC OF CULTURE

by **Lawrence S. Cunningham**

Long before his death in 1968, Thomas Merton exercised an enormous influence on the Catholic life of this country. As his letters, now in the process of publication, attest, that influence was also felt outside the American Catholic fold. When one begins to focus with precision on the character of that influence the clear lines of understanding begin to blur. He was a poet but his poetry is not decisive; he was a literary critic but one rarely finds his criticism anthologized today. His autobiographical writings from *The Seven Storey Mountain* down to the posthumous *Asian Journal* and other volumes still sell thousands of copies in a variety of languages. At least one of his books — *New Seeds of Contemplation* — has reached the status of a minor classic of the genre. He wrote on an enormous variety of topics but one is inclined to agree with the great monastic historian, Jean Leclercq, that he was a master of nothing. It is a judgment that Merton himself would not have resisted. In a 1967 letter to Rosemary Ruether, he said of himself: "I am not a pro at anything except writing. I am no theologian."[1] That such a sentiment was not false modesty is attested by the now famous chart in which he categorized his writings from "awful" to "good."[2]

Nonetheless, twenty years after his death, there is no diminution of interest in his writings and no stopping the writing about him. As I write I

---

1. Thomas Merton. *The Hidden Ground of Love: Letters on Religious Experience and Social Concerns*; ed. by William H. Shannon (New York: Farrar, Straus & Giroux, 1985), p. 510.

2. See Thomas Merton, *Honorable Reader: Reflections on My Work*; ed. by Robert E. Daggy (New York: Crossroad, 1989), pp. 150-151.

* This paper was delivered on 10 November 1988 at the conference, *Thomas Merton: Concerned Religious Writer for a Secular Society*, Oakhurst Baptist Church, Decatur, Georgia.

can hear in my inner ear the word processors clacking as graduate students, admirers, and professors spin out yet another volume which, inevitably, will end up on my already overloaded Merton bookshelf. Tellingly enough, I await those volumes with anticipation just as I look forward to the volumes of Merton's own writings which are, as it were, waiting in the wings to be launched out on a public life of their own.

My first acquaintance with Thomas Merton came in the early 1950s when I was barely in high school. A next door neighbor lent me a copy of *The Seven Storey Mountain*. I must have been about fourteen at the time but I can still recall — born and bred of a Catholic though I was — the somewhat ominous photographs of the Trappist monks with their shaved heads and peaked hoods. For my high school graduation I received a copy of *The Sign of Jonas*. By that time I was so hooked that I think I can now say of Thomas Merton what the great fifteenth century humanist Pico della Mirandola said of all books: that I have read everything Merton has written which has been published.

But let me go back to the question I have already raised: what is the character of Thomas Merton's influence? Not, surely, because of the sustained power of all that writing since, as Merton himself realized, there is a good deal of dross among the gold. Not, equally, for the judicious balance of his insights because, as Michael Mott shows in his acclaimed biography, he could be irritatingly apodictic in his enthusiasms or naive in his judgments. Nor, finally, because of the systematic beauty of his thought because his thought was not systematic and, in a sense, was not thought at all if one means by "thought" an organized body of reflection. He was not, in short, a Karl Barth (who, incidentally, died on the same day in the same year as Merton) about whom Merton cunningly dreamed in the opening pages of *Conjectures of a Guilty Bystander*.

Let me tell you how I came to understand how one might approach the mystery of Merton's influence.

A few years ago Trappist author Basil Pennington organized a series of papers on Thomas Merton to be read in conjunction with the annual meeting, The International Medieval Conference, which is held on the campus of Western Michigan University in Kalamazoo, Michigan.[3] The Merton sessions attracted large numbers of people who ordinarily would not attend a conference on medieval studies. A dozen or so ordinary lay

---

3.   The papers were later published in the volume *Towards an Integrated Humanity: Thomas Merton's Journey*; ed. by M. Basil Pennington, O.C.S.O. (Kalamazoo, Michigan: Cistercian Publications, 1988).

folks drove down from Canada. I met a young woman, a recent graduate from Bryn Mawr of no particular religious persuasion, who worked with the homeless and the undocumented alien population of Milwaukee. She had read Thomas Merton in college and, to the despair of her parents, decided to do something, as she told me, to "make her life add up."

That young woman is not unlike other people I know: a painter who read Merton regularly because she thirsts to be something other than simply a painter; a Jewish woman who told me that reading Merton was an anchor in her desire to live an orthodox life and keep her family orthodox in its style of life. My suspicion is that every monastic guest master or gate keeper in this country can tell similar stories. The monks at Gethsemani tell me that there is a steady stream of people who come to their doors seeking simply to visit Merton's grave or to talk with monks who knew him. Almost any book on Merton will sell modestly well and good books on Merton as well as Merton's own books sell very well indeed. Merton, a theologian once said to me, expressed modern religious longing better, and more authentically, than any other writer in this century.

Once I began to take note of this phenomenon I began to see that it was Thomas Merton *as a person* — the person, to be sure, who spoke through his writings (and the vast bulk of his writing was autobiographical but often disguised under other genres) — who exercised such a profound influence on people. Thomas Merton, in short, strikes me as a paradigmatic person not in the sense that everyone could use him as a model to emulate but because, in his life, there are clues as to how we might live and how we might view the world even when we find ourselves in circumstances quite different from his own.

We might pause at this point to note quickly what a rather unlikely model Thomas Merton is for Americans, Catholic or not. While he attained American citizenship as an adult, he was born in France to an expatriate American mother and a father who was from New Zealand. His early education was garnered from both French schools (he was bilingual) and, to his chagrin, English ones. He travelled on the continent a good deal from his youth and, due to circumstances of his home life (or lack thereof) moved across the Atlantic more than once as a child.

His first sustained encounter with American educational culture came in the 1930s in the heady atmosphere of Columbia University. In 1941, when he was in his mid twenties, Merton entered a rural Trappist mona-stery in Kentucky and, rare forays aside, remained there until his death in 1968 which occurred, almost implausibly, in Thailand. His youth was spent in restless moving but his adult years were firmly anchored in a place. From 1941 until 1968, he was a traveller of the mind with his most common mode of mental travel being the letter, the essay, the poem, and the journal. His letters reflect an enormous range of correspondents from Pope Paul VI and Nobel laureate Czeslaw Milosz to Henry Miller, Erich Fromm, and an ersatz hippie teenager in California.

Furthermore, Thomas Merton was a monk. He is inexplicable without constant reference to that fact. I have argued in print, and state once again here, that this is the key datum about him. Monasticism, a hallmark of the Catholic tradition, is not one of the primary things most Catholics think of when they consider what Catholicism means. In fact, most American Catholics probably go through life with little direct contact with monasticism. Even a comprehensive survey of American Catholic life like Jay Dolan's recent *The American Catholic Experience* spends little space on monasticism in this country. Despite that benign neglect, monasticism exercised an enormous influence on the very shape of Catholicism in everything from the liturgy and asceticism to our understanding of scriptures and the shape of our prayer. A good deal of that influence has been absorbed into Catholic life, and given the hidden style of monastic life, it is easy to overlook its influence.

It may well be — at least I will advance this argument — that it is the very marginality of the monk that provides a starting point for our reflections on the significance of Thomas Merton. It is a vantage point with which Merton himself would be sympathetic. Anyone who reads the posthumously published essays collected in his volume *Contemplation in a World of Action* will recall his repeated assertion that a monk is, by definition, a person on the margin. There is delicious irony in the fact that during the decade that made relevancy its war cry, Merton insisted repeatedly that it was irrelevancy that was central to the monk's life. He himself lived that marginality both in terms of the kind of life that he had chosen and the place where he lived out his monastic vow of stability. In fact, one can trace an arc of marginality in his own life as he moved from the energetic life of the campus of Columbia University in New York to a rural monastery in Kentucky and, from there, to the edge of the monastic enclosure and his hermitage in the woods. Each step in his maturity was, as it were, a step further away from the "center of things."

Merton was not being flatly ironic in his description of marginality. From its early beginnings in Christianity, monasticism always prized the practice of *fuga mundi* — flight from the world. This was as true of the early desert fathers and mothers as it was of the medieval Cistercians who sought out the wilder parts of France for their foundations. There is, historically, a real tension in monasticism which can be called the dialectic of the desert and the city. The weight of the tension favors the desert because history tells us that monasteries are most successful when they are away from the energetic bustle of urban life. It is a tension that has its foundational roots in that same tension of the gospels where we see the almost sacred dance of Jesus as he enters and leaves cities to spend time in desert places or mountain tops alone with Abba in prayer.

Where the paradox arises is that when monks flee the world for authentically religious reasons, the world, in time flees to them, either for spiritual counsel or to find havens of peace and recollection. What happens, in brief, is that monks exemplify certain gospel values which may be under appreciated or undervalued but which have a power to attract if they are lived out. I would make my own, in this regard, some words of the noted Yale liturgical scholar, Aidan Kavanaugh:

> Monasticism was not the creation of medieval bishops but of early Christian lay people. It flowed directly into Christian life out of Jewish prophetic asceticism which received new focus through the lens of Jesus' own teaching. One must therefore take the continuing fact of organized asceticism in Christian life as a given which provides access to whole dimensions of Christian perception and being. The existence, furthermore, of specifically monastic asceticism is a theological datum which lies close to the very nerve center of Christian origins and growth. One cannot study Christianity without taking monasticism into account. One cannot love as a Christian without practicing the gospel asceticism which monasticism is meant to exemplify and support. A Christian need not be a monk or nun, but every monk and nun is a crucial sort of Christian, and there have been too many of these people over the centuries for their witness not to have considerable theological importance.[4]

That same sentiment has been expressed more succintly in a meditative essay recently published by the Trappist monk, Matthew Kelty:

> There is no need to become a monk. It is not necessary. The reason: monastic life is not Christianity. It is rather one way of being a Christian. A very ancient way. A very good way. And a way that is of great appeal to some, even if of interest to many.[5]

How effectively monks provide this witness is not for me to judge. What does seem patent is that in every age, monks who live in the silence of their cloister and the prayerful quiet of their choir stalls suddenly "open their doors" (to use the wonderful phrase of the Russian monastic tradition)

---

4. Aidan Kavanaugh, *On Liturgical Theology* (New York: Pueblo, 1985), pp. 6-7.
5. Matthew Kelty, "The Making of a Monk," *Cistercian Studies* 23 (1988), p. 262.

to speak to the world. Thus it was that a talented literary person, seized by Christian faith, entered a monastery in 1941 and, after some years of silence, "opened his doors" through the publication of his spiritual pilgrimage which he called, using a schema from Dante's Purgatorio, *The Seven Storey Mountain*. With the publication of that book, the monk who fled the world discovered the world fleeing to him.

Why?

The reasons are most likely as various as the persons who came but, it does seem to me, that one can hazard some generalizations that would not count as being too far of the mark. In the bicentennial year of 1976 the novelist Walker Percy wrote a wonderful essay on bourbon for an issue of *Esquire* that was devoted to the celebration of Americana (e.g., baseball, mom, apple pie). In that piece Percy sums up middle American malaise: a man comes home late in the afternoon to the suburbs of anywhere. The kids look past him briefly before turning again to the cartoons. His wife gives him a distracted hello from the kitchen. He sits down, amid the smell of pot roast, to catch the evening news. He looks around and says quietly to himself: "Jesus, is this all there is?"

Percy's vignette captures in essence a general complaint common to the post-Freudian age. It manifests itself in our culture in literally thousands of ways in everything from the thirst for immortality amid the fitness crazies to the incredible growth of the therapy industry and on to the wild blue yonder of sexual revolution. Let me not overly sermonize on the point but I do want to insist that an authentic monk — of whatever religious tradition — is one answer to the question that haunts every person who is not distracted by the primordial struggle for sheer existence: who am I? and where am I going? The monk is one who engages those questions, not as philosophical conundrums, but as naked existential facts.

The thesis I would urge is that Thomas Merton advanced an answer to that question both in his life and in his writing. His answer, roughly, was something like this: we are human beings who are neither the creatures of blind destiny or of absolute autonomy. We are people whose lives have meaning and that "meaning" somehow finds itself in a connectedness with an absolute center which is called, in our culture, God but who, as the Book of Exodus makes quite clear, is beyond name.

Thomas Merton, in short, was an authentically religious person (religion: from *religare* — to be bound) who could communicate what it meant to be religious. Such persons, despite the statistics, are in short supply. If we accept that description a number of things about Thomas

Merton become clear. In the first instance, it helps us to put into some kind of order the many facets of Merton's life.

Merton as monk. We tend to think of the monk as the participant in a highly regimented form of life devoid of personal choice and personal freedom. The monastic tradition, however, argues that the monastic life is a life of freedom. It is a freely chosen way of being that says, in essence, here is how I will organize my earthly pilgrimage: as a life which will have as its fundamental focus the absolute center which is God. Peter Brown, in a number of very elegant essays, has argued that early Christian asceticism, especially sexual asceticism, was not motivated by a gnostic hatred of the body, but by a desire to exercise the freedom to refuse the biological necessity imposed by late antique culture which demanded that women bear children and men sire and sustain them. Asceticism, in short, was an alternative way of living rooted in a concept of free choice that could nay say the expectations of culture as well as the imperatives of biological destiny. Obviously, people make such choices of freedom without being monks but the point is that being a monk is one way to choose to live a life that is examined and centered. Merton chose such a life.

If we keep that point in mind then we can see that there is a kind of unity to his writing that absolves him of the charge of mere intellectual dabbling or cerebral curiosity. In fact, his disparate writings only begin to make sense when we see them in the context of this freely chosen life and its fundamental assumptions.

His long essays on Albert Camus — that Algerian ascetic, as Merton once called him — dwell almost exclusively on Camus' affirmation of integrity, purity of purpose, constant struggle, thirst for freedom, and the desire for authentic meaning — all themes that recur like a fugue in monastic writings. His studies of the fiction of Boris Pasternak emphasize what Merton calls the "sophianic criticism" of Pasternak whose world was suffused with the mystical affirmation of the Russian Christ.[6] His essay on Shaker art is drawn to the Cistercian values of simplicity, spareness, and purity just as passion for Blake centers on the white heat of Blake's imagination.[7] Again, both his longlived romance with Byzantine art (first encountered when he was still a teenager) as well as his appreciation for the gestural marks of calligraphy and the austere contentless painting of his

---

6. For the essays on Camus and Pasternak, see *The Literary Essays of Thomas Merton*; ed. by Brother Patrick Hart (New York: New Directions, 1981).

7. See Thomas Merton, "Introduction," in Edward Deming Andrews & Faith Andrews, *Religion in Wood: A Book of Shaker Furniture* (Bloomington: Indiana University Press, 1966), pp. vii-xv.

friend Ad Reinhardt were not simply enthusiasms at either end of the artistic spectrum. He loved Byzantine painting because of its symbolic power just as he loved the flat black canvasses of Reinhardt because they were congenial to his own apophatic experiences of silent prayer.[8] What, at first glance, seem like contradictory experiences are, on closer examination, simply variations on a spirituality which was common to the monastic tradition. It was all part of what Merton called "monastic culture."

What I am groping to indicate goes something like this: Thomas Merton freely chose to live a kind of life that put a high value on certain values. He absorbed those values and was able, in turn, to highlight them in a culture that had under-appreciated them. Merton spoke to a Catholicism, for example, which highly prized doing. Merton came to monastic maturity at a time of heady expansionism for the American Church. It was a time when the "beau ideal" of the Catholic clergy was Bing Crosby of *Going My Way* and *The Bells of St. Mary's* — the not overly pious, but solidly faithful cleric, who could save a parish or a school, jolly it up with his Protestant and Jewish neighbors, and demonstrate a more than competent swing at home plate. That ideal found its lay expression in the post war period in the highly mythicized portrait of John F. Kennedy: cool, ironic, worldly, and Catholic.

To that culture Merton spoke a different language. It was the language of silence, interiority, asceticism, other worldliness, prophetic resistance, and transcendence. The numbers of Catholics who tried their vocations with the Trappists of the 1940s and 1950s are small tokens of just how receptive an audience there was for such a vocabulary and the life that it promised.

We might also note that it was not only the rather restricted culture of American middle class Catholicism that was ready for these words. In the post war period, there was an artistic *avant garde* that also had counter-culture aspirations. It was more than mere rhetoric that caused Merton in the 1960s to see the monk as pursuing a life trajectory not unlike that of the Beats and, later, the Hippies. Merton's own sympathies for Eastern religions, experimental poetry, abstract art, jazz, and social protest make a lot more sense when viewed against the background of that counter-culture. In that sense, Merton's interests coincided with a deep cultural current that was abroad in the land — a current which he had encountered

---

8. See Donna Kristoff, O.S.U., " 'Light That is not Light': A Consideration of Thomas Merton and the Icon," in *The Merton Annual II* (1989), pp. 85-108 and Lawrence S. Cunningham, "The Black Painting in the Hermit Hatch: A Note on Thomas Merton and Ad Reinhardt," *Merton Seasonal* 11: 3 (Autumn 1986), pp. 10-12.

in the 1930s at Columbia where, it should be remembered, Jack Kerouac tried his hand at higher education.

Wilfrid Sheed has recently made this point with reference to Thomas Merton and that literary hermit, J. D. Salinger. Let me simply cite, in a somewhat abridged fashion, some words he wrote while reviewing Ian Hamilton's biography of Salinger:

> Merton makes an instructive parallel in several respects. *Seven Storey Mountain* came out in 1948 and *Catcher in the Rye* in 1951, and both of them took off like thunder, against all conventional expectations. The generation they spoke to would later be referred to derisively as "silent" to which it may well have answered, out of the din of promotion that followed the war, there was a lot to be silent about then; Salinger called it "phoniness" and Merton called it "worldliness," but for most young readers there was only one enemy.
>
> . . . And both, significantly, turned to Zen Buddhism among other things to soothe this torment of awareness . . . .
>
> Thomas Merton's very tone conveyed a spiritual and intellectual authority which made his divagations into orientalism sound rock solid; but Salinger in those days was still obliged to work with the cap and bells of his profession — by which I don't mean that he was funny about his Eastern discoveries, but that he was doomed to entertain whatever his subject . . . .[9]

One could argue that the counter-culture broadly conceived had strong, albeit eccentric, religious impulses. I would not wish to rehearse that argument here but I would point to the preoccupation of the Beats with the ecstatic; with the 1960s counter-culture's desire for self-transcendence; and the *avant garde*'s preoccupation with erasure and simplicity as it is manifested in everything from the minimalism of a John Cage or Samuel Beckett to the apophatic abolition of form and content in abstract expressionist art. In an influential essay on the role of silence in the *avant garde*, Susan Sontag argued a generation ago that the role of silence had its ancestral roots in a tradition of apophatic mysticism whose wellsprings are in the writings of Pseudo-Dionysius.

This is not to argue that the monastery and the counter-culture are two sides of the same coin. What the counter-culture lacked were the very elements that have kept monasticism alive over the millenia: discipline; a distrust of self-indulgence; and a positive appreciation of asceticism. During the heyday of the Flower Children I read a letter in the *Berkeley Barb* which told of a commune that dissolved because of a futile argument over who was to do the dishes after the evening meal. Who does the dishes

---

9. Wilfrid Sheed, "The Exile." Review of *In Search of J. D. Salinger*, by Ian Hamilton. *New York Review of Books* (27 October 1988), pp. 40-41.

is not a problem in monasteries. A monk does not do his thing; monasteries do *their* thing.

Merton could speak to these constituencies and, as his interest in the peace movment and the civil rights struggle intensified, increasingly did so. Anyone who has read *The Cold War Letters* — unpublished circular letters sent in mimeograph to a large number of people — cannot help but be struck by how Merton could write and talk of profoundly religious matters without relying on the explicit religious language of piety and devotion. By turns, light hearted, ironic, scathing, serious, and informative he, nonetheless, had a point of view; a place from which he wrote; and convictions that shaped what he had to say.

What he did say was not always on target. He got his news of the outside world in bits and pieces (he muses half ashamedly how he had to hide his copy of *Newsweek* lest the abbot should find it on a visit to the hermitage) and responded, at times, with instant analysis. Yet, he knew when to pull back. As a leading energizer of the 1960s peace movement, he was not slow to react when violence raised its head either as a gesture of suicide on the part of a young Catholic Worker or when he spoke to the Weathermen begging for non-violence. In the same way he could see rather quickly the ephemeral nature of much of the "Death of God" movement and was cool in his judgments about the 1960s romance with secularity. Likewise, he welcomed the renewal of the Second Vatican Council but he was not slow to criticize the more zealous activities of its less thoughtful cheerleaders.

If one were to categorize Merton in terms of his publications, we would have to say that he was a spiritual writer but we would have to understand that description in the broadest sense of the word. Pose this question to yourself: can you think of another religious writer in this century writing in English who commanded a greater and more diverse audience than Thomas Merton and whose writings and influence outlived his own life time?

To answer my question would produce a very short list, indeed. The only parallel that readily comes to mind is C. S. Lewis who, like Merton, has penned books which continue to sell in the millions; whose life is of intense interest to many people; and who has had a demonstrable influence on a whole range of people. Again, like Lewis, a whole industry ranging from the scholarly to the commercial rose up after his death to fill the insatiable need of people to identify somehow with their respective personae. When, some years ago, someone sent me a Thomas Merton desk calendar, I thought to myself: "What next? Merton T-shirts and coffee mugs?" Such excesses should not scandalize; they are predictable enough given the kind of culture in which we live. Anyone who wishes to understand what Merton stood for needs to go beyond (or under) these epiphenomena to tease out the values that he represents which make him a lodestar for others to follow. Merton is hardly alone in being ill served by his most passionate admirers.

In his biography of Thomas Aquinas, the splendid English author G. K. Chesterton said that the saint is the person who exaggerates those values which the world has forgotten. Merton was not a saint in any conventional sense of the term but he certainly enfleshes the truth of Chesterton's aphorism. He brought to the three worlds he addressed — the worlds of monasticism, the church broadly conceived, and human culture outside the previous two — the truths which he had refined in nearly thirty years of ascetic discipline and deep prayer. He did that by harnessing both his omnivorous intellectual curiosity and his disciplined life into a drive for understanding at its most profoundly human level.

A concrete example might illustrate what I have in mind. In his journal, *A Vow of Conversation*, Merton writes on 2 February 1964:

> The religious depth of Ammonas, the perspicacity of Merleau-Ponty, even the tedious subtlety of Sartre, and always the bible. Meetings of opposites, not carefully planned exclusions, not mere acceptance of the familiar. A life of clashes and discoveries, not a life of repetitions. Deep dread before God, and not trivial excitement.[10]

In those three crisp sentences Merton juxtaposes his readings in a primitive desert father, the phenomenologist Merleau-Ponty, and the philosopher-atheist Jean Paul Sartre; to which he adds the sharp stop: "and always the bible." Readers with good antennae would also pick up other allusions: the "meeting of opposites" is a possible reference to the old mystical doctrine of the *coincidentia oppositorum* while the refusal of the life of repetition and the phrase "deep dread before God" may contain an echo of Soren Kierkegaard which saturated Walker Percy's novel *The Moviegoer*, a novel Merton had just read with relish.

I cite those sources and allusions not to prove that Merton read a good deal but to show how his reading was absorbed and channeled towards an end. He was "catholic" enough to take the French moderns and the ancient ascetics, not as an amalgam, but as a holding together of

---

10. Thomas Merton, *A Vow of Conversation: Journals, 1964-1965*; ed. by Naomi Burton Stone (New York: Farrar, Straus & Giroux, 1988), p. 20. Hereafter referred to in the text as *VOW.*

tensions and insights ("clashes and discoveries") that help lift us from the trap of the accustomed to the state of being before the awe-ful otherness of God. The cluster of references in that short paragraph was not meant to express wide ranging erudition but to seek some sense of connectedness among writers who were, on the surface, quite diverse and seemingly at odds. In that sense, Merton is a truly *catholic* writer — catholic with a small "c." Any careful reader of Merton soon realizes that his serious writing needs a good deal of "unpacking" both because Merton was a poet who understood the polyvalence of language and because he had absorbed so much reading in his contemplative years in the monastery.

A decade before the journal entry cited above, Merton wrote some words on reading that well describe what it means to be a contemplative reader:

> Books can speak to us like God, like men, or like the noise of the city we live in. They speak to us like God when they bring us peace and light and fill us with silence. They speak to us like God when we desire never to leave them. They speak to us like men when we desire to hear them again. They speak to us like the noise of the city when they hold us captive by a weariness that tells us nothing, gives us no peace, and no support, nothing to remember, and yet will not let us escape.[11]

There is a further point. That drive for understanding to which I alluded above was a drive rooted in his Christian faith. Let us not forget that fact because Merton was at pains to affirm it clearly. Again, in *A Vow of Conversation*, he puts the matter bluntly:

> Here in the hermitage returning necessarily to the beginnings. I know where my beginning was: hearing the name of God and of Christ preached in Corpus Christi Church in New York. I heard and I believed. And I believe that He has called me freely, out of pure mercy, to his love and salvation. (*VOW*, p. 116)

It is well to dwell on those words and ones similar to them. The facile judgment that Merton was a syncretist or a step removed from Catholic faith does an injustice both to him as a man and, more importantly, strays away from a full appreciation of his writing. I think both judgments derive from a failure to appreciate just how unique he was as a Christian writer. He didn't always sound "Christian" in the sense that his writings were not studded with those pieties that one often identifies with Christian writing. Nor did he always sound "theological" because he did not write in the style of the theologian nor did he use its technical vocabulary or jargon. He did

---

11.   Thomas Merton, *Thoughts in Solitude* (New York: Dell, 1961), pp. 75-76. Hereafter referred to in the text as *TS*.

very much sound like those cultural critics who range over issues political, social, and literary but his criticism always had a kind of shape and heft to it that derived both from his deep faith and from the twenty-seven years of disciplined asceticism and prayer that molded his persona.

As one goes through his writings there are those almost unexpected flashes of the mystic who sees whole. It is texts like those that stand as a deep background to all of his concerns for racial justice, purity of intention in writing, peace among nations and peoples, the necessary dialogue of all religious believers, and the drive to see meaning and love in all human artifacts.

Early in his monastic life Merton learned that the monastic life could be a vehicle for values which were anti-human. He had to rethink his excessive disdain for the world; his sharp demarcation of grace and nature; his austere notion of contemplation; and so on. All students of Merton point to those shifts in his thinking whether it be on the issue of poetry versus contemplation or on his slow awareness that to be a monk did not absolve him from being a member of the commonweal. I should like to close this essay with the positive side of that learning experience, to wit: Merton's increasing conviction that he would only be a good monk and a good Christian if he learned to be a full human being; that being fully human and fully monastic was no more a paradox than being fully a spouse or parent and being fully human. Here are some words that he wrote midway in his monastic life. They remained true at the end of his life as they remain true for us today. They will serve as a coda for this paper:

> Christianity is not stoicism. The cross does not sanctify us by destroying human feeling. Detachment is not insensibility. Too many ascetics fail to become great saints precisely because their rules and ascetic practices merely deadened their humanity instead of setting it free to develop richly, in all its capacities, under the influence of grace . . . .
>
> The ascetical life, therefore, must be begun and carried on with a supreme respect for temperament, character, and emotion, and for everything that makes us human. These too are integral elements in personality and therefore in sanctity — because a saint is one whom God's love has fully developed in the likeness of his creator. (*TS*, pp. 25-27)

.

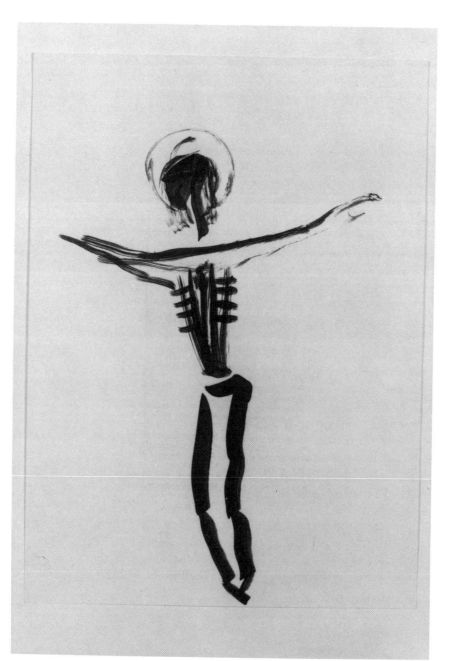

THE CHRISTIAN MYSTIC AS

paganus redevivus:

A Hermeneutical Suggestion

by **Roger J. Corless**

For some time there have been panels on East-West Mysticism at the International Congress on Medieval Studies at Western Michigan University. These panels have grown out of an attempt, inspired by Thomas Merton, to understand Christian mysticism in a worldwide context. I believe that, were Merton still living, he would be an enthusiastic supporter of and original contributor to such panels. Merton sought, in his contacts with non-Christian mystics, a vision of what mysticism was as a whole. Yet, except for some oblique and tantalizing phrases in his prose poem "Hagia Sophia," he paid very little attention to the pagan roots of Christian mysticism.[1] This essay attempts to do this, and suggests that Christian mysticism is a reclamation and enrichment of the power of its pre-Christian origins.

A STORY

My name is Margaret. You know me as Julian since I was, while on earth, an anchoress attached to the church of St. Julian in Norwich, England, during the fourteenth century of our salvation. I have come to tell you

---

1.   Thomas Merton, *The Collected Poems of Thomas Merton* (New York: New Directions, 1977), pp. 363-371. Hereafter referred to in the text as *CP*. I am indebted to Stephen Daney for drawing my attention to this important text.

*   This paper was delivered on 8 May 1989 at the *24th International Congress on Medieval Studies*, Western Michigan University, Kalamazoo, Michigan.

something of my secret thoughts. When I received my first showings from Our Lord and Saviour I was much troubled, although much delighted. It seemed to me that what He showed me was not that which Holy Church taught, and so I kept my counsel, writing only shortly and circumspectly of what I had seen. Many years later, after continued communion at the motherly breast of my Saviour, I was emboldened to write more largely and more plainly. Your clerkes have now collected both of my poor attempts and solemnly published them as the *Short Text* and the *Long Text*. Pardon me if I find myself somewhat amused by this!

Now that I have passed beyond the world of history, I know more, but I still do not know all. Some of you may think that, after having gone through the gate of death which, through the merits of Our Lord's Passion, is now the gate of eternal life, I should have come to know everything. You will even say that I wrote "suddenly our eye will be opened . . ." That is true, but to what is our eye opened? It is opened to the infinity of God! Into this infinity, this boundless ocean of love and wisdom, I continue to grow, and its end has not been shown me.

As the hands of my Lord never leave off His work, and as I am His joyful and willing servant, so I find that my own hands are commanded never to leave off the work of God until all time shall be ended. My Lord has other sheep, who are not of the fold which I knew while I was on earth, and I must assist my Lord in calling to them.

That in my Lord's showings which most delighted yet most troubled me was the absence of any showing of hell. The clerkes taught that there was hell, the Word of God spoke of it, and all around me the Black Death was raging as a living hell. How could it be that my Lord would say that hell did not exist, that the world was all good, when so much of what I heard and saw was pain, ungood and suffering?

He replied that all was good because He loved it. All that He had made was as nothing, seen in itself. The immensity of the universe was in His sight no more than a hazel nut (or, as you say in the New World, as a filbert) and, except that He loved it, it could not survive a single instant. As our brothers Thomas of Aquino and the Master Eckhart have said, we live perpetually on the brink of the abyss of non-being, and we are held in being only by the goodness of God.

I am, now, beginning to understand more of what Our Lord meant when he showed me this. Hell is division, it is separation from God. And who can separate us from God? No human nor non-human being, and no distressful thing at all, as the blessed Apostle Paul assures us. It is our own willfulness that separates us from God. All our unpeace, I have written, comes from failing of love on our part. This means, to speak plainly and without dissimulation, that hell is our own creation. When our minds are hellish, all we see, think and feel is hellish.

This is how it was during the terrible days of the Black Death. You who have to deal with the pain and fear of AIDS can only dimly, as in a mist, imagine the Black Death. Anyone, it seemed, might be struck down. We could see no reason for it. We did not know about what you call germs, and had someone suggested the flea as a cause, we would have laughed them to silence. All we could imagine was that God had turned against us, and that we needs must out from this stinking world and ascend to the world of light above. We threw ourselves on the mercy of God, and despised the world which He had created.

But I was told, amidst the screams and the stench, that all would be well, that all manner of thing would be well, that God despised nothing that He had made, and that He comes down to us in the lowest part of our need to succor us. Indeed, He is not only with us, He is under us, for He is the Ground of our beseeching.

I was shown, I now believe, the world of God as the temple of God, and mankind as its priesthood. This, therefore, I now say:

> Look within, and look without. Look very far in, and very far out. Do not stop at how you feel or how you think, nor even at how God appears in the letter of His Holy Word or the writings of the learned clerkes. Commune with Him heart to Heart. See your soul as a mirror of God the Creator of all. See His creation as His clothing, as did our brother Francis. Know that you and God are already oned in His opening, and that He has put all His creation in your soul. Your God became flesh for you. Do you become enfleshed for Him.

COMMENTARY

In the foregoing fantasy, I imagine Mother Julian (whom I pretend is called Margaret) coming to push us on, in this day and age, to a more incarnational and therefore more Christian mysticism: what Cornelia Jessey has called the prayer of *cosa* or things as distinct from the prayer of *nada* or "no-thing."[2] I will now try to present a hermeneutic of Christian mysticism in terms of this incarnational or "thingful" (*cosa*-full) perspective.

---

2. Cornelia Jessey, *The Prayer of Cosa: Praying in the Way of Francis of Assisi* (San Francisco: Harper & Row, 1985), p. 6. Hereafter referred to in the text as *Cosa*.

An Evolutionary View

The evolution of religion, still less of mysticism, is not a popular subject today. It is even embarrassing for a scholar to admit to some ideas on the subject. But, as we now seem to understand the world, evolution is a given, and it is unclear how religion, or mysticism, could escape from the theory. Perhaps we avoid the subject because the theory has been simplistically applied. Some reputable scholars of the fairly recent past argued that religion evolved as the number of gods decreased, or as it became more rational, or more like the Church of England. This is not dissimilar to Condorcet arguing that the pinnacle of the evolution of the human spirit is the French Republic. We cannot take the examples seriously, yet we need not on that account dismiss the theory itself.

A full demonstration of the fact and nature of religious evolution is well outside the scope of this essay which, as it says, is merely a suggestion. Some day (or year!) perhaps I will attempt the Hegelian (as it would literally be) task of composing a thorough proof. But let us for the moment assume that there is an evolution of religion, or of mysticism, and see what we find.

The Axial Age and World-Denial

Karl Jaspers suggested in 1948 that history had gone through a crisis which he called the Axial Age, somewhere between 800 and 200 B.C.E.[3] He noted first the extraordinary clustering of major religious figures around, especially, 600 B.C.E. Many of the major so-called "world religions" owe their origin, or their distinctive "modern" form to some teacher who lived at about that time: Confucius, Lao Tzu, Buddha, the anonymous composers of the *Upanishads*, the mysterious gentleman whom we call Second Isaiah, and the pre-Socratics (as founders, in effect, of the scientific world view). This clustering is immediately clear to the most superficial student of history, yet it is hardly ever mentioned in introductory courses in religion.

Jaspers claimed that the Axial Age was the time when *logos* took over from *mythos* and that "[m]an became aware of consciousness itself" ("Axial," p. 431, column 1). He characterized the main Axial Age vision as follows:

---

3. Karl Jaspers, "The Axial Age of Human History: A Base for the Unity of Mankind," *Commentary* 6: 5 (November 1948), pp. 430-435. Hereafter referred to in the text as "Axial."

> Imprisoned in a body fettered by passions, separated from the light and only dimly aware of himself, man longs for liberation and redemption . . . whether it is by ascent to the Idea; or in *ataraxia* — passive resignation; or by immersion in thought; or in the knowledge of himself and the world as Atman, the Universal Self; or in the experience of Nirvana; or in harmony with the Tao — the cosmic order; or in surrender to the will of God.
>
> ("Axial," p. 432, column 1)

In short, Jaspers is saying that, in the Axial Age, religion became *soteriological* in its emphasis. The world was seen as a trap, or as a prison, and means were sought to escape it.[4] This vision of the world which, when we are being rude, we may call Gnostic is what Gilbert Murray calls "the failure of nerve."[5] He observes that: "The religion of later antiquity is overpoweringly absorbed in plans of escape from the prison of the seven planets" (*Five*, p. 147). Murray says that "[w]e seem to have travelled far from the simplicity of early Greek religion" (*Five*, p. 149f). There comes into being "what seems to us such a commonplace truism, the difference between Man and God" with a consequent movement "away from the outer world towards the world of the soul" (*Five*, pp. 152, 160).

Before the Axial Age, or the Age of the Failure of Nerve, religion had "something unawakened about it" ("Axial," p. 433, column 2). We might understand this in Erich Neumann's neo-Jungian terms as "The Original Unity" which then moves on to "The Separation of the Systems."[6] That is, the consciousness associated with early religion was something like the consciousness of the infant: everything came from the all-providing mother. The world was *Mother Earth*, and she gave life, but she also punished (for perhaps mysterious reasons) and brought death. One needed to accept this, for there was, at that level, no other source of either life *or* death. The religious mode, I would say, was *celebrational* and *this-worldly*. The world was seen as *cosmos*, an ordered place which was one's home, and one (primarily) gave thanks for it.

This is the mode of the surviving pre-Axial traditions — those which we used to call "primitive" or "pagan." It is nicely illustrated by Shinto, a pre-Axial tradition which has, because of the peculiarities of the Japanese

---

4. Curiously, Jaspers does not seem entirely to follow his own logic. In the quote above I have omitted a key phrase. The relevant part of the quote, with the omitted section italicized, is: ". . . man longs for liberation and redemption; *and he finds that he can achieve liberation and redemption in the world, whether it is by ascent* . . ." Since I am not following Jaspers, but building on him, I have removed what appears to be an aberrant reference to this-worldy (because "rational," as he calls it) religion.

5. Gilbert Murray, *Five Stages of Greek Religion* (London: Watts & Co., 1935), lecture IV, "The Failure of Nerve." This is a reprint of the original (1912?) Clarendon Press edition. Hereafter referred to in the text as *Five*.

6. Erich Neumann, *The Origins and History of Consciousness*; Bollingen series 42 (Princeton, New Jersey: Princeton University Press, 1954), section headings A and B in Part II.

genius, continued as an integral part of Japanese culture. Shinto worship, which is primarily a ceremony of gratitude to the *kami* (gods) seen as *Oyasama* ("Parent" or "Mother-Father"), has four elements: purification (*harai*), offering (*shinsen*), prayer (*norito*), and feasting (*naorai*).[7] Christian liturgists will note at once the absence of *confession. Harai* is, quite simply, washing. It is the removal, as it were, of dust.[8] In contrast, Buddhism, which is definitely post-Axial, speaks of the defilement of the passions, using a Chinese character which literally means "to dye cloth." That is, Shinto sees faults as minor, superficial obscurations while Buddhism, although claiming that the defilements are in the last analysis adventitious to mind, finds the defilements staining the mind through and throughout.

If, then, as Jaspers seems to say (or perhaps as I make him say) the post-Axial religious consciousness is *soteriological,* it is so because it sees the world no longer as an ordered *cosmos* but as its opposite, a *chaos.* From this chaos, which is variously defined, the practitioner desires release.[9] The religious mode is now world-denying or "redemptive."

The so-called New Age religions appear to set themselves up in opposition to this world-denying or redemptive consciousness. They are, by and large, religions of the earth, that is to say of the flesh and of the "now" and they call themselves, sometimes, pagan.[10] And it is significant, I think, that New Age religions typically are suspicious of what they call "institutional religion" but are accepting of the "mystical" or "inner" traditions.[11] When we look at the Christian mystics as *pagans,* I think we can see the connection.

We sometimes hear it said that, for primitive humankind, "everything was sacred." We might as well say that, for fish, everything is water. We can make this statement because, as somewhat amphibious animals, we can distinguish water and air. Pre-Axial humankind, it seems, did not distinguish "sacred" and "secular" and so it would be more meaningful

---

7. Sokyo Ono, *Shinto: The Kami Way* (New York: Tuttle, 1962), p. 51.

8. Tenrikyo, one of the most popular of the "New Religions" of Japan and which has a strong Shinto element, refers to defilements as "dust" in explicit contrast to post-Axial "sin": "Thus we can say that man is not to be accused of any original sin but rather is covered now and then with dust." Tadamasa Fukaya, *The Fundamental Doctrines of Tenrikyo* (Tenri City: Headquarters of Tenrikyo Church, 1960), p. 8.

9. I once taught a course on "the great world religions" (i.e., the post-Axial religions) from the standpoint of their soteriology: i.e., what is the problem, what is the answer, and how does one get from one to the other? It seemed to work.

10. Margot Adler, *Drawing Down the Moon: Witches, Druids, Goddess-Worshippers, and Other Pagans in America Today*; rev. & expanded ed. (New York: Beacon Press, 1986).

11. An engrossing semi-popular journal, *Gnosis,* is devoted entirely to "The Western Inner Traditions" and includes many articles on mysticism but none on the kinds of goings-on described in *The National Catholic Reporter.*

to say that "the sacred was everything." That is, in our (post-Axial) terms, the sacred could not be localized as either objective or subjective. It simply *was*.

By contrast, the God of Monotheism manifests as Sacred Object in opposition to the profane. God exists before, and outside of, creation. Genesis 1: 1 says: "In the beginning, God . . ." (or, more correctly, *bara elohim*, "he, that is God, created . . ."). The Bible stigmatizes the identification of any object with God as idolatry, and, in the tradition of the Church, the limitation of the sacred "to this world" (note that the wording implies "another" world) has been regarded as the heresy of pantheism. That is, the God of Monotheism is a God of the post-Axial consciousness, of the split between the sacred and the secular, of a down-playing of "this world" and therefore of a need for salvation, escape, or redemption.

Mysticism and World-Affirmation

But, of course, that is not the whole story. The God of Monotheism is experienced as inside as well as outside the soul. The Holy *Qur'an* (50: 15) says that Allah is closer to us than our jugular vein, and Augustine wrote that God is *interior intimo meo et superior summo meo* (*Confessions*, III. 6. 11). And Christianity, in addition, claims that God became flesh, that is, became intimately connected with, indeed indissolubly united with, this-worldly reality.

Whatever it is that we call "mysticism" (and I keep using the word although I am not sure what it means) seems to have something to do, at least in Christianity, with this experience of the immanence of God. Theology, on the other hand, seems to have to do with the transcendence, or the pseudo-objectivity, of God. I once read a prayer that began with the misprint "O external and almighty God . . ." Such an external God is not by any means the God of the mystics. The mystics see God in the depths of their souls and at the heart of created things.

A catalogue of citations on this point would fill a weighty volume. I will only cite a few examples which I believe are representative.

In the New Testament, the Gospel of John holds pride of place amongst Christian mystics because of Jesus' repeated assertions that he is within us as we are within him, and that he and the Father are likewise within each other. This is the co-inherence which, it seems to me, is the hallmark of the developed spiritual consciousness.[12] The remark of Jesus recorded at Luke 17: 21 that "the kingdom of God is *entos humon*," although literally meaning "among you," was taken by Cassian to mean "within you" and has been so interpreted by generations of Christian mystics.[13]

Many saints are remembered as being on intimate terms with animals. Wild animals often became their pets (or, as we now say, "companion animals"), so that the distinction between "useful" (or domesticated) and "useless" (or dangerous) animals disappeared. Saint Jerome, after healing a lion, put it to work fetching food for the monastery. A raven brought bread each day to Saint Benedict during the time that he was a hermit. A noble Italian lady of Saint Francis' day was awakened for prayer by a devout lamb.[14] Saint Roch was accompanied to his hermitage by his dog. Saint Philip Neri, when the time came for him to live in community, insisted that his cat be left in his apartment and that the brothers should go there to feed it. And, of course, Mother Julian is presumed to have had a cat, as permitted by the *Ancren Riwle*.

Perhaps the most well-known and greatest expression of the Christian mystical experience of communion with the so-called "natural" world (again, note that the word implies "another" world) is the *Canticle to Brother Sun* by Saint Francis. There is, indeed, a strong immanentist feel in Franciscan spirituality as a whole.[15] The incident of Saint Anthony of Padua preaching to the fishes comes across as positively pagan:

> So one day, by an inspiration from God, St. Anthony went to the mouth of the river near the sea. And standing on the bank between the sea and the river, he began to call the fishes ... and ... all of a sudden such a great throng of large and small fishes gathered before him near the bank as had never been seen in that sea or river. And all of them held their heads a bit out of the water, gazing intently at St. Anthony's face. There you would have seen ... a great and very dense crowd of small fishes come in a hurry,

---

12. I have argued for this in many places. My fundamental position paper uses the modality as a way of understanding Buddhist-Christian relations. See Roger J. Corless, "The Mutual Fulfillment of Buddhism and Christianity in Co-inherent Superconsciousness," in *Buddhist-Christian Dialogue: Mutual Renewal and Transformation*; ed. by Paul O. Ingram & Frederick J. Streng (Honolulu: University of Hawaii Press, 1986), pp. 115-136.

13. "Conferences 1: 13," in *Western Asceticism*; trans. by Owen Chadwick; Library of Christian Classics (Philadelphia: Westminster Press, 1958), 12: 202. The *New Jerusalem Bible* (footnote in loc.) allows "within you" only as "a third possibility [which] would not furnish as direct an answer to the Pharisees' question."

14. "When [Lady Jacoba di Settesoli] was late getting up in the morning, the lamb nudged her with its horns and roused her with its bleats, urging her to hurry and get to church." Bonaventure, *Major Life of Saint Francis* 8: 7, in *English Omnibus of the Sources for the Life of St. Francis*; ed. by Marion A Habig (Chicago: Franciscan Herald Press, 1983), p. 694. Hereafter referred to in the text as *Omnibus*.

15. "Many commentaries on the writings of Saint Francis have overlooked this aspect because of a weak pneumatology." *Francis and Clare: The Complete Works*; trans. by Regis J. Armstrong & Ignatius C. Brady (Ramsay, New Jersey: Paulist Press, 1972), p. 11. Hereafter referred to in the text as *Francis & Clare*.

like pilgrims going to receive an indulgence, and approach closer to the
holy Father as to their protector. And so first the smaller fishes near the
bank, secondly the middle-sized, and thirdly the largest fishes, where the
water was deeper, attended this divinely arranged sermon of St. Anthony
— all in very great peace and meekness and order.' [Then] St. Anthony
solemnly began to preach, saying: "My fish brothers . . .' [and so forth]."
    At these and similar words and preaching of St. Anthony, some of
the fishes began to open their mouths, and all of them nodded their
heads, and by these and other signs of reverence they praised God as
much as they could. (*Omnibus*, pp. 1391-1393)

Except for the phrases "inspiration from God," "pilgrims going to receive
an indulgence" and "they praised God," we might be reading here of the
activities of a shaman who understands the voices of the beasts and is
understood by them.

Much of Celtic spirituality exhibits a similar this-worldliness. Many
Celtic saints, although far from other humans, had lively exchanges with the
local animals.[16] *The Breastplate of Saint Patrick* calls Christ and the Trinity to
the protection of the Christian as the pre-Christian Celt called the elemental forces. Saint Columba could say "Christ is my Druid," that is, the Wise
One of the Wild, and the Cross of Saint Martin on Iona, as other Celtic
crosses, is a tree of life as much as it is the gallows of the Saviour. Heaven and
earth, as A. M. Allchin pointed out in his film on Celtic spirituality shown on
B. B. C. television, cannot be clearly separated by people who live in the
British landscape where sea, mist and sky commonly blend into each other.
There is, I would further suggest, a feeling of closeness to the earth, of
indeed Mother Earth in the pre-Axial sense. It is, perhaps, out of this Celtic
heritage that Mother Julian could hear Christ say, in the midst of the plague,
"How could anything be amiss?"[17]

And then, there is the vexed case of Meister Eckhart. Hailed as a great
mystic, denounced by the Vatican, in process of being reclaimed by
present-day Dominicans — whatever the outcome of the debate, one thing
is certain. He was accused of Pantheism, a very significant charge. Eckhart
was regarded by his enemies as having gone back to a pre-Christian spirituality in which "this world" is the only world there is.

---

16.   Fortuitously, another member of the panel at which the original version of this essay was read, Esther
de Waal, mentioned to the delight of the rest of us many such instances in her paper "The Concept of
Dysart/ Disserth: East/ West Encounters in Early Celtic Monasticism."
17.   For the creation spirituality element in Mother Julian, see Grace Jantzen, *Julian of Norwich: Mystic
and Theologian* (London, SPCK, 1987), pp. 128-137.

Affirmation, Negation and Transfiguration

The question arises, from these few examples, whether the mysticism of *cosa* is atypical of Christian mysticism, and, indeed, opposed to the "orthodox" mysticism of *nada*. Dom Cuthbert Butler catalogues the difference between the mystics of light and the mystics of dark but does not solve the problem for us.[18] Cornelia Jessey tries to assure us that there is no opposition. Citing Niels Bohr that "the opposite of a profound truth is another profound truth," she tells us that:

> The prayer of *cosa* goes in a direction opposite to the prayer of *nada*, as north is opposite to south, but it is only another profound truth. The profound truth of the prayer of *cosa* is as old as the profound truth of *nada* — perhaps older. (Cosa, p. 6)

But she is a little slippery. *How* is it another profound truth? I suggest we go back to Erich Neumann. If, as his book maintains, the ontogeny of personal integration is (in some analagous sense) a recapitulation of the phylogeny of myth, then perhaps the Axial Age is equivalent to adolescent rebellion and a maturer spirituality would entail a reconciliation with Mother. If, further, we might legitimately claim that the mystics are maturer Christians than the rest of us, then we might find that they (or, at least, the mystics of *cosa*) have resolved the tension between the experience of God as transcendent, or "external," and as immanent. And, I believe, we do find just that.

Saint Francis, in his *Canticle to Brother Sun*, praises the sun and other "natural" phenomena as creatures of God, not as objects in themselves, and he uses the particle *per*. This means in Italian "for," "by" and "through" (*Francis & Clare*, p. 38f, n. 5). In English, we must choose one of these translations (Armstrong and Brady in the note just cited explain why they chose "through") and thereby lose the richness of the original.

In pre-Axial mode, one might praise the sun as sun: the sun *himself* would be a god, *Sol Invictor*. In post-Axial mode, one acknowledges that behind the sun (and other phenomena now called "natural" in contrast to "supernatural") there is another force, a force indeed without which the "natural" world would be dead. Whereas the Monist (or Pantheist) holds that the universe is Itself Being and that it created Itself by its own inherent power, life and consciousness, the Monotheist teaches that God, who alone has (or is) Being, says to the inert universe: "Let there be . . ." (Genesis

---

18. Cuthbert Butler, *Western Mysticism*; 2nd ed. (London: Constable, 1926).

1: 3, 6, etc.).[19] Such an inert universe could not *in and of* itself be anything but "a vale of tears" from which all right thinking people must desire deliverance.

The vision that "nature" herself was dead and therefore could not be worshipped as such was a startling revelation which distinguished the religion of Israel from that of its neighbors. The Temple of the Most High, to the frustration of looting conquerors, was empty. There was no god who could be carried back to Babylon in triumph. The prophets and the psalmists made fun of those who bowed down to images which "have noses and smell not" (Psalm 115 [113]: 6). The religious festivals, beginning as agricultural and possibly fertility festivals, were transformed into celebrations of God's redeeming acts in history.[20] Centuries later when Islam became known as a religion, daily prayers were ordained to be said (amongst other items) just *after* dawn, noon and dusk, as if to say very clearly: "We tell time by God's sun, we do not worship the sun as a god."

Today, when "redemptive theology" is somewhat under a cloud and, like vinyl records, seems quaint and old-fashioned, we need to remind ourselves of its power. The proclamation "I am the LORD, there is no other," and the realization by the post-Exilic Jews that the Lord did not need a Temple made with hands for his temple was the entire universe, and by Micah that God did not need animal sacrifices (Micah 6: 6-8), liberated the Monotheist from subservience to natural forces. One saw how one could go beyond and behind the pesky earth-spirits and (later) the gnostic archons into friendship and communion with "he who made the Pleiades and Orion" (Job 9: 9). In a word, one had grown up and realized that Mother was not God, she was just mother.

And this is where the Christian mystic comes in to resolve the tension between the transcendence of God (which in its clean, post-Axial way fits neatly into a systematic theology) and his immanence (which is pre-Axial, murky, and quasi-pantheistic). The mystic is, above all, one who *experiences* God. And the Christian God is not only (as in other Monotheisms)

---

19. "That (One-With-No-Second) thought, May I be many, may I grow forth. It sent forth fire. That fire thought, May I be many, may I grow forth . . . ." *Chandogya Upanisad* VI. 2. 3. in *The Principal Upanisads*; trans. by S. Radhakrishnan (London: Allen & Unwin, 1953), p. 449. Radhakrishnan comments that "thought" (*aiksata*) is "literally saw. This word indicates that pure being is conscious." Note that although I agree with Jaspers that the Upanishads are post-Axial, I believe that there is a spectrum from minimally to maximally post-Axial, and that traditions such as Monistic Hinduism and Taoism are on the low (pre-Axial) end of the spectrum, while the Abrahamic traditions (Judaism, Christianity and Islam) are towards the high end. There is no space here to offer proof for this view.

20. For example, during Sukkoth one sits in a booth decorated with the fruits of the harvest but thinks, not of the fecundity of Mother Earth, but of how one's ancestors, being nomads, lived in temporary shelters (Leviticus 23: 42-43).

above and beyond the universe while also being somehow deeply within it, he also became flesh, was crucified, and rose beyond birth-and-death into dimensionlessness. By accepting death (and a real, not a docetic, death) Christ assented to the post-Axial vision that all is not well with the world, true satisfaction is not to be found in it. He then passed into the earth, sanctifying and transforming the Earth Mother, and from thence ascended in the resurrected flesh, post-Axial but celebrational.[21]

Some forms of Christianity have stopped at the Cross: the rottting and twisted Christ of the Isenheim Altarpiece by Grunewald (ca. 1509-1515) is its icon. Such a Christianity makes no sense, even on its own terms, for it sees Christ as a failure. Creation Spirituality is a needed antidote, but, I believe, it goes too far. It is not clear what it does with sin and suffering.[22] The cosmic Christ of Matthew Fox has not been crucified (although the planet, which is "Mother," but also somehow Christ is "being" crucified).[23] By going experientially through the crucifixion to the resurrection, the Christian mystic, especially the mystic of *cosa*, accepts the reality of sin, of the post-Axial vision, and then recaptures the vision of power in creation, seeing it however as divine not by reason of itself but by reason of its redemption, and therefore its participation in the resurrected life by having become, I dare to say, co-inherent with Christ in the Blessed Trinity.

CONCLUSION

My claim, then, is that there is an ancient view of the world as sacred in such a way that sacred and secular are indistinguishable or, better, are not yet distinguished. For the purposes of this essay, and to be a little

---

21. That Christ's contact with earthly things sanctified them is a commonplace of patristic theology. For example, at his baptism, it was said, the water did not purify him (as it would us) but he purified it, so that all water became sacred and suitable for baptism. However, I have not come across a patristic suggestion that, by his burial, Christ sanctified the very earth herself. (The germ of this idea was suggested to me by Thomas Sherratt, a former Franciscan friar).

22. This was a question which the Vatican asked of Teilhard de Chardin and to which, in my view, he never adequately responded. An article by Kenneth Woodward on Thomas Berry in *Newsweek* (5 June 1989 — "A New Story of Creation," pp. 70-72) concludes with the remark: "But Berry's theory . . . does not take into account the existence of moral evil . . . ."

23. The front cover of Fox's *The Coming of the Cosmic Christ* (San Francisco: Harper & Row, 1988) depicts a young man identified as Christ and Holy Wisdom and holding the planet earth. The note inside the back cover explains that: "There is a traditional icon of Christ as Holy Wisdom from Russia. This is a modern variant of that theme . . . based on Matthew Fox's discussion of God as a child and Meister Eckhart's vision of the beautiful naked boy." This remark is too offhand. Whatever a vision of a naked boy may have meant to Meister Eckhart, it is not at all clear that it has much to do with Hagia Sophia who is, in Eastern Orthodoxy, almost always female and different from Christ (see, for example, Samuel D. Cioran, *Vladimir Solov'ev and the Knighthood of the Divine Sophia* [Waterloo, Ontario: Wilfrid Laurier University Press, 1977]). If Christ is straightforwardly identified with Sophia and the planet earth, how is this not pre-Axial religion *tout simple?*

provocative, I call this the "pagan" viewpoint. This view is then replaced by that of a Sacred standing over against, or transcendent to, what comes to be known as the "secular" or "this world." But such a view is both personally unsatisfying (it alienates us from our immediate environment) and unfaithful to the rich ambiguity of the Christian experience in which God is known to be at one and the same time immanent and transcendental, personal and transpersonal, invisible and incarnate.

It is then left to the mystic to explore the *terra incognita* between these apparent opposites and, in the process, to risk being accused of heresy. The typical accusation, I have suggested, is Pantheism (or Monism) and Pantehism is, it seems, typical of the "pagan" viewpoint. Therefore, I claim, it might be fruitful to regard the Christian mystic as a neo-pagan or *paganus redevivus*. But, just as the Christ of Matthew's gospel is *Moses redevivus* but is not Moses himself, so the Christian mystic is not "merely" a pagan but one who has recovered the ancient vibrancy of nature and brought it into the Christian sanctuary.

Pre-Axial consciousness looks at a flower and celebrates the beauty of creation: that, and nothing more.[24] Post-Axial consciousness regards this as superficial, reminding us that all flowers die. As the Zen saying has it: "Life is like getting into a boat that sails out to sea and sinks." Therefore, it pulls away from creation and seeks redemption. The Christian *mystical consciousness*, that is, that of the experiential contemplative or "friend of God," sees, as it were, a dogwood flower — the white flower whose red tips are said to have been acquired after its wood was used for the Cross. The Christian mystic of *cosa* celebrates the "original blessing," accepts and mourns the subsequent corruption (the oddly named "original" sin) and goes on, through redemption, to celebrate resurrection and cosmic transfiguration.

And so we come back to what it might have been that Merton was hinting at in "Hagia Sophia." The poem begins with a notably pre-Axial or "pagan" statement: "There is in all visible things an invisible fecundity, a dimmed light, a meek namelessness, a hidden wholeness. This mysterious Unity and Integrity is Wisdom, the Mother of all, *Natura naturans*" (*CP*, p. 363). Merton continues in a very "thingful" way, with scenes in a hospi-

---

24. The devas (earth spirits) of the Findhorn Garden explicitly ask us to see the beauty of creation by contemplating flowers: "We suggest that you appreciate the beauty that we present to you in our flowers. See the positive in them in as many ways as you can, and then look at the rest of life in the same way." Larkspur Deva, quoted for the month of June in the Findhorn Nature Calendar for 1989 (Findhorn Foundation, Forres, Scotland).

tal: very concrete, not at all a mysticism of *nada*. His hospital shows us the reality of pain: the world is not entirely as it should be, and the "awakening of one man . . . in the hospital" is the awakening of the Axial Consciousness. Then "the helpless one" goes through the Cross and "Naturé [is] made wise by God's Art and Incarnation . . . (*CP*, pp. 364, 365). The poem closes with a vision of Mary, seen at "Sunset. The Hour of Compline. Salve Regina" (or, indeed, the hour of Vespers and of the Magnificat), who gathers in herself the energies of *Natura* and is "a personal manifestation of Sophia" (*CP*, pp. 369-370).[25]

Herein, Merton presents us with a way of relating to God which is entirely Christian, yet which carries with it, fulfilling rather than escaping from, the telluric powers of paganism. He suggests, I would claim, that the Christian mystic is *paganus redevivus*.

---

25. Merton's identification of Sophia with Mary seems to me at once more recognizably Christian and more spiritually satisfying than Matthew Fox's ambiguous equation of Sophia with Christ and the planet earth.

SOCIAL INVOLVEMENT

AND SPIRITUALITY

by **E. Glenn Hinson**

Spirituality has to stand on four legs: the social, the institutional, the intellectual, and the experiential. Take away any one of these and the spiritual life will wobble. Take away more than one and it will fall. Without a social dimension spirituality may result in little more than a search for self-gratification. Without an institutional dimension it may lapse into emotionalism and a continuous quest for religious "highs." Without an experiential dimension it may surrender its motive.

There is a real problem here in our age and culture. Our tendency is to go from one extreme to another. In the 1960s, for instance, many heard the call of Dietrich Bonhoeffer to "worldly holiness." They hurried out of sheltered sanctuaries, away from liturgies and prayer, and immersed themselves in the life of metropolis. Commendable as their goal was, to be "the Man for others," they soon found themselves having nothing to offer which the others did not already have. In reaction against their extremes, in the 1970s, many sought new sanctuaries, monasteries and retreat centers and churches, where they could cultivate the life of the spirit. They joined sects and cults with an Oriental flavor. They became charismatic in a quest for religion of spirit and power, rather than for form or intellect or social slant.

One essay will not allow enough time to say anything significant about all four of these dimensions. Consequently, I'd like to focus on one, namely, social involvement and spirituality. My thesis will be that spirituality and social service or action can and should have a reciprocal relationship. Contrary to what many have supposed, these do not stand in opposition to one another. In Christian history, spirituality has impacted heavily on social perceptions and particularly on social involvement and action, as the record of medieval monks and Quakers will readily demonstrate. On the other hand, social involvement has produced changes in spirituality. Baron Friedrich von Huegel, as Douglas Steere has pointed out, acted on good instinct when he directed Evelyn Underhill, who came to him for spiritual guidance, to devote two afternoons a week to visiting the poor, with the explanation that this, "if properly entered into and persevered with, will discipline, mortify, deepen, and quiet you" and "as it were, distribute your blood — some of your blood — away from your brain, where too much is lodged at present."[1] Many saints have found their hearts quickened by contacts with human need and come to their deepest insights through this.

Spirituality and Social Perceptions

There is a widespread but erroneous assumption that piety dampens social concern and involvement. Historical evidence and, more recently, sociological data prove quite the contrary. Admittedly it is true that some kinds of piety have had a negative effect, especially the "pie in the sky bye and bye" kind, but the bulk of the evidence shows that pietists have been the doers and shakers in society. Let me comment on four groups representing different periods of history and then look at contemporary sociological evidence.

1. First, the monks of the high middle ages. Most of us think of otherworldliness when we think of medieval monasticism, and there is little question that the monastic life often had that slant to it. Nevertheless, we must not close our eyes to the record even cloistered monks compiled. Cluny, the great Benedictine monastery in France, distinguished itself more than once by emptying its stores to feed the hungry during the recurrent famines of the tenth and eleventh centuries. It played a role in the reform of church and society, and arranged the so-called Truce of God, which halted fighting between combatants part of the week so that peasants could work the land. Bernard, abbot of Clairvaux, was not only the most noted mystic of the twelfth century but also the most important political figure. He intervened in a dispute over the papacy, in effect installing the new pontiff. He preached the ill-fated Second Crusade in 1145. He took an active part in

---

1. Douglas V. Steere, *Together in Solitude* (New York: Crossroad, 1982), p. 57.

numerous political settlements.

2. The mendicant or begging orders which developed during the early thirteenth century — Franciscans and Dominicans — were designed to bridge a widening chasm separating church from society. Taking a cue from the military orders which had come into existence during the crusades, they united piety and activity in a way the cloistered monks could not. Francis of Assisi yearned more than anything simply to follow Jesus in caring for the poor. His first Rule consisted of four passages of scripture: "Let the one who would come after me deny self, take up a cross, and follow me;" "Go. Sell what you have. Give to the poor. And follow me;" and two passages about hating one's family for the sake of Christ. Francis, as he put it, "married Lady Poverty." He liked to call himself "Il Poverello," Little Poor Man. Repudiating the bellicose temper of his times, Francis crusaded for peace, going to the Sultan of Egypt himself to persuade him to become a Christian. He made peacemaking a part of the prayer called "The Canticle of Brother Sun." Francis inaugurated a new approach to missions, based on love and reason rather than violence, which came to its best expression in the work of Ramon Lull, a Franciscan martyred by Moslems in North Africa. The Franciscans did a lot of things their founder never intended, but none can doubt their effort to exhibit a socially active piety.

The Dominicans are, perhaps, best known for their teaching in the universities and for their work as inquisitors, but the great fourteenth century German and Dutch mystics, most of whom were Dominicans, deserve mention for the accent they placed on social responsibility. They knew persons who argued that faith alone matters; yet they were quick to repudiate these. From their influence emerged "The Friends of God," pious groups of lay persons who spent time in earnest Bible study, prayer, and service of the needy, and later the "Brethren of the Common Life," forerunners of the Protestant Reformation and of German Pietism. Writings coming from these groups are saturated with exhortations to social responsibility. Typical is John of Ruysbroeck's directive: "If you are praying and some needy person comes to you for help; leave your prayer and meet that need. Love is more important than anything."

The fourteenth century incidentally, a century characterized by deep human suffering and searching, gave impetus to the renewal of social sensitivity. Besides those already mentioned, Catherine of Siena and Catherine of Genoa exemplified the essential linkage between piety and social responsibility. Catherine of Siena, who died at age thirty-three, has been called a "social mystic," which she indeed was. She took an active role in the reforms of the papacy, and her intervention had much to do with the return of the papacy from Avignon, where it had been dominated by the French monarchy, to Rome. In the fifteenth century Catherine of Genoa spent her life in a hospital ministry.

3. Protestant Pietism, originating in reaction to Protestant scholasticism, followed on the track of "The Brothers of the Common Life." In its initial phase, with Philip Jakob Spener and August Hermann Francke, it produced not only the *collegia pcetatis*, cell groups for prayer and Bible study, but schools, orphans homes, hospitals, and other charitable endeavors. In its second phase, through Count Nicholas von Zinzerdorf's influence on the Moravians, it inaugurated the modern mission movement in 1732. In its third phase, where it impacted the American churches in the form of revivalism, it contributed significantly to the development of a strong social consciousness. Timothy Smith has argued that "whatever may have been the role of other factors, the quest for perfection joined with compassion for poor and needy sinners and a rebirth of millenial expectation to make popular Protestantism a mighty social force long before the slavery conflict erupted into war."[2] Though some preachers fostered an exclusively spiritual faith, the majority sounded a call for social and economic responsibility in the form of care for the poor and needy or of opposition to slavery.

4. The Quakers, one of numerous offshoots of English Puritanism who also claim roots in the fourteenth century in German and Dutch mysticism, have been the most consistent in combining spirituality and social responsibility. Protestant contemplatives, they had existential reasons for prison reform in England, for they spent plenty of time in the worst of England's jails. There they were incarcerated in the dankest cells without sanitary facilities, feces to their shoe tops. Early on, too, they got involved in the abolitionist movement. In the American colonies, John Woolman began his journey around the colonies in 1746, pleading with Quakers to free their slaves. Though he died in 1772 with the goal still ahead, by 1787, largely as a consequence of his efforts, no American Quaker owned a slave. Woolman also set a powerful example regarding other injustices: whites breaking treaties with Indians, attitudes toward the poor, abuse of sailors in the shipping industry, and disregard for human and animal life in the stagecoach traffic in England. The Quakers have also been one of the three

---

2. Timothy Smith, *Revivalism and Social Reform: American Protestantism on the Eve of the Civil War* (New York: Harper & Row, 1965), p. 149.

"Peace Churches," alongside German Baptist Brethren and Mennonites.

So many individual examples could be added to show that spirituality not only does not inhibit but rather enhances social responsibility. To the historical data supplied above, however, I would add one important bit of information from a study of lay attitudes in the United Church of Christ. Thomas C. Campbell and Yoshio Fukuyama reported that persons in the UCC who scored high in devotional orientation also scored higher on a scale of social acceptance of minority groups and involvement in civil rights, despite the fact that such persons usually came from the lower socio-economic classes. Campbell and Fukuyama concluded that such persons are "modern 'inner-worldly ascetics' " who combine "a sense of personal discipline with concern for others.[3] Having proper rational perceptions about social matters is not enough to cause anyone to act to change them. People have to be touched affectively, in the heart, and not merely in the head.

Social Involvement and Spirituality

At this point I want to turn the question around to ask: How does social involvement affect spirituality. What wisdom will we find in the comment Baron von Huegel made to Evelyn Underhill? Here, I think, we must recognize that social involvement will not automatically generate saints. It can help, but something else has to accompany the experiemce of social solidarity, for some have emerged from crunching human experiences horribly scarred, not saintly at all. Those who have some awareness of grace to begin with, however, may find their social crucible turning out a better brew than they began with.

To look at the matter in light of von Huegel's comment to Underhill, then, how does active social involvement de-intellectualize, discipline, mortify, deepen, and quiet one with resultant benefit to the life of the Spirit? In Underhill's case it is not surprising that von Hugel underlined the intellectual more emphatically than the others. She had grown up in affluence. Though she had a brilliant mind, well educated, she lacked common sense and feeling for reality. Her popular book on *Mysticism*, which she had already written by this time, shows that. In contemporary language I

---

3. Thomas C. Campbell & Yoshio Fukuyama, *The Fragmented Layman* (Philadelphia & Boston: Beacon Press, 1970), pp. 167, 214.

suppose we would say she needed to shift from the left to the right brain or, on a Myers-Briggs scale, from the rational to the feeling side.

Quakers, I think, have grasped this insight better than any other Protestant group. Though they have attracted a throng of intellectuals from the days of George Fox on, they have mellowed their minds with the practical realities of life and thus fostered a spirituality which blends head and heart. Here thought is not abstracted from life and experience. Rufus Jones, the brilliant American interpreter of Quaker thought and life, has put it well:

> We need to learn how to think of God as a resident presence cooperating vitally with us and in us here and now as an Emmanuel God, and at the same time we need just as urgently to see how our human lives can and do open out into a Beyond within ourselves. Almost every person who has attained to a mature spiritual life has had experiences which convinced him, at least in high moments, that he was *more than himself.* Help comes from somewhere and enables us to do what we had always thought could not be done. We find somewhere power to stand the universe when its waterspouts are let loose and even when they have gone over us. We discover strength from beyond our own stock of resources in the midst of our crises.[4]

Oh, how many have had these words confirmed in experience! Recall Alfred Delp's poignant words in a reflection on his trial and sentencing to death by a Nazi court. The whole charade seemed unreal, the sentence as well as the proceedings. Yet Delp could say:

> Up to now the Lord has helped me wonderfully. I am not yet scared and not yet beaten. The hour of human weakness will no doubt come and sometimes I am depressed when I think of all the things I hoped to do. But I am now a man internally free and far more genuine and realized than I was before. Only now have I sufficient insight to see the things as a whole.[5]

In these same comments we can discern also the *discipline* von Hugel spoke of. Spirituality *toughens* up when it confronts social realities, just as it wisens up. Catherine de Hueck Doherty related that on a visit to Dorothy Day, founder of *The Catholic Worker,* Day invited her to spend the night in her own "Hospitality House" in New York City. Fifteen people slept in one room, Catherine and Dorothy on a double bed together. As they prepared for bed, a woman of the streets, nose rotted off and actively syphilitic, walked in and asked if she could stay. Dorothy welcomed her, saying, "Of course." She put a mattress in the bathtub for Catherine and shared the double bed with this woman. When Catherine, a nurse,

---

4. Rufus Jones, *Pathways to the Reality of God* (New York: Macmillan, 1931), p. 199.

5. Alfred Delp, *The Prison Meditations of Father Delp;* introd. by Thomas Merton (New York: Herder & Herder, 1963), pp. 161f.

reminded her that syphilis was contagious, Dorothy replied: "Catherine, you have little faith. This is Christ come to us for a place to sleep. He will take care of me. You have to have faith."[6]

A lot of spirituality today, particularly in the United States, is what Martin Marty has called "summery." It likes the sunshine and warmth. For many persons, however, the times call for a "wintery" spirituality, like that found in the Psalms, which can face the thunder of storms all around. I've found participation in the peace movement calling for this kind of spirituality. The more resistance one meets, the more one must gird up the loins of mind and heart. Social experience of this type toughens spirituality.

Social involvement may also help us to *overcome self-centeredness*, which is what I take von Huegel to mean by *mortification*. Truly to follow Christ, we have to die to self and live to God and others. One of the most truly selfless persons I have had the privilege of knowing was John Howard Griffin. I didn't know him before he undertook his research on racism in America by becoming black with the aid of drugs and sun lamp treatments. Merely to undertake such a thing, at the risk of life and limb as well as health, says something about his faith and life and self-mortification. He told me several years ago that taking the drugs had caused a deterioration of his bones which necessitated seventy-five operations on his face alone. Yet he did not complain. He would have done the same thing over. The physical aspect, however, was only a part of the mortification. John Howard Griffin became another human being. In *Black Like Me*, he described his first shock.

> Turning off all the lights, I went into the bathroom and closed the door. I stood in the darkness before the mirror, my hand on the light switch. I forced myself to flick it on.
> In the flood of light against white tile, the face and shoulders of a stranger — a fierce, bald, very dark Negro — glared at me from the glass. He in no way resembled me.
> The transformation was total and shocking. I had expected to see myself disguised, but this was something else. I was imprisoned in the flesh of an utter stranger, an unsympathetic one with whom I felt no kinship. All traces of the John Griffin I had been were wiped from experience . . . .
> The completeness of this transformation appalled me. It was unlike anything I had imagined. I became two men, the observing one and one panicked, who felt Negroid even into the depths of his entrails.
> I felt the beginnings of great loneliness, not because I was a Negro but because the man I had been, the self I knew, was hidden in the flesh of another. If I returned home to my wife and children they would not know me . . . .

---

6.   Catherine de Hueck Doherty, *Fragments of My Life* (Notre Dame, Indiana: Ave Maria Press, 1979), p. 108.

I had tampered with the mystery of existence and I had lost the
sense of my own being.[7]

This was only the beginning of a death to self. There followed the experience of being treated as a "tenth-class" citizen in a racist society. Chased
threateningly down a dark street by a redneck calling him Mr. No-Hair,
Baldy, and Shithead. Having a door slammed in his face as he prepared to
step off a bus in New Orleans and being carried eight blocks beyond his
destination, refused exit at each stop. Showered with obscenities by a
carload of white men and boys as he walked down a street in Hattiesburg,
Mississippi. "I knew I was in hell," he commented about this moment of
terror. "Hell could be no more lonely or hopeless, no more agonisingly
estranged from the world of order and harmony" (*Black*, p. 81). Conversed
with as if he as a black man could do nothing but say, "yes, sir," and mumble
four-letter words. Warned by a white from Mobile who gave him a ride:
"I'll tell you how it is here. We'll do business with you people. We'll sure as
hell screw your women. Other than that, you're just *completely off the
record as far as we're concerned.* And the quicker you people get that
through your heads, the better off you'll be" (*Black*, p. 124f). Stared at with
hate and served contemptuously just for being black. Watching a white
man in Atlanta crimp his face as though he stank and snort, "Whew!"

Blacks have had more than their share of mortification, and I wonder
if this does not go a long way toward explaining the vitality of their spirituality. All of us, of course, are aware that black churches have spawned the
Negro's search for racial and economic justice. In Atlanta, according to
Martin Luther King, Sr., the Civil Rights Movement, led by Martin Luther
King, Jr., during the 1960s, went back at least to the early twentieth century.
A. D. Williams, "Daddy's" father-in-law and Martin Luther King, Jr.'s grand-
father, led in the organizing of this early phase at Ebenezer Baptist Church
in Atlanta.[8] We should recognize equally how struggle, from the slave
period on, has shaped black spirituality. You will find evidence of that in the
spirituals, in the sermons, and in the lives of black people. Nothing better
exemplifies the end product, however, than the effective campaign of
non-violent resistance led by M. L King, Jr., in Birmingham, Alabama, in
1963. In a letter responding to eight clergymen who protested the boycott,
King attributed this mediating Christian approach to the influence of the

---

7. John Howard Griffin, *Black Like Me* (London: Catholic Book Club, 1960), pp. 19-20. Hereafter referred
to in the text as *Black*.

8. Martin Luther King, Sr., *Daddy King: An Autobiography* (New York: William Morrow & Co., 1980),
pp. 85-87.

Negro church.[9] "The Negro," he explained, "turned his back on force not only because he knew he could not win his freedom through physical force but also because he believed that through physical force he could lose his soul" (*Why*, p. 25). He expressed disappointment at the white churches and ministers who had stood on the sidelines and mouthed "pious irrelevancies and sanctimonious trivialities" and "blemished and scarred that body through social neglect and through fear of being nonconformists" (*Why*, pp. 94, 95). What is the source of difference in these spiritualities? They share geography. They share Judaeo-Christian roots. They share much of the same history. The major difference lies in the fact that black spirituality is born and bred in a climate of oppression and suffering, whereas white spirituality has had a privileged upbringing in a culture dominated by whites. White spirituality could use some mortification.

Social involvement will also *deepen* spirituality, a point directly applicable to King's complaint about Protestant churches and ministers in the struggle for civil rights. Protestant spirituality is superficial. It is afflicted by a profound dualism, denying the worth of the physical. Religion is compartmentalized and set in a realm outside everyday experience.

Getting involved in the cares and struggles of fellow human beings can deepen piety. That, at any rate, is what Francis of Assisi and many others who have followed in his footsteps have discovered. "One cannot expect to become a saint without paying the price," Mother Teresa of Calcutta, one of the modern imitators of Francis, has said, "and the price is much renunciation, much temptation, much struggle and persecution, and all sorts of sacrifices."[10] The chief thing in saintliness, she never tires of saying, is to grow in love. We grow in love by exercising it. We do not love God in the abstract but through service. Thus the object of Mother Teresa's Missionaries of Charities is "wholehearted free service to the poorest of the poor." To feed the hungry, give drink to the thirsty, and those other things cited in Matthew 25: 40-46 "is our only way of expressing love for God," she insists. "Our love must pour on someone. The people are the means of expressing our love of God" (*Love*, p. 15). Contrariwise, as Rufus Jones has warned, "To withdraw from the human press and struggle and seek only the selfish thrill of individual salvation is the way of spiritual danger."[11]

---

9. Martin Luther King, Jr., *Why We Can't Wait* (New York: Harper & Row, 1963), p. 90f. Hereafter referred to in the text as *Why*.

10. Mother Teresa, *The Love of Christ: Spiritual Counsels;* ed. by Georges Gorres & Jean Harbier (San Francisco: Harper & Row, 1982), p. 21. Hereafter referred to in the text as *Love*.

11. Rufus Jones, *Our Social Task and What It Demands* (pamphlet, n. d.).

Finally, social involvement may quiet our spiurituality. A lot of contemporary spirituality is rather noisy. Some can't seem to get enough of talk about experience or exercises in religion, others enough of spiritual extravaganzas and orgies, still others of church hopping to find a bigger demonstration of religion of Spirit and power. I'm reminded of Talkative in *Pilgrim's Progress*:

> This man is for any company, and for any talk; as he talks now with you, so will he talk when he is on the alebench; and the more drink he hath in his crown, the more of these things he hath in his mouth; religion hath no place in his heart, or house, or conversation; all he hath lieth in his tongue, and his religion is to make a noise thereof.

Behind such noisiness may lie a serious doubt about the reality of one's spirituality and perhaps of its worth. The measure of religion is always what it produces, and if ours is doing nothing more than bringing personal gratification and mouth wagging, it is bound to leave an emptiness, a void which we try to fill with more religious activities. The emptier we feel, the noisier we become. Contrariwise, the more we know God, the more we become silent.

A partial antidote to this problem can be found in social involvement. Love of neighbor is self-validating. It doesn't require a lot of noise to assure the doer. Bunyan's word to Talkative, based on James 1: 22, 27, is: "The soul of religion is the practical part: . . . This Talkative is not aware of; he thinks that *hearing* and *saying* will make a good Christian; and thus he deceiveth his own soul."

Catherine of Genoa (1447-1510) had a noisy spirituality until God directed her to work among the sick as he life's vocation and commitment. Born into an aristocratic family, she wanted to enter an Augustinian convent at age thirteen, but, because of her age, this was denied. For strictly financial and political reasons her family arranged a marriage with Giuliano Adorno, an aristocrat, at age sixteen. Subsequently, she suffered ten years of loneliness and melancholy as a result partially of her husband's unfaithfulness. She withdrew almost completely from public life for five years and then partially for another five. On 22 March 1473, she experienced the love of God in an overwhelming way. After an extended period of penance and soul searching, accompanied by her husband's declaration of bankruptcy, she and her husband, who also experienced conversion, moved into a modest house near the Pammatone Hospital, where they spent the rest of their lives in service of the sick. According to *The Spiritual Dialogue*, a work attempting to record Catherine's inner history, Catherine had struggled mightily up to this point to overcome self-love and human frailty. Her work in the Pammatone Hospital became the way her heart was subdued to obedience to God through submission to others. God's words to her as recorded in the *Dialogue*, are worth quoting:

> So that you will have something to do, God said to her,
> you will work for a living.' [She had never had to work before!]
> You' [Catherine] will be asked to do works of charity
> among the poor sick,
> and when asked you will clean filthy things.
> Should you be conversing with God at the time
> you will leave all and not ask who sends for you or needs you.
> Do not do your will but that of others.
> You will have the time you need,
> for I intend to crush all disordered pleasures and discipline you —
> and I want to see results.
> If I find that you consider some things repugnant
> I will have you so concentrate on them
> that they will no longer be such.
> I will also take away
> all those things that gave you some comfort
> and make you die to them.
> The better to test you,
> I will have you endure a corresponding version of spiritual things
> of those that give and take away pleasure.
> You will have no friendships, no special family ties.
> You will ove everyone without love,
> rich and poor, friends and relatives.
> You are not to make friends,
> not even special spiritual or religious friendships,
> or go to see anyone out of friendship.
> It is enough that you go when you are called,
> as I told you before.
> This is the way you are to consort with your fellow
> creatures on earth.[12]

Not many of us will carry obedience to the extremes Catherine did. Unable to bear the sight of lice which covered the sick she ministered to in the hospital, according to divine instruction, she put a handful of them in her mouth and swallowed them. In this way she overcame her nausea: "Learning to handle them," *The Spiritual Dialogue* says, "as if they were pearls" (*Spiritual*, p. 131). After that, care of the desperately sick came easier. So did selfless love.

---

12. Catherine of Genoa, *Purgation and Purgatory: The Spiritual Dialogue*; trans. by Serge Hughes (New York: Paulist Press, 1978), pp. 128-129. Hereafter referred to in the text as *Spiritual*.

Involvement and Spirituality: A Reciprocal Relation

Just as spirituality heightens social awareness, therefore, social involvement enhances spirituality. Neither will do so automatically, but they will do so if we let them. What is sought is not the subservience of one to the other but mutuality. In a reciprocal relationship each will reach a higher level. The same, of course, should be true of all four of the legs on which spirituality stands — the social, the institutional, the intellectual, and the experiential.

Within the American religious context we will probably need to push people toward the social more than the experiential, especially today, because their natural inclination will lead them toward the latter. American religion has always put its accent on the individual, and revivalism has heightened this inclination. How do we get people more involved socially in the cares of their fellow human beings?

I would say, first of all, not by cajoling or trying to coerce, perhaps not even by shocking or frightening. Confronting people with the stark reality of such things as a nuclear holocaust may awaken some, but it may turn others off, cause them to deny the reality, and introvert still more. It may overwhelm them completely.

We must begin, rather, with humility. For most of us humility should come naturally, first, because neither we nor anyone else have solutions to the world's problems, and, secondly, because we have not done a lot to solve them ourselves. What solution do we have to offer concerning economic justice in the Third World, for example? Most of us are more a part of the problem than a part of the solution, and we have done precious little to change even our lifestyles, over which we have some control, much less engaged in effective social action to change our society, over which we have little or no control.

Humility suggests a "Come, let us reason and pray together" approach. The Quakers have done this with great effectiveness for centuries. Rather than bending even the will of a single person to the group will, they have taken time to let the Spirit of God speak to all. John Woolman relates a moving instance of this in his *Journal*. In 1763, Indians had massacred a settlement of whites living along the Delaware River. Woolman felt the leading of God to go among them and do what he could to effect peace. When he told his wife, she did not agree. Rather than run rough shod over her feelings, he held an all-night prayer vigil, during which, as he phrased it, "In this conflict of spirit there were great searchings of heart and strong cries to the Lord, that no motion might in the least degree be attended to but that of the pure spirit of truth." Quakers often hold protracted and exhaustive meetings until they can be confident every person has assented voluntarily.

Concrete opportunities combining the journey inward and the journey outward should also be set before people. Many devout persons do nothing simply because they don't know where or how to begin. They know about the problems of hunger, injustice, persecution of minority groups, and war in the abstract, but they need specific direction to feel they can do something. The Church of the Savior in Washington, D. C., has done a marvelous job of "calling out the called." They set before the faithful a bundle of specific options — peacemaking, employment for the unemployed, housing for low income people, etc. — so that none need flounder helplessly trying to do something that matters.

The "journey inward" is exceedingly important here. If people are to be touched at a deep enough level they will be moved to action. They have to learn to look at the world through God's eyes. Reading a long statistical chart will not suffice. Thus we come back to our major point, about the reciprocal relation of social involvement and spirituality. God Himself has to break through and fill our hearts with love and compassion, our heads with wisdom, and our spirits with strength. Yet we are often unable to open them wide enough to invite God to enter until the human situation — a "Hell's Kitchen" for a Walter Rauschenbusch — compels us to open wider. The major thing is an enlargement which must go hand in hand with the operation of grace.

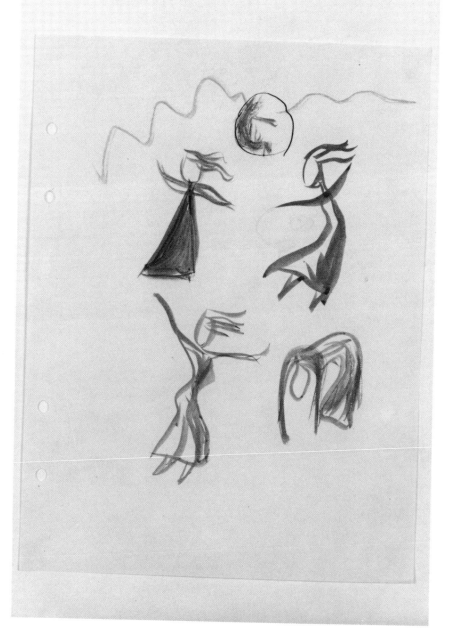

THOMAS MERTON

AND THE GREY MAN

by **Michael Rukstelis**

People who care to look at art, for example at Fra Angelico's *Annunciation*, sometimes say they experience moments when they feel engaged by something other than their own efforts to make sense of what is before them on the canvas. They may feel they have been set free from trying to know about the picture, and in the process, have been able to enjoy an experience of taking part in what the artist is trying to do when representing "another" world. After undergoing such a moment, their responses to the picture may suggest how alike some experiences of art and religion really are. On the face of it, Thomas Merton's early reflections about aesthetic and religious experience frequently point to a pattern like the one I have just outlined. During the process of writing his 1939 Columbia University thesis on William Blake, for example, Merton draws a conclusion that will later influence his own development as a contemplative. It is that the artist and the mystic seem to share the same kind of intuition about God: "This seizure of intelligible realities without using concepts as a formal means is something analogous in both the poet and the mystic, but they operate differently and on different planes."[1] If we pursue Merton's responses within the context of a particular experience of art, we can bring to view his struggle for identity empowered by something other than an impulse, as one of his biographers has put it, "to interpret life in terms of sociological and economic laws."[2]

---

1. Thomas Merton, "Nature and Art in William Blake: An Essay in Interpretation," in *The Literary Essays of Thomas Merton*; ed. by Brother Patrick Hart (New York: New Directions, 1981), pp. 444-445. Hereafter referred to in the text as *LE*.

2. Monica Furlong, *Merton: A Biography* (San Francisco: Harper & Row, 1980), p. 75.

In Thomas Merton's thesis, "Nature and Art in William Blake: An Essay in Interpretation," this claim for an analogous relationship between the artist and the mystic seems rooted in his reading of Jacques Maritain's *Art and Scholasticism.* A key source for the thesis, Maritain, in part, argues that the artist in "pursuing the line of his art . . . tends without knowing it to pass beyond his art."[3] Since the artist's activity resembles the mystic's in this way, there is especially in the fine arts a sort of divine horizon "where matter comes into contact with spirit" (*Art*, p. 27). And for Maritain, because the purpose of art is to "prepare the human race for contemplation," one object of the fine arts is "to produce an intellectual delight, that is to say a kind of contemplation . . . whence the beauty of the work ought to overflow" (*Art*, pp. 27, 62).

That Merton's opinion resembles Maritain's is evidenced in a 25 October 1939 entry from his "Perry Street Journal," printed in *The Secular Journal of Thomas Merton.* For example, in this passage Merton argues that discovering the action of Fra Angelico's "Temptation of St. Anthony" leads to an aesthetic stillness like that of contemplation: "Just as prayer leads to stillness and timelessness in contemplation, so the action of this picture leads to contemplation on an aesthetic level."[4] Thus, for the viewer, as much as for the artist, the task becomes one of "realizing what constitutes the action in a good picture" in order to gain "some basis for talking analogically about the joys of heaven" (*SJ*, p. 16). A viewer's efforts, then, will be an on-going discernment of the central action of a good picture. This discernment will not just alter a viewer's responses to the picture. It will effect a new response to its subject matter as well. Only when a viewer's initial perception of a good picture is reformed by the more hidden action or movement of the picture can the person be led into an experience like that of contemplation.

At this juncture, I want briefly to shift the focus from the viewer's responses to a work of art to the effect the artist's work has on a viewer. Some of Merton's thinking about what an artist does when he makes a good picture had already been formulated in his thesis on Blake. There Merton saw in Blake a model of a Christian artist who had "found in art a way of knowing and loving the principle of all Being" (*LE*, p. 430). As early as 1938, Merton was beginning to see the "way" of the artist, not as contradictory to,

---

3. Jacques Maritain, *Art and Scholasticism*; trans. by J. F. Scanlan (Freeport, New York: Books for Libraries Press, 1971), p. 66. Hereafter referred to in the text as *Art*.

4. Thomas Merton, *The Secular Journal of Thomas Merton* (New York: Farrar, Straus & Cudahy, 1959), pp. 14-15. Hereafter referred to in the text as *SJ*.

but as complementary with the religious vocation he has in mind at the time. The quest in the thesis is an intellectual one, and it looks into a question about how the discipline of art brought about in Blake a unified awareness of God: "Everything Blake ever wrote, painted, or said," writes Merton later in his St. Bonaventure University teaching notes, "is directly or indirectly concerned with the steps towards achievement of mystical union with God."[5]

In the context of religious experience, then, the question became: how is the discipline of art related to the discipline of contemplation? Merton answered by analogy. Both the artist and the mystic, through their respective disciplines of poetry and contemplation, see alike because they share an awareness of "the possibility of direct intuitive contacts with pure intelligibility" (*LE*, p. 444).

Thomas Merton's analysis of Blake's Imagination brings to view his own early thinking about how the experience of the artist is like that of the mystic's. In the thesis Merton decided favorably on Blake's visionary genius as a defiantly uncritical force, which links the artist and mystic in relationship, and which consequently sets Blake apart from other poets. His genius, argues Merton, "implies a highly developed habitus of art" (*LE*, p. 433). The more usual experience, however, is that the "virtue or habitus of art does not spring fully grown in the artist's mind; [but] it has to be cultivated by definite means" (*LE*, p. 448). Just how the artist develops a habitus of art like Blake's seems to become a primary question for Merton in his life-long search to find a shared ground between mystic and aesthetic experience.[6]

While Thomas Merton recognizes the strength of Blake's poetic genius as making "no distinction between truth and beauty, knowing and loving, but puts them all together in 'Imagination'," he also decides that "it is here that Blake becomes an extremist." Instead St. Thomas becomes the

---

5. Faddish-Siracuse File, Friedsam Memorial Library, St. Bonaventure University, Olean, New York.

6. For example, in his essay "Poetry and the Contemplative Life," in *Figures from an Apocalypse* (1947), Merton pushes this discussion of aesthetic experience even further. Here he again invokes aesthetic experience as an analogue to "mystical experience which it resembles and imitates from afar." In this discussion he argues that the "mode of apprehension" of an aesthetic experience "is that of 'connaturality' " in that "it reaches out to grasp the inner reality, the vital substance of its object, by a kind of affective identification of itself with it." Recalling blake in this context, Merton says: "So close is the resemblance between these two experiences that a poet like Blake could almost confuse the two and make them merge into one another as if they belonged to the same order of things" (pp. 101-102). In the 1947 essay, Merton argued that between aesthetic and mystical experience "there is an abyss." In his 1958 revision of this essay, "Poetry and Contemplation: A Reappraisal," although he maintains almost identical language in this passage, Merton cuts the sentence — "And yet there is an abyss between them" (i.e., a "division of life into formally separate compartments of action and contemplation"). In this essay aesthetic intuition becomes recognized as a way of participating in God's creative action: "Aesthetic intuition is not merely the act of a faculty, it is also a heightening and intensification of our personal identity and being by the perception of our connatural affinity with 'Being' in the beauty contemplated" (*LE*, p. 339).

model who best represents a "sense of balance" rather than an extreme for the artist, who is also a mystic. While Blake "inextricably link[ed] up the poetic instinct with his own mysticism," St. Thomas makes distinctions between the role of judgment in art and the artist's intuition of beauty. Thus Merton sees St. Thomas's balance achieved in his ability to couple an artist's delight in or love of beauty in created things with the artist's ability to use judgment: "St. Thomas balances the love of beauty with judgment in the artist: *perfectio artis consistit in judicando.*" Insofar as the "apprehension of beauty implies at once knowledge and ecstasy," St. Thomas recognizes, like Blake, the possibility of an artist enjoying beauty connaturally, that is, "directly and intuitively" and without "any effort of abstraction and analysis" (*LE*, pp. 445-446).

Merton actually understands Blake's concept of Imagination within the scholastic idea of "virtue" or "habitus" (i.e., "the permanent condition perfecting in the line of its own nature the [subject] which it informs"), and then suggests that Blake's genius "implies a highly developed habitus of art" (*LE*, p. 431).[7] Having noted Blake's genius as an exception to the usual circumstance of the artist, Merton then looks to St. Thomas Aquinas as one who models the necessary sense of balance between the artist's subjective or connatural involvement in some thing's beauty and the disciplined judgment inherent to art. In this context contemplation is integral to the artist's ability to judge, not just because as a discipline contemplation implies asceticism and sacrifice of physical pleasure for the sake of spiritual good. Contemplation also becomes the important discipline because it involves training the intellect to judge or discern God's essential self as it bursts forth from creation. Because judgment is seen as a practical sign of the habitus of art at work in the artist, the perfection of the artist consists in an on-going discernment of God's presence shining through created things (*LE*, pp. 442-448).

Merton also uses scholastic categories of thought to account for what the Imagination reveals to the poet when he sees God's splendor burst forth from matter. For example, he borrows again from Maritain's discussion ideas about "form," or the "principle determining the peculiar perfection of everything," and about "claritas," or "the glory of form shining through matter" (*LE*, p. 443). While Merton identifies form as the "revelation of essence," claritas is seen as the condition of form that best satisfies

---

7. It should be noted that Merton reads "virtue" and "habitus" as the same in meaning: "The idea of virtue is the ancient's idea of *habitus.*"

the intellect's demand, not just for intelligibility and light, but also for essential beauty.

Merton's analysis of Blake's Imagination suggests something about his own early thinking about the mission of the artist. While the mission of the artist is to reveal God's transcendent intelligence to the world, this mission also presupposes the artist's fundamental "virtue" to discern God's being already active in the world. Imagination in the thesis becomes understood as a process that directs the artist's attention to the transcendent in matter. It gives the artist the freedom to look through nature and "into the very essence of things" (*LE*, p. 445). The mission of the artist, then, is not just a transformation of the natural world, but a transformation of the attention one gives to that world. Because the Imagination directs the artist's attention to discern what is essentially there, the artist will necessarily "see" beyond the typical categories of thought and consequently be freed from the constraints of normal perception. Thus for an artist like Blake, the object of any portrait will always be to show a person's perfection, one's essential likeness to God (*LE*, pp. 435-436).

Christian response to art is based on the intellect's grasp of a portrait's form. What a viewer does when paying attention to a good picture is to share in the same kind of imaginative activity as the artist. That is, as a viewer is engaged by the central action of an artist's work, understanding about what constitutes normal perception is also reformed. One moves, albeit on a different level, towards an awareness of direct and intuitive contact with essential being. The Imagination, then, is a kind of discipline of art that engages perceptual activity in what is eternal and transcendent. Someone who has an intellectual grasp of a "good" picture shares in God's stillness and significance, participates in God's self-creative activity, learns what prayer is, and comes even to participate in the joys of heaven (*SJ*, pp. 14-16). What I have just described is in part a theory of reading, a poetics, that Thomas Merton began to develop while writing his 1939 Columbia Masters thesis. An analysis of Merton's early poetics tells readers something about what is involved in a "Christian response" to a created thing like a picture; but it also suggests how Merton constitutes his version of a "Christian artist." In order to demonstrate what may be involved in, or in this case excluded from, the Merton version of a Christian artist, I want to return to some of the early works and highlight the negative terms of his poetics.

I have already suggested how Merton's analysis of Blake's Imagination gains force through Thomistic assumptions and takes shape through

Thomistic language. In the thesis this analysis of Blake is set up against a critique of naturalism and idealism in art. The issues raised by this critique, especially when they are related to the identity of the artist, establish another model of the artist — the technician artist. The technician artist, as well as the landscapes he fashions, are represented in the novel *My Argument with the Gestapo,* written in 1941, just two years after Merton wrote his thesis. These artists and their landscapes seem to be a function of Merton's critique of naturalism and idealism in art and are therefore worthy of attention.

Merton's critique of artistic idealism actually begins with Plato whose emphasis is on the role of the intellect as it relates to the right working of the state. Thus his inquiry into the nature and function of art is made within the context of the question: what "pursuits make° [human beings] better or worse in private or public life."[8] Plato's theory of knowledge makes an extreme distinction between true existence and human making. True existence presupposes that there is a transcendental idea or form for a particular class of created matter. (For all the shoes in the world there is a corresponding form or idea). A cobbler's knowledge about making shoes is closer to ultimate reality and therefore inherently more valuable to society than what an artist does when he makes a picture. Indeed, unlike the cobbler, the artist "will make a likeness of a cobbler though he understands nothing of cobbling." Thus, the work of the artist is an imitation of nature. It is a copy of a copy and therefore is "ruinous to the understanding of the hearers" (*Plato,* pp. 658, 666). Based on this rationale, Plato makes his moral condemnation of poetry.

Of course, Merton is critical of Plato's understanding of art. In fact, Plato's moral condemnation of poetry is, according to Merton, based on a misconception of the function of art. Plato, argues Merton, overemphasizes the role of cognition in the quest for truth. Plato's dependence on cognition, moreover, leads to a perception of the soul divided into good and bad parts, by means of "clear-cut, arbitrary distinctions." The philosopher in the quest for the true nature of things "relies on measurement and calculation" which is "the best part of the soul." By contrast, Plato saw the artist as merely one who imitates or copies nature and therefore as one who does not exercise well the rational principle of the soul. Consequently, the philosopher assumes poetry affects only emotions and not the intellect,

---

8.   Plato, *The Portable Plato* (New York: Viking Press, 1948), pp. 664-665. Hereafter referred to in the text as *Plato.*

and he understands poetry only as stirring up "the meaner instead of the better parts of the soul." Thus the artist's pictures would adversely affect the citizens of the Republic. Such a dichotomy, in Merton's view, leads ultimately to a "complete misunderstanding of the nature of the artistic process" (*LE*, p. 439).

As it is represented by Merton, the "generalizing" of the eighteenth century seems to be partly a consequence of Platonic idealism. Such idealism gives way to the creation of "a standard of beauty by which we might presumably judge all men." This impulse to generalizing Merton resists for a couple of reasons. First, Plato's understanding of the soul is based on an assumption that being is "external to the world, entirely separate from it, and above it," [and] . . . faintly reflected in the things of this contingent world." Because Merton assumes that being is integral to the matter of the world, he sees Plato's transcendentalism as a kind of distortion of a particular thing or subject's essential identity. As a consequence, Merton is critical of the eighteenth century's penchant for generalizing for the same reason (*LE*, p. 441).

Secondly, Merton resists Plato's transcendentalism and the eighteenth century's admiration for standards of beauty for a more pragmatic reason. Standards of beauty inevitably distort individual human feeling and lead to dehumanizing behavior. In other words, the people who utter abstractions, who reduce an individual's God given identity to an ideal form or type, are also the people who sanction the destruction of cities like London and Paris.

Within this critique of artistic idealism, Merton implies that a standard of beauty, because it is an abstraction, can easily be appropriated as propaganda to advance the political interests of the state. In *My Argument with the Gestapo*, the cinema is one artistic medium by which to represent the belief that destroying a city is a legitimate action, and by which to advance one nation's standards of "home" over another's. For example, a German officer, whom the Merton narrator meets in the deserted streets of Paris, speaks of his wish for an ideal home. When the narrator asks this officer where his home is, the German describes "a droll little house in a village or dorf."[9] This is an ideal home, fashioned from movies which he has seen. In fact, the officer claims the "house in the movies is more really Germany than the real places where [he] lived" (*MAG*, p. 216).

---

9. Thomas Merton, *My Argument with the Gestapo* (Garden City, New York: Doubleday & Company, 1969), p. 216. Hereafter referred to in the text as *MAG*.

The German officer does not regard his own experience as valuable. Instead, it is the experience of the romanticized Lew Ayres character from the film of *All Quiet on the Western Front* who is regarded as worthy of attention. Moreover, while this officer emulates Ayres's sadness and loneliness, he also seems to use Ayres's death as the reason to justify his own army's role in the destruction of Paris:

> When I entered Paris with the Fuehrer's victorious regiments . . . I remembered that little butterfly [which Ayres reached for before he was shot]. I thought then that Paris ought to have been leveled to the earth, but I really don't care. Besides, it was only a film. (*MAG*, p. 219)

The consequence of propaganda is clear: human feeling is constantly undermined by abstraction.

Thomas Merton's critique of naturalism in art is as severe as that leveled against idealism. Merton describes eighteenth century society as "largely skeptical or Deistic." The natural religion of this age sought God's will by consulting nature. This version of religion then presumes that human rationality will put one in touch with God's transcendental form. However, because their natural religion focuses exclusively on the use of human sensation and rationality as the means to mediate the quest for transcendental experience, the Deists and their natural religion only fostered a sharper split between humanity and God. As a result, Deists created a passionless religion that in Merton's eyes reduced God to "little more than a good feeling pervading the universe" (*LE*, p. 412).

Thus Merton reacts to another of this age's extremes: its emphasis on the senses and rationality as primary shaping agents of artistic vision. Because the naturalist artist relies "on the evidence of his senses," this artist copies nature and creates a work whose subject matter portrays an object's recognizable image. The danger here is that an extreme type of naturalism "aims to yield 'sensations as nearly as possible identical with those aroused by the model itself.'" This artist's purpose is not to reveal a person's "essential" portrait. The end instead is an emotional or sensual delight in the subject matter (*LE*, pp. 436-437).

For Merton the consequence of such an aim is clear: artists who forget to "stress the essential, intellectual character of art," reduce themselves to the status of "trickster, or a clown," who "achieve their effects by trickery, by technical dodges" (*LE*, pp. 437 & 438). In other words, manual dexterity, the artist's facility or technical achievement, does not constitute the true nature or function of art (*LE*, pp. 433-434). By implication, a person who views such a work can be seriously misled. In this case, response becomes identified with the subject matter of the picture. A viewer's response to this kind of picture leads to "the love of creatures as they are in themselves and not as they are in God" (*LE*, p. 437). Such a response, that is, leads to idolatry.

In *My Argument with the Gestapo*, Merton uses landscapes to illustrate the impact idealism and naturalism in art have on the human spirit. For example, at one point the narrator and a group of friends go to the movies. Once inside the theater the narrator notices a little girl named Anne who "just looked solemnly at the screen" (*MAG*, p. 81).[10] This solemn child waiting for the movies to begin overwhelms the narrator with sadness, because she reminds him of his own childhood: "It was like remembering my whole life." As in his own past experience, the inside of this theater is both gaudy and macabre. The walls are "painted up with marble columns" and are touched up "with the illusion of horrible balustrades over the top of the proscenium arch." The "gray arching ceilings" are full of "dead decorations," which are "peopled with distorted, half-draped figures among painted clouds . . . all asking to be swallowed up by the merciful darkness" (*MAG*, pp. 82).

The narrator's memory of the little girl, Anne, and his description of the theater's interior suggest the consequences of the technicians' idealism upon the child's belief and innocence. His memory of the particular place dramatizes his own recognition of how this landscape functions. In situating Anne within the midst of this place, the scene offers an image of a child buried within a landscape that promotes belief in illusion. In other words, the narrator's description of the movie theater emphasizes that the theater functions as a kind of tomb. Thus, while inviting the child's belief in what is fundamentally illusory — movies are copies of nature which in turn is a copy of eternity — the technician artist creates structures (of which the movie theater is a symbol) in the world that aggressively contradict the human spirit, and so form a world picture that denies the need human beings have for contact with transcendental being.[11]

---

10. In Michael Mott's *The Seven Mountains of Thomas Merton* (Boston: Houghton Mifflin, 1984), he points out that the name Anne was important throughout Merton's life: in "St. Anne's (Soho), Anne Winser, St. Ann, and many later Anns and Annes . . . there is a coincidence in the way the names come together and play off one another" (pp. 63-64; see also p. 424).

11. In a later work like *The Seven Storey Mountain* (New York: Harcourt Brace, 1948), the need for, and the lack of, a radically transformed vision is often dramatized by the way the narrative episodes are organized. Merton's rendering of his mother's death is a case in point. In the autobiography, Ruth Merton writes a death bed letter to her son "informing [him] by mail, that she was about to die, and would never see [him] again" (p. 14). But while the narrative speaks of the original toll — "I was very sad" — that his early experience had taken, it is the way the scene is represented here which is telling. The structure of the scene emphasizes the boy's isolation from his mother. In fact, his isolation is intensified through the writer's focus on the place. The detail that supposedly absorbs the young Tom's attention includes "buildings, thick with soot [with] rain dripping from the eaves." The sky is "heavy with mist and smoke," and the "sweet sick smell

That these structures of contradiction are integral to the landscape of the world is consistently dramatized throughout the novel. For instance, in chapter twelve the landscape of the present is first introduced when the narrator's car "swings over the brow of a hill" to reveal a "wide country [that] seesaws down and up with space full of fields, trees, lines of identical houses." In fact the landscape projects only a veneer of tranquility and peace in which its sky is like that "in an eighteenth century landscape painting" and its soldiers stand at ease "with their helmets off their heads and their arms folded" (*MAG*, p. 100).

But the reader may also notice that in this description there is a pattern that organizes the space itself: the "wide country seesaws down and up with space." The images of guns "all pointing at the southeast sky" and of "gunners˙ [who] stand against the sky" reproduce a pattern of potential violence hidden in the midst of this landscape. In other words, pervading this space is a shifting "down and up" pattern that reveals the landscape as an elaborate camouflage for the material of war. Moreover, by disclosing how the space in this landscape is organized, the narrator also exposes the manipulative and self-destructive actions of its creators (*MAG*, p. 100).

From this initial perception about how the space of this landscape is organized, the narrator, some ten pages later, is able to "turn again and look once more at the landscape." As he sees it reappear within the context of war, the narrator understands not only why it seemed in the past to be "without harmony, in a state of contradictions," but also to see how the landscape itself now is "incomplete without the anti-aircraft battery." Responses to this landscape, especially as they pertain to the past and childhood, connect the narrator's new understanding of "the relation between idealism and ugliness" with the childhood penchant for romantic distortion and self-deception. The child's view of the landscape ranged from a nostalgic longing for "what the landscape had been once," to a vague and utopian wish for "what the technicians dreamed it ought to have

---

of the hospital and gas-house" (p. 15). Like the little girl Anne in the novel, the narrator situates the boy within a landscape that virtually boxes him in: he sits in a car, which rests in a yard which is surrounded by "black brick buildings, thick with soot."

This episode relocates Merton's critique of naturalism and idealism within the conventional wisdom of the day. While the scene dramatizes a boy's separation from his mother, it also identified Ruth Merton as an important source of his isolation. Ruth Merton's ideas about child rearing help to create the situation of her son's isolation: "And since I was destined to grow up with a nice, clear, optimistic and well-balanced outlook on life, I was never even taken to the hospital to see mother .... And this was entirely her own idea" (p. 14). The boy's "subconscious rejection" of the fact of his mother's dying reflects a critique, not so much of his mother, but of the conventions that create conditions offering no relief from the pain and grief of death. Indeed Merton asks what good it would have been for him to be exposed to death without the means — "any prayer, any Sacrament" — to "make some kind of meaning out of it."

been." Within the context of peace, then, childhood "misunderstandings" had, in effect, displaced the present landscape's reality and permanence: "I could never see what it' [i.e., the landscape] was, and I believed it was temporary" (*MAG*, pp. 110-111).

The child's romanticizing of the past is, however, only a part of the picture. It is finally the technician who makes the ugly believable and who legitimizes the ongoing "dialectic between disorder and all the confident techniques behind disorder" (*MAG*, p. 110). The so-called dreaming technician is the builder of a landscape that invites and sustains the childlike belief in what is fundamentally a pattern of aggressive contradiction. In this same chapter, the narrator meets another character who is tagged the "officer of artillery." This officer represents that class of technicians I have just described; and he reflects their fundamental misconceptions about the nature and function of art.

The officer speaks a paean of praise to Cambridge, but his praise takes shape within a dematerialized landscape. Images like shining "pools of ice" and "brittle buildings" characterize this supernatural place. The rooms and buildings, the very architecture of the place itself, become spiritualized and without foundation in the earth. Moreover, the officer celebrates Cambridge as a kind of sacred place in which "the most abstract whisper of discord" is expelled, leaving only the "cleanliness of mathematics" to "shine still in my mind." Meanwhile titles like "old Cambridge" and "Gray Cambridge" emphasize the personal feeling that the officer attaches to the place. Thus, besides describing it as a sacred place, the officer memorializes Cambridge as a great, wise parent who begets a happy society of faithful servants, of which he is an example (*MAG*, p. 107).

For the officer, Cambridge embodies a wish for a place secure from "the time of disorder." In his speech, images and terms of geometry shape his memory of Cambridge, but in so doing, they reorder life experience, turn memory into "new mental structures," and place both memory and experience outside of time. Within this landscape, life is realized within "one polygonal experience of order." Church bells sing out "Quantum, Quantum," and water sliding under a bridge bears the sound of the name of Euclid. Time itself becomes converted into "three lucid and concentric spheres" that "murmur the harmonious names of Newton and Kepler." The officer's memory of this place takes on the appearance of permanence and unity (*MAG*, pp. 106-107).

The world the officer represents, however, is available to him only indirectly, built as it is "upon the base of your' [i.e., Cambridge's] abstract isosceles peace" (*MAG*, p. 106). Here disorder and discord are not a part of the picture, because the picture itself evolves out of the perspective of geometry. But the reality of a world of peace and harmony is undermined by the officer's own perceptual practices.

The so-called "mental structures" which the officer generates finally rely on evidence communicated by his senses. The officer produces a picture of a rigid and spiritualized landscape because his feelings of praise for Cambridge are identified with an intellectual activity that intends only to measure out and define the material world. Ultimately, immediate experience and transcendental intuition are shut out in order to accommodate his wish for a timeless order of peace and harmony. The mind's reliance on sensual evidence undermines the spirit of praise the officers intend to convey.

This discussion of Merton's early works has come to suggest the following: Thomas Merton puts into question the meaning of "normal perception," posits a series of opposing terms and produces any number of formulations for the differences between normal seeing and imagination, or the subject matter and the central action of the picture.

As I have represented them, the issues raised by both the critique of idealism and naturalism in art and the analysis of the Blakean Imagination, especially as they relate to the person of the artist in the world, establish two opposing identities. In the novel they are conveniently identified as the "crazy poet" and the "dreaming technician" artist. What I have tried to suggest thus far is that the technician's identity is a function of the critique and the analysis.

Merton's critique, on the one hand, calls into question the meaning of ordinary or normal perception. As we have seen, normal perception tends to maintain the negative and secondary terms of these early poetics. Normal perception suggests the technician artist creates a landscape, or fashions a subject matter, or devises a pattern that denies a person's fundamental need for direct and immediate experience of God.

The German officer, the woman character named B., the officer of the artillery, and the little girl Anne all suggest the power of the technician to circumscribe systematically the identity of a person to the will of the state. Although motivated by dreams of a world ordered by peace and harmony, these technicians achieve their ends through perceptual and intellectual practices ordered exclusively by the rules of empirical science and Platonic logocentrism. The effect of their efforts on the human community is political uniformity, moral deterioration of the institutions of society, spiritual denial, and intellectual contradiction.[12]

On the other hand, Merton's analysis of Blake's Imagination brings to view the more hidden dynamics of visionary sight. I have already suggested that Merton saw Blake as the poet who perfectly realized a unified conception of the religious artist. For Merton, Blake's genius lay in his ability to know and love God through the Imagination. The category of the Imagination, then, becomes the special type of vision by which one comes to see God's glory bursting forth from the created world. This vision is not dependent on perception of natural phenomena as these are mediated through the senses. Nor does this vision especially value or even rely on the intellect's ability to reason or to have discourse about nature. Instead, Merton sees Blake's Imagination as the vehicle for a radical transformation of the individual's normal perceptual activity which, in its "usual" tendency towards analysis and definition, excludes transcendental intuition and shuts out immediate experience of God.

The process of moving from seeing things by virtue of normal perception to seeing things by virtue of a transformed perception is often reflected in Merton's journals. Certain episodes of a life, especially when represented in the act of writing, allow the writer to reflect on the differences between a pattern, event, or person as they exist in an apparently random physical space or context and the interpretive moves by which that pattern or event is made into a personal meaning, symbol, or history of one's own. One of these moves involves a distinction between normal perception and the "consciousness of perception," and for Merton, the

---

12. The mythic figure inspiring Merton's critique of naturalism and idealism in the novel is Blake's Urizen, a figure who "represents empiricism and doubt, and also dogmatism, because he is blind to imagination, passion, and spirit" (*LE*, p. 427). In the character of Mrs. Frobisher is suggested the effects of Urizen upon daily, family life: manners, duty, allegiance to country, the worship of science, all of these take precedence over the individual, imagination, spontaneity, or love of God. Mrs. Frobisher makes speeches comparing horsemanship to good manners and *noblesse oblige*; she gives sermons on the duty the narrator has "to run with the pack;" and she teaches her children "a lot of lessons in utilitarian morality" (*MAG*, pp. 59-71).

The Merton narrator's analysis of Cambridge represents the moral deterioration of the institution to which the individual has been subjected. The narrator hears the decay of "dried scraps of putty falling from [Cambridge's] windows onto the linoleum floors," and sees the sun color the streets of Cambridge "like the parchment skin of dying protestant bishops." The narrator smells a sort of pollution that bespeaks moral contradiction of "the awful cleanness of soap in the dank showers" but which cannot remove the stain of suicide "where the soccer player hanged himself." Even the "thought of Cambridge . . . empties like old gin out of a glass that has been standing several days, among the clean plates." Here the action of emptying out suggests how the thought pervades and unobtrusively contaminates "the clean plates" from which others will feed themselves.

The narrator's responses to his memory of Cambridge also depict one of the causes of past suffering. In an important way, these responses become a poetic anatomy of the more demonic aspects of Cambridge. This anatomy is achieved by generalizing particular memories in order to suggest the individual's suffering. For example, while we notice that the narrator tastes Cambridge "in the broken skin of [his] lips," the meaning of the sentence is completed by virtue of a comparison: "I taste you . . . like the bloody leather . . . boxing glove." The narrator tastes a force of physical violence, of which the broken skin of his lips is a sign. Thus the poet identifies Cambridge as an obscure and malevolent force which does psychological and finally even physical violence to the individual (*MAG*, pp. 107-109).

recognition of such a move yields an important moment of self-discovery.

"The big discovery I made there in 1938," writes Merton of a train ride he took through the Delaware Valley, "when riding with [Robert] Lax was only, after all, that I was capable of reflecting upon an act of consciousness of my own." It was only "since then that [he had] been able to write any poems." Some of what this discovery means is spelled out in an entry from his "Perry Street Journal" from the fall of 1939. In this entry, Merton indicates that the "big discovery" made clear the difference between simply seeing a random pattern of things and seeing the pattern in relation to an act of thought: "I recognized it [a billboard seen on another train ride, this time through Long Island] as something I had seen before, but I happened to be thinking about it, in relation to some telegraph poles moving in front of it." In other words, what is clarified is a "distinction between a normal perception and a reflection upon the consciousness of perception." The big discovery makes clear the relationship between, in this case, the random memory of "a series of things that just happen to be there" and which "never meant anything," and an action of consciousness which makes "something I had seen before" into a "part of a pattern" and, we might add parenthetically, into a meaning "of my own."[13]

By making the scene "a pattern of my own," Merton also discovers an identity that accounts for a change in the way he attends to the scene. Merton's negotiation of random events into a personal meaning suggests a symbolic transformation, not so much of material or events, but of the kind of attention he gives to the things or events within a particular scene or context. Perception is now transformed by virtue of his power to recognize or to make his own patterns. Thus the meanings he fashions as poet alter attention habitually tied to or associated with "normal perception." While this interpretive move yields a moment of self-discovery that shifts attention from perception of patterns to reflections "upon an act of consciousness of my own," such a move also links Merton to symbolic relationships friendly to his newly discovered identity as poet or writer.

In an October 1939 "Perry Street Journal" entry, Merton writes about various paintings of Fra Angelico, El Greco and Breughel that he saw while at the World's Fair Art Exhibition. In this entry he does a close analysis of one of Breughel's works, "Wedding Dance." This particular reflection is

---

13. For the two journal entries to which I refer, see Michael Mott, *The Seven Mountains of Thomas Merton*, pp. 114 and 136. I found Mott's chapter, "The Pasture, Merton's Heart," especially helpful in pointing out Merton's early concerns and struggles as a writer.

valuable because it manifests the major tendencies of the poetics which I have just outlined.

In this analysis of the Breughel, Merton identifies a "pyramidal arrangement of people formed by the central dance," which he calls "the basis of composition" in the picture. This first pyramid contains the more active elements of the wedding feast, and these images seem ordinary enough at first glance. At the apex of the pyramid, Merton notices two cartoon-like couples. From this point, his perception of the work moves to the right, encompassing a first line of spectators, and then moving to a group of pipers in the lower right corner, finally to a sudden notice of the red and white colors which emerge from, but which also animate, the crowd of onlookers. Merton's attention to the first pyramid then gives way to a second one; but the second pyramid captures his attention even more suddenly and forcefully. At its apex is "one, rigid, solitary, little man in grey with his back to the whole business, simply looking away at nothing" (SJ, p. 17).

Merton's interest in how the artist and the mystic share in a direct and intuitive knowledge of God without the benefit of concepts finds expression, ironically enough, in his analysis of the Breughel painting. As viewer Merton participates in the action of this picture by virtue of the symbolic figure — the solitary, grey man. In this solitary figure, Merton has found the key to the whole composition because the grey man "is paying no attention to anything, doing nothing . . . ignoring everything about the subject matter." The grey man, who is associated with a meaning of not paying attention to the subject matter, is the central "objective" action of the picture itself. However, this figure also directs Merton's "subjective" response to the picture. The grey man, then, symbolically orders the attention Merton now gives to the subject matter. Thus, on one hand Merton is now free to review and discover an area of the picture that had gone previously unnoticed. On the other hand, Merton's original response to Breughel's accomplishment as an artist is profoundly reformed (SJ, pp. 17-18).

That his appreciation of Breughel as an artist has been deepened directs our attention as readers to at least one kind of relationship that Merton was choosing to establish and develop at this period of his life. But to see the importance of this kind of relationship, I want first to invoke another: the relationship possible here between Thomas Merton and his contemporaries who view the pictures with him at the exhibition. According to Merton, individuals in the crowd frequently reflect their own attitudes to art as a sort of commodity. They memorize the subject matter of the picture and use the knowledge they have gained as a kind of currency to buy themselves social status. While they have appropriated a certain rote learning about great art from their guidebooks, there is no guarantee that they will penetrate to the unknowing heart of the picture's form. On the contrary, crowd responses to the El Grecos seem to reflect emotional reactions to the images of sickness and suffering which betray only the thinnest veneer of understanding, and which lead them away from a deeper sharing in, and even enjoyment of, what the artist has done (*SJ*, pp. 19-20).

Such reactions awaken in Merton a sort of horror about the "subject matter" of the world and towards his contemporaries. The people at the art exhibition do not wake up to themselves and talk like people when they view the El Grecos. Instead, they themselves talk "like the possessed." And in his own reaction to these responses, Merton indicts his age as one "of hypocondriacs and murderers and sterilisers." His question is finally about the pictures that "we" make: can "*our* pictures . . . be said to die, when the can't even come to life" in the first place? (*SJ*, pp. 20-21).

That Merton chose to establish another kind of relationship during this period of his life is made apparent by the way he developed aspects of his own understanding about art. This particular passage makes us aware of the relationship that Merton attempts to create between himself and the absent artist, in this case, Breughel. By identifying the grey man as the key element or central action in the picture, Merton has enriched an implied relationship between himself and the absent artist. Merton comes more fully to appreciate Breughel and then to situate him in a modern context of experience. Even more importantly, however, the grey man brings together in tentative synthesis earlier reflections about William Blake and St. Thomas. I have already suggested that, with his back turned to the wedding dance, the grey man becomes the central action of the Breughel painting. But the grey man also recalls the Blakean identity, that is his genius, and the "meaning" of that identity — that the artist and the mystic share the same kinds of intuitions about God. In their own way, either meet God "face to face," without using concepts or having recourse to analysis. The grey man suggests just this aspect of such a meeting.

The grey man, however, also reintroduces some of the values that St. Thomas represents in his ability to strike a balance between emotions and the intellect. As transforming agent of the way Merton initially attended to the scene, the grey man represents an identity that is free from habitual control or domination by "normal perception," as suggested, for example, by the responses of the people at the exhibition. In this sense, the grey man does not come to mean "rejection" of these responses or of the subject matter. Instead, the figure represents an attitude of refusal to have attention shaped or identity claimed by responses like these alone. Merton's negotiation of the subject matter into a personal meaning suggests a symbolic transformation, not of the patterns perceived, but of the attention he gives to possible life-giving relationships which are otherwise hidden by the subject matter, distorted by contemporary responses, or finally excluded altogether by the technicians' empiricism and idealism.

As a result of following Merton's perceptual activities through from the dance to the grey man, one begins to gain a feeling for the quality of this transformed attention. While perceived in relation to the subject matter, the grey man disappears from sight, the sight that is of the people watching the celebration of the wedding feast. (I have tried to suggest that the people caught up in the dance include not just the figures of the painting but also the people at the art exhibition who are moved only by the subject matter of the painting.) If, as we have seen, the "meaning" of the grey man is "not paying attention to the subject matter," what is left out, or what has gained Merton's attention as the central action of the picture, is a figure or a form which undermines the very importance, the significance, the very meaning of the wedding dance. The grey man at the margin of this dance appears as the secret center or activity of the dance itself and sustains this center only insofar as he disappears from the view of the crowd which engages the general dance.

Ultimately, the grey man represents the sort of identity necessary for Merton actually to participate in the subject matter of the picture, if not the world. As "perceived" in relation to this secret center, the grey man presents the most radical and enlivening action in the picture, because he revives in Merton a response of wonder or admiration. This figure is a new revelation of the self, of a free and creative identity, situated in the midst of a subject matter, or world, that is normally perceived as being hostile to such identity. Thus Merton's response of profound admiration for, if not wonder at, "just how much Breughel had done with his pattern" enforces, in this case, a movement away from the world's apparent hostility and towards the artist's efforts to bring good pictures to life. Such a response makes the absent artist present, or in Merton's language, "very modern looking." What is also made available for Merton is the healthy, fertile, and life-giving meaning that the artist and his picture has come to represent. In establishing this link between himself and the absent artist, whether he be Breughel, Blake, or Aquinas, Thomas Merton has chosen relationships, largely symbolic, but vitally friendly to his own creative efforts within the domain of the modern and public world.

By way of conclusion, I would like to reflect briefly on my "method" of reading some of Merton's early texts because out of this activity of mine has come a different view, I think, of the origins of an "identity" of interest to many readers of this historical person named Thomas Merton.[14] As a consequence of my analysis, I am able to establish the grey man's status within the picture. This suggests two things: first, that there is something strange or paradoxical about the quality of experience inherent to Merton's interests and perceptual practices; second, that my account of the grey man is possible because I become aware of the operations Merton used to make sense of a concern he had about artistic experience leading him to contemplation. From this concern, so goes my argument, Merton created a poetics, or a set of "reading procedures" that allowed him to distinguish between other related concerns: for example, to distinguish between the historical person of Blake and the Blakean Imagination, between genius and judgment, between contemplative and artistic experience, between normal perception and artistic vision, between the subject matter and the central action of the picture. I have called these procedures Merton's early poetics because they reflect some of the rules he uses to reduce the strangeness or the paradox of someone like Blake, who came to know and love God through his art.

My observation of his perceptual practices or my outlining of some of the conventions he makes use of when writing are ways I have, or anyone has, to talk about an identity of interest to us — in this case, the artist-contemplative. But this is not really the point of this reflection on "my method of reading" Merton's early texts. The point is to suggest that my method has an effect on me. In other words, producing a text which pays attention to Merton's practices of observation and response has influenced what I do when I read or write. And when this awareness is situated within a particular community of readers, as I am attempting to do here, I believe a shift will occur in the way readers of Merton will read and discuss this person and the concerns he laid before us.

---

14. Jonathan Culler's *Structuralist Poetics: Structuralism, Linguistics, and the Study of Literature* (Ithaca, New York: Cornell University Press, 1975) helped me to find the language I needed to describe my reading experience of Merton's early works. See especially his chapter, "Convention and Naturalization."

WEEK OF A VISITOR

IN A STRANGER'S HOUSE:

A Man without a Season
From Merton's Hermitage

by **David Kocka**

SUNDAY, Merton's Hermitage, Abbey of Gethsemani

This is a house — a warm house with cool concrete walls. I'm too old, too gone by myself to play hermit. Those desires have faded into the romantics of my youth. I live on new romantics though I'm not quite sure of their characteristics. (My first ritual). My first action here, once I unpacked, was to create a ritual. I believe in the need and purpose of rituals, though in these days they seem odd and obsolete. Dogs sniff out their turf — poets sniff out poems. And I feel a need for a ritual.

I got a bowl, filled it with water, blessed it and walked through the house reconsecrating old memories, past events and thoughts, and the pains and joys that dwell here. I prayed that the sadness might become creative energy and the insights might re-abound. Then outside, once the square house was blessed, I walked a large circle around it and blessed the earth. I feel more at home now and ready to settle in.

† †

The bumble bees are mating in their bumbling sort of way just off the porch in mid-air. Maybe that is the ecstasy one has to learn in a place like this: all this takes place in the blue haze — green sun-filled thick avenue of woods. I see the hills in the spring distance and wonder who and how many have gazed out from this window.

Such thoughtful seeds feel good in this solitude. They simply scamper in my skull like the mouse patters scrambling above my head in the ceiling. The monk steel cup is half-filled with water — here on the old prophet's desk. A lizard steadily guards the wood box and butterflies burst wild from the tall grass.

The old wagon wheel looks at me from the foot of the cross. Twenty years it has been there near the crowded lilies. Like an ancient cyclops eye — with two spokes missing tooth-gaped — it stares at me. The old thing is rusty and worn out, rim tottered, tilted, decaying, exhausted from too many fiery ascensions. Elijah doesn't live here any more.

However, his ravens do (we call them crows). They can be heard in the distance. They it must be who leave me bread and cheese at the doorstep.

The cheese stench lingers on my fingers with no one here to comment. A fox, a beautiful grey fox, strutted by this evening as the sun was going down. It stopped and looked at me like a monk upon whose solitude one has intruded.

This is a good place to come back to like an old familiar home — not a hermitage. It's my first visit. Here no one will stone your poems and make you famous. You can read them to the trees and they'll applaud when they're ready — if aided by a drifting wind. But that might be weeks away when I'm in another home.

Perhaps good poems need to be mulled over and after for a long time by a metabolism that is as natural as they are.

RITUALS:

For a fledgling hermit mind, someone need define the rituals of living here. For this reason the only book I brought of Merton's was for this purpose. (*Day of a Stranger*).

The outhouse is inside now — (development comes to those who wait). The king snake near the outhouse is to be addressed such-wise upon entry: "Are you in here, you bastard?"

Reply: "Why are you?"

† †

The bees have gone to bed. It's 9:00 p. m. Sounds change to wood night songs. Bugs are attracted to my night light — kamikaze-ing the window screen. Light can do astounding things to creatures, but so can darkness. I shut off the light and wait for dreams to come — sleeping in Merton's hard simple bed.

Dream

(1)   I saw myself reaching to touch the night reading light — then pulled my hand back quickly — too hot (then I woke up).

(2)   In a green wooded forest a deer appears before me (then I woke up).

MONDAY

At six o'clock a slip of grey white light snuck through the corner of the blinds and hit me in the face. I heard a bird or two. I slept much too well for a fake hermit.

† †

THE HERMITAGE

Photo by Thomas Merton

I put on my ritual garb (shorts and a sweater) and marched to the indoor outhouse. It's funny how these rituals become so easy with time. Boiled water for tea — sat on the porch and I knew that a hermit day had begun; the bumble bees were beginning to mate and work, fight and buzz under the wide eaves as a streak of red sunlight crashed into the green wood onto the grass — an early point of light.

In the simple quiet chapel I prepared for Eucharist. Icons on the wall supported my prayer. Elijah attended and so did the Virgin Mother.

Thick, brown and moist Trappist bread about the size of a silver dollar was placed on the patten. The sweet wine could be smelled as it mingled with the aroma of candle wax. I prayed the Mass of the Holy Spirit — prayed for peace from this place of peace — prayed for the healing of my genetic line on back as far as God would go.

Then I prayed the rosary. Simple prayer forms are best for me now. Unconditional love cannot be conjured.

†   †

Well, here I am, Merton. What does a hermit do now? I've prayed. I know your answer, Merton, and yes, the wind has come through the trees and I had no choice but to breathe it. I'll put on my pants now and try to live with this day.

†   †

How many wish they could be here in my stead this week? Many, I'm sure. Some retreatants sneak up here to get a glimpse of the house. They have great reverence for this bit of concrete on a hill stuck in the pines. But it was you whom they really sought. No, it is something much more than you. You just contained that which we all contain and seek to gain, looking in strange places to find. I really didn't care to come here now. Ten years ago — maybe even five — would have sparked me more. But here I am, without even trying, I've come to visit. You invited me and must have thought me ready. Years ago when I would have thought I needed to come, I would simply have been an intruder. Glad to meet you, Mr. Stranger.

†   †

As a matter of fact I'm looking for my own home. A place in which I can put on, without fear and in freedom, the primal mind in order to make apparitions. Solitude is dangerous.

And the danger makes it holy — can't get too comfortable or you'll run the risk of being a hermit or a monk, an artist or a poet or a seer, soothsayer or shaman. No, when solitude becomes too comfortable — shoot it — because you are in the wrong place.

† †

Primal minds possess no word for art. They have a concept for living, which the western mind might interpret as art. Their immersion in the vast life of tribal experience and its expressions through art and ritual the West calls culture. Their art and their life is only visible, not tangible. They use mystery to celebrate mystery, not to explain it. Perhaps this is my hermit's week task.

† †

Our tribes have hidden themselves in the woods somewhere. And the keepers of the symbols have gone with them. Up here no one knows my name and, if they do, they don't care and if they care, I don't know it. Perhaps this is a house for strangers to visit. Estranged egos looking for a place to strip off their shells and be, without trying, all that they can be, because there is no way to be anything else.

† †

There is nothing here but the apparition of life. Nothing or at least not too much to distract you from your state of not being with that of which you are a part.

Breakthrough is at our fingertips daily if we are willing to take off Perceval's homespun or break Perseus' shield and turn around to discover that the one who spoke to us out there in a mirror darkly was living in the back of our brain.

Such thoughts strike me gently in your house, Mr. Stranger, but this is not the place for too many thoughts — I'll just pick up my Nikon-icon-maker and contemplate with a third eye.

† †

Returning from a long walk in the mid-day sun, sweating well and feeling the cool breeze as I ascended toward the house, I was struck, almost halted, by the pattern of the road. About two years ago I had a dream of ascending a mountain. The road was paved for a while, then it turned into gravel — then dirt — then a simple worn path with grass untrampled.

Two ducks waddled by in front of me. At the top of the mountain was a shelter. From the heights I saw a house in the valley under clear water. Then upon entering the shelter I saw Merton in a pool. He invited me in and together we played with a girl about three years old, splashing and almost dancing in the clear water.

Then a woman figure handed me a bronze sculpture. It was very primitive, like a deer head, the kind primal minds of Africa might make (I awoke).

The road conjured up that dream. It brought it back as clear as day and I recognized that this was the road.

Is this why you invited me up here, Merton? To play in some fresh spring pool with a little child and with you?

If you did, what does it mean — or is meaning out of the question here? Primal people celebrate mystery with mystery itself. I'd like to learn the lesson of living where meaning and life are not distinguished and given private categories.

I'd like to think you've invited me here to unmask what little is left of my illusions of you. Maybe it will just simply drain and dribble out of me so as to allow me the freedom of not having ever to identify with you again.

This is my home right now, Merton, and the one who gave it to me is the same one who gave it to you in the first place.

† †

Merton, I imagine many wish to come here to play a game that they thought you played. I would have been one of them a few years back. But the funny thing is you didn't even know the game you were playing. There were no rules or rites and no wrongs. You just simply tried to play and at times got caught in the thought of thinking. That same game needed to emerge. Useless undefinable uselessness — no scheme no context no pretext for living. All the good works have gone home to hell — all the self-made puppets who try and prop up a dying culture are busy about many things. The ecclesiastical marionettes do their stringed dance, program after program. hoping something will save our desperate diaspora.

A crucified "corpus christi" of which our best efforts are no more than nails being pulled from the palms.

It is sadness that built this house, not pessimistic retreat. Sadness because this house wants to be everywhere. Not a novelty, but a norm, not fringe, but requisite like breathing is to the lungs.

† †

Transformation — a term that western minds find hard to understand. This is America, Merton. The myth in this land is what transformed you. The natives of this earth have taught you the secret of the grandfathers. They live in the trees outside your cabin. Transformation can be done only with a primal mind. Metamorphosis of one thing into another for the sake of knowing and relating with the other. Did Kafka follow me up here?

† †

Sitting on the porch today gazing southward in the blue-green horizon I felt myself transformed:

My eye lashes felt like the wide eaves. My feet felt like a concrete porch. The trunk of my body was built of living blocks and at the center was the hearth. What is it like to be a house on a hill in the woods of Kentucky?

Cords of wood lean against my left side, little lizards play in the cracks. The sun bakes the top of my head and I take it without a sound until the cool night air allows me a crack of relief.

My porch is surrounded by tall green plants. It is a cool moist earth under those footings. I am a shelter for more than men. A spider lives in the sink. Cobwebs are suspended like bridges in secret corners. The branches of big trees scrape me on all sides while hordes of ants tickle my bricks in their rummaging work. The pump of the cistern begins when the toilet is flushed — it seems as though I have gas. My ceiling is soot-soiled from old fires — they are the only remarks I will make of what has gone on here in prayer or in play. No need to tell my secrets. I'm a hermitage. Silence is my final word.

I am maturing in my old age. There are cracks in my facade which make me a little more distinguished than before. I imagine that someday I'll be even more honored than now, not unlike the caves of St. Francis. Yes, that day may well come, being unwelcome, when they make me a sanctuary.

People will gawk at my nakedness then. Pilgrims in need of a touch from their center. And they will go home being disappointed that I am so simple. O yes, the future may be like that but I hope they realize by then that what they obscurely seek in me is not here and never was. Go build your own house. This one is filled, like a widow, with beautiful memories.

†   †

When one chooses to come to a wilderness such as this, one sees how routine the days are. Even the animals, most often unnoticed, retrace their paths and replay their rituals. One just never knows with them when they play and when they work.

We make our lives all too important, just too commodious for a sacrament. Then the time comes in convalescence, in nursing homes or on the death bed, when we wrestle and begin to deal with the face of solitude. Sitting in a rocker looking out at the beautiful landscape reminds me of the old men and women who stare out of their windows, nothing to live for and too healthy to die. They are like fisher kings, but aren't we all? The difference between the hermit — fake or true — and these folks is choice, or is that even valid? Perhaps some attend to the inner choice of spirit earlier than others.

†   †

The life of unconditional love is a life of humility and transparency. If we could only learn somehow to become human spores, letting life in, its sounds and colors, charm, and aroma, letting it all pass through us and out from us without blocking or clinging. This place is a place for mad men, wild men, who know they have bodies and balls, hands and feet, nostrils and hearts, ready to be engaged and ruffled a bit in their encounter with life.

Dare I roll in the grass up here — hug a tree — stand naked in the Kentucky forest at dawn or at midnight — sure I want to — don't we all deep down and secretly. But if we did, could we still make a distinction between the dancer and the dance?

It is dangerous for our western minds to do that free and honest a thing. Maybe if we're drunk enough we'd do it. But then our egos have dissolved in solution and become numb. The freedom of choice is gone and only freedom can spawn that contemplation. No wonder places like this are filled with mysterious wonder and great dread. You're on the edge of being what you always were and unsure if you want to be what you've always longed for and sought in the oddest of places. The funny thing about daring to touch that wild uncontrollable side is not that someone might see (although there is a collective voice that rings in the back of the brain) . . . what is worse is if I'm not wholeheartedly involved in it, then I might have to watch myself be a fool. If I take the plunge this week into my wild sanity, I won't tell you. Only my shaman knows for sure.

TUESDAY

This place is built for aboriginal "dreamtime." That is what our culture refers to as poetry. People all over the world join me here when the question "where are we when we think?" is asked.

Dreamtime is sacred time — the realm of myth and inspiration. It is a time when someone speaks to me with my own voice. A marvelous familiar stranger appears. William Blake suggested "if the doors of perception were cleaned, man would see everything as it is, infinite." To cultivate the imagination is to attend to the sacrament of the psyche (soul).

Perhaps the real need of places like this is to fulfill the need that our culture has lost so long ago. When western culture stepped out of its primal mind, we set our course on a journey which is difficult to retrieve. We've become perpetual spectators of the world vicariously living (or thinking to live), outside the nature that governs us by "natural law." But the physicists (specialists), to whom we have given away our power, are only now discovering from their objective spectator sport that they are unsure of what the "natural law" is.

I wonder if that doesn't also happen in ecclesiastical circles. We've locked up our mystics. Joseph Cupertino flew around when he celebrated Mass — lock him away ... kill the medicine men, censor the shaman . . . why? Because death is a universal threat to the existence of the physical body — but "heresy" is a threat to "existence" itself. (At least one perspective of existence).

View from within THE HERMITAGE

Photo by Thomas Merton

I think that Christ came and grew here as a cult figure because the west needed him more than most. He didn't appear in China or in the Americas. He came to the center of the "civilized world," even the physical center of that time. Why? To show us how to become God. Or rather to return to us our lost humanity, that is, "to open the doors of perception — to cleanse it so that we could see things as they are": "infinite."

† †

What did you go out into the desert to see? Someone dressed in fine clothes or one naked rolling in the grass and hugging trees — speaking with birds and dreaming dreams?

Isn't that why the desert Mothers and Fathers went out to the solitary places? The primal peoples made a life of such an adventure. They could not be whole if they hadn't attempted a vision quest. The quests would rely on sacred songs and hardships, fasting, sleeplessness, nakedness, cold, living for days in the wilderness as a means of stimulating visions.

We seem to laud the saints and revel in their glory as opposed to celebrating their substance by similar practice. Jung is correct when he states that we are living in a mythless society. Our rites, rituals, symbols and art are so banalized that those who feel the great call are either victims of the collective unconscious or make great strides to create their own myths.

The spectators among us will then critique their life and work as *avant garde* and laudable or as trash that upsets our taste. Van Gogh and Gauguin are good examples.

Our religious deserts seem to suffer the same onslaught. Even the most vigorous of them can too often get caught up in the comfortable and familiar. When the desert becomes an oasis the suburbs will move in. Then the church and even its potential bright stars will become gypsies and tourists, no longer pilgrims and strangers.

† †

Yes, this place, Merton, is still primitive enough to scare you to death and rebirth. Dare I tell you what I saw from your old porch last evening when the sun was almost set and darkness crept in? Did you know there was a shrine to a virgin about seventy yards from the cabin? There is. She is only three feet tall and low to the ground under a canopy of trees, very simple. I was watching the night descend when I looked her way.

As I stared I'm sure I saw her move. I remembered how as a child waiting to go to confession in the dark church halls, I would gaze in a similar way at the Sacred Heart statue. It would move for me then, too. I'm sure that has happened to many of us when we were children. Well, I looked again and looked dimly at what was dim. For fifteen minutes I looked that way and the more I looked the more she moved, that is she danced, really danced with soft curves and gentle motions. It was as if I was being invited to dance with her. Did I tell you that Kafka followed me up here? I won't tell you what I did. That is too personal.

† †

It rained early this morning and was rather cool. I built a fire and prayed in the rocking chair. The tea kettle brought me to the kitchen for breakfast, oatmeal and toast. When the sun came out I spread some blankets on the grass to burn out the musty smell. It's noon and time to pray again.

† †

On my third day as a part-time hermit, it has come to my attention that a schedule must be created. Though hermits must be wild and free that does not mean they can be lazy and indulgent.

What should a hermit's day be like?

— get up and out of bed when you wake up. the sun helps you out that way.

— first ritual leads you to the indoor outhouse . . .

— sit down and wake up — listen to the day begin. what can you expect from the day — the sun helps or the lack thereof.

— boil water for tea.

— pray for awhile — while the water is boiling.

— eat breakfast.

— celebrate Eucharist and pray for awhile.

— work time — find something that will move your blood. Make you sweat — stretch your ligaments and loose your mind from the thought that you're playing hermit. Now don't overdo it — there is nothing to be gained in working to get too much done quickly. If you do that there will be too much time for thinking of things to do. No rush, take it easy and enjoy splitting wood, or cutting grass, or cleaning the cabin.

— take some nourishment — take a nap — the Lord gives to his beloved in sleep.

— now sit on the porch and feel free to think how being here makes no sense at all. Think, too, how dull you are and how dull you were before you came here.

— take a walk someplace without direction — just walk 'cause it's good to walk while you can. Enjoy walking and breathing. Walk till you think of something to do, then keep walking and don't do that good thing you thought of doing.

— read for awhile. Pick something out to read by your intuition. Read on the porch till a bee distracts you or a thought spins you off into a blank stare . . . let the thought walk on by and read . . .

— write if you feel it and then write when you feel that you don't feel it.

— be attentive to the little things — like the rotation of the fan — the overhead mouse — the bird chirp — squirrel rattle — dog bark and bee buzz — feel your butt on the bench — feet on the flour — heart beat — breath — hand scratch — itch on the face.

— eat when you are hungry and sleep when you are tired.

— go pray — BREATHE.

— take some time to think on how bad you are at being a hermit . . . .

† †

Two of Elijah's ravens came today, one on foot, the other on a bike. The foot raven brought me some eggs, corn and margarine. He must have been a Mayan in a former life. The bike raven brought beer, poetry and conversation. We shared a beer, read a poem about the "Luxuriant Apocalypse" and talked about *pointe vierge* and the Immaculate Conception.

† †

There are holy men in this place — sensitive men who struggle like the rest of us — more intensely at times perhaps — with the terrors of Paradise. If we could only clean the doors of perception and see things as they are.

WEDNESDAY

Overslept and missed the sunrise — then I completed my usual rituals and went to the desk to finish reading the poems Paul [Quenon] gave me. They are good poems — honest and straightforward — humorous — deep when depth is called for. Irony must be a Trappist trait or rather, in attempting seriously to live out a solitary life (an impossible ideal), irony becomes a tool — a vantage point whose message is simply: "Your ego's been nudged — now laugh at it creatively and stop taking yourself and your ideas so seriously."

I read a poem on the porch which was my response to his poetry — got choked up a bit and made him read my awful writing. Then I tried again with great ease —

Paul brought the graveling lawn cutter up to let me get some exercise and tidy up the tall grass. I felt like one of the horsemen of the apocalypse behind that bright red and white machine — uphills — near the lilies — into a tree round the building — nicked the fence post — into mole ruts — over an anthill — into a ditch and parked.

The exercise felt good — sweat, dirt in my face, stretched body and mostly losing myself in the process. Modern man on the whole is sick because of a sick outlook on leisure and labor. Sure, some get exercise but that's different somehow. An old Indian shaman said: "It doesn't matter too much what you eat or drink, etc... but somewhere somehow you've got to sweat." What's that commercial that is ringing in my ear? Never let 'em see you sweat? — In other words never let them see you vulnerable or human — keep up the image, the persona mask — you might die young and frustrated — but you sure as hell will look and smell good.

Sweat — that's the only message I have received here — sweat and do what you will.

This is a catholic hermitage — with a small "c." And I find it most amusing that in every hermitage I've been to from the Franciscan hermitage of Monte Casale — LeCelle — LaCarceri — St. Anthony's in Egypt and an isolated home in the Arizona desert — certain animals are required. Most of them contain the same creatures. Lizards are a must, so too are crows, butterflies, wasps, bees, moths and mice. Here I've got them all and they are important. They are the only ones who give you a sense of life that is at least familiar. I missed the bumble bees today for about an hour. They must have been napping.

† † †

For lunch: I took the ravioli left from Sunday which Brother Anthony kindly gave me and added some ginger — hot sauce — peppers — altar wine — cheese and tomatoes, onions and a few other odds and ends and ate well and in peace. The turmoil will come later but I brought some Maalox. Yes, I believe even hermits can't digest everything. Especially after having to deal with all the beasts —(i.e., as mentioned above). Those creatures are more than empirical data on the paper from *National Geographic* — they live in the psyche —

Or at least so I'm told as I sit here with a glass of Yellowstone reading Jung. Yes, I forgot to tell you, he and an American Indian name Jameke Highwater followed me up here too.

Before my discussion with them, however, I needed to get air in my pickup's tire. So I got gas as well and, while I was at it, some beer and bourbon. Well, you have to help out the local economy and this is bourbon country — you wouldn't want to offend them.

Besides if some monk is inspired to visit this time I can offer him a beer. Actually it is wise to have no booze if you are attempting to get in touch with the divine. However, wine and bread do help in an unbloody sort of way. But I've come to appreciate that, like solitude: if you are too routinely comfortable with it, the possibility of breakthrough is impossible. You might just as well have a drink. With the danger of overindulgence at hand, I find inebriation a possibility every step of the way. Drink — solitude-monastic life-art-mysticism and the lot — compulsion comes in many forms. That's why you see snakes — beatles — bats, birds and virgins dancing — well, not the only reason.

In other words, life everywhere is dangerous, especially if you take yourself too seriously or not seriously enough. Monks, hermits and the rest of us should learn a lesson. Firstly, there are no monks nor hermits nor the rest of us. Just people stuck with a bundle of grace and love that twists and squirms in our bellies and bowels, sometimes making it to the head where dreadful disease gets worse like the curse that came from the garden. To each his or her own darkness and light. Let's allow justice and peace to kiss and make up and unfold into a compassionate new being. That sounds catholic to me.

If there are any monks left over, any hermits or pretenders, there's beer left in the fridge: "Drink it and do what you will" — the cows have all gone home.

† † †

This place needs a woman's touch — but what masculine place doesn't. *Anima mea* please get out of here, this is not a place for women, at least as far as I know. Let's cut down the flowers — separate the bees — harvest the forests — kick out our souls — damn it, David, stop writing poetry — Sophia just jumped into the bedroom and Proverb slipped out of the lectionary — can't you see that we are overrun by that spirit called woman. Boy! — I mean — Girl! that bourbon does do strange things.

Anyway, whoever reads these lines probably thinks I'm a heretic — well, that might be so. I read in *Conjectures of a Guilty Bystander* that little minds undid Meister Eckhart in that fashion.

Merton didn't live long enough to see that they now call him a saint. So much for a defense. The cows still have gone home. Besides, I sing Kyrie and Sanctus in the liturgies I'm privileged to celebrate — how's your local pastor?

† †

THE HERMITAGE FIREPLACE

Photo by Thomas Merton

In a vision I saw a cope crucified to an apse wall — waiting for some symbol loving fable child to pull out the nails like the youth Arthur of the Round Table and Holy Grail, who pulled out the sword from the stone.

Then I saw the nostalgic saccharine souls with bodies beyond the sixties or stuck in the early part of the century who want to return to the old unconscious rites (familiar no longer) or make a return to that which they've never known. Sweet Jesus, I'm with you, come softly with your rouge and lipstick heart throbbing in your hand. Don't laugh — there's something to be learned — don't long for it — it's got you already —

When you take the icons out of churches, posters abound in the stores . . . read the signs of the times, that's a sacrament too.

Where have all the poets gone? — long time passing, where
have all the poets gone.
. . . long time ago — ?

Could it be and should it — that our mythless West — to say a society without a season or reason to live — which undoes every culture because we ourselves are undone — has as some ungodly vocation from God the call to do just that?

And if and when we've undone and done them in with our great western aggression imposing our principles, our norms and our mission (let no culture remained unturned).

Then, perhaps, all of us on the same fragile and vulnerable turf can look at one another in wonder and weep — saying: "Wasn't it good, that variety, those songs and those stories, that color and dress, those eyes terrorized by the plow of paradise lost, longing to gain their own garden."

Then it could be that we agree, being commonly common, that the old stories and songs, color and dress would return on their own to give us a grace unexpected, engaging us in a peace that is beyond our limited view.

Could it be and should it?

THURSDAY

Well, I've got two new piles of wood to stack today as well as finish cutting the grass. My meeting with the Abbot and a small committee to interview for a possible sculpture commission will be held tomorrow evening at 6.45 p.m.

I'm not too sure the monks here are ready to "cannon-ize" Merton in bronze. I can understand and appreciate that. I'm sure they weren't too hot on doing the same for Benedict either. But until people come to the awareness that they too contain that virginal point (*point vierge*), we will always have need to project our hidden inner goodness outward onto someone else — we'll make others live out or represent our unlived call to holiness. Some sort of image of Merton will arrive here in a public way sometime, I'm sure of that, perhaps if not now, maybe in fifty years or so.

† †

I didn't sleep all that well last night. You know they don't have springs on the beds. That must be one of those techniques for subverting your sleep in order to induce visions. Do you really think so?

This is no place for hermit-asters. I'm sure many of us will come here to have a retreat with Merton, but don't you listen to them. Merton doesn't live here any more. Resurexit — sicut — dixit.

This is just a place where someone tried to live a simple life with all its mystery and struggle, who failed at times, was unsure of the code, caught some glimpses of the Kingdom — was smart enough to see beyond the hills, wanted to be everywhere where he wasn't and knew that being here was just as good a place as any, seeing that everywhere and nowhere were the same. That was his genius.

To catch the wave of that spirit authentically would mean to build your own house, in your own place, according to your own nature. But you have to have a nature first in order that "Grace's House" can be edified. When you ride on the shirttails of someone else's wake, it usually means you are uncertain of your nature and certainly out of touch with your creativity. We Catholics have always been good at capitalizing on the dead bones of our saints and mystics. As long as that saint or mystic is locked up in a flesh-eater sarcophagus — behind glass or in the gilded reliquary, in pieces all over the world, they're safe enough to have around. Let's all jump off the Merton bandwagon. Anyway, the wheel is broken and leans up against the cross decaying day by day.

Don't get me wrong, Mertonians — I think he should be honored and thanked, celebrated and remembered. More than that we should learn what he was in the process of learning.

Sanctuaries and images, candles and pilgrimages are good, right and wholesome to my mind. But they are a little less than conscious events (effective perhaps at one level) if we don't allow them to point back to ourselves. They are a little like gazing at the finger that points to the moon.

†   †

Is that enough preaching, Kocka? Are you satisfied that you got it out for yourself and you are convinced? Go mow the grass, you Hermit-aster. You'd like to have people read this just as much as the next guy. Who do you think you're fooling — are you channeling Merton now?

†   †

Perhaps the Metaphor of Paradox is not only Merton's but, in fact, is the image of our age. Maybe that's why we can connect with his experience.

†   †

Brother Patrick' [Hart] is coming up for supper. I'd better get the cheese and bread ready — clean up the lawn and pray some. In his office is a watercolor of the hermitage (painted by Jim Cantrell), right on the wall and if you could see through it, you'd be looking right at this site. So, according to the time-space consciousness of the Hopi Indians, if I walk out the front door of this place, I should be in his office. Hello, Patrick!

This is a universal point, if you take the Hopi consciousness into consideration. The mud daubers build their houses out of mud (obviously) and they are reminiscent of the adobe pueblo cultures. Then the meat eaters (wasps) are excellent technicians ... they build their units like cells in a monastery — but then I'm not sure if they are monks or not — I think each cell is a pentagon. Anyway, they are guarding the four corners of the great porch. You can see by the mud smears on the porch trim, somebody undid most of the pueblo — mud dauber homes. So much for the third world.

But the bumble bees are the fat cats. They're as big as half of your thumb. They live in the house like the rest of us — (dominant culture that we are). Oh well, so much for projection.

†   †

God? I'm not going to talk about God here — that's in another notebook.

†   †

I don't miss the TV except for Ted Koppel. Anyway the hearth with a fire in it serves a similar purpose. Perhaps a better one. To dream dreams or tell stories around that bundle of energy is better than most TV programs I've seen. Besides there are no commercials.

† †

Most people don't want to be monks or hermits but they want to be holy — maybe even most monks and hermits don't want to be monks and hermits, they just want to be holy, too. The possibility of holiness is all over the place.

FRIDAY

Brother Patrick came for supper last night. We had cheese, bread and beer — lots of good conversation and some good laughs as well. He stayed an hour and a half beyond his bed time. I'm sure it was 9.30. They get up early here, you know.

† †

Well, I've decided that after my meeting with the Abbot I'll be on my way. There is still a good part of the day ahead of me and I hope to get the wood up in stacks before I leave.

† †

The longer one stays here the more attached you become to the idea and experience of solitude. Something in the brain's mechanics changes. I'm not sure if it's the air or the water but whatever it is, I find my thoughts calmer and clearer. There is no rush to get things done because of a deadline. Things get done in due season even in a senseless place.

At this stage in our evolution, it seems we are a society of instant replay. It used to be certain individuals would do a work or live a life and sometime down the road they would either be theologized, philosophized or historically criticized.

With the instant replay capability and mind set — we attempt an assimilation in the middle of the game, whatever that might be. This place has reinforced for me the need for contemplative pause, over and after the events of life. Otherwise we run the risk of a superficial interpretation to the happenings.

I think that I have to live a life which counters our cultural thrust. That seems to be in accord with the Christian ideal. I've met too many people in my work who in some way could be called successful — but what kind of life was it? What good was it if you've never done the thing you wanted to do in all your life? We must go where our body and soul want us to go. Follow your bliss —

That is a very different call from being successful — it's a call to fidelity, to a knowledge of oneself. It's normally called conscience. One may even end up challenging the orthodox community of which he is a part. That's what happened to Jesus — he died as a heretic. Why should we be so amazed that in the history of our tradition we've burned many mystics as heretics? Follow your bliss and burn at the stake.

It seems to me the function of any orthodox community is to give the mystic his desire and scope: which is union with God — through mortification and death. But then let him go there. Give him the Judas-called "friend" kiss.

† †

It's been suggested by Hugo Rahner that the Church must live out, as the body of Christ, the elemental stages of his life. These stages are movements of transformation. Then it sounds as though he is suggesting that the Church must die and resurrect. I wonder if we're not on one of those death edges now.

Could it be that the Spirit Jesus sent us after his ascension, received at Pentecost, was taken and compiled in a collective vessel "the Church." Then the individual tongues of fire were consolidated in one fire (together — together). A union of this sort is not community, but we live under that assumption. To each his or her own flaming tongue. It's the relation that makes community possible — but individuals need to stand on their own grace-filled two feet in order to relate.

If the collected — unconscious — grace-filled vessel is on the verge of breaking, then some individuals had better be prepared to lap up what spills out or it will be lost.

† †

Now seems the hour when the Spirit of the Lord and Her Holy operation is once again presented to individuals who are willing to allow the Word to become incarnate in their lives. That's a tremendous task because it infers that no longer will an institution or group or one individual live your holiness for you.

†   †

That, it seems to me, was the underlying message of Thomas Merton as well as all the great mystics.

†   †

On his death bed, St Francis said: "The Lord has taught me what to do. May he teach you what is yours to do."

†   †

THE HERMITAGE CROSS

Photo by Thomas Merton

Doing their doing and trying to become their being means we have lost the possibility of becoming our unique Christified selves who in concert with other Christified selves could illumine the world.

† †

Merton wrote on Franciscan eremitical life. Perhaps there is something of a vision for the future in that little essay. If this place of his wants not to be eccentric but concentric in relation to the world, if it does not want to be a novelty but a norm of sorts, then there may be truth in that statement.

The Franciscan eremitical life is a neighborhood of hermits with mothers and children. It's a little clustering of "church" in relation to one another and the world. Personally I feel that this rule for hermits could be expanded and developed in such a way that without creating a ghetto church — lively *communidads de base* — could emerge. Some people already have their mission and call and are not following their bliss. That is tragic for the church, our nation and our world. Those who are accomplishing this in the — God be praised — variety of expression, I pray may be blessed.

The rest of us will just have to reflect on the possibility and hope our time will come.

I didn't want to write about you, Merton, especially in your own home. I'm sure that after twenty long years in eternity you know pretty much about yourself anyway. Besides I just wanted to pick up where you left off — isn't that what you'd have us do, rather than simply spin our wheels over your grave?

† †

They told me that Elijah's cloak is neatly packed away in the closet of your bedroom — it's been said he left it after his last fiery ascension, you know when the wheel broke off in the front yard: do you think it would fit?

† †

I read Robert Lax's poetry to the trees this afternoon after I packed. His picture is great. When I grow up to be white-haired like that, I want to comb my hair like Lax's.

By the way the trees applauded and so did I.

†　　†

I have to go and hug the trees now and bid this place farewell. Perhaps I will return some day. If not, it is because I have found my own hill and built my own house. And if that happens, then here and there are not distinct for a man without a season.

THE CONTINUING TSUNAMI:

1989 in Merton Scholarship & Publication

by **Robert E. Daggy**

David D. Cooper — in the only major book published about Merton in 1989, *Thomas Merton's Art of Denial: The Evolution of a Radical Humanist* — says that in recent years "a near-tsunami of biographies, critical analyses, reminiscences, primary source materials, reprints, and ephemeral bric-a-brac have spilled over the floodgates of Merton studies." He goes on to say: "Even more books and collections have been launched upstream."[1] I would probably change the imagery here to accord with the Japanese conception of tidal waves rising from the ocean floor by saying that, in 1989, even more Merton materials have welled to the surface. It may not have been a flood, but more than a trickle of material has been published.

1989 saw the culmination of the various events commemorating and celebrating the twentieth anniversary of Merton's death in 1968 in The First General Meeting of *The International Thomas Merton Society* (titled "The Pattern in the Seed: Thomas Merton's Glimpse of the Cosmic Dance"), held at Bellarmine College in Louisville and the Abbey of Gethsemani from 25 to 28 May. The program at this meeting, the largest conference yet held on Merton, included a presidential address (William H. Shannon), five general session talks (James Conner, O.C.S.O.; Robert Giroux; Robert Hale, O.S.B.Cam.; Paul Marechal; and Mary Luke Tobin, S.L.); papers and presentations by thirty-four Merton scholars and writers; and music and dance performances (Lee Brunner, G. Philip Koonce, and the Richard Sisto Jazz Quartet). No

---

1. David D. Cooper, *Thomas Merton's Art of Denial: The Evolution of a Radical Humanist* (Athens, Georgia: University of Georgia Press, 1989), p. ix. Hereafter referred to in the text as *Cooper*.

plan for gathering the various talks and papers into a "Proceedings" has developed, but several have been published. Five — those by James Conner, Sidney H. Griffith, Michael W. Higgins, Douglas R. Letson, and Karl A. Plank — are included in this *Merton Annual*. Robert Giroux's keynote address, "*The Seven Storey Mountain*: The Making of a Spiritual Classic," was basically the same text as his "Editing *The Seven Storey Mountain*" in *America* (22 October 1988). William H. Shannon's presidential address, "The Farmer from Nelson County," and the two homilies given at Masses by Flavian Burns, O.C.S.O., and Paul J. McGuire, S.C.J., appeared in the Summer 1989 issue of *The Merton Seasonal*. Elena Malits's "The Meaning of *The Seven Storey Mountain*" will appear in the Winter 1990 issue of *The Seasonal* and David D. Cooper's "Merton's Letters to Literary Figures" in the Spring 1990 issue of *Katallagete*. Additional papers from the First General Meeting may be included in *The Merton Annual IV*.

The bulk of Merton publication in 1989, however, was not generated by the many 1988 commemorations and the ITMS General Meeting. In looking at the year as a whole certain things stand out: 1) the appearance of a significant amount of previously unpublished or obscurely published Merton material; 2) the reprinting of several Merton texts (at least one of which was modestly revised); 3) an upsurge (perhaps resurgence is better) of Merton publication in England; 4) an impressive amount of participation in Merton studies by Canadians; 5) the introduction of some less explored topics in shorter writings about Merton; and 6) the publication of an inevitable number of reminiscences and what Cooper terms "ephemeral bric-a-brac."

Two books and three articles presented previously unpublished Merton writings. The second volume of the Merton correspondence was published by Farrar, Straus & Giroux in August: *The Road to Joy: Letters to New and Old Friends*; selected and edited by Robert E. Daggy. This volume, intended as a celebration of the lasting friendships in Merton's life, is divided into five sections: I. To Mark Van Doren; II. To Family and Family Friends; III. Circular Letters to Friends; IV. To Some Special Friends (Mahanambrata Brahmachari), Seymour Freedgood, John Howard Griffin, Robert Lax, Sister Therese Lentfoehr, Thomasine O'Callaghan, Beatrice Olmstead and Family, Ad Reinhardt, Edward Rice, Saint Bonaventure Friends, John H. Slate, Daniel Clark Walsh); and V. To and About Young People. *The Road to Joy* is reviewed in this volume by Sister Jane Marie Richardson.

Walter H. Capps edited (from a tape transcription) and introduced Merton's remarks delivered at the Center for the Study of Democratic

Institutions in Santa Barbara, California, on 3 October 1968. Titled *Preview of the Asian Journey*, it was published by Crossroad. The remarks were made only days before Merton left for Asia and the basic text gives insight into what he thought he might do while there and certain inklings as to what he thought he might do when he returned. Two essays — "The Sacred City" and "The Wild Places" — which appeared in *The Center Magazine* are included, but they have appeared elsewhere and neither enlarge upon nor bear on the remarks themselves. Bonnie Bowman Thurston reviews the book in this *Annual*.

Brother Patrick Hart continued his serialized edition of Merton's "St. Aelred of Rievaulx and the Cistercians" with a fifth instalment in the first number of *Cistercian Studies* for 1989. Two early letters of Merton's, written during his undergraduate days at Columbia, were offered for sale this year. They were published in the Autumn issue of *The Merton Seasonal* under the title "Thomas Merton and Alfred B. Hailparn: Two Recently Discovered Letters Concerning the 1937 *Columbian*." Merton was editor-in-chief of the yearbook and the letters deal primarily with yearbook activities, documenting as well Merton's well-known fondness for beer. *The Merton Annual II* featured three articles by Merton which were new to readers of English. "Answers for Hernan Lavin Cerda: On War, Technology and the Intellectual" and "Letter to a Poet about Vallejo" had previously appeared only in Spanish translations. "List of Works submitted for the Approval of the Most Reverend Fathers Capitular, O.C.S.O, Meeting at Citeaux, May 1946," written by Merton in French, was translated by William H. Shannon and gives clues to Merton's writing and projects in the mid to late 1940s.

A number of writings and projects, though not from the 1940s, were reprinted during 1989. New Directions issued a trade edition called *Thomas Merton in Alaska: Prelude to* The Asian Journal: *The Alaskan Conferences, Journals, and Letters*. This edition, available in both hardcover and paperback, included the journal and letters and retained the introduction by Robert E. Daggy and preface by David D. Cooper which constituted the limited edition, *The Alaskan Journal of Thomas Merton*, published by Turkey Press in 1988. Eight of the conferences which Merton gave in Alaska (previously published in *Sisters Today* and *The Priest*) were added. Abbess Diane Foster reviews this new edition in *The Annual*.

Unicorn Press which had originally published *Introductions East and West: The Foreign Prefaces of Thomas Merton*; edited by Robert E. Daggy, in 1981, decided to allow this edition to go out of print. (As an aside, the death of Teo Savory in November 1989 ended a long tradition of Merton publishing stretching back to the days when Merton himself first published in *The Unicorn Journal*.) This text was slightly revised by the addition of three more "foreign prefaces" and seven letters on proposed translations of Merton books. It was published by Crossroad under the new title of *"Honorable Reader": Reflections on My Work*, a title taken from the Preface to the Japanese edition of *The Seven Storey Mountain*, where Merton says in the closing paragraph: "Therefore, most honorable reader, it is not as an author that I would speak to you, not as a story-teller, not as a philosopher, not as a friend only: I seek to speak to you, in some way, as your own self."[2] Michael Downey reviews the book in this volume.

Most people familiar with Merton are aware that he decided in 1967 that he would edit his own "underground" magazine, filling it with prose and poetry contributed by his friends and "friends of friends." He called it *Monks Pond* and edited four issues, all of which appeared in 1968. The fourth and last issue was completed after his departure for Asia and in it Merton indicated that there would be no more: "So the pond has frozen over — as planned."[3] It was produced at the Abbey of Gethsemani and the four issues themselves are rare items. It is unclear how many of each issue were actually printed. In order to make this hard-to-find Merton item available to a larger public, it was decided to "unfreeze the pond" and issue a facsimile edition. *Monks Pond: Thomas Merton's "Little Magazine"*, edited by Robert E. Daggy, was published by the University Press of Kentucky. Brother Patrick Hart supplied an afterword. Jonathan Greene, Kentucky poet and one of the original contributors to *Monks Pond*, reviews it in this *Annual*.

Barry Magid has printed a limited edition of one hundred copies of Merton's translation of *Dialogue about the Hidden God*, by Nicholas of Cusa. Magid points out in his brief introduction that Merton's interest in Nicholas never developed beyond this translation. It has appeared, before this edition, only in *The Lugano Review* (1966) and has not been collected in any editions of Merton's writings. Doubleday and Company, a house quick to remainder their books and send them into out-of-print status, has apparently grasped that interest in Merton is swelling rather than receding and has reprinted four Merton titles in paperback (with new covers and, as one

---

2. Thomas Merton, *"Honorable Reader": Reflections on My Work*; edited with an introd. by Robert E. Daggy (New York: Crossroad, 1989), p. 67.
3. *Monks Pond: Thomas Merton's "Little Magazine"*; edited with an introd. by Robert E. Daggy; afterword by Brother Patrick Hart (Lexington, Kentucky: University Press of Kentucky, 1989), p. 212.

might expect, higher prices): *Conjectures of a Guilty Bystander, Contemplative Prayer*, and *A Thomas Merton Reader.*

Finally, among primary Merton materials, the continuing wave of Merton's taped lectures published by Credence Cassettes must be mentioned. Ten more tapes (approximately twenty lectures), under the headings "Prayer" and "Mysticism," were issued on cassette in 1989. The tapes on "Mysticism" are re-edited versions of tapes published originally in the Electronic Paperbacks *Mystic Life* series and are, of course, Merton's lectures on Sufism. Dewey Weiss Kramer examines the entire "Second Series" of *The Merton Tapes* in a review-essay included in this volume.

The "upsurge" of interest in Merton in England is due in no small part to the conferences, seminars, and retreats instigated by William H. Shannon and several English confreres in the last few years. Shannon's "Study Week" at Clare College, Cambridge University (where Merton attended one year before being rusticated to the United States), has helped in prompting Clare to acknowledge Merton as one of their more prominent matriculators. The English Mertonites have organized themselves into *The International Thomas Merton Society (European Chapter)* with The Reverend Canon A. M. Allchin as President, The Reverend Arthur Middleton as Vice President, and The Reverend Stephen J. Hotchen as General Secretary. Middleton's address, "The World in a Grain of Sand," delivered at one of the Merton conferences, appeared in *The Merton Annual II.* The group is in the midst of developing a newsletter, an English version of *The Merton Seasonal*, with the title *New Seeds.* John F. X. Harriott's remarks in *The Tablet* in November 1988 indicated that interest in Merton has reached England. He said:

> Supposing the bets could be collected, which of this century's prophets and sages would a gambler back to show the greatest staying power? . . . My own money, however improbably, would be on an American monk who lived most of his life in a Kentucky monastery and much of that in a small hermitage, who rarely travelled outside its boundaries and was professionally dedicated to silence and solitude: the Trappist, Thomas Merton . . . . Out of that silence and solitude spoke an authentically twentieth-century voice, articulating with power and grace this century's fevers and frets and, with growing confidence, their relief and remedy.[4]

Another indication of renewed interest in Merton came early in the year when Monica Furlong, known for her well-received *Merton: A Biography* (1980), re-entered the Merton arena after statements that she had

---

4. John F. X. Harriott, "A Man for Our Time," *The Tablet* 242 (26 November 1988), p. 1354.

"done" Merton and was getting on to other things. She contributed two articles, drawn from her basic research — and premise — for the biography, to *The Tablet*. Titled "Thomas Merton Reconsidered: A Monk and His Abbot" and "A Prophet Reassessed," they appeared in the 28 January and 4 February issues. Furlong also contributed an introduction for the short volume, *The Shining Wilderness: Daily Readings with Thomas Merton*, edited by Aileen Taylor and published by Darton, Longman & Todd. This and the even shorter *Thomas Merton on Prayer*, compiled and edited by Tony Castle and published by Marshall Pickering, constitute two unique "English" publications. They are reviewed in this *Annual* by Donald Allchin, President of the English ITMS. Marshall Pickering, under its Pickering and Lamp Press imprints, has been most forward among English houses in publication of Merton and Merton-related material. *A Thomas Merton Reader* has been published and *The Hidden Ground of Love: Letters on Religious Experience and Social Concerns* and *The Road to Joy: Letters to New and Old Friends* are in preparation. They have issued William H. Shannon's *Thomas Merton's Dark Path* as well as a Merton-inspired book (what I call a "Merton spin-off) by an English Franciscan, Brother Ramon. This book, titled *Soul Friends: A Journey with Thomas Merton*, is about Brother Ramon's encounter with Merton in his own life and he weaves Merton's biography into his own life story. Late in the year Collins brought out two books in their Fount Paperbacks series, the first an edition of *"Honorable Reader"* using only the American subtitle, *Reflections on My Work*, as the title. The second was another Merton "spin-off," Melvyn Matthews's *The Hidden Journey: Reflections on a Dream by Thomas Merton*. Matthews, Director of the Ammerdown Centre for Study and Renewal, uses Merton's account of a dream in *Conjectures of a Guilty Bystander* as the springboard for this book on prayer and understanding ourselves.

Nicholas Dunne has written an article about Merton's last trip which appeared in *The Catholic Herald* in London in 1988 and was reprinted in 1989 under the title "Thomas Merton's Final Journey" in *Catholic Asian News*, published in Singapore. Many of the Englishpersons interested in Merton are, in fact, Anglicans and that connection in Merton's life was explored by Terry Tastard, an Anglican Franciscan, in "Anglicanism and Thomas Merton," published in the London journal *Theology*. Earlier in the year (6 February) the BBC broadcast a somewhat unsatisfying play by Bruce Stewart called *Me and My Shadow*, the title taken from the 1927 hit song by Al Jolson, Billy Rose and Dave Dreyer which pulsatingly punctuated this strangely non-spiritual account of Merton's life. But what the play indicates, along with the various publications, is that the English are claiming Merton, who did after all receive much of his education in England and undoubtedly thought of himself as at least partially English, as one of their own.

On the other side of the Atlantic but still from the British Commonwealth, work by Canadians remains significant in Merton studies. The Reverend Frank A. Peake's "Self, Sexuality and Solitude in John Cassian and Thomas Merton: Notes from a Retreat" was featured in *The Merton Annual II*. Four Canadians participated in the First General Meeting of the ITMS — Donald Grayston of the Shalom Institute in Vancouver, Douglas R. Letson and Michael W. Higgins of the University of St. Jerome's College in Waterloo, Ontario, and Jacques Goulet of Mt. St. Vincent University in Halifax, Novia Scotia. Grayston and Higgins were the organizers and coordinators of the first large Merton conference, *The Thomas Merton Symposium*, held at the Vancouver School of Theology from 11 to 13 May 1978. They collected and edited the papers from this symposium in *Thomas Merton: Pilgrim in Process* (Toronto: Griffin House, 1983). As mentioned, the ITMS papers by Letson and Higgins are included in this *Annual*. Michael Higgins's lecture, "Making and Remaking: The Many Masks of Thomas Merton," delivered at St. Thomas More College of the University of Saskatchewan, appeared as a separate publication and in the April 1989 issue of *The Canadian Catholic Review*. J. S. Porter's *The Thomas Merton Poems: A Caravan of Poems*, published in 1988 by Moonstone Press in Goderich, Ontario, is a collection of poems, *not* by Merton but inspired by and patterned after him. Porter's book was reviewed rather widely in Canada and is reviewed in this *Annual* by John Leax. Ross Labrie of the University of British Columbia, whose *The Art of Thomas Merton* was published some years ago by the Texas Christian University Press, discusses Merton at some length in his latest book, *The Writings of Daniel Berrigan*.

Back south of the border in the United States, several books in 1989 contained significant sections about Merton. N. S. Xavier, born in India, has a chapter, "Thomas Merton," in his *The Two Faces of Religion: A Psychiatrist's View*, in which he attempts to look at Merton from a psychoanalytical viewpoint. In a book published in 1988 but which reached the Merton Center in 1989 — Eugene Kennedy's *Tomorrow's Catholic / Yesterday's Church: The Two Cultures of American Catholicism* — there is a chapter called "Thomas Merton Died for Our Sins." Kennedy identifies Merton as a "Culture Two Catholic," one of those who sought to undergo religious experience in a creative, indeed an artistic, way. According to Kennedy,

Merton's "life was thus a model for legions of creative people who baffled the institution and who paid high prices for being originals who did not fit easily into precut placements."[5] Thomas M. King, a Teilhard de Chardin scholar, had a new book titled *Enchantments: Religion and the Power of the Word.* In a chapter called "Merton and *Aseitas,*" he discusses Merton's "enchantment" with that word, often used to describe the "Of Himself-ness" of God. According to King, the word itself delivered Merton from thinking of himself as *aseitas* and enabled him to emerge from his selfish identity into a state where ethics became possible and God, as He should, became *aseitas.* "Thomas Merton and His Poetry," a chapter in James Laughlin's *Random Essays: Recollections of a Publisher,* falls into the reminiscence category. It is basically an account of Laughlin's contacts with Merton as publisher of all his volumes of poetry. The essay does, however, offer insight into how Laughlin thinks Merton developed as a poet. *The Catholic Counterculture in America, 1933-1962,* by James T. Fisher of Yale University, contains a chapter "Jack Kerouac and Thomas Merton, the Last Catholic Romantics" which presents Merton as a paradigmatic Catholic liberal. Fisher says however: "Merton's sophisticated resignation to authority appealed to the many Catholics who no longer reflexively followed the dictates of the church but were far from ready to risk the ostracism which might result from direct questioning of authority."[6] Finally, Charles J. Healey, a Jesuit priest who has written on Thomas Merton in the past, has written a book published by Alba House, *Modern Spiritual Writers: Their Legacies of Prayer.* The book is an introduction to nine writers on spirituality, including Merton.[7]

Two interesting catalogues of Merton exhibits appeared during 1989. *An Easter Anthology,* an exhibit devoted to religious art, Merton's drawings and photographs, and images of Merton, opened at the Owensboro Museum of Fine Art in February. The catalogue, also called *An Easter Anthology,* carried photographs of several of Merton's works and nearly all of the images of him and included a biographical reflection by Robert E. Daggy and a short essay on Merton's art by Brother Patrick Hart. Sister Therese Lentfoehr, longtime friend and correspondent of Merton's, left

---

5. Eugene Kennedy, *Tomorrow's Catholics / Yesterday's Church: The Two Cultures of American Catholicism* (New York: Harper & Row, 1988), p. 155.

6. James Terence Fisher, *The Catholic Counterculture in America, 1933-1962* (Chapel Hill: University of North Carolina Press, 1989), p. 232.

7. See, for example, Charles J. Healey, S.J., "Thomas Merton: Growth in Compassion," *American Ecclesiastical Review* 168 (November 1974), pp. 579-594 and "Thomas Merton: Spiritual Director," *Cistercian Studies* 11 (1976), pp. 228-245.

her extensive collection of Mertoniana to Columbia University when she died in 1981. Long attached to the Catholic Campus Ministry at Columbia, the collection has now (to the relief of Merton scholars) been deposited in the Rare Books and Manuscripts Division in Butler Library, a much more secure location than its former housing. The collection has been processed and catalogued and featured in an exhibit which opened 6 December 1989. A prospectus (or collection summary) called *Thomas Merton, the Poet and the Contemplative Life* has been published. It contains a foreword by Kenneth A. Lohf, an introduction by Patrick T. Lawlor, and the text of the labels which accompanied items in the exhibit. Lawlor, who processed the collection, also contributed an article to *Columbia Library Columns* about Merton's letters to his Columbia teacher, Mark Van Doren. The letters themselves are now available in *The Road to Joy*.

Merton is now included in many standard reference works. In William S. Ward's *A Literary History of Kentucky*, published by the University of Tennessee Press, Ward places Merton in his section on modern poetry. He discusses Merton primarily as a poet, basing this on the fact that when *The Seven Storey Mountain was published in 1948, Merton was described as "a young American poet" and his published work consisted of three volumes of verse. Merton has also made the pages of The D. A. B. —The Dictionary of American Biography*, Supplement Eight, 1966-1970. William H. Shannon wrote the entry and brings perspective to several aspects of Merton's life within the short framework of such an entry. The following paragraph, for example, sums up his involvement with social issues and his interest in non-Christian traditions.

> Merton's contemplative experience explains his involvement with social issues and his dialogue with other religious traditions in the East and West. During the 1960s he became, from behind his monastery walls, a recognized leader for many in the struggle for racial justice, for world peace, and for nonviolence as a way of life. He expanded his involvement in interreligious dialogue, eager to enrich his own faith by contact with other Christian traditions as well as with Judaism and the religions of Asia. His interest in religious dialogue was not primarily ecumenical; his concern lay not so much in resolving differences in religious formulations as in discovering the fundamental unity underlying different religious traditions — namely, the unity of the religious experience. (p. 431)

Merton is also popping up in children's textbooks, usually as a one page entry giving brief details and including questions for the students about him and about monasticism. A fifth grade text from Silver Burdett & Ginn — *This is Our Faith*, by Carl J. Pfeiffer and Janaan Manternach — features such a page, "Thomas Merton — Man of Prayer," and is in use in several parochial schools. In England (once again), Collins has published an elementary text called *Communication, Celebration, Values* which includes a page on Merton.

Speaking of younger readers (though not necessarily confined to them), Merton made the Sunday Comics in 1989 in Paul Howie's syndicated column "In Their Own Words." His 2 April column featured a "Merton word game." Clues are given to form words leading to a quotation from an unidentified Merton source, the quotation being "Happiness is diminished when we do not share it with others." Certainly this and other items — such as Gregory J. Ryan's *Munx Pond Magazine: A Collection of Humor Inspired by Thomas Merton* — can be classified as what Cooper calls "ephemeral bric-a-brac." Ryan's computer produced pamphlet, which he calls "Number One & Only" and which he has offered for sale, while it may be bric-a-brac, points up the neglected area of Merton's humor which often gets inundated by heavier analyses and it underscores something of the inexplicable appeal of Merton. Ryan includes fictional correspondence, "concrete" poems a la Merton, and various word games, including crossword puzzles with clues drawn from such Merton books as *The Seven Storey Mountain* and *A Vow of Conversation*.

Quotations from Merton and comments about him surface in many publications, such as a quote about Shaker chairs in *The National Geographic* (September 1989); an account of his friendship with John Howard Griffin in *American Heritage* (February 1989); a long quotation from *Love and Living*, complete with a drawing of Merton against low craggy mountains, in *Blue Marble* (November 1989); and an abridged version of Elizabeth Kristol's "The Monk from Manhattan: Thomas Merton's Tantalizing Message for Modern Catholics" in *Catholic Digest* (April 1989).

Only one major study of Merton, however, was published in the United States in 1989, that by David D. Cooper mentioned at the beginning of this essay. *Thomas Merton's Art of Denial: The Evolution of a Radical Humanist* sails some new waters in Merton studies because it approaches Merton from a more secular viewpoint than other studies and it raises several provocative questions. It is reviewed in this *Annual* by Ross Labrie.

Shorter works on Merton continued to appear in journals and periodicals, most of which were reviews of the various books by and about Merton which have been published in the late 1980s. Other work included scholarly analyses and the usual number of reminiscences and "Merton spin-offs." Four issues of *The Merton Seasonal*, published at the Thomas Merton Studies Center at Bellarmine College, carried short articles, reviews, verse, and images of Merton. Highlights of the year included articles by Anne Page Brooks ("Job and Thomas Merton: Their Experiences of God and the Realization of Integrity") and David Kocka ("A Song of Syllables: Merton an Artist in Art"), various materials from the ITMS General Meeting or inspired by it (such as Martha Bartholomew's "Seeds for Generation: A Poem written at the ITMS General Meeting"), and a review symposium of *The Road to Joy: Letters to New and Old Friends* (Michael Casey, O.C.S.O.; Robert Grip; Jane Marie Richardson, S.L.; and Bernard Van Waes, O.H.C.).

Analysis of specific texts by Merton or the development of a theme in a particular text has not loomed large in Merton studies, but some forays into textual analysis did appear in 1989. Brother John Albert used a Merton text in his "The Christ of Thomas Merton's *Monastic Peace* and Victor A. Kramer explored one of Merton's "monastic orientation texts" in "Patterns in Thomas Merton's *Introduction to Ascetical and Mystical Theology*." Both appeared in *Cistercian Studies*, the first in the third issue and the latter in the fourth. Brent Short drew references from Merton texts to develop his "Thomas Merton on Genesis: A Way of Seeing" (*Spiritual Life*, Spring 1989). Interest in Merton's relationship with the nurse has yet to crest, but, except for review articles by Anthony T. Padovano and Paul Wilkes, no one had examined closely the so called "Nurse Poems," published in limited edition with the bland title *Eighteen Poems*. Doug Burton-Christie stuck his oar into these waters with his interesting article "Rediscovering Love's World: Thomas Merton's Love Poems and the Language of Ecstasy," *Cross Currents* (Spring 1989). Burton-Christie uses a different approach but concludes, as others have, that Merton's writing was informed and articulated by his experience. In a different watercourse, Janet S. Horne has examined Merton's writings as a form of direct communication in her "Beyond Rhetoric: Thomas Merton on Silence" in *The Speech Communication Annual* (February 1989).

Some much touched themes in Merton scholarship were in evidence also in 1989: Zen, nonviolence, prayer, self. Worthy of mention are John Dear's "Glorifying the God of Peace: The Nonviolence of Thomas Merton," *Fellowship* (December 1988); Robert Imperato's "Merton's Way of Prayer," *Living Prayer* (March-April 1989); George Kilcourse's "Personifications of the True Self in Thomas Merton's Poetry," *Cistercian Studies* (no. 2); Belden C. Lane's "Thomas Merton as Zen Clown," *Theology Today* (October 1989); and Gregory J. Ryan's "Merton, Main, and the New Monasticism," *Monastic Studies* (Christmas 1988).

Translation of Merton works into languages other than English continued, but Barry Magid at his Dim Gray Barr Press in New York paid tribute to Merton's own work as a translator into English by publishing his translation of *Dialogue about the Hidden God*, by Nicholas of Cusa. This short production, just twenty leaves, is a limited edition of 100 copies and contains a one page introduction by Magid. The first known translation of a Merton book into Finnish appeared this year. The translation of *Thoughts in Solitude* was done Pia Koskinen-Launonen, titled *Ajatuksia Yksinaisyydessa*, and published in Helsinki by Kirjanelio. A unique translation of Merton material was a cassette tape produced in Freiburg, West Germany, by Verlag Hermann Bauer. Called *Betrachteugen uber die Leben*, it consists of readings of three chapters from *No Man is an Island* with musical interludes. Horst Warning did the readings and the three chapters (translated into German) are "Love Can Be Kept Only by Being Given Away," "The Wind blows where It Pleases," and "The Measure of Charity." Early in the year the translation of Merton's *Love and Living* into German (*Lieben und Leben*), translated by Christ Broermann and published by Benziger Verlag in Zurich, appeared.

Work continued outside the United States in studies such as Zoltan Dukai's "Thomas Merton: Nemzetkozi Tarsasag," *Agape* 2 (1989)* [published in Hungarian in Novi Sad, Yugoslavia]; Yasuo Kikama's "Tomasu Ma-aton no Shu-uhen," *Journal of Kobe Kaisei Joshi Daigaku* 27 (December 1988); Cyrus Lee's "Merton and Chinese Wisdom," *Chinese Culture* 30 (June 1989); Vivian Ligo's dissertation, "The Language of Paradox in the Life and Writings of Thomas Merton" (done at the Katholieke Universiteit Leuven in Belgium); and Uwe Schroeder's "Kontemplation in einer Welt des Umbruchs: Thomas Merton gegen die Tauschungen im kontemplativen Leben," *Erbe und Auftrag* 65 (August 1989).

Undoubtedly the largest controversy of the year was engendered by George J. Evans, an exclaustrated Cistercian, whose article, "Merton: Trappist Monk or 'Monastic Sport'?," appeared in the 22 September issue of *The National Catholic Reporter*. Evans concluded that Merton was a "sarabite" who had "a pernicious effect on traditional Trappist life."[8] The article prompted a minor tsunami of response in letters to the editor by George Darling, Joseph A. Eisenberg, Robert Grip, Robert Hale, Terrence G. Kardong, Mary Luke Tobin, and Frank X. Tuoti (these appeared under the title

---

8. George J. Evans, O.C.S.O, "Merton: Trappist Monk or 'Monastic Sport'?," *National Catholic Reporter* 25 (22 September 1989), p. 17.

"Merton Melange" in the 13 October issue). Several letters were not printed. The response centered on the fact that the writers did not share Evans's view of Merton's negative influence on monasticism in general and Trappist life in particular, but also on the fact that it seemed inappropriate that a monk who had found various ways of living away from his monastery should accuse Merton (who did not do so though he may have considered and even planned at times to do so) of sarabitism. So, all writing did not adulate Merton, but Evans's remarks showed that a certain kind of negative criticism can cause immediate and solid defense.

One other publication reflected a growing trend, the desexing of language — and this trend has both its defenders and detractors, particulary in regard to Merton's writings. Some feel that these writings, all completed by the end of 1968 and long before inclusive language became an issue, should be allowed to stand as he wrote them. Others feel that some texts, especially the more popular ones, should be revised to eliminate *any* gender references. In any case, Pax Christi USA in Erie, Pennsylvania, issued a desexed selection of texts from *Thomas Merton on Peace* (retitled *The Nonviolent Alternative* in the 1976 edition). This fifty-two page pamphlet is called *Words of Peace: Thomas Merton on Nonviolence* and the introduction says in part: "The manuscripts in this publication have been adapted to reflect gender inclusive language . . . ."

1989 — it was not an astonishing year, but it was an interesting one. The continuing waves of work on Merton, of drawings and paintings of him, of poetry written to and for him, of conferences and meetings, to quote David Cooper once again "surely [stand] as a testament to Thomas Merton's durable and enduring message for our increasingly confused and troubled era" (*Cooper*, p. ix).

REVIEWS

Thomas Merton
"HONORABLE READER":
Reflections on My Work
Edited with an Introduction by Robert E. Daggy
Preface by Harry James Cargas
New York: Crossroad, 1989
ix, 172 pages   — $16.95 clothbound

Reviewed by **Michael Downey**

The title of this work derives from the celebrated preface to the Japanese edition of *The Seven Storey Mountain*. What we have in the volume under consideration is an expanded version of *Introductions East and West: The Foreign Prefaces of Thomas Merton*, originally published by Unicorn Press in 1981. In addition to the prefaces Merton prepared for foreign editions of his works, editor Robert E. Daggy provides appendices including other material which will undoubtedly be of interest to those already somewhat familiar with Merton studies: (1) a reproduction of the graph Merton used to rank his books from "awful" to "best" (he judged none worthy of placement in the latter category); (2) seven letters in which he discusses proposed translations of his works; (3) a comprehensive list of the various editions and foreign language translations of Merton's works. It may also be of use to note that the preface to *Martha, Mary and Lazarus* is unique to the volume insofar as it was not intended to introduce a translation but a possible English publication.

This is a rather strange sort of book: a group of prefaces, with its own preface by Harry James Cargas. What could possibly be its merits?

That Merton went through many changes in the course of his lifetime is not news. But unlike the others of great religious or literary reputation, Merton never took up his pen to describe specifically how his mind had changed over the course of a given period. No such personal retrospective exists, and it is difficult to imagine what Merton's would look like had he left one. It is safe to venture, however, that he would not attempt to validate positions presently held by arguing that, at least implicitly, he held them all along.

In lieu of a personal retrospective, *Honorable Reader* may be understood as a collection of some of Merton's "second thoughts," or further reflections. His prefatory remarks often indicate that he had come to see things differently between the time of publication of a given work in English and its later translation into another language.

To enumerate such changes would be to repeat what is already generally recognized by those in Merton studies. What is useful to note is that Merton himself seemed willing to "eat his words" and to acknowledge his embarrassment in the face of some of the things he had written earlier. It may also be instructive to note that Merton did not write these prefaces for works which were "doctored up" before or after translation. With rare exception (i.e., *New Seeds of Contemplation*), Merton allowed his work to stand as originally published, thus allowing the loose ends of his earlier thinking to be exposed, even though his own mind had arrived at points of greater clarity.

There is a second merit to the volume. In addition to the many other "second thoughts" which are disclosed in these pages, Merton admits to his foreign readers that some of the difficulties with his writing stem from his attempt to adopt a style and a voice, or a theological posture, foreign to himself. This he indicates clearly in the prefaces to the French editions of *Exile Ends in Glory* and *The Ascent to Truth*, neither of which, incidentally, received high marks on Merton's "Graph of My Work, Feb. 6, 1967." Though he did not rank *The Ascent to Truth* "awful" on the graph, it is perhaps the clearest example of the problems Merton encountered in attempting to use the scholastic idiom at the expense of his own monastic, existential voice.

We are in Robert Daggy's debt for assembling the prefaces together with the material in the appendices. His own introductory remarks to each of Merton's prefaces are particularly helpful. But greater editorial care might have been taken in this work. There is the usual flurry of typos found in most publications today (the first appears on the first page of Daggy's introduction [p. 3]). A bit more jarring are the footnotes in the preface to the French edition of *Martha, Mary and Lazarus*, while endnotes are provided for the other prefaces. Why break stride? No explanation is offered.

Further, it may have been advantageous to update the editor's introduction (originally published in the 1981 edition of the collected prefaces) before inclusion in this 1989 publication. When Daggy notes the enduring value of Merton's work "more than a decade after his˙[Merton's] death in December, 1968" (p. 6), the careful reader notes that this volume appears over two decades after his death, and that much of note has occurred in Merton studies during the second decade.

Those with interest in Merton studies are likely to find little of value in this work. But for those who are close and careful readers of the Merton corpus, this volume will be useful because of the nuances in Merton's thinking which can be discerned in these "second thoughts."

Thomas Merton
MONKS POND:
Thomas Merton's "Little Magazine"
Edited with an Introduction by Robert E. Daggy
Afterword by Brother Patrick Hart
Lexington, Kentucky: University Press of Kentucky, 1989
xv, 349 pages — $30.00

Reviewed by **Jonathan Greene**

In 1965 Thomas Merton realized "a dream deferred" — becoming a hermit, living in a small concrete block building on the edge of a field a short walk from the main buildings at Gethsemani. Far from shutting out the world, these remaining years of his life were his most activist. He thought long and hard about peace and was much concerned with the struggle for racial equality. Living in the midst of a traditional monastic community, he was always interested in the cutting edge of what was happening in the Catholic world, in other religions, in politics, and in the literary and philosophical worlds.

In the late 1950s and into the 1960s, the literary world witnessed an explosion in the number of both small presses and "underground" literary magazines. While most of Merton's books went to mainstream houses (Harcourt, Brace; Doubleday; Farrar, Straus & Cudahy), he was familiar, as a publishing poet, with small literary magazines. Though some of his poems appeared in the "giants" such as *The Atlantic Monthly, The New Yorker, The Hudson Review* and *The Sewanee Review,* many appeared in the "little magazines" such as *El Corno Emplumado, Journal for the Protection of All Beings, Pax, Unicorn Journal,* etc. Attuned as ever to the *zeitgeist,* inspired by the monastery's purchase of an offset press, Merton decided to join the fray and doff an editor's cap as well as the cowl.

Monks Pond was the result. It was named after a real pond created by a concrete dam in the monastery's woods. He planned four issues: "The purpose of this magazine is to publish a few issues devoted to poetry and to some unusual prose and then go out of business." Merton was in touch with many writers and I would guess some of the contents of the first two issues were on hand when he conceived the magazine: his old Columbia friend Ad Reinhardt's aesthetic statement; the religious/philosophical texts of Shen Hui, John C. H. Wu, Reza Arasteh, etc.

Once the idea of the magazine was in place, Keith Wilson, Jonathan Williams and I acted as unofficial "contributing editors," sending in texts and exhorting writers we thought in sympathy with the project to send in material. The poetry Merton was writing had taken on a sea change with the recent *Cables to the Ace* and his work-in-progress, *The Geography of Lograire,* some of which would appear in *Monks Pond.* Also recent was his interest in photography and the magazine featured his work along with experimental work by his photographer-friend from Lexington, Ralph Eugene Meatyard. Merton also used some of his calligraphic drawings that he was turning out prolifically at the time. And another new interest found its way into these pages — concrete poetry, both by himself and by others. *Monks Pond* was an outlet for Merton's enthusiasms — both his own new exploratory writing and art, and his co-conspirators working in these realms. It is a rich record of the ferment taking place within him at this time.

The first two issues were rather select and intimate affairs of sixty-four and forty-eight pages. But, by the time help arrived in the person of Philip Stark, a Jesuit visiting at the Abbey of Gethsemani during the summer of 1968, the floodgates had opened and the third and fourth issues on which Stark worked became large grab bag anthologies of ninety-eight and 140 pages. The scope, too, had expanded to include translations of French, Latin American, Chinese, Polish and Finnish poets, as well as African myths and proverbs.

The whole idea of the magazine, as well as its contents, was a bit anarchistic. No money was sought (though contributions to cover expenses were accepted). Copies were sent out to those who requested them and many went to contributors. Less than 200 copies of each issue were printed. So it was not empire-building, but a quick sand castle waiting for an incoming tide. Mott, in his biography, has snidely remarked that "Merton made the mistake as editor of including the work of poets who were friends and of friends who claimed to be poets." Robert Daggy, in his informative introduction, quotes this with the rejoinder that "Mott may interpret this as a mistake, but it was precisely what Merton intended."

Reading through this 350 page reprint, though, one can see that Mott's low opinion of the magazine might have some justification. There is a wealth of worthwhile material in its pages, but *Monks Pond* has amateurish work, especially in the last two mammoth issues. Although Merton did not accept everything submitted, with his active mind I suspect he could often "read in" qualities to some of the work, qualities not so visible to others. *Monks Pond* was a light diversion for Merton that quickly became more work than he intended (any editor of a small magazine will corroborate this experience). With all the demands on his time, it might just have been easier to hand over work to Stark to type than to write a rejection letter.

Merton was sincere when he said that he thought there was much good work, "good poets hiding around in the bushes." This discovery of other experimental writers, his enthusiasms for the work of others writing in a similar vein, probably helped feed his own work (for example, one could make a case of like methods being used in *The Geography of Lograire* and in Paul Metcalf's work). The conjunction of this hermit with the community of writers is recorded here during a time that the writer, monk and man were undergoing new energies and changes. This is the main value of this reprint.

It may seem unfair to close with a few quibbles, but I think more time and care put into the reprinting would have made it a better volume. For example, on page 106 the unattributed second poem dedicated to Tu Fu is by Li Po which explains its juxtaposition to the one above which is about Li Po written by Tu Fu. And even though the introduction claims that only pagination has been changed, the deletion of an accent mark in CAFE on page 38 has rendered the poem meaningless. Also, although the title page announces that the Introduction is by Robert Daggy and the Afterword by Patrick Hart, their names are not in evidence with their words. But aside from such quibbles, we should welcome back into print one of Merton's last projects.

Thomas Merton
PREVIEW OF THE ASIAN JOURNEY
Edited with an Introduction by Walter H. Capps
New York: Crossroad, 1989
114 pages   — $13.95 hardcover

Reviewed by **Bonnie Bowman Thurston**

Readers who are familiar with Merton scholarship will remember that Walter Capps wrote one of the best articles on Merton's significance that was produced in the flurry of analysis and scholarly activity ten years after his death. "Thomas Merton's Legacy" appeared in the March/ April 1979 issue of *The Center Magazine* and described Merton's contributions to the new contemplative and social era in religion. Now, twenty years after Merton's death, Capps has edited the dialogue which Merton engaged in at the Center for the Study of Democratic Institutions in Santa Barbara, California, on 3 October 1968, a few days before he left on his Asian pilgrimage. Like the article, this longer work helps us to put Merton's importance as an intellectual into perspective.

A thin volume, *Preview of the Asian Journey* contains an introductory essay, the transcription of Merton's dialogue, and two short essays (one on the ancient Mesoamerican city of Monte Alban and one a reflection on Roderick Nash's *Wilderness and the American Mind*) which were published in *The Center Magazine* and which have appeared elsewhere. The value of this volume is the dialogue, which with *Thomas Merton in Alaska*, makes an important contribution to our knowledge of Merton's thought in the last year of his life. As the introduction notes, the dialogue is part of the record of Merton's first extended period away from Gethsemani, is one of the only times Merton met with a group of intellectuals, is an indication of why he wanted to travel to Asia, and is a record of the manner and style in which Merton thought and spoke. This final aspect is of importance and might well have been problematic. Those who have listened to any of the Merton tapes have an idea of how difficult! The problem of transferring the spoken word to the written are gracefully handled by Capps through inclusion of "stage directions" which give the reader visual clues and atmosphere and through footnotes introducing the other speakers.

The participants in and the subject matter of the dialogue are wide-ranging. Merton is introduced by W. H. "Ping" Ferry and fields questions from Donald McDonald, Frank Kelly, Edward Crowther, John Seeley, Bishop James Pike, Gerald Gottlieb, Judy Saltzman, Peter Marin, John Wilkinson, Rex Tugwell, William Gorman, and John Cogley. We are able to hear Merton in conversation with some of the best minds of the time, sometimes holding his own — and sometimes not. The substance of the conversation ranges over monastic renewal and marginality, the Pentecostal movement, the influence of Eastern mysticism on Christianity and on "pop spirituality," idolatry and prosperity, and what was then termed "the underground church."

Perhaps what will be most interesting to those familiar with Merton will be to see how he handles himself with his intellectual equals and betters. In this context he does not have the "monastic mystique" on his side, and, while his partners in dialogue are respectful, they push him in a way others with whom we have seen him did not. Frequently issues are raised and then dropped. Merton picks up and then discards a tantalizing idea. While we might wish he had finished many of his thoughts, we recognize Merton's characteristically agile, if not entirely focused, mind.

The dialogue helps us to see more clearly the reasons why Merton wanted to travel in Asia and what he was expecting to discover. While the language sounds slightly dated at points, the basic themes (authentic religious experience, the need for genuine community, idolatry, the contemplative life and social action) are still timely and important.

Turning to the essays, the reader will certainly wonder if they were not included to make a book-length work. "The Sacred City" on Monte Alban reveals once again the variety of subjects on which Merton wrote with apparent authority. Merton evinces a certain romanticism about things ancient which is unsettling. "The Wild Places" also deals with the primitive, but in a literary and intellectual context that curbs Merton's romanticism.

Merton enthusiasts might well have gotten along without reading of his enthusiasm for the Zapotecs, but they would have missed an important introduction to his Asian experience had this dialogue not been made available. What it contains and what it suggests is well worth the hefty price of the volume. Having seen how well dialogue can be edited to work in print, we might hope that others who have access to Merton's informal conversations might be encouraged by Capps's volume to prepare their material for publication.

Thomas Merton
THE ROAD TO JOY:
Letters to New and Old Friends
Selected and Edited with an Introduction by Robert E. Daggy
New York: Farrar, Straus & Giroux, 1989
xvi, 383 pages   — $27.95 hardcover

Reviewed by **Jane Marie Richardson**

A faithful friend is a sturdy shelter:
one who finds a friend finds a treasure. (Sirach 6:14)

Three years before his death Merton wrote: "I could fill another page with names of people I have loved to be with and loved to hear from. Lax, above all, and Mark Van Doren and all the old friends, Ad Reinhardt and so on." It is especially these "old friends" who are celebrated in *The Road to Joy: Letters to New and Old Friends*, although readers will certainly be glad for the "new" ones included, the term being used quite broadly. All of these friends, new and old, underscore the kind of spontaneous bonding that Merton could establish so readily. Making and keeping friends came as easily to him as praying.

This gift of identifying so simply and honestly with his correspondents is, of course, characteristic of Merton's writing as a whole. The personal nature of letters, however, accentuates this trait and accounts so much for Merton's continuing power to speak to an ever-widening community of earnest searchers. It is this ability to create bonds and to express them, even in letters hastily written, that helps us to realize how deeply integrated into his being was Merton's awareness of everyone's fundamental oneness in Christ. In a special way, *The Road to Joy* abounds with glimpses of Merton at his most lovable, sensitive, and vulnerable best.

Merton had many more friends than acquaintances and, in some way or other, the majority of his correspondents would fall into the former category. For this reason, the editor had to make some difficult choices in his actual selection of which letters among the 3,500 extant would most appropriately be published in the collection. Robert E. Daggy, director of the Merton Center at Bellarmine College in Louisville, has done an excellent job of making such a selection and of editing this volume, the second in a projected series of five. There are brief and pertinent introductions to each of the five chapters, as well as notes sprinkled between and throughout the letters, enabling the reader to place them in proper context. Daggy's additions are very helpful without being intrusive.

As in *The Hidden Ground of Love*, the initial volume in this series, published in 1985 and edited by William H. Shannon, general editor of *The Merton Letters*, the reader will find so much simply to enjoy: singularly good writing, uncommon insights, breadth of vision and concerns, irrepressible humor, deep compassion, flagrant exaggerations, striking metaphors — and pervading it all, an extraordinary and dynamic faith. As is usual with Merton texts, these letters quickly focus our attention and compel us to think and feel profoundly. But there is a certain warmth and nonposturing in these letters to friends that puts us at ease, sharpens our perception of how good life is, and invariably calls us home to ourselves. There are occasional expressions of vulnerability and nostalgia that come as a surprise, accustomed as we are to a certain kind of reticence from Merton even in the act of self-disclosure: "Well, it seems like a totally different world from that in which we used to spend Christmas together at Fairlawn in the old days. . . . One had so much fun then: children do not know how fortunate they are to be children!"

It was a child of ten who ultimately gave this book, so manifestly the work of a free spirit, its lovely title. When little Grace Sisson sent Merton her drawing of a house, it "had no road" leading to it. Five years later she sent him another drawing which she called "The Road to Joy." Merton responded sensitively: "I am glad you still draw things with love, and I hope you will never lose that. But I hope you and I together will secretly travel our own road to joy, which is mysteriously revealed to us without our exactly realizing." How could a book whose special focus is friendship be better named? Friendship creates its own joys and enhances all others. These Merton letters, so strongly rooted in the awareness of God's love for all of us, make that happiness unmistakably clear.

There are degrees of friendship, of course, and the division of these letters into five sections recognizes that fact. The first chapter consists of letters to one of Merton's oldest and dearest friends and mentor, Mark Van Doren. Dating from March 1939 to November 1968, these sixty-five letters, unfailingly rich in respect, appreciation, and self-revelation, give us another perspective from which to view Merton's development, both as a poet and literary artist and as a human being always reaching out for truth. From Columbia to Darjeeling, the remarkable and congenial Van Doren, a Pulitzer Prize poet and an outstanding teacher, accompanied Merton on his life's journey, always a stimulating and sustaining presence. Letters to this faithful friend, twenty years his senior, drew forth from Merton some of his most beautiful writing: "Love's debts have this in them that they are too great to be paid, and that therefore one loves to remain in debt. I hope that I will owe you more and more that I can never repay, and I fully expect to. You are certainly one of the joys of life for all who have ever come within a mile of you." Merton's solicitude for the Van Doren family in time of stress is touching. No wonder that on receiving the news of Merton's death, Van Doren would offer this deeply-felt tribute: "I shall mourn for him as long as I live."

It is in his letters to another lifetime friend, Robert Lax, that Merton's unrestrained spontaneity, wit and imagination have their heyday. One gets the impression that nothing was ever held back from Lax, that underlying the clever playfulness and outrageous humor rampant in these letters was an unshakable trust in the recognition that here was someone who understood and accepted him thoroughly. Merton was a man of many words; Lax, of few. (In *The Seven Storey Mountain*, Merton describes Lax, in part, as "a mind full of tremendous and subtle intuitions, and every day he found less and less to say about them.") These letters to Lax, their casual style notwithstanding, register a gamut of significant cares, ideas and reflections. In the summer of 1965, as the war in Southeast Asia was escalating, Merton deplored the apathy of his country and Church. He wrote to Lax, then living on the Greek island of Kalymnos: "Here all is forgetfulness of the morals and of the Vietnam, everybody just want to forget issues. The doors slam and people retire to forget the issues and stick their heads all the way into the TV where the issue is befuddled and made comfortable." Looking back sixteen years after Merton's death, Lax would say, with typical reserve: "I certainly felt I'd lost a correspondent; if I had something funny I wanted to tell him about it would be a little more difficult now, but I didn't feel lost.

I felt that he'd gone on to another stage, and I really felt that if it happened, it must have been the time for it."[1] But on that fateful day in December 1968, Lax could only respond in his telegram to Gethsemani: "Sorrow."

The eruption of joy in Merton's letters to Lax is somewhat complemented by the more or less even keel of those addressed to Therese Lentfoehr, a Salvatorian sister, a teacher and a published poet. This correspondence makes up the largest set of letters (135 of them) in the book. Sister Therese was invaluable to Merton in her skills of typing, recording and preserving his manuscripts and he consulted her on occasion. Therese first wrote to Merton in 1939, telling him how much she liked one of his poems, but it was not until 1948 that their correspondence actually began. Daggy suggests that these letters were an "alternate form of journal keeping" for Merton. Certainly, there are long, personal passages not common to other letters. He writes at length about his books in process, about prayer, about situations at the monastery, about other people's writings, about her work and his health. He continually discourages her from making him bigger than life but her praise seemed to nurture his humility. There is about these letters something that suggests that Merton really did find in Therese the sister he never had. In any case, he appears to have had no difficulty in writing to her from the heart when he so wished: "I walk around saying 'Love!' Or I just mentally keep slipping the catch that yields my whole soul to Love."

Family love constitutes a special kind of relationship, one that resembles friendship even though distinct from it. *The Road to Joy*, therefore, includes a chapter of letters "to family and family friends." These letters to relatives — three aunts, an uncle and a cousin — and others connected in one way or another with the Merton family put us in closer contact with some less familiar Merton roots and influences. In writing to "Aunt Kit" (Agnes Gertrude Stonehewer Merton), one of his father's four sisters, Merton seemed particularly at ease. Once, after sharing with her some of his thoughts on the Christian life, he added: "We live in the belief that God loves us and will let nothing happen to us that is not for our good. He is in fact always with us and indeed in us . . . ." One cannot but believe that Aunt Kit remembered this when, four years later in a tragic ferry accident, she met her own death after being "a tower of courage" to others on board the sinking ship.

---

1. *Merton: By Those Who Knew Him Best*; ed. Paul Wilkes (San Francisco: Harper & Row, 1985), p. 74.

There is much more in *The Road to Joy*, like letters to Dan Walsh and John Howard Griffin and other people special to Merton. There is a whole chapter of "Circular Letters to Friends," a form Merton adopted out of sheer necessity in order to communicate with the growing number of persons who found in his words and understanding a source of strength and clarity in their struggles. It was not simply courtesy or interest or even kindness that motivated these letters. It was a conviction that this was part of his vocation, as he himself states in the first circular letter. There are, finally, letters "to and about young people," in which we see once again Merton's exceptional ability to accommodate himself to others, whatever their age or experience, background or concerns. He could and did attract younger readers, dialoguing with these "new friends" and taking seriously their questions and values. Each of them must have been grateful that Merton never did speak down to them.

Early on, Merton had expressed a desire that his writing be "frank without being boring." Small chance. One has only to read a little of these letters to see how powerfully his prayer was answered. His enormous talent for straightforward and engaging speech blesses us all. Still, I was struck by how much Merton owed to these people — and many others — and by how much he needed them to become and to be all that he was. Never one to point to himself (not seriously, anyway), Merton implicitly invites and even challenges us in these letters to examine our own friendships, our own relationships to God, to others and to ourselves. After spending time with him, one is never left in total comfort, but, paradoxically, one never feels more alive. This is the way Merton gifts his true friends, never failing to open up for them new pathways to joy.

Thomas Merton
THOMAS MERTON IN ALASKA:
Prelude to The Asian Journal:
The Alaskan Conferences, Journals, and Letters
Introduction by Robert E. Daggy / Preface by David D. Cooper
New York: New Directions, 1989
xvii, 162 pages — $19.95 hardcover / $9.95 paperback

Reviewed by **Diane Foster**

Bardo Thodol — your own true nature confronts you as Pure Truth, "subtle, sparkling, bright, dazzling, glorious, and radiantly awesome . . . Be not terrified . . . From the midst of that radiance the natural sound of Reality, reverberating like a thousand thunders simultaneously sounding, will come. That is the natural sound of thine own real self. (p. 5)

Not the properties of an individual nature, but the unique relationship of each being with God — a relationship by the Holy Spirit and realized in grace — is what constitutes the uniqueness of a human person. (p. 17)

Sunday 6 a.m. on KHAR Anchorage . . . . A good thought from a respectful potato. (p. 17)

Bluegreen Juneau. The old cathedral. The deserted hospital. The deserted hotel. The deserted dock. The deserted school. (p. 27)

Noise of heat walking around in the walls. I am hungry. (p. 28)

. . . copies of Ave Maria on the table but I did not get to look at them to see if my statement on draft record burning was there. Nor have I had any repercussions. A letter from Phil Berrigan . . . He does not mind prison life. But demonstrations & draft card burnings are not understood. (p. 28)

Dillingham — grey sky, smelling of snow. Cold wind. Freezing. Brown tundra. Low hemlocks . . . Another distance with snow covered mountains vanishing into low clouds. Lake Aleknagik speaks to me. A chain of lakes far from everything. Is this it? (p. 31)

The journal entries of *Thomas Merton in Alaska* offer yet another kaleidoscopic view of the personality, Thomas Merton. One senses with him the tundra, thunder, cold, cutlery and crockery, bays with small islands, the old town of Valdez, an enormous jigsaw puzzle, a lovely, ageless Eskimo woman, the smell of bacon, fallen birch leaves, seagulls flying by in the rain, a volcano to which one speaks with reverence, a chain of lakes far from everything. "Is this it?" Merton is, as ever, on the scent of his quest for God, being with God in ever deeper ways, ever more inclusively. His journal entries, a potpourri, imbue the reader with his here and now as he wends his way through Alaska with Asia on the horizon.

The letters, sixteen in all — to four people, principally address business or social concerns, with scattered descriptions of Alaska. For the Abbot [Flavian Burns], he goes into further details depicting all the potential sites for a true solitary life. Though predominantly prosaic, when inserted in their chronological sequence with the journal entries, the correspondence reveals the "complex self-contradictory temperament" of the author.

A superficial reading of the six workshop conferences and two "day of recollection" conferences fails to disclose the gems hidden in the midst of Merton's bright ideas and farfetched connections. If one tastes the conferences in a *lectio* type of rumination and allows them to engender further questions leading to deeper personal exploration of one's perception of oneself, God, neighbor and world, a continuity of monastic process appears through one conference to the next. In "This is God's Work," Merton weaves together a description of contemplative life including one's depths where God's voice is heard, the problem of alienation, a way to freedom for what really matters.

> "contemplative life" . . . The main point is the action of God's grace in our life . . . . God's work in us is a very, very deep call which is heard in silence in the deepest part of our being . . . . The covenant consists in listening to the call and believing the promise, and always listening and always believing . . . . Alienation . . . somebody who is never allowed to be fully himself. . . . the truth will make us free. This relationship to God through the Word of Jesus makes us free because it does not merely give us political liberation, it gives us the Holy Spirit . . . . What really matters is that God is here and now and loves us and dwells with us and we are called to realize this.
> (pp. 71-74, 76, 79-80)

In "Prayer, Personalism, and the Spirit," Merton continues with the Holy Spirit and freedom addressing the need to allow for differences in the life of prayer, moving freely with the Spirit "without violating the rights of others, and to fulfill love without violating love" (pp. 88-89).

> All the old ways are good and all the new ways are good. We can't do everything, so you pick the way that is good for you at the time that it is good for you . . . . let's respect indidviual differences and let each one do what is best for him or her and not feel badly if nobody else is doing it . . . . We are not used enough to the idea that several people can be right in different ways, and there can be different ways of being right. (pp. 89, 91)

It is clear that the author is not advocating individualistic practices, rather the more difficult asceticism of being led by the Holy Spirit to a "freedom to be ourselves without infringing on others" (p. 88).

In "Building Community on God's Love," remembering what really matters with a spirit of freedom, Merton touches basically upon the necessity of not preferring things to people, believing in the power of God's grace to enable the solving of problems, and trusting one another while knowing that trust can fall and be rebuilt.

> ... community ... is God's work and the basis ... is not just sociability but faith.... the importance of poverty is that we are supposed to be free from things that we might prefer to people ... people come here ... to see you as a community of love .... When we live together with people we have strong feelings of rebellion against them ... tend to repress this ... they cause anxiety.... You have sufficient grace to solve all your problems in the ordinary human way; ... to deal with them, not to be without them. You have to work at it all the time.... the power of God's love will be in it. We are going to make mistakes, but it really doesn't matter that much.
> (pp. 97, 98, 101, 102, 105)

Much of the context of Merton's words on building community on God's love is quoted from Eberhard Arnold. I found it appropriately based upon God's grace and somewhat simplistic when considering the specific work required personally and comunally to realize a community of love.

In "Community, Politics, and Contemplation," Merton tells us: "We have to be where love is and it is really the harder position, but it is also the creative position and the constructive position .... you can't have any real non-violence unless you have faith in God" (p. 109). Again, quotations from Arnold on community provide the backdrop for Merton's own commentary on a community built by God, where love prevails over power and a longing for the sacred working in people's lives brings nonviolent revolution.

> Contemplation is the realization of God in our life ... prayer is our real freedom ... liberation from ... alienation .... It is in prayer that we are truly and fully ourselves and we are not under any other power, authority, or domination. (p. 113)

In "Prayer, Tradition, and Experience," Merton moves to the heart of the matter.

> It is always hard to talk about prayer because everybody prays in private and everybody is different.... You speak from your heart.... That is what prayer is and that is what we have to do.... after a while the only rule that there is in prayer is that you never say anything that you don't mean ... you seek a deeper level to just *be* with God, just to listen to God.... We used to have in monastic life a sort of guru-disciple relationship ... someone who knows intuitively how to bring out what is deepest in a person and, believe me, that is what we really need.... We know it is there and yet we can't get to it. That is really why I want to go to Asia. I want to find out how Asian

> Buddhists are trained ... to get down into the depths of a person .... in the Desert Tradition ... if the old man was really charismatic, he would bring out in the novice the deepest power of prayer .... There is no reason for contemplative monasteries to exist if you are not able ... to develop a different kind of consciousness from that experienced outside.
> (pp. 118, 119, 122, 123, 126-127)

Contemporary Western monasticism is found lacking by the author. Where indeed are those who "would bring out ... the deepest power of prayer?"

In the next conference, "Prayer and Conscience," Merton further develops his notion of the relationship of prayer, consciousness, identity and conscience.

> Who is it that prays? ... Where is conscience? ... What is it? ... It is by the activity of my conscience that I create my identity and make my life what it is .... the deepest sense of conscience is conscience with grace, not just me, but the Holy Spirit and me. ... Prayer is opening up this deepest conscience and consciousness, a mystical conscience and a mystical consciousness, in which God and I work together. (pp. 129-131)

It is perhaps from this mystical place that Merton says:

> ... I am not just an individual when I pray, and I am not just an individual with grace when I pray. When I pray I am, in a certain sense, everybody. The mind that prays in me is more than my own mind, and the thoughts that come up in me are more than my own thoughts because this deep consciousness when I pray is a place of encounter between myself and God and between the common love of everybody. (pp. 134-135)

Merton speaks eloquently and experientially of distractions. In part he says:

> You have to take God and creatures all together and see God in His creation and creation in God and don't ever separate them. Then everything manifests God instead of hiding God or being in the way of God as an obstacle. (pp. 139-140)

"The Life that Unifies," a conference given at a day of recollection, concluded with these words: "Down deep in you there is something that sustains you because you are letting it sustain you, and, if you let it, it will" (p. 155). Sufi mysticism and Martin Buber in *The Way of Man* assist Merton in his evocative portrayal of the essence of contemplative and monastic life, the power of God in one's soul and the secret/yes in the task of one's final integration.

> The whole essence of contemplative prayer is that the division between subject and object disappears .... final integration ... real maturity is for a person to become a mystic. That is what man is made for .... The purpose of monastic life is to create an atmosphere in which people should feel free to express their joy in reasonable ways. This final integration and unification of man in love is what we are really looking for .... real people ... in the core of our soul the Divine force in its depth is capable of acting on the soul, changing it, binding the conflicting sources together, amalgamating the diverging elements. It is capable of unifying it .... our life

demands breakthroughs . . . we must break through and go beyond where we are . . . . Sufism looks at man as a heart and spirit and as a secret, and the secret is the deepest part. The secret of man is God's secret; therefore, it is in God . . . . this secret . . . is the word "yes" or the act of "yes." . . . My destiny in life — my final integration — is to uncover this "yes" so that my life is totally and completely a "yes" to God . . . . Deep in our hearts is the most profound meaning of our personality, which is that we say "yes" to God, and the spark is always there. All we need to do is to turn towards it and let it become a flame. (pp. 144, 146, 147-151, 153-154)

The last piece in the book is a day of recollection for priests, entitled "Prayer and the Priestly Tradition." Herein, Merton paints a picture of contemporary challenges and the choices needed to meet them.

Today, the ony way we priests can live and keep our sanity amidst all the complications of life is by breaking through to a deeper level of simplicity. The real level of course is the level of death, and that can only be reached by prayer . . . . to be a Christian today is to be in trouble . . . . we have to live in this trouble on the deepest level, not on the level of apologetics, but on the level of faith and personal commitment to Christ . . . . self-knowledge . . . I must find myself. I must solve my identity crisis, if I have one, then find myself as one loved by God, as chosen by God, and visited and over-shadowed by God's mercy which I now experience as totally in terms of God's mercy . . . . To wonder if you believe is not to doubt God, it is to doubt yourself.

In the "Introduction" and "Preface," Robert Daggy and David Cooper carefully situate and describe details of *The Alaskan Journal* period of Thomas Merton's life that might not be found elsewhere. Until Merton gives conferences, his words are sensual, direct from whatever level is finding expression, and then, the reader — if a seeker — will be awakened as the author risks the edges of deepest darkness with its hidden power of prayer. All in all, the book is not stellar, not immediately gratifying. It simply exposes yet another facet of the piece of a star that Merton is, the spark of which may possibly ignite the piece of a star that the reader is, that each person is.

Thomas Merton
THOMAS MERTON ON PRAYER
Compiled and edited with an Introduction by Tony Castle
Christian Spirituality Series
London: Marshall Pickering, 1989
9 pages   —   £1.50 paperback

Thomas Merton
THE SHINING WILDERNESS:
Daily Readings with Thomas Merton
Edited by Aileen Taylor with an Introduction by Monica Furlong
London: Darton, Longman & Todd, 1988
xvi, 62 pages   —   £2.50 paperback

Reviewed by **A. M. Allchin**

Thomas Merton is not all that well known in England, at least to judge from the story with which Tony Castle introduces his little booklet. A Salvation Army officer giving an address in a Catholic girls school during the week of prayer for Christian unity, compliments the pupils with the words: "How fortunate you Catholics are to have the wonderful writings of Thomas Merton," only to discover that none of the girls had ever heard of Thomas Merton. It looks, however, as though there is at present a revival of interest in his work, particularly among Anglicans. Tony Castle's little book is one sign of it, and he manages to pack a good deal of Merton's teaching on prayer into its pages. *The Shining Wilderness* is also a little book, but it has a more substantial feel to it. The sixty passages from Merton's writings which it contains have been skillfully chosen by Aileen Taylor, former warden of the Retreat House at Pleshey in Essex, made famous sixty years ago by the retreats of Evelyn Underhill. Monica Furlong contributes a vigorous and characteristic introduction, making of the book an admirable introduction to Merton's writings.

More recently other and larger studies of Merton have begun to appear on this side of the Atlantic. Terry Tastard devotes a chapter to Merton's work in his recent book, *Spark in the Soul*, a study of the interrelationship of spirituality and social justice (Darton, Longman & Todd, 1989). Brother Ramon, an Anglican Franciscan, has produced a very personal account of Merton's development in his book, *Soul Friends: A Journey with Thomas Merton* (Marshall Pickering, 1989). As the destructive efforts of ten years of Thatcher government become clearer and clearer in British society, so the social teaching of Merton becomes more and more relevant to our situation. We need his voice now more than ever.

Thomas Merton

THE MERTON TAPES
Second Release of Lectures

Kansas City, Missouri: Credence Cassettes, 1988 & 1989
Thirty casette tapes [Sixty minutes each]   — $7.95 each

Reviewed by **Dewey Weiss Kramer**

The goal of all Christian formation is to become formed in the image of God. Of all human institutions, the monasteries, especially contemplative ones, see as their *raison d'etre* the creation of an environment and program which makes this goal possible. The monk has but one "work," to seek God alone. Thus the practices of monastic formation can be expected to help all serious Christians in their attempt to image Christ, and methods used in the monastery can be expected to work for non-monastic Christians as well.

This is particularly the case when the director of such monastic formation is one of the era's most gifted spiritual teachers, Thomas Merton, a writer whose published works, while intended primarily for non-monastics, were the fruit of his monastic experience. Thus, it is no surprise that the two series (now made available to the general public by Credence Cassettes) of Merton's lectures to the novices at Gethsemani during the 1960s have enjoyed tremendous success. This second group of tapes brings the number of tapes released in unedited versions to forty-nine. Used judiciously, and most effectively in groups of lectures wherein relationships between and among the various talks can be absorbed, these lectures give insight both into Merton as teacher and novice master, as well as into the nature of the monastic community itself in which he played a significant role. His awareness of that role stands out clearly in these tapes.

One wonders, however, if there might not be a large number of perplexed or disappointed listeners among the various purchasers of the tapes. For, while the series is undoubtedly of value, one does not receive the concentrated, carefully crafted and thought-out fare of Merton's books. Rather, insights and guidance come out in bits and pieces during the sixty-odd lectures. These are lecture-discussions, not formal lectures, nor were they meant to be. They are a record of Merton and other monks in the process of learning more about the monastic life. Merton as teacher is eliciting responses, assisting others to think and to contribute basic answers to his questions. Seen in this light even the "small talk" which frequently begins a tape is valuable. Merton may ease into a discussion by telling about something which has recently occurred in the monastery. The final tape to be discussed in this review, "Spiritual Direction" (AA2137), for example, begins with some talk about a just completed "Tricenary," thirty days of prayer for the dead, and he uses explanation of this tradition to lead into discussion of the tradition of spiritual direction, a tradition vital to the Cistercian vocation and to the serious Christian life. Still, a caveat is in order. These tapes are not for the Merton beginner who will do better to turn to the books. But they can prove valuable, perhaps even invaluable, for the person knowledgeable in Merton matters, or monasticism, and this is so for several reasons.

First, there *is* a wealth of sound advice on how to live the spiritual life meaningfully, and the compilers have facilitated this by arranging the twenty-nine tapes under review in thematic sets and color-coding the cases accordingly so that one can keep track of the groups. Secondly, and closely related to the first point, there is a wealth of suggestions for further study provided. Merton frequently advises his novices to get hold of this or that book, contemporary, ancient, classic, and the listener would do well to follow his advice. Further, Merton is drawing constantly on his copious reading, and the references to his sources are simultaneously references to crucial foundations of spirituality. The works of Cassian, Origen, the Cistercian Fathers are now all far more accessible to the general reading public than they were in the 1960s, and this is due in part to Merton's own pioneering efforts at bringing them back into the mainstream of contemporary spirituality. Merton's use of such thinkers gives insight into his method and provides a clue to his own position in the history of twentieth century spirituality. In his talks on conversion of manners, for example, he develops his own thought and that of his novices by going back to the sayings of the Desert Fathers, to Origen, Cassian, bypassing eighteenth and nineteenth century authorities to return to the sources of perennial wisdom. It has been this return to the sources that has contributed greatly to the renewal of contemplative spirituality in the present era and we see Merton playing early on a major role in this renewal. In the lecture on Mary, as a further example, he presents his novices with *the* Cistercian Father, Bernard, thus trying to teach Cistercian essence by delving deeply into the original Fathers. Other novice masters have since done comparable work, perhaps more careful work, but the ease, grace, and liveliness of Merton's use of and integration of an immense range of essential original sources was seminal and explains his importance in the re-emphasis of Cistercians on their contemplative charism.

Two final points should be made in regard to the value of these tapes, both of which relate to the decision to offer the lectures without editing. The original Merton tapes produced by Norman Kramer in the 1970s were edited with a heavy hand, omitting pauses, Merton's ubiquitous "see?," comments by students, all small talk and joking. The sober teacher who spoke from those tapes was a far cry from the mirthful and witty Merton treasured by those he had taught personally. The editorial policy followed by Credence Cassettes which omits nothing has, in turn, elicited some virulent criticism, especially in regard to the inclusion of commentary (sometimes barely audible) of his students. Such pauses, the references to personal matters, to specific events at Gethsemani or in the world, account in part for the point made in the beginning that the essential "teaching" is sparse and has to be gleaned in pieces.

Understandable as such criticism is, the unedited versions are preferable. One hears Merton as mirthful, can observe his teaching style, and is brought to the realization that spiritual direction is a long, slow process. The emphasis on the building of community which constitutes a vital part of the content of the series of lectures is viscerally realized here in the give-and-take of the dialogue, the groping for words, the repetitions. Even though some answers are inaudible, Merton's responses almost always restate the material so that the sense is not lost. Beyond the personal repartee documented, one gains invaluable clues into the nature of Gethsemani. The accents of its novices, the trivia, the bantering all produce something akin to a time capsule. What has been lacking in the biographies of Merton thus far has been the essential monastic element of his life. These tapes could help supply that to the future definitive biographer.

Individuals, librarians, spiritual directors, and researchers who use these tapes should seek to perceive how they fit together as a whole. The following discussion of these taped classes has two aims: to give some brief indication of their content, and to demonstrate how they feed into one another. Merton's job, the job of his Gethsemani auditors, and our job as we listen, is to become aware that Christian formation is first and foremost a process, sometimes a painful process.

I.

Two groups of lectures, on "conversion of manners" and on "poverty," can profitably be evaluated together. Both deal with fundamental aspects of monasticism difficult to comprehend because of the emphasis on interior change. (Other aspects of monastic formation — silence, chastity — to be discussed later seem at first glance more understandable; refraining from talking or sexual abstinence appear to be, at least superficially, quite concrete. Merton, however, points his audience to the subtlety beyond most initial assumptions.) Taken together, the six tapes on the subject of conversion of manners (AA2228 - AA2233) provide a valuable index to Merton's thinking about the positive dimension of renunciation. The same is true of the discussions on poverty.

Conversion in the radical sense Merton discusses it is a mode of life wherein renunciation of self is fundamental. In his first lecture ("The Vow of Conversion" - AA2228) he observes that people in the modern world are trained never really to find themselves: "Today's culture is one where we are floating." To take a vow which demands a complete change, "the baptismal vows pushed a little further," is to allow God's will to become realized as one's own will. Such conversion is thus not a matter of imposition, but rather it is like becoming a saint, "one who acts because the root of the willing is in God." Rootedness is essential to all conversion of manners; you cannot just float. The next tape in this set, "Conversion in Christ" (AA2229), treats the monastic commitment in relation to its sacramental aspect. With reference to Bede Griffiths (side A), Merton explains how conversion is a simple change whereby the individual "lives closer to God," yet in which the community is crucially involved; thus the rituals of, for example, tonsure or washing of feet stress community relationship and mutual responsibility. On side B, he examines Peter of Celle's "Nine Letters to Carthusians" as a continuum of the basic idea that within a monastic setting, a theocentric setting, one works to make a "cultivated place full of light and peace." In such a setting, made possible by a loving community, it is possible to "get one's self together."

All this leads naturally into the next lectures on "Becoming Our True Self" (AA2230) where Merton considers finding "our true self" in discipline. These two lectures also contain an intriguing excursion into avoidance of the "Old Directory" (it is *not* a matter of "progress") (side A), and into Indo-European languages and an anecdote about a Zen monk (side B). Two Zen monks met a woman at a stream who did not want to get her skirt wet. The one monk obliged her by carrying her across the water while the other fretted. The punch line comes in the former's reply to his companion: "I dropped her ten miles back; you're still carrying her." The story exemplifies well both Merton's own attitudes and his teaching methods.

"Permanent Conversion to God" (AA2231) stresses that one's vow truly changes life. "The Patience of Conversion" (AA2232) emphasizes the need for choice, and the realization that according to the Rule of St. Benedict "to prefer absolutely nothing over Christ" is a process which allows an individual gradually to be so disposed that he or she cannot easily do something contrary to God. This then leads naturally into "The Commitment to Conversion" (AA2233), a set of lectures which examines the relationship of commitment to obedience. Side A considers the Blessed Mother as model, noting her importance for the Cistercian Fathers. Side B alludes to Cassian, observing that certain of his fundamental ideas were later abridged: Merton says, with a sense of irony, that Cluny "was a place [for producing] future popes." His point is that conversion of manners is not primarily a concern with externals. Fulltime Christian renunciation means "we do everything so that Christ lives in us."

The six tapes discussed thus far, while sometimes rambling, clearly emphasize the need for perseverance. Given the nature of the subject, repetition is justified, even necessary. The same might be said about the next group of four on poverty (AA2101 - AA2104). The first, "The Modern Cult of Efficiency," is also perhaps the most interesting in its discussion of a paradox endemic to religious life. The life depends on a "spirit of poverty," yet Merton must admit that the contemplative orders "need to have a modicum of security." Detachment is, of course, the key. These four tapes are probably the weakest set within the series, not because the material is bad, but because Merton relies heavily upon lists and examples: canonical vows discussed in relation to money; specific terms defined; sins outlined; and finally the difference between "Inner and Outer Poverty" (AA2104). Occasionally boring, they are not without their worthwile insights. In fact, the last mentioned includes a valuable discussion of and revelation of Merton's thinking on poverty in contemporary Central America, and specifically in Nicaragua, with reference to sins of large landholding families.

Merton's task as teacher is to help his listeners see their job as monks as a lifelong process. Thus, as implied above, if we listen to the six tapes on conversion, or these four on poverty, the stress is very much upon the Christian life as a process to be consciously lived out. It is never merely a matter of a vow being taken but rather of the vow being a reminder of the direction in which a life must grow. The next set of tapes to be discussed demonstrates this.

II.

Four lectures are devoted to humility, and while of varying quality and containing much student discussion (the first tape of this group, "The Holy Rule — On Humility" [AA2105] is headed with the publisher's commentary: "This talk contains more dialogue than some."), they remind us what work it is to be saintly. Merton returns to the Rule to get his students thinking about how the "ladder of perfection" works; how "we ascend by descending" and how there is a fundamental paradox in the Christian or monastic life. He explicates Chapter 14 of St. Luke, about taking the lower place, to make his point and to stimulate discussion. On side B, using Peter of Celle and Benedict, Merton discusses the need to avoid pride.

In "Conversion" (AA2106) he analyzes "Sermon Number Seven" of Bernard's, "On Humility," to make the point that we must learn to rely upon humility in *all* things, to learn that nothing is against God's will. He explicates the same ideas *via* Benedict on side B. Benedict says that "formation of consciousness of the last things is basic." Keeping such a fact clearly in mind should convince us that *our thoughts* do matter. This content leads naturally into the next set of lectures on "Formation of Conscience" (AA2107). Self-will is to be avoided: any "will which is exclusively ours and thus not in union with others" is bad. Merton observes in an overview of Western history, and as a commentary on what is wrong with the present moment, Renaissance humanism's glorification of that which is good for the self. This, he maintains, is subversion of nature. It is precisely self-will which "we have to avoid." On side B he develops these ideas and discusses the difference between an aggressive and a passive fortitude, the one bad and the root of many troubles, and the other good. The problem is one Merton discusses in many places and is fundamental to his view of life: "The great problem is that in ourselves there are two selves: a real self; and, the ego.... The outer self is what has to be removed, despised...." The fourth tape in this group, "The Fourth Degree of Humility" (AA2108), discusses scripture texts which give insight into the practice of humility.

This release includes one group of two lectures about "The Virgin Mary" (AA2128), probably occasioned by the need for some feast day commentary. Though containing some awkward comments, these lectures are ultimately focused and tie in nicely with the preceding four on humility, for Mary is the model *par excellence*. On side A Merton cites Bernard on Mary as mediatrix. As a type (and in the writings of Bernard, a metaphor), Mary is beheld as a model for the spiritual life. On side B Merton develops the connection between Mary and our need for a mother ("as long as we don't get sloppy and sentimental"). A mother beyond an earthly mother, says he, heightens our awareness of the presence of God. This tape also contains some important comments on bad art and the impossibility of combining art with the spiritual life if the art is weak — "like Muzak."

All of the fifteen tapes discussed above (six on conversion, four on poverty, and five on humility and Mary) emphasize the need for interior change. While useful, they tend toward the abstract. Discussion of the second fifteen tapes here will focus on more specific and practical matters, a shift which the subjects themselves enjoin. In the foregoing lectures, Merton stresses matters of attitude and the heart. In these remaining ones Merton tries to give *specific* hints about the monastic life: about how to read; think; and live. One hears him, as it were, thinking along with his students about the difficulty of the monastic life and its relationship to the wider world — historical and contemporary — about the community beyond themselves, when considering the Christian life as lived, for example, by married people. Thus, as these lectures develop, Merton seems increasingly concerned to make sense of the monastic life by tying it in with the world beyond the life of one Abbey, or one person.

Two sets of lectures (AA2234 and AA2235) treat communism. Fairly fundamental, they provide a good basic picture of the difference between the Christian approach and "the whole idea of Marxism [which] is that God is the big illusion." Especially valuable here is Merton's willingness to point out problems with both communism *and* capitalism. In both systems, humans are alienated from themselves. In tape AA2235, "Communism versus Capitalism," Merton discusses a Czech economist-philosopher, Hromadka, whose valid point is that to a great extent the Communists are "our fault." Merton ties in this dialectical thinking with the "God is dead" movement. These lectures offer thoughtful introductions to challenges made by communism.

Two additional tapes expand on the concern of how one lives as Christian in a world so completely different from the Christian ideal. The lectures on St. Augustine (AA2236) and St. Jerome (AA2237) provide basic introductory material about these Fathers. Because their subjects are so vast, these two tapes are a bit disappointing; but like most of the others, in context, they are worth hearing. The lecture-discussion on Augustine centers on the need to discern which signs are of value for Christians. This material grows out of a discussion of *De Doctrina Christiani*, and basic points are clearly explained, most importantly that as readers of scripture we need "to distinguish between reality and sign." Ultimately "sign is to be used; reality is to be rested in."

In the lecture-discussion on St. Jerome we learn of the significance of the use of scripture, as well as the significance of a small Christian community. Both these tapes are essentially a series of hints to be followed up on later. Merton urges us, for example, to look up Jerome's Letter No 125 to Rusticus (side B of AA2237). His hints are intriguing and might well lead his latterday listener to further exploration.

III.

Quite valuable for monks and for lay people are the several tapes on silence. Why is genuine silence more than the absence of vocal speech? In "Silence" (AA2133), Merton explains: "In a certain way my word *is* myself . . . the capacity to make things intelligible. Like all natural gifts, it needs to be controlled." Within the religious (or monastic) context "refraining from speech is, therefore, an act of worship." Also, to restrain from useless words has a human value. This leads into discussions of "Solitude" (AA2099), and some interesting commentary on Merton's departure from the novitiate. (This must have been in 1965 just as he was becoming a hermit).

Side B of AA2099 is then about hermits and the purpose of (Merton's) life in the hermitage. Significantly, what comes across most strongly is the relationship of this kind of life to that of the larger community. "Solitude and Resurrection" (AA2100) also pulls together various good insights in regard to silence and the life of the solitary. Merton speaks of Zen "bringing you back into the realm of straight being;˙ [its] purpose is to get you detached." And then emphasizing the relationship between "solitude and resurrection": "The whole meaning of our life is to say *yes* to God. The only real affirmation is the affirmation of the Risen Christ." Side B continues this discussion in relation to the Modernist controversy, a crisis, says Merton, which was sixty years behind the times. "The reality of tradition is not a spirit with a small 's'. The reality is that Christ lives in us *NOW.*"

The four tapes on "Chastity" (AA2129 - AA2132) contain considerable dialogue and are best heard as part of the larger grouping, where each may be seen as part of the whole. Merton has to establish the meaning of chastity; the meaning of "Authentic Friendship" (AA2130); the "Uses of Charity" (AA2131); and "The Symbolism of Chastity" (AA2132). There is much of interest about the sacrament of marriage, especially in AA2131. The theology of the monk's vow of chastity emphasizes the mystical aspect of marriage; yet chastity for the monk has to be seen as a gift, and a calling not extended to all.

What comes across in the lectures on chastity is Merton's conviction that because the sexual drive is such an exceedingly strong force, "if put aside, it has to be replaced by something else." And this is all for the good. Merton's view of life as essentially a paradox built on a natural contradiction is basic to this discussion: "If one yields fully, one yields to death." Conversely, "true life *is* a mortification of nature." All the lectures on silence and chastity show that denial of natural goods is a means of finding a higher good, not some kind of perverse loss.

IV.

Many of the tapes discussed thus far are ultimately about community. The same is certainly true of the final group to be evaluated here, those on love and spiritual direction. The last block of three (AA2134 - AA2136) are essentially discussion of points made by St. Bernard on the nature of love. In "Love Casts Out Fear" (AA2134), Merton also outlines how his students might become aware of Bernard as an artful user of words, one concerned about how, as preacher, he could make people of God aware of God's plan, yet also aware of the limitation of words: "The sum total of all we should strive for cannot be written down."

The lectures on love — "In the Image of God" (AA2135) and "Pure Love" (AA2136) — are valuable expositions of their topics. While defining terms and guiding his listeners, Merton demonstrates that the love we need to strive for "is a dynamic force." In many different modes of living, no matter the cost, we must and will love. If we do not love well, we will love badly. There *is* always this force toward unity. Therefore at every moment each person *is* loving. You cannot avoid this fact.

Merton's distinctions (based on Bernard's types of love — of the slave, of the mercenary, of pure love for the sake of love) are examined carefully on side A of AA2135. On side B he comments upon the "Meditations of Guido the Carthusian" and relates them to life in today's world. Over and over we hear that "You put nothing away for love which you do not recover at a higher level."

AA2136, "Pure Love," continues the consideration of these same ideas derived from St. Bernard. There is a good bit of chatting, but the comments on love and conversion are worth attending to, and especially so in relation to the other lectures in this grouping. A major idea is that in a Cistercian monastery everything is arranged so that "a change in one's whole self . . . a revolution in one's whole life is possible."

How such a conversion is to be effected is, of course, the point of the whole course in formation preserved on these tapes. But a crucial element in the formation is "Spiritual Direction" (AA2137, mentioned already at the beginning of this review). This set of two lecture-discussions examines the significance of spiritual direction, bringing out the fact that it is so necessary and simple, and yet so difficult.

It is "a matter of guidance. A becoming is taking place." Merton refers to other traditions in which spiritual direction is crucial, such as Sufism. On side B he outlines the veils that have to be removed if we (as also the Sufis) are to find our way on the spiritual path. It is also on this tape that Merton recounts a conversation with D. T. Suzuki who had asked him about his work as Novice Master and spiritual director: "Are you teaching those novices to be mystics?" Merton answered: "No!" and added that any answer would be "Baloney," for "this development I'm talking about is much closer to home." And home is essentially being at home!

Occasionally rough or sketchy, these lectures are definitely worth hearing. Merton constantly demonstrates his love of his fellow monks, his community, and thereby the church and the world. These *are* classroom performances, but accepted as such they provide a unique witness to the work of monastic formation.

David D. Cooper
THOMAS MERTON'S ART OF DENIAL:
The Evolution of a Radical Humanist
Athens, Georgia: University of Georgia Press, 1989
xiv, 304 pages   / $35.00 hardcover

Reviewed by **Ross Labrie**

There seem to be two kinds of books and articles about Thomas Merton, the one anecdotal, personal, and sometimes pious, the other analytical, scholarly, and generally more objective in tone. David Cooper's *Thomas Merton's Art of Denial: The Evolution of a Radical Humanist* belongs distinctly in the second category. Unlike much of the mind-numbing prose that has come out of academia in recent years, however, his study is not only carefully researched and judiciously considered but a pleasure to read. While the book is primarily a biographical study, it covers a good deal of Merton's writing, and is often informative about this writing, especially regarding the history of Merton's thinking about art and religion. As a biographer, Cooper is particularly persuasive in revealing the psychological meaning underlying Merton's eulogistic memories of his father.

Cooper's central thesis is that, because of dialectical forces embedded in Merton's personal history and psyche, he changed gradually from an ascetic with a hostile view of the modern world to a Christian humanist who finally accepted the idea that Christian awareness, even emanating from a monk such as he, not only could but should be incorporated into contemporary culture. Cooper's analysis includes an epilogue in which he sets forth the ideas of psychoanalyst, Erik Erikson, to explain Merton's need to restructure his identity at various periods of his life, usually producing some innovative writing as a creative windfall in these otherwise difficult periods. The restructuring of identity characteristically involved a collision between "negative identity fragments" remaining from previous "developmental stages" and "positive identity elements" which related to the person he was on the way to becoming. While the framework of Erikson's ideas does not surface in detail until the end, it seems evident to the reader in retrospect that they helped Cooper to organize his thinking about Merton's life throughout the study.

The advantage of using someone like Erikson is that his analyses clarify our understanding of what has surely been one of the most paradoxical and complex minds of recent intellectual and religious history. An implicit disadvantage of such an approach is the danger of reductive thinking, a risk that Cooper tries carefully to avoid by merely appending Erikson's views to a study that focuses primarily on Merton's own life and words. Nevertheless, there are times when one feels one's vision of Merton narrowed by Cooper's adopting of the Erikson analysis — as, for example, in Cooper's rather negative view of *The Seven Storey Mountain* and *The Sign of Jonas*: "A book like *The Sign of Jonas*," Cooper writes, "excluding its headnotes and epilogue and its rare moments of extrospection — reveals a man whose wings are clipped by his apophatic spirituality, his vision frequently clouded by life at Gethsemani closing in on him."

Such a view seems to me to lead to an undervaluing of Merton's writing at this time. While it is true that Merton himself turned his back on the isolationism and clericalism that characterized his early writings, these writings are evocative reminders of the turbulence of youth and of the drama of the individual soul on a journey to God. In addition, in spite of some of the ecclesiastical platitudinizing, both *The Seven Storey Mountain* and *The Sign of Jonas* are powerful examples of Merton's literary skill, a matter that, although it is not Cooper's primary concern, might have received more attention. Cooper spends a good deal of time analyzing Merton's *Cables to the Ace*, for instance, as an example of Merton's experimentalism following an identity shift, but it is worth pointing out that, as art, *Cables to the Ace* is arguably inferior both to *The Seven Storey Mountain* and to *The Sign of Jonas*. While, in other words, Merton may have moved through the patterns of growth described by Cooper, the words negative and positive as applied both to Merton's psychological growth and to the classical modes of contemplative thought, do not necessarily reflect an aesthetic ascent.

The matter comes up again and again. In connection with Merton's poetry of the late 1940s and early 1950s, for example, Cooper writes that the writing "was stunted by a poetics of negation." Similarly, in connection with *Figures for an Apocalypse* (1948) and *The Tears of the Blind Lions* (1949), Cooper believes that whether "denying human companionship, renouncing the claims of sense impressions, or condemning the ethos of secular civilzation, Merton's poetics of denial produced, above all else, a series of poems which comment on their own impotence." The reason, Cooper believes, arose from Merton's internal division whereby the contemplative and writer were engaged in ceaseless combat with each other so that the poems read more like "laments on Merton's distrust of language than as meditations on prayer, solitude, and the contemplative life." That Merton was so divided there can be no doubt. Nonetheless, the early poetry itself is often successful *as poetry* in conveying the spiritual beauty of contemplative solitude and what I have elsewhere called the mood of "celibate joy." Furthermore, it is noteworthy that two of the poems in *Tears of the Blind Lions* shared the Harriet Monroe Poetry Prize for 1949. Indeed, many readers, including Wendell Berry, with whom I discussed the matter some years ago, prefer the poems written before Merton turned his poetry over to social criticism in the 1960s.

The problem which Merton faced in attempting to reconcile his dual vocation as contemplative and writer is sensitively dealt with by Cooper, who quotes liberally from Merton's writings at different points during his life. Essentially, Cooper argues, the issue was decided when Merton conceded that he would never be a mystic and when coincidentally he became interested in the relationship between his views as a religious thinker about the moral state of modern society. Cooper is especially illuminating in showing the relationship between the development of Merton's central ideas in the 1960s and his debt to writers like Erich Fromm, Boris Pasternak, Albert Camus, and Herbert Marcuse.

Cooper is most effective in tracing the changes in Merton's understanding, which led him eventually to accept the possibility that "art could play an important role in the growth of a more integrated man." Nevertheless, while developing into a Christian humanist, Merton did not necessarily deal successfully — on an intellectual level at any rate — with his old problem of the role of art in the contemplative life. It was not so much that he did not become the mystic he would, according to Cooper, have liked to become. Rather, it was that the contemplative life itself was inevitably disturbed by the artist's excitement in seizing upon the artistic possibilities of thoughts and images which entered the contemplative's head. In retrospect it would seem that the artist in Merton was indeed irrepressible but that Merton came to see that the artist in him did have his uses — to the world — if not to the frustrated mystic. At the same time, while Merton came to regret his earlier alienation from the larger society around him, he continued to show, as Cooper parenthetically concedes, an interest in the contemplative life in his writings throughout the 1960s. In other words the contemplative calling, which had attracted him into the Trappist Order in the first place, continued to attract him up until his death in 1968 — even if certain aspects of his earlier attitudes were later abandoned.

For this reason it is salutary to bear in mind that even if, as Cooper rightly argues, Merton arrived at a Christian humanism "relevant to modern realities," an important part of that relevance relates to his writings about the universal need for contemplative solitude. In particular, as Merton wrote to Daniel Berrigan, if the Christian was correct in confronting secular powers on significant moral issues, the Christian activist must prior to such action, withdraw for a time from organizing protest in order to bury himself in the mind of God. This was not only Christian but monastic humanism — of a sort which only a cenobite who had separated himself from the world could articulate.

I should not like these modest reservations about Cooper's book to cast a shadow over it. Compared with the many books which have been published about Merton in recent years, I would say that this is one of the strongest and most original both in conception and structuring. Thomas Merton is one of the most mercurial and elusive figures, both in his life and in his writings, to have emerged in this century. That Cooper's book throws a fresh and distinctive light on Merton there can be no doubt.

Anthony T. Padovano
CONSCIENCE & CONFLICT:
A Trilogy of One-Actor Plays:
Thomas Merton, Pope John XXIII, Martin Luther
New York / Mahwah: Paulist Press, 1988
xii, 102 pages   — $7.95 paperback

Reviewed by **Richard Moir**

I found *Conscience & Conflict* by Anthony Padovano an inspiration. As an actor with the desire for what might be described as a "theater of the spirit," I have found that this trilogy of one-actor plays achieves what all good theater, film or television must achieve — that is, its whole be greater than the sum of its parts. I approached the trilogy with a fair knowledge of Thomas Merton, a slight acquaintance with Luther and hardly any awareness of Pope John XXIII. To say that my understanding of, and feeling for, these three "rebels" of the Catholic Church has increased would be an understatement.

Padovano states in his introduction that drama is less passive than a book or a lecture and indeed I believe strongly that the time is fast approaching when we shall be seeing *The Seven Storey Mountain* on television or, even better, on the big screen. Drama, as Padovano explains, is about magic and mystery. There is a latitude in the creation of drama which allows the protagonist's path of personal growth to be charted and plotted as in no other form. Because the life journeys of Merton, Luther and John are seen so very clearly in this collection, it follows that the presentation of the plays on stage, their intended purpose, would be a most entertaining and inspiring night at the theater.

What is most interesting about these three "solitary human journeys" is their very marked similarity. Each monologue begins with the seed of an inner conflict and for each man this conflict is the same. In *Winter Rain*, Thomas Merton mourns the death of his mother but, more than that, he mourns the fact that she would not let him near her. There was not even a farewell embrace, just a letter between mother and son explaining her approaching death. This single event colored Merton's life and because this is drama and Merton is "speaking" to an audience then that audience is able readily to comprehend the interpretation that Merton became a writer in order to gain the embrace of the world. The play also suggests that Merton became a monk in order to write. So it is seen that Merton's twin vocations grew out of this early dilemma — a lack of demonstrable love from his mother.

In *His Name is John*, Angelo Guiseppe Roncalli, the future Pope John XXIII carries an image of his earthly father hoisting the young Angelo on to his shoulders to catch a passing parade. He states: "I looked often for another father — not to supplant mine, only to supplement a little." He says later that he never knew his father and in his speech to the Conclave speaks of his mother, Marianna, and the great dilemma he faced in not coming home to see her one more time before she died. "She waited and waited, an advent with no Christmas, expectation without birth, longing and no rejoicing." Later in the speech he confesses that he cannot get to God without going through his mama and papa. So Pope John's story is influenced throughout with the connections between fathers and sons, mothers and orphans. He wonders what matters more — doctrine or parents: "The world calls me father though I feel like an orphan."

In *Summer Lightning*, Martin Luther is obsessed with his earthly father. His earliest memories are the beatings he received. "A kind father is not easy to come by, on earth or in Heaven." But he accepted this: "My father at least paid attention to me. I never pleased him but even his displeasure was better than my mother's indifference." Later he states: "I shall become a loyal son if only I can find the right father." The play suggests that Luther became a priest to find a father. Going against his earthly father's wishes, "he tried to invent himself to make himself his own creator."

The relationship between child and parent has an important resonance in the lives of each of these "church outsiders." In a dramatic context and from the point of view of an actor, this leads to an interesting possibility — that *Conscience & Conflict* is perhaps three scenarios with essentially one character. While I am not suggesting that Merton, Pope John and Luther are not three unique individuals, I am suggesting that their presentation in this collection would be best served by being played by one actor and preferably all in one performance. Their stories echo and mirror one another in such a way as to show the universality of the lifelong quest for meaning and peace. By treating the trilogy as "one" I believe this important message of the plays would become apparent and, very importantly, *Conscience & Conflict* would be seen as a strong piece of theater.

It is not only similar parental problems and influences that create this idea of three parts of a whole. Merton, John and Luther were all essentially outsiders and rebels. They all went against the established grain of the Church of the day and they all faced up to the question of social justice. Merton saw a link between holiness and human passion. He wanted to know why he found "a compatibility between things my church tells me I should find incompatible." He was a monk who was to follow a rule of silence but who would not shut up. In the world of Vietnam and nuclear weapons, he wanted to achieve peace. On his Christian journey, he found Buddhism bringing him closer to God. Through it all he kept writing and growing in the face of disapproval and censorship from church authorities.

In the course of his life, Pope John "made popes angry, lit candles for Bulgaria, removed walls in Turkey and saved twenty-four thousand Jews." He entertained Communists and produced "Pacem in Terris" — a letter on peace. His convening of the Second Vatican Council met, at first, with silent disapproval from his Cardinals. Martin Luther burned a papal bull in public and nailed his ninety-five theses to a church door in Wittenberg. From being a celibate monk, he married and had children. He was responsible for the beginnings of a reformed church. There is a line from *Winter Rain* which I think sums up these three very human and holy men: "When you don't cause trouble in a world as troubled as today's world, you're in trouble."

So the similarities between the three subjects in *Conscience & Conflict* obviously suggest that they be treated as a whole with one actor perhaps portraying all three. This, of course, would be a mighty task and something of a problem. The "monologue" is often an area of theater in which it is hard to sustain audience interest. There is no interaction between characters and, apart from lighting and some costume changes, we have only the voice and the words. I have read other plays using a similar method of portrayal (including some on Merton) and I know that just the voice and the words would not be enough in these plays to make them theatrical events. I have no such worry with *Conscience & Conflict*. There are scenes here capable of creating strong emotions and thought: Martin Luther grieving over the death of his daughters; Merton talking about "Margaret," the woman whom he "would cry for at night but not go to at night;" the simple love of John as he visits the children's hospital. As an actor, the thought of playing any one of these men, let alone all of them, would be a very fulfilling challenge.

Above all, these plays are the stories of men who possess the courage to face up to the conflict both within and without their lives. As Padovano says:

> To struggle with the same issues as they did is to suffer pain with them but also to achieve liberation and peace. All three plays conclude on a tranquil note. Is there anything more we could ask for our Church and for each of our lives?

J. S. Porter
THE THOMAS MERTON POEMS:
A Caravan of Poems

Goderich, Ontario, Canada: Moonstone Press, 1988
84 pages   — $8.95 paperback

Ron Seitz
MONKS POND, OLD HERMIT, HAI!:
A Haiku Homage to Thomas Merton

Monterey, Kentucky: Larkspur Press, 1988
92 pages   — $15.00 paperback / $65.00 special

Reviewed by **John Leax**

Though these two works are as unlike as one could imagine, pairing them raises an interesting question. Is it possible successfully to derive literature from literature? These books suggest that it is, but that success may depend on choices made before a writer begins.

Both of these works take the life of Thomas Merton as their subject matter. Porter chooses to build a narrative opening his poems with the line, "I, Thomas Merton." From there he proceeds, in a re-creation of Merton's voice, to meditate on some of the better known incidents in Merton's life and themes in his work. Seitz chooses to shun narrative. He instead assembles a sequence of fifty haiku, fifty moments of insight. While some of them can be placed in direct relation to events in Merton's life, most cannot. All of them, however, are related to the hermit life lived by Merton and can be read as an intuitive commentary on or identification with that life.

Porter's book is obviously ambitious. He seeks to interpret Merton, to make him speak clarities he refused to speak himself. But where Merton's voice was subtle and elusive, the voice Porter gives his Merton is pedestrian. This is nowhere clearer than in the lines recording Merton's vision at Polonnaruwa. Porter writes:

At Polonnaruwa
sleeping buddhas
look so restful,
sleeping to awake
from water to land
— moving on air.

touch the elements
each and all
water, earth and air
the last journey —
fire.

Compare these to Merton's account, quoted by Porter in his introduction:

> The silence of the extraordinary faces, the great smiles. Huge and yet subtle . . . I was knocked over with a rush of relief and thankfulness . . . jerked clean out of the habitual half-tied vision of things, and an inner cleanness . . . as if exploding from the rocks themselves. . . .

Merton's words have energy, and they have a natural restraint, for Merton knew when he was reaching the discursive limits of his words and accepted them. Finally, Merton's voice, well established in the reader's ear, is too strong for Porter. The illusion that Merton is speaking, necessary to the success of the poems, fails.

Ron Seitz, writing from a closer relationship to Merton, is more aware of the danger in deriving literature from literature. Without side-stepping the debt of his poems to Merton, he evokes the spirit of Merton by choosing a form that is complementary rather than derivative. The tradition of the haiku is older and larger than Merton. Consequently Merton's presence hovering over the work cannot overwhelm it. What is more, Seitz evokes the spirit, not so much of Merton's poems and voice, but of his photographs:

maybe the year's last —
that snowflake on the dog's ear
quickly melting now.

Small objects, distant voices of children, clouds, the moon, bells, the cold, the ordinary surroundings of the hermit's life are, in themselves, filled with meaning. They become revelatory when the hermit (and the poet) has eyes to see and words to say. When Merton appears in these poems, he is observed in some small act that opens into significance:

waiting for two monks
to drag a log up the hill
he removed his hat.

Monks Pond, Old Hermit, Hai! is a beautiful book. It is beautiful to read. Slowly. One haiku at a time over many days. It is also, as book lovers have come to expect from Larkspur Press, beautiful to look at and beautiful to touch.

Patrick G. Henry & Donald K. Swearer
FOR THE SAKE OF THE WORLD:
The Spirit of Buddhist and Christian Monasticism
Minneapolis: Fortress Press / Collegeville: Liturgical Press, 1989
256 pages   — $10.95 paperback

Reviewed by **William H. Slavick**

With the richness of the Christian contemplative tradition still so largely unexplored in our time, the growing interest of Christians in Eastern spiritual experience may suggest, in some quarters anyway, curiosity, in others a departure from Christian prayer life. Concern about the latter occasioned Cardinal Ratzinger's letter in October 1989 on aspects of Christian meditation, reminding Christians of the personal and communitarian nature of Christian prayer — focused on God as revealed in the Scriptures as against impersonal techniques and preoccupation with self, and of the Christian's prayer as participating in the Church at prayer.

Ratzinger's concern about efforts to overcome the distinction between creature and Creator as if the gap is inappropriate and to reduce pure grace to the level of natural psychology suggest that Eastern methods are not always being used "solely as a psychophysical preparation for a truly Christian contemplation" but put the "absolute without images or concepts" of Buddhism "on the same level as the majesty of God revealed in Christ" — or obscure the divinity. The letter identifies the Christian way to Christ as doing His will, not dissolving the personal self in the absolute, so that Christian prayer "always leads to love of neighbor, to action, to the acceptance of trials." His obvious fear is that resort to Eastern techniques may lead to syncretism.

Cardinal Ratzinger's letter provides one useful context for Patrick G. Henry and Donald K. Swearer's *For the Sake of the World: The Spirit of Buddhist and Christian Monasticism*: whatever the parallels, Buddhist monasticism is of limited value to Christian prayer and life. The need for a spirituality that can weather the pressures of the modern world and transform it, and the Western Church's estrangement from its own tradition of meditation and from monasticism as its prime resource in meeting this challenge — for laity and religious alike — offers another challenge. The patient reader will find Henry and Swearer carrying forward both discussions in the process of offering a comparison of the two monastic traditions and an assessment of their present usefulness.

This discussion falls into no vacuum, of course — long preceded by Dom Bede Griffith's writings about what the East has to offer Western Christianity and by Dom Aelred Graham's *Zen Catholicism*, which identified, in the 1960s, the shortcomings of Zen to Christians and its usefulness in bringing the soul to a peaceful reconciliation with the painfulness of the human situation through an attitude of simplicity and surrender of self, docility regarding things as they are, and development of an ability to live in the present — a usefulness that justifies exploring more extensively the likenesses and differences in Buddhist and Christian monasticism. Understanding of both monastic traditions has been enriched immensely in the past three decades. In fact, except for classical texts, all of Henry and Swearer's suggested readings are from these decades. Thomas Merton's interest in Zen would, alone, constitute a radical growth in interest.

For the Sake of the World is rewarding in what a "side by side" study highlights and in its discussion of what monasticism has to offer modern folk. That the authors are close observers of monasticism rather than monks defines their perspective — sometimes too remote, at other times helpfully objective for the newcomer to either or both institutions.

The initial chapter, "Contemplation and Action," illustrates the advantages and disadvantages of their stance. To the uninitiated, focusing on Thomas Merton and Thich Nhat Hanh as exemplars of the two traditions and of the basic paradox of withdrawal and engagement in monastic life, is helpful and attractive. Merton saw the necessity of interior solitude and monasticism as the vocation in which one is most "poured out into the world" in love of all and he was the most articulate of modern monastic voices in discussing both — and the common aim of Buddhist and Christian monasticism — a radical personal transformation. The Vietnamese Nhat Hanh's writings likewise relate meditation and action, wisdom and compassion, and develop the Zen understanding that truth is awakening to things as they are, "the heart of reality." For both, true community "develops from transformed persons rather than from political ideologies and manipulation of political structures." As Parker J. Palmer observes, "the world is within us," and, in contemplation, one lives "for the sake of the world." Merton and Nhat Hanh ideally serve the authors' purpose, as articulate monks, and the thesis of this book. But how representative are these two gifted poets of contemporary — and historical — monasticism?

Each chapter explores one area of comparison. Both traditions share in an essential but moderate asceticism in overcoming the "limitations of the mundane world in order to actualize another kind of being or reality, or to transform the mundane." For Buddhism, the Eightfold Path of moral virtue, constant attentiveness, and transcendent wisdom takes one beyond the limitations of his *karma* — if pursued variously, as a wandering or cenobitic monk. Henry and Swearer point to parallel Matthew and Luke references to Jesus as a drunkard, but Jesus who goes apart to pray, who fasts, who exemplifies humility, also is, like Buddha, a model of ascetical practice. Diversity in Christian asceticism is reflected in the eremitic and community traditions, the Manichaean departure, Luther's rejection of asceticism in his affirmation of the created world, Calvin's restoration of renunciation, and such a decline in asceticism in our time that Christians now look to the East to rediscover it. The difference in the Buddhist and Christian traditions is fundamental: Christian asceticism leads to Jesus.

The historical chapter wisely focuses on the early traditions. From the outset, Buddhists left ordinary life — some came naked — and gathered around a proven teacher. The degree of austerity varied. The purpose was discovery of truth about suffering, its cause, the way to cessation of suffering in absolute freedom: "walking through the world and leaving no imprint." Only in time did Buddhism develop rules, building complexes, and a hierarchy. Christian monasticism grew out of the example of the early community of the Apostles — but slowly, from the *Life of St. Anthony* to Pachomius and Basil in the fourth century when it became, arguably, the best practical realization of Jesus' "disengagement from conventional structures" and Paul's account of "a new age."

A chapter on the Benedictine Rule emphasizes the very unmodern view that freedom and self-direction come through discipline. Buddhism involved a three-stage ordination ceremony that included hundreds of rules. *The Book of Discipline* regulated community life — if variously from place to place, abbot to abbot. The rules recognize the centrality of study — and allow for female monks, though Buddha saw them as an eventual weakening force.

Discussion of the rule in Christian monasticism recognizes Benedict as choosing from ten generations of monastic lore and the gradual acceptance of his rule over two centuries, a rule marked by covenants with God and the community and establishing a family, authority, and a school of the Lord's service in which obedience to an abbot as holding the place of God is the ordering principle of one's ascent of the ladder of humility. *Ora et labora* replace study as the focus of community life. Where Buddhists generated prayers, Christian monks chanted the Psalms and readings come from the Scriptures, the Fathers, and lives of the saints. Henry and Swearer use this chapter to identify several anomalies of Western monasticism —the monastery as an often gigantic economic enterprise in the Middle Ages, the increasing proportion of ordained priests, the Eastern Church tradition of consecrating only abbots as bishops, the Russian Staretz tradition, the all male Mount Athos. Final emphasis is on the common tradition everywhere: hospitality.

As a social institution, Buddhist monasteries were centers for learning — spiritual, moral, literary, and technical. Western monasticism served as the great transmitter of medieval culture for a millenium, and the monasteries developed strong schools of classical learning. But another tradition develops in seventeenth century Trappist houses — teaching by example alone: "Monks have not been appointed for study, but for doing penance . . . to weep and not to teach," a controversy prefigured in St. Bernard's criticism of Abbe Suger's pomp and patronage of art and architecture. Such differences, however, are secondary to Benedict's sustaining vision of the monastery as a place of spiritual wisdom, transitory though it may be in a violent world — a tradition that included such prominent and diverse figures as Hildegarde of Bingen, mystic and musician; the Staretz Amrosy who is the source for Dostoyevsky's Father Zossima in *The Brothers Karamazov*; and St. Francis of Assisi who took his asceticism and humility among the poor.

Ironically, as interest in Buddhism has spread westward, Buddhism in Asia is seriously threatened by the influence of the West, political change, secularism, and materialism. After surveying monasteries in Japan and Thailand, the authors ask how a tradition of compassion and non-egoism can survive in today's competitive world. But Buddhist meditation is spreading to the laity and new institutions are being established, such as Bhikku Buddhadasa, which includes meditation and political and social involvement.

Modern Christian monasticism, attentive to early tradition but with much higher educational standards, is adjusting, shifting from slavish obedience to authority and uniformity to a developmental model with authenticity rather than a traditional view of holiness as its goal — with a strong emphasis on formation of candidates.

Henry and Swearer make their strongest contribution in the short final chapter which looks at what monasticism has to offer in the modern culture described in *Habits of the Heart* and *After Virtue*. In a society where community is disappearing and the past is a void, monasticism offers rules for harmony, a community of memory, and an ordered rhythm of community life. Important habits of the heart are found in the monastery. Monks know "things take time," a response to today's dismissal of the past and demand for instant results. "Things must be done together" answers the American individualism the authors see as now being elevated to a world wide crisis, the obsession with the new, and readiness to abandon one course for another. As Joan Chittister, O.S.B., observes: "Community leads to conversion." "Habit breaks habit" is monasticism's answer to the slavery of undisciplined freedom. "Things are seldom what they seem": the monk's renunciation of wealth allows for the perception of reality within a world of illusions, of forces we do not recognize. Monastic asceticism, Henry and Swearer argue, establishes an ascetical attitude toward the world that challenges the "assumptions of a getting and spending world," one "where competition leaves little room for compassion."

Can such habits survive today? They have survived other "modern world" challenges, and Merton's own story is illustrative of retreat from and engagement with the world. Certainly, Henry and Swearer conclude, the monastery has something to offer: "For it is a real home where real people dwell." My particular delight in a spectatorial study that does not always engage me is the authors' repeated reference to Father Zossima, who observes, modestly but accurately, that "a monk is simply what every person ought to be."

NOTES ON CONTRIBUTORS

ARTHUR MacDONALD ALLCHIN is a Canon of the Anglican Church and currently resides in Oxford, England. He is President of *The International Thomas Merton Society* (European Chapter). He is the author of *The World is a Wedding: Explorations in Christian Spirituality* (London: Darton, Longman & Todd, 1978), which includes a chapter, "The Writer and Tradition: A Common Theme in Henry Vaughan and Thomas Merton."

FLAVIAN BURNS, O.C.S.O., is a monk of the Abbey of Gethsemani at Trappist, Kentucky, and served as Abbot from 1968 to 1973. He is the author of "The Consciousness of God and His Purpose in the Life and Writings of Thomas Merton," *Cistercian Studies* 14 (1979).

JOAN CHITTISTER, O.S.B., is Prioress of Mount St. Benedict Monastery in Erie, Pennsylvania. Her talks on feminist theology — *Sexism in the Church: Agenda for the Next Decade; The Future of Religious Life and Ministry*; and *Of Moses' Mother and Pharoah's Daughter* — are available from Credence Cassettes.

JAMES CONNER, O.C.S.O., is Chaplain at Osage Monastery in Sand Springs, Oklahoma. He is a member of the Board of Directors of *The International Thomas Merton Society*. He is the author of "The Original Face in Buddhism and the True Self in Thomas Merton," *Cistercian Studies* 22 (1987) and "The Experience of God and the Experience of Nothingness in Thomas Merton," *The Merton Annual I* (1988).

ROGER J. CORLESS is Professor of Religion at Duke University in Durham, North Carolina. His essay, "Fire on *The Seven Storey Mountain*: Why are Catholics looking East?," appeared in *Toward an Integrated Humanity: Thomas Merton's Journey* (Kalamazoo: Cistercian Publications, 1988).

LAWRENCE S. CUNNINGHAM is Professor of Theology at the University of Notre Dame in Notre Dame, Indiana. He is the author of *The Catholic Heritage* (New York: Crossroad, 1983) and of several essays on Merton, including "Thomas Merton: Firewatcher," *The Merton Seasonal* 15 (1990).

ROBERT E. DAGGY is Director of the Thomas Merton Studies Center at Bellarmine College in Louisville, Kentucky and President of *The International Thomas Merton Society*. He is the editor of *The Merton Seasonal* and of *The Road to Joy: The Letters of Thomas Merton to New and Old Friends* (New York: Farrar, Straus & Giroux, 1989).

MICHAEL DOWNEY is Professor of Sacramental Theology at Loyola Marymount College in Los Angeles, California. He is the author of *A Blessed Weakness: The Spirit of Jean Vanier and l'Arche* (San Francisco: Harper & Row, 1986) and *Clothed in Christ: The Sacraments and Christian Living* (New York: Crossroad, 1987).

DIANE FOSTER, O.C.S.O., is Abbess of the Trappist community at Redwoods Monastery in Whitethorn, California. She met Thomas Merton during his visits to and conferences at Redwoods in 1968.

JONATHAN GREENE is publisher and editor of Gnomon Press in Frankfort, Kentucky. He was a contributor to Thomas Merton's "little magazine," *Monks Pond* in 1968 and wrote the "Foreword" for Merton's *Early Poems / 1940-42* (Lexington, Kentucky: Anvil Press, 1971). His poem, "On Hearing of Merton's Death," was included in *A Merton Concelebration* (Notre Dame: Ave Maria Press, 1981).

SIDNEY H. GRIFFITH is Director of the Institute of Christian Oriental Research at the Catholic University of America in Washington, D. C. His doctoral thesis was titled *The Controversial Theology of Theodore Abu Qurrah (c. 750 - c. 820 A.D.): A Methodological Study in Christian Arabic Literature* and was completed at Catholic University in 1976.

PATRICK HART, O.C.S.O., is a monk of the Abbey of Gethsemani at Trappist, Kentucky and a member of the Board of Directors of *The International Thomas Merton Society*. He is editor of *Cistercian Studies* and of several books on Merton, including the third volume of Merton's correspondence, *The School of Charity: Letters on Religious Renewal and Spiritual Direction*, scheduled for publication by Farrar, Straus & Giroux in 1990.

MICHAEL W. HIGGINS is Assistant Academic Dean and Professor of English at the University of St. Jerome's College in Waterloo, Ontario, Canada. He is editor of *Grail: An Ecumenical Journal* and author of several articles on Merton (including "Making and Remaking: The Many Masks of Thomas Merton," *Canadian Catholic Review* 7 [April 1989]). He is an International Adviser of *The International Thomas Merton Society.*

E. GLENN HINSON is David T. Porter Professor of Church History at Southern Baptist Theological Seminary in Louisville, Kentucky. He is Treasurer of *The International Thomas Merton Society.* His writings on Merton include "Expansive Catholicism: Merton's Ecumenical Perceptions," in *The Message of Thomas Merton* (Kalamazoo: Cistercian Publications, 1981) and "Merton's Many Faces," *Religion in Life* 42 (1973).

DAVID KOCKA, O.F.M.Conv., is a poet and sculptor who lives at the community of Saint Francis in Mt. St. Francis, Indiana. He is the author of "A Song of Syllables: Merton an Artist in Art," *Merton Seasonal* 14 (1989).

DEWEY WEISS KRAMER is Professor of German and Humanities at DeKalb College in Clarkston, Georgia. She is the author of *Open to the Spirit: A History of the Monastery of the Holy Spirit* (1986).

VICTOR A. KRAMER is Professor of English at Georgia State University in Atlanta, Georgia and a member of the Board of Directors of *The International Thomas Merton Society.* He is the author of *Thomas Merton: Monk and Artist* (Kalamazoo: Cistercian Publications, 1987) and of several essays on Merton, including "Patterns in Thomas Merton's *Introduction to Ascetical and Mystical Theology*," *Cistercian Studies* 24 (1989).

ROSS LABRIE is Professor of English at the University of British Columbia in Vancouver, British Columbia, Canada. He is the author of *The Art of Thomas Merton* (Fort Worth: Texas Christian University Press, 1979) and *The Writings of Daniel Berrigan* (Lanham, Maryland: University Press of America, 1989). His essays include "The Ordering of Thomas Merton's Early Poems," *Resources for American Literary Study* 8 (Spring 1978) and "Thomas Merton's War Novel," *Renascence* 30 (Spring 1978).

JOHN LEAX is head of the Writing Department and Poet-in-Residence at Houghton College in Houghton, New York. His poetry has been published in four collections, including *The Task of Adam* (1985). He is also the author of "Poetry and Contemplation: The Inner War of Thomas Merton," *Christianity Today* 19 (23 May 1975) and "Thomas Merton: Abiding in Christ," *Christianity Today* 20 (9 April 1976).

JEAN LECLERCQ, O.S.B., resides at the Abbaye St-Maurice in Clervaux, Luxembourg. A friend and correspondent of Merton's, his writings include "The Evolving Monk," in *Thomas Merton / Monk: A Monastic Tribute* (Kansas City: Sheed & Ward, 1974); "Maritain and Merton: the Coincidence of Opposites," *Cistercian Studies* 19 (1984); "Merton and History," in *Thomas Merton: Prophet in the Belly of a Paradox* (New York: Paulist Press, 1978); and "Merton and the East," *Cistercian Studies* 13 (1978).

DOUGLAS R. LETSON is President of the University of St. Jerome's College in Waterloo, Ontario, Canada. He is co-author (with Michael W. Higgins) of *Portraits of Canadian Catholicism* (Toronto: Griffin House, 1986) and *Women and the Church: A Source Book* (Toronto: Griffin House, 1986).

THOMAS F. McKENNA, C.M., is Professor of Theology at St. John's University in Jamaica, New York. His doctoral thesis, completed at the Catholic University of America in 1982, was titled *Conversion and Growth: The Theological Interpretation by Henry Nelson Wieman and the Doctrine of the Council of Trent*.

RICHARD MOIR is an actor/producer who lives in Chatswood, New South Wales, Australia. His films include *27A* (1973), *Going Down* (1982), *Plains of Heaven* (1982), *Heatwave* (1982), and *Wrong World* (1985). He has twice been nominated as Best Actor by the Australian Film Institute for his performances in *In Search of Anna* (1977) and *An Indecent Obsession* (1985). He is currently at work on a film with the production title *Deadly*.

KARL A. PLANK is Associate Professor of Religion at Davidson College in Davidson, North Carolina. He is the author of *Paul and the Irony of Affliction* (Atlanta: Scholars Press, 1987) and his writings on Merton include

"Harvesting the Fruits of Monastic Contemplation," *Books & Religion* 14 (October 1986) and "Meditating on Merton's Eichmann," *Christian Century* (9 October 1985).

JANE MARIE RICHARDSON, S.L., is a Sister of Loretto and lives at Cedars of Peace in Nerinx, Kentucky. She has often reviewed Merton books, particularly in *Worship*. A setting for a text from *The Sign of Jonas* was included in her *Musical Reflections* (1980).

MICHAEL RUKSTELIS lives in Rock Hill, South Carolina. His writings on Merton include the poem, "The Pasture (Thomas Merton's Heart)," *Merton Seasonal* 13 (Spring 1988), and the essay, "Thomas Merton's Understanding: The Claritas Strategy," *The Merton Annual I* (1988).

WILLIAM H. SLAVICK is Professor of English at the University of Southern Maine in Gorham, Maine. He studied at St. Bernard Abbey in Alabama and is an oblate of Abtei Grussau, Wimpfen, West Germany. An article on Benedictine monasticism will appear in *The Catholic Digest*.

BONNIE BOWMAN THURSTON is Chairperson of the Department of Theology and Religious Studies at Wheeling Jesuit College in Wheeling, West Virginia. She is Vice President of *The International Thomas Merton Society*. Her writings on Merton include "The Man of Letters," *America* 159 (22 October 1988); "Why Merton Looked East," *Living Prayer* 21 (November-December 1988); and "Zen Influence on Thomas Merton's View of the Self," *The Merton Annual I* (1988).

INDEX

Index

Index